Forty Niners
50th Anniversary
Collector's Edition

by Joseph Hession

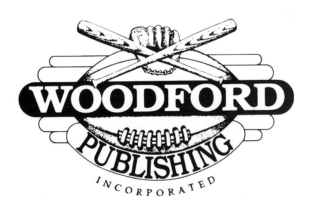

ISBN 0-942627-33-4

52495>

9 780942 627336

Woodford Press
660 Market Street, Suite 206
San Francisco, CA 94104
415-397-1853

Distributed to the trade by National Book Network

To order individual books, please phone
Woodford Press at 1-888-USA-BOOK.

Forty Niners—50th Anniversary Collector's Edition/
by Joseph Hession.

ISBN 0-942627-33-4
Library of Congress Number: 96-061271

Forty Niners

50th Anniversary
Collector's Edition

by Joseph Hession

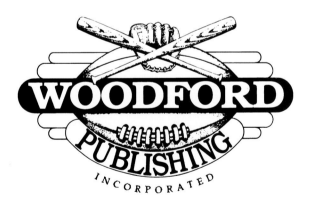

WOODFORD PUBLISHING INCORPORATED

Photo Credits

AP/Wide World Photos: pp. x, A-9, 31, 35, 38-39, 40, 45, 49 (all), 54, 57, 60, 65, 67, 76, 80, 86, 87 (top), 88, 133, 170, 179, 187, 189, 191, 193, 199, 200, 203, 204, 258

San Francisco 49er Photo File: pp. 39, 55, 62, 63, 68, 69, 72, 73, 77, 79, 81, 84, 97, 111, 130, 143, 165, 175, 195, 197, 210
    Dennis Desprois: pp. 95 (top), 122
    Frank Rippon: pp. 33, 53, 71, 75, 91 (bottom)

Pro Football Hall of Fame: pp. 28, 41

Stanford University Archives: p. 5

UPI/Bettmann Archives: pp. iv-v, 2, 4, 7 (top), 8, 9, 11, 12-13, 14, 17, 18, 23, 25, 30, 32, 36, 43, 44, 47, 48 (both), 50 (both), 51, 87 (bottom), 89

B. Andres: p. 153

Michael Zagaris: Cover and all color photos; pp. viii, xii, A-20, 91 (top), 92 (all), 93 (both), 94, 95 (bottom), 96, 99, 100-101, 102 (both), 103 (all), 104 (all), 105, 107, 109 (both), 110, 114 (both), 115, 117 (both), 118-119, 124 (both), 127 (all), 128-129, 132, 134, 135, 137, 138, 139, 142, 145, 146, 147, 149, 152, 153, 155, 156, 157, 159, 160, 161, 164, 165, 167, 168, 172, 174 (both), 181, 182, 184, 185, 188, 201, 205

Thanks to Lido Starelli, Clarence Amaral, Bobby Ferretti and Tim Lynn for use of their 49er programs and memorabilia.

Acknowledgements:

Liam Brady and Trevor Anthony for research and technical assistance. Sam, Liam and Michele for hot meals, cold feet and warm laughter

CONTENTS

Foreword   ix

Introduction   xi

50 Years of 49ers   A-1

Chapter One: The Formative Years (1946-1949)   1
The Morabito dream, recruiting from local college and military teams, highlights of the near championship season in the All-America Football Conference. Profiles of Frankie Albert, Alyn Beals, Len Eshmont, John Strzykalski and Joe Vetrano.

Chapter Two: Joining the National Football League (1950-1959)   27
The switch to a new league, the development of the Alley-Oop Pass, the Million Dollar Backfield, the heartbreaking 1957 playoff loss. Interviews with Hugh McElhenny, Leo Nomellini, Joe Perry, R.C. Owens and Y.A. Tittle.

Chapter Three: The Lean Years (1960-1969)   59
The Shotgun Formation is a hit, the 49ers prepare to leave Kezar Stadium, John Brodie replaces Y.A. Tittle. Interviews with Bruce Bosley, Charlie Krueger, Jerry Mertens, Dave Parks and Abe Woodson.

Chapter Four: From Championship to the Cellar (1970-1979)   83
The team's first appearance in the NFL Championship Game, the bitter losses to Dallas, Eddie DeBartolo buys the club. Interviews with John Brodie, Len Rohde, Gene Washington, Dave Wilcox and Delvin Williams.

Chapter Five: The Super Bowl Years (1980-1989)   121
Winners at last, Bill Walsh takes control of the team, Joe Montana develops into the game's best quarterback, and the Team of the Eighties reigns supreme. Interviews with Dwight Clark, Ronnie Lott, Joe Montana, Bubba Paris, Ray Wersching, Keith Fahnhorst, Roger Craig, Jerry Rice and Bill Romanowski.

Chapter Six: Era of Excellence (1990-1996)   171
A new era takes hold as Coach George Seifert replaces Bill Walsh, quarterback Steve Young succeeds Joe Montana, and the 49ers become the first team to ever win five Super Bowls. Interviews with Harris Barton, William Floyd, Brent Jones, Ken Norton, Jr., Deion Sanders, Jesse Sapolu, George Seifert, Steve Young, Tom Rathman, Merton Hanks, Ricky Watters and Gary Plummer.

Chapter Seven: Records & Statistics   229
The 49ers all-time draft, all-time roster, all-time coaches, a complete year-by-year look at every game played and the score. Records for 49ers' coaches and club leaders.

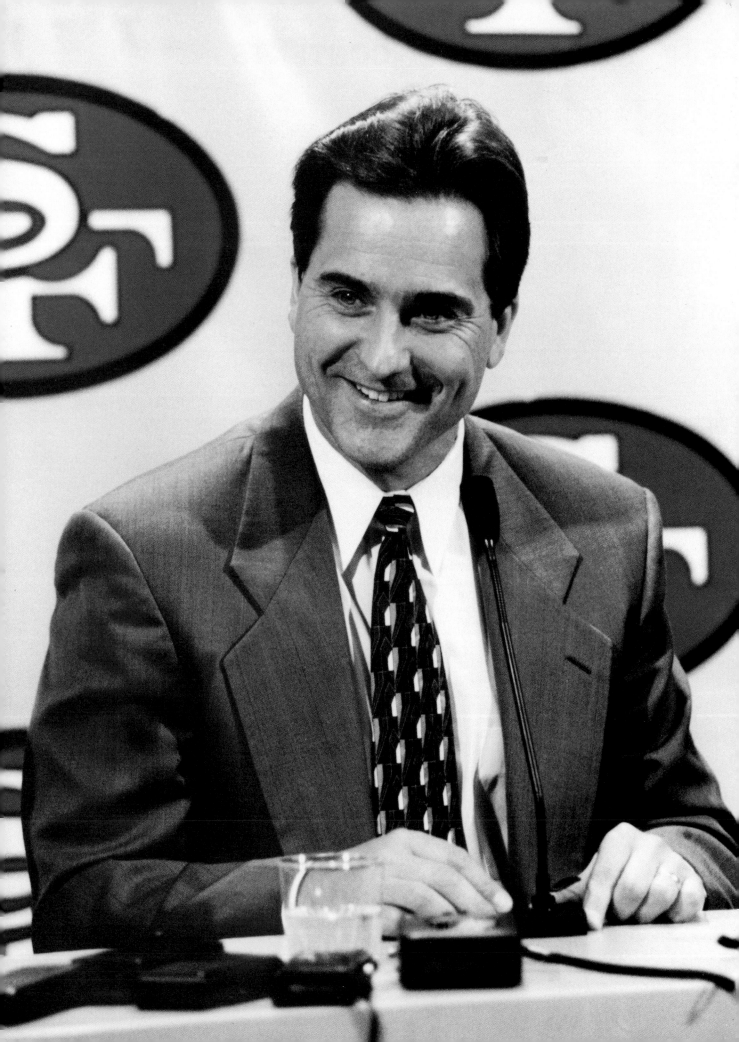

FOREWORD

Five Super Bowl Trophies. Five Super Bowl rings.

It's the first thing we see when we walk into the lobby at the Marie P. DeBartolo Centre, headquarters for the San Francisco 49ers. And they aren't there by accident.

After I became head coach of the 49ers, one of my first duties was to address the squad before our initial mini camp. I told the team that those trophies and rings are there *because* of the high standards this franchise expects and demands every time they step onto the field. They are also a product of the work ethic and dedication that has been maintained throughout the years, making this one of the model franchises in all of sports.

During my years in Green Bay we spent countless hours learning the 49ers' way. We implemented the 49er offensive and defensive systems, how they practiced, their approach and philosophies. It all starts at the top with Owner Ed DeBartolo and President Carmen Policy. They have molded this franchise into something that is emulated by others. Then you have players like Steve Young, Jerry Rice, Ken Norton, Merton Hanks, Brent Jones and Tim McDonald just to name a few. As an opposing coach, I always respected their abilities and talents on the field and now have seen the class and integrity in which they conduct themselves off the field as well. It's comforting to be on the same team.

I'm very honored and excited to have been named head coach of the San Francisco 49ers. Needless to say, it's a huge responsibility and challenge to follow a Hall of Famer like Bill Walsh and the man with the highest winning percentage in NFL history in George Seifert.

The torch has been passed.

There may be new faces both on the sidelines and on the field but one thing will remain the same: We are here to make sure this organization stays on top —this year and into the next century!

— *Steve Mariucci*

INTRODUCTION

The San Francisco 49ers celebrated their 50th anniversary in 1996 but my life-long love affair with the club began over 30 years ago, in the early 1960s.

It started as a lark. Three mischievous nine-year olds from the city's Sunset District decided to try something new on a sparkling fall morning. Armed with free 49ers tickets clipped off Christopher Milk cartons, my friends and I set off in search of adventure.

I'd never been to a football game and I wasn't sure where Kezar Stadium was located. But I convinced my pals that the Muni's 72-line, which ran on Sunset Boulevard near our homes, would take us in the general direction of Kezar Stadium. Once on board I asked the driver for directions. He eyed us with the tired expression of a man who'd been driving a bus for 30 years and said to get off with the rest of the crowd.

The bus was packed with men who could only be described as "eccentric." Some wore bright red and gold jackets, others sported tattered caps that looked as if they'd been handed down for generations. There was loud chatter and even louder transistor radios tuned to pregame shows.

As we approached Third Avenue, near the eastern edge of Golden Gate Park, everybody on the bus suddenly got up and disembarked. Following the bus driver's directions we jumped off too. It was then that I spotted Kezar Stadium for the first time. It might as well have been King Arthur's castle. I was overwhelmed. The size of the stadium and the enormity of the crowd as it moved along Lincoln Way toward the entrance gates were a spectacle hard for a nine-year old to comprehend.

We waded through the crowd and innocently tried to convince a ticket-taker that our ducats entitled us to admission near the 50-year line. He patiently directed us to an area reserved for Christopher Milk patrons.

Inside, we realized it was a very special section. It was fenced off from the rest of the crowd and intended for young fans under the age of 17. But the age requirement was loosely enforced. Men old enough to have served in World War I sat near us chain-smoking Lucky Strikes and occasionally sipping from a bottle wrapped in a brown paper bag. Between sips they cussed at quarterback John Brodie, using words I'd never heard at St. Gabriel's grammar school.

I immediately disliked the men. I hated cigarette smoke and Brodie was the only player with whom I was familiar. Before the day was over I would know about another 49er star.

It wasn't far into the game that I noticed Brodie connecting on passes to a wide receiver named Dave Parks. It wasn't the receptions that were so striking, it was the way Parks got to the football. He was like an acrobat, leaping and twisting to catch everything in his direction. Midway through the second quarter he hauled in an 80-yard touchdown pass.

I was hooked. That game opened a whole new world for me, at the center of which were the 49ers. Little did I know that my new addiction would force me to suffer through years of despair as I watched the 49ers stumble and bumble their way through the 1960s and 1970s. There were brief glimpses of brilliance as the 49ers came close to NFC crowns in 1970, 1971 and 1972. But each time the season ended in heartbreak at the hands of the Dallas Cowboys.

The dejection was finally lifted in 1981 when the messiah, Joe Montana, led the 49ers to their first Super Bowl crown. Since that first championship, the 49ers have put together one of the most remarkable runs of any team in any sport.

After 50 years the 49ers are acknowledged as one of the most successful teams in professional sports, a franchise emulated and admired throughout the NFL. It is a standard they hope to improve on over the next 50 years.

—*Joseph Hession*

50 Years of 49ers

The 1996 season marked the San Francisco 49ers' 50th anniversary.

It seems hard to imagine that in 1946 the 49ers were playing their first home game at Kezar Stadium against the Chicago Rockets in the newly formed All-America Football Conference. The team's founders were unsure whether professional football would fly in the Bay Area. It flew. Now the 49ers are at the top of their game in the NFL and playing to sold-out crowds at 3Com Park.

What a history! To celebrate this anniversary, 49 fans recount their favorite team memories in this special section, "50 Years of 49ers."

The Christopher Milk section

Kezar Stadium was a wild place. As a kid, I used to sit in the Christopher Milk section, which was right next to the tunnel where the players came on and off the field. It was separated from the rest of the stadium by a cyclone fence.

We would buy a quart of Christopher Milk, which cost about 15 cents back then, then pour out the milk and clip the coupon off the back to get into the game. The section was supposed to be for kids. You were supposed to be under 15 or something like that.

Once you got in the Christopher Milk section, you realized the age rule was loosely enforced. There were guys old enough to be my grandfather sitting in there, and they were drinking whiskey and smoking cigarettes. Obviously, they weren't kids.

The worst part of the section was that people threw stuff at the players: bottles, hot dogs, peanuts, whatever they could get their hands on. Most of that stuff was thrown by the drunks and their aim was off, so once in a while a bottle or something would come flying into the kids' section since it was so close to the player's tunnel.

As I look back on it now, I realize how dangerous that place was.

—Bill Baxley

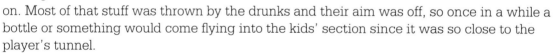

I recall the pass that Jerry Rice caught when he broke the record of most touchdowns. That was one of the most memorable 49ers moments. With that catch and throw by Steve Young, there was a kind of rhythm. The greatness of Jerry Rice and Steve Young really affects me. They really know how to do it. I've been a fan since Y.A. Tittle was a quarterback. I really became a fan when Mr. DeBartolo took over. He wanted it to be a truly great team, not a mediocre one.

**—Reverend Cecil Williams,
Glide Memorial Church**

Ricky Watters plays X-Men

One time our family was up at Lake Tahoe for a celebrity golf tournament. My brother and I were hanging out at Caesar's arcade, while my dad was hanging out and gambling with some of the celebrities.

I was playing the X-Men video game and some guy came in and said, "Excuse me. Do you mind if I play?"

I didn't know who he was. In fact, I didn't even look at him because I was playing the game. I just said "Sure."

For a long time I was playing the video game with this guy. After a while, my brother came over to watch and he whispered to me, "That's Ricky Watters you're playing with."

Then I looked and realized it was Ricky Watters and I almost died. I thought it was cool that he played with me, although I was getting mad because earlier he kept bumping into me while we played.

—Tony Lorber

49ERS FANS REMEMBER

You snooze, they lose

I was at Kezar Stadium in 1957 when the 49ers played the Detroit Lions in a playoff game. Both teams ended the season tied for first place and they needed the playoff to see who would advance to the NFL Championship Game.

San Francisco played fabulously in the first half and had a 24-7 lead. They got another field goal in the third quarter to go up 27-7. By that time, everybody was celebrating in the stands. We figured the 49ers had the game won and we left to hit the bars on Irving Street. We were really having a great time and I overindulged a little.

The next morning I woke up with a big hangover and read in the paper that the 49ers lost. I couldn't believe it. I went to bed happy, thinking the 49ers were going to play in the NFL Championship Game.

—*Bridget O'Sullivan*

For better or worse

I have held season tickets since the first year the 49ers were in Candlestick Park in 1971. I relocated to Orange County in 1986 but have continued to follow the team at home and away—against the Los Angeles Raiders, the Los Angeles Rams and the San Diego Chargers.

I can be in a constant state of euphoria or depression because of a game, but I still shoot. My job is to capture it all. It's the eye of the hurricane.

—Michael Zagaris,
49ers Team Photographer since 1973

My wife, Karen Meyer, and I picked our wedding day as the Saturday after Thanksgiving, November 24, 1990. We felt that a holiday weekend would allow more friends from out of the area to join us in our celebration.

Only after consulting our calendar and 49er schedule did we discover that our planned honeymoon would interfere with not one but two 49er home games. My bride graciously and lovingly assented to enjoying our honeymoon between the two games!

The capper was that my brother and his family posted a congratulatory message to us and 66,000 of our closest friends on the Candlestick scoreboard during the Sunday Rams game.

—*Paul Duggan*

More than a feeling

Super Bowl XXIII against the Cincinnati Bengals was a great moment. I remember thinking it didn't look good for the Niners late in the fourth quarter. Then Joe Montana took the field with about two minutes to go and I figured if anybody could take the 49ers 90 yards for the winning touchdown, it was him.

After the 49ers crossed the 50-yard line, I knew they were not going to give up and die. As they got closer to the goal line I could feel it coming. I knew they would score.

Finally, Joe lined up behind Randy Cross, took the snap and dropped back. He saw John Taylor in the end zone and hit him with a pass. Joe Montana's arms shot straight up into the air like they always do when he throws for a touchdown. That was a scene I'll never forget.

—*Dan Twomey*

50 YEARS OF 49ERS

A real old-timer

My memories of the 49ers go back to the very beginning of the franchise in the 1940s. Professional football was virtually unknown on the West Coast when the All-America Football Conference began in 1946. As a youngster of 10 or 11, it was very exciting to go to the 49er games.

Me and my brothers would hitchhike to the games from Burlingame after going to church, then we'd try to find a way to sneak into the stadium. One of the gatemen knew our family and he'd allow us through his gate if there was no supervisor around. Sometimes we were given tickets from adult fans who had extras.

One memorable Sunday we were at a game during which Norm Standlee was knocked out and was down for a really long time. Coaches and trainers and doctors were working over him and the crowd was hushed. We were told that Norm had swallowed his tongue and couldn't breath. One of the trainers knocked out some of his teeth with a knife handle and reached in and pulled out the blockage. Norm finished the game.

I found out just recently that what Norm had actually swallowed was a chaw of tobacco. Apparently, before mouth guards were common, the old pros chewed tobacco to keep their teeth clenched together and keep them from getting broken.

During the 1950s, once the franchise became established, I operated a parking lot at St. Mary's Hospital and paid for my college education, earning $85 to $100 a Sunday. Although this was great money at that time, I was unable to attend the games anymore.

—*Jim Monahan*

Why I hate the Cowboys

The 49ers broke my heart. I grew up in San Francisco and watched the 49ers religiously as a kid.

In the early 1970s I was a college student at Santa Clara and I still followed them pretty closely. They made the playoffs a couple times back then, but never went very far.

One year, 1972, I was at Santa Clara and listening to the 49ers-Dallas playoff game on the radio. San Francisco was up by about two touchdowns in the final couple minutes (San Francisco led 28-16). I thought for sure the 49ers would finally win a big playoff game and get to the Super Bowl. I was esctatic.

Instead, Roger Staubach came off the bench for Dallas and threw two touchdown passes in the final two minutes.

One of the 49ers (Preston Riley) fumbled an onside kick and the Cowboys recovered. When that happened, I knew the 49ers would probably lose but I refused to believe it.

When Staubach threw the winning touchdown pass, I literally fell on my bed and cried. I was heartbroken.

I've hated Staubach and the Cowboys ever since.

—*Steve Williams*

49ERS FANS REMEMBER

No Joe? I won't go

When the 49ers let Joe Montana go, I was disappointed. I remember his last game with the 49ers against the Detroit Lions. I really liked him and was looking forward to seeing him play. I don't recall his stats for the game, but I do remember the Lions defense kind of took it easy on him. Instead of pounding him hard when they had the opportunity, they would just shove him out of bounds or bring him down easy, which I thought was pretty cool.

Late in the game he threw a touchdown pass and he threw his hands up in the air like he always does. The TV reporters commented on how it was Montana's unique trait to throw his arms straight up after a touchdown, and they said it looked like he was healthy. I was looking forward to seeing Montana play the next season.

In the offseason, the 49ers traded Montana and I couldn't believe he was gone. I knew the team would never be the same again. He provided all those magical moments, the last minute drives. He'd always be able to find the open man.

Since then I haven't cheered for the 49ers or even liked them. I probably never will again because of what they did to Joe Montana.

—*Simon Seiba'a*

Best moment was playing the Rams in '89. I grew up as a Rams fan originally. The 49ers were down 17 points in the last quarter when Montana threw a long pass to John Taylor. It was my second year covering the team and it was so amazing to see the comeback. It was magical. Especially Montana. You knew that this player was really special. After the game, the Rams' faces coming off the field looked so down, like they were saying, "We'll never beat this team." It was very dramatic. As a journalist I know it's so much easier to interview players after a winning game. They are so much more effusive. Try asking a 350-pound guy why he missed a tackle and you'll know what I mean.

Kevin Lynch, Editor, 49ers Report

I saw "The Catch"...well, almost

The play that I'll always remember was toward the end of the 1981 season when the greatest quarterback ever hooked up with Dwight Clark on a touchdown pass that put the 49ers into their first Super Bowl.

Plays like the "Immaculate Reception" and "Hail Mary" were nothing compared to this play. It was dubbed "The Catch" and will go down in history as one of the greatest plays ever.

I was only five years old at the time, but I will never forget the effect it had on my life. It was a very dreary December afternoon and I was sipping on my fourth cup of hot chocolate because it was so cold. I had been to 49er games before and since, but none had an atmosphere like that one.

As I think back on the game, I realize I wasn't paying attention to much of it. I was whining and complaining because my father wouldn't buy me one of those large yellow fists with one finger sticking up.

I eventually got my toy and as I settled back down into my seat, the fans erupted. Not knowing what occurred, I began to cry because I could not see anything and it was very loud. I jumped up on my seat. Down in the end zone I recall seeing Joe Montana with his arms up in the air and the entire 49er squad jumping around like a bunch of maniacs.

I looked at my father and asked him what happened. I couldn't make out what he was yelling at first. After a few seconds, I realized he was screaming, "It's a touchdown! It's a touchdown!"

—*Tom Brady*

Nothing like the first time

A favorite memory I have of the 49ers is my first time going to a 49er game. My uncle had season tickets and he asked me to go to a game with him. It was on Christmas Eve against the Chicago Bears.

When my uncle came to pick me up I was all ready to go. I had on my 49ers sweater and a 49ers hat. Before going to the game we stopped at a hotel and got hot dogs and soft drinks, then we took a bus that went to Candlestick Park.

I remember walking in and wondering how many people were there. I had never seen so many people in one place in my life. As we walked in and sat at our seats I thought the park looked strange. I had been to many Giants games before and the stadium seemed different. There were so many more people, there was no baseball diamond, and the field looked a lot smaller.

I remember seeing Joe Montana throw a touchdown pass and Jerry Rice score a touchdown. It seemed different seeing it at Candlestick Park instead of on television.

Before I knew it, the game was over and we were going home. The 49ers won the game and I had a great time. As we left, I felt disappointed because I had to go home. That night all I could think about was the game, the excitement and all the people. It was one of the best times of my life and I'll never forget it.

—Tony Sciandri

The best Christmas present

When I was growing up, I lived fairly close to the 49ers practice field in Redwood City. My father would take me down to the field in the afternoon. I remember there was this green mesh woven into the fence. It was hard to see inside but there were areas where the mesh parts left a crack. I would put my eye in the crack and stare at all the players. Sometimes one would come up to me and talk. When all the players would head inside, I quickly would run to the door where they came out.

Usually the door was crowded with kids like me eager to get a hello, or the ultimate, an autograph. As soon as the players came out, kids would swarm all over them. I was small at the time and usually got shoved out of the way. But still it was fun to be there. I got extremely excited when I received an autograph from a player. I would show my mom as soon as I got home.

My uncle was a major 49er fan. He always had season tickets and would go to all the games. He loved the 49ers. So for a Christmas present one year I drew a poster with the 49ers helmet on it. I went down to the practice field one evening and tried to get it signed. I got Bill Walsh's signature, Ronnie Lott, Joe Montana and a lot more. It took me several evenings but I eventually got the majority of the team's signatures.

That Christmas, when my uncle opened the present, the look on his face was unbelievable. He loved it. It made me feel special when he told me it was the best present he ever received.

For years he had the poster on his wall. It was one of his most prized possessions. When he died he was buried with the poster in his coffin and a pair of 49er tickets in his hand.

—Aaron Meister

49ERS FANS REMEMBER

Up close and personal

One of my favorite memories as a 49er fan took place at Kezar Stadium on December 19, 1965.

My high school buddy and I would attend the 49er games through the Christopher Milk section. On this particular Sunday, the 49ers were playing the Green Bay Packers. The 49ers weren't very good in those days, but this last game of the season would be a special one.

The 49ers tied the Packers in the closing minutes of play at 24-24. John Brodie had a great game and threw the tying touchdown pass to an obscure player by the name of Vern Burke. It wasn't the score that was so memorable but the events that took place during those last couple of minutes.

My buddy and I went down on the field and were standing behind the Packers bench. In those days, Kezar didn't have a fence surrounding the field and fans could get down on the field easily.

So here we were standing close to all the great Green Bay players: Bart Starr, Paul Hornung, Jim Taylor, Boyd Dowler, Jerry Kramer, Ray Nitschke and Herb Adderley.

The best part was seeing Packers coach Vince Lombardi up close. Lombardi was outraged, to put it mildly, that the 49ers were able to tie the Packers. He was yelling and swearing at his players. He just couldn't believe what was happening.

The tie caused Green Bay and the Baltimore Colts to end the season tied for first place. It forced a playoff game the following week between the two of them. The Packers eventually won the playoff and the NFL title that year.

—*Bob Ferretti*

Never say die

The 49ers were trailing the New Orleans Saints 35-7 at Candlestick Park on December 7, 1980. Lon Simmons was nearly falling asleep while doing the radio commentary. It looked like another blowout.

Being a 49er "die-hard" since 1957, I never gave up. Fans were booing. Then I witnessed something miraculous.

Somehow the 49ers climbed back into the game, tied it in regulation and won in overtime. Ray "Mochine" Wersching kicked the field goal in overtime to give San Francisco a 38-35 win. At that time, it was the greatest NFL comeback

> *The greatest memory? It's still "The Catch." Everything that has happened since is because of it.*
> **—Hal Ramey, Sports Director, KCBS Radio**

ever. A guy named Joe Montana engineered the win.

The 49ers ended the year with another losing record at 6-10, but this time it was different. The team never gave up. They played a lot of close games and made it exciting. Yeah, the 49ers were out of the playoffs again and had to hope that next year would be a better season. And what a year it was.

The New Orleans game seemed to be a springboard to the 1981 season, which started off 1-2, but ended 13-3. It ended at Super Bowl XVI in the Silverdome at Pontiac, Michigan.

—*Bob Bachecki*

50 YEARS OF 49ERS

A bird's-eye view

Having been a 49ers fan trapped in Texas, I was excited to come to college in California so that I could experience being a Niners fan as a local.

Without a car and unable to afford game tickets, I had been content to read the various articles about the team in the local newspapers and watch all the games in their entirety. But when it was the week before Super Bowl XXIX, 49ers vs. Chargers, and the 49ers had moved their final West Coast practice to Stanford because the Santa Clara field was a swamp, I seized the opportunity. I went over to the enclosed field where the team was practicing, camera in hand. I found that I could not see clearly through the shielded fence unless I was right up on it and the security guards kept me from being able to do that.

The first time I peeked through I was told to move on after only a few seconds. I tried to find a spot on the other side, but I was turned away again. I circled the field but nowhere was there a spot from which I could view the practice in peace. I must have been told to move away about eight times by these guys, and I still hadn't gotten anything more than a glimpse of the team.

Unwilling to give up this once-in-a-lifetime chance to personally see my heroes in action, I decided the only way I would get to see the practice would be to climb a tall tree, out of the view of the myriad security guards. So I waited for an opportune moment and then climbed into the foliage of this tree until there was nowhere higher to climb. I must have been some 30 feet off the ground and, after I cleared away a couple branches, there I saw the 49ers in their practice gear.

I was awestruck! I looked over to the sideline bench, where I saw the great Deion Sanders and his trademark Do-Rag, hanging out with Merton Hanks and Eric Davis. Then I shifted my focus to the offense, which was running some passing and running drills against the practice squad. There was MVP Steve Young, handing off to Watters. Then a pass, Young to Rice, perfect. I was seeing all of the guys in person: Sapolu, Taylor, Floyd, Wallace, Plummer, Norton, McDonald, Stubblefield, Seifert. I was able to watch for about 45 minutes before the team rushed off to the buses and headed back to Santa Clara.

I managed to get a few pictures, which came out fairly well, though I wish I had had a high-powered lens. In any case, I had just gone to great lengths to watch the Niners exactly eight days before they would destroy the Chargers 49-26 for their fifth Super Bowl victory.

Without a doubt, that is my greatest 49er memory.

—Andrew Milk

> *My most memorable 49er moment was sharing in San Francisco's love affair with the team following the 1995 Super Bowl. I had the privilege of riding in the victory parade as thousands upon thousands of people from all walks of life lined the streets in a tremendous outpouring of congratulations and pride in our hometown champions.*
>
> **—G. Rhea Serpan, President and CEO, San Francisco Chamber of Commerce**

It's so hard to take one memory from this team, like asking a parent to name their favorite child. But I'd have to say it was the feeling in our locker room after Super Bowl XXIII, because it had been such a tough season after starting with a 6 and 5 record. I've been in a lot of championship and Super Bowl locker rooms, but this was magic. It was above and beyond.
—Michael Zagaris, 49ers Team Photographer since 1973

Those were the days...

The 49ers were playing at Kezar Stadium. It was one of those rare hot Sundays in the city. I was about 12 years old, so it must have been around 1966.

Before the kickoff, the Armed Forces color guard came marching out on the field. They looked great in their dress uniforms with the highly polished chrome helmets and white gloves.

After the National Anthem, they marched toward the west end zone. As they were approaching it, a drunk spectator let fly with a bottle of Budweiser. It hit one of the color guardsmen, the guy who was second from the left, square on his chrome helmet and dropped him.

Of course, there were some patriotic fans in the west end zone. Either they were war veterans, or they were mad because this guy wasted a whole bottle of beer. Anyway, they went after the guy who threw the bottle.

Soon enough, there was a huge fight in the west end zone. One spectator got beat up and was knocked all the way down the concrete stairs to field level.

I forget who won the game.

—Tom Monaghan

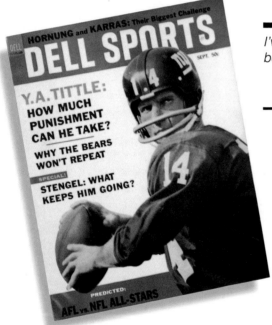

I've played tennis with a dozen or so 49ers. I had never realized before that tennis was a body contact sport.

—Arthur Hoppe, Columnist, San Francisco Chronicle

Riding coach

Whenever the 49ers played the Chicago Bears, it brought out the best in the fans. Or maybe it was the worst, depending on how you looked at it.

One time, in the 1950s, the 49ers were playing the Bears and the fans were riding "Papa Bear" George Halas pretty good. There were a couple of guys behind me who called Halas every name in the book.

Finally, as the game was nearing halftime, Halas turned around and looked at these guys and said something. You couldn't hear what he said, but he was definitely talking to the guys who had been yelling at him throughout the first half.

A few minutes later the half came to an end and the Bears all ran off the field. Halas was walking behind the team talking to another coach.

Then one of the guys who had been doing all the yelling got out of his seat and walked down by the side of the field. You could tell he was up to something. He obviously had a snoot full of booze in him. Suddenly he hopped the little fence and ran onto the field. He ran up behind Halas and kicked him in the seat of the pants as hard as he could. Then he turned and ran back into the stands before anybody could catch him.

Halas turned around and didn't know what happened because the guy ran away so fast.

It was one of the funniest things I've ever seen in my life.

—Phil Butler

49ERS FANS REMEMBER

Chance encounter

I was walking through this shopping mall in San Mateo. It must have been about 1968. I had just moved to the Bay Area from back East and I was still kind of a New York Giants fan.

If I remember right the 49ers weren't having a great season, but John Brodie was one of the most visible players on the team. He was about the only player I was familiar with.

Anyway, I saw Brodie at the mall. I approached him and asked for an autograph and ended up talking to him for about 20 minutes. He seemed like a really nice guy. After that, I became a 49er fan and a couple years later I bought season tickets. I've had them ever since.

You don't see players mingle with the fans like that anymore. They charge you for autographs or they're rude. But it was that chance encounter with John Brodie that made me a 49er fan.

—*Susan Margoli*

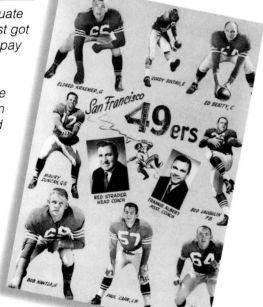

I was very partial to the 49ers in 1946 because I was a Stanford graduate and they had the great Stanford alum Frankie Albert playing. I had just got back from the war and it was a thrill to go to Kezar on Sunday. You'd pay $1 to get in and sit anywhere. I used to love watching Frankie Albert perform. The passing combination of Albert to Alyn Beals was as powerful as anything the Cleveland Browns had. The Browns were the dominant team in those days. In 1947, '48 and '49 I worked at the San Francisco Examiner promotion department and we always sponsored the opening pre-season games with the Los Angeles Dons. There I'd find myself in the end zone, catching the drop kicks and punts from (Jim) Thorpe. I've had a very interesting career going all the way back to the beginning in '46.

**—Lloyd McGovern, Founder,
49ers Report and Sports Historian,
Stanford University**

It was great—even if it was 20 below

My greatest day as a 49er fan was going to the team's first Super Bowl game in 1982 against Cincinnati. I flew back to Pontiac, Michigan on the red-eye flight with a bunch of friends.

I've been a 49er fan since the early 1950s and that was something special. First of all, there was the weather. It was snowing like hell and about 20 below zero. For us guys that grew up in the Mission District, that was a hell of an experience. I've only seen snow three times and I've never been in weather like that.

Then we got to the dome there in Pontiac. We were all bundled up and you walk in there and it's about 80 degrees. We had to take half our clothes off.

The 49ers jumped out to a big lead in the game. They were ahead 20-0 at halftime and everyone started celebrating. My friend Jack Sloan brought a pint of whiskey in the game and we polished that off, thinking the game was won. But the Bengals made a good comeback and actually could have won the game, except for a great goal line stand by the 49ers.

I remember how exuberant everyone was after the game. It was the first time the 49ers ever won anything. I'd been following the team for 30 years and that was their first championship so it was special.

—*Dan Stillman*

Future Football Players of America

My favorite 49er memory was around 1983 when my father took me to my first football game. It was when the 49ers were playing the Miami Dolphins and I was about seven years old.

I remember getting up early and going to the Candlestick parking lot for a tailgate party. It was a beautiful day. The sun was shining and there was just enough of a breeze to keep it from getting too hot.

I remember my dad telling me about his favorite player, Joe Montana, and telling me about some "rookie sensation" from the Dolphins who had a "pretty good arm."

I couldn't tell you who won the game, but I watched them march up and down the field and it seemed like each guy could throw the ball a million miles and run so fast. I thought, this is what I want to do. I want to play football.

I still remember everything about that day: the smell of popcorn in the air, the vendors walking by, and how cold my ice cream was when my dad handed it to me. I remember the breeze running through my hair and how the crowd screamed when the 49ers scored. I remember high-fiving the guys next to me and doing the wave every time it came by.

And I remember running up the stairs as we were leaving.

After we left the stadium, we waited around for the players to leave, and seeing them made me feel small and weak. But my mind was made up. I wanted to be just like them: big and strong.

I'll always remember that day: the sights and smells of the stadium, the roar of the crowd. But the thing I remember most is being on my father's shoulders as Joe Montana walked by. He looked at me and said, "Hey kid. How are ya?" and I thought, here's where I want to be someday, too.

—*Tim Podesta*

My first full year at Channel 2, I got to cover the Dallas-49ers game when the 49ers went to the Super Bowl. I was on the field during the game. The tension and electricity were incredible. It was so loud. My own palms were sweaty. I turned to my cameraman and said, "These guys deserve every penny they make to play under this pressure and tension." When Dwight Clark made The Catch, I was standing in the end zone about 25 feet away from him. It was the highlight of my broadcast career. I was 24 years old and to think I was also getting paid for this— it was a dream come true.

—Mark Ibanez, Sportscaster, KTVU

On the shoulders of giants

I was at the San Francisco Zoo for 49er Night. My family and I were walking up to the new monkey cages when I saw a guy with a 49er jersey on. It was number 50, so I knew it was Riki Ellison. He was one of my favorite players. I walked up to him and said, "Hi." I remember him being really tall. He put me up on his shoulders and took a picture with me, then walked me up to the monkey cages on his shoulders.

—*Mike Rudd*

49ERS FANS REMEMBER

Shut up, Sergio!

There was one game that really stands out for me. It wasn't a Super Bowl game or a playoff game. It was an exhibition game at Candlestick Park against the Raiders.

The year before I went to Los Angeles to see the 49ers play the Raiders, but the Niners failed me and lost. All the way home, my friend Sergio, who is a die-hard Raiders fan, was giving me a bad time. Even my uncles were getting sick of him and told him to shut up. I told him to wait until next year.

For the rest of that season, every time we saw the Niners play, Sergio would bring up the Raiders game.

Finally the new season came around and the Raiders and 49ers played at Candlestick this time.

We got to Candlestick early and had a barbecue in the parking lot. My uncles, friends and I were having a great time when Sergio showed up and started the Niner bashing. We told him to wait for the game.

This time the 49ers dominated from the opening kickoff. They were making great plays, scoring touchdowns, making tackles. By the end of the game, I was all over Sergio. All the way home I told him how great the Niners were. Every time I see him I still bug him.

I remember this game because of all the fun I had. Even though it wasn't a great game, it was a great day for me with my family and friends.

—Danny Navarro

My greatest 49ers memory was at Super Bowl XXIII, Miami, sitting with my husband Paul and two of my children in the end zone, surrounded by Cincinnati fans already celebrating their 16-13 victory over the 49ers. On the far side of the field, in the opposite end zone, Joe Montana huddled with his teammates with minutes to play. The beauty of what is now the legendary "Drive" is that Joe, Jerry, Roger and John were coming at us, and with each yard closer, the Bengals fans around us were awed into silence by its efficiency and ultimately, its inevitability. Montana to Taylor. 49ers 20, Bengals 16. The thunderous cheers rocked the stadium as the 49ers roared to victory.
—Congresswoman Nancy Pelosi

Bubba wins—hands down

One time I met Bubba Paris at a car dealership and got his autograph.

I was wearing a 49ers jersey that day with number 16 on it. He said that he protects anybody who wears that number.

I couldn't believe how big he was. I challenged him to arm wrestle. He won easily.

—Ricco Rodondi

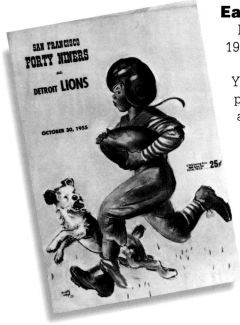

Early Steve Young fan

I was at that game against the Minnesota Vikings, I think it was 1988, where Steve Young broke about 10 tackles on a touchdown run.

I was sitting near the five-yard line in the roll-out seats. Steve Young came in at quarterback and the 49ers were losing by four points. The place was going nuts. There were 65,000 people yelling at the top of their lungs.

Young took the snap and couldn't find anyone to throw to. He took off running from about the 35-yard line. He was getting hit left and right by the Minnesota defense, but wouldn't go down. He must have got hit 10 times, and he almost tripped over his own feet a couple of times. By the time he got to the end zone, his helmet was halfway off. He must have run about 100 yards altogether and was so tired he just kind of fell into the end zone.

When he scored we were high-fiving and yelling at the top of our lungs. Then I got hit in the head with a bag of peanuts. I turned around and there was this drunk Vikings fan yelling, "The Niners are bums." I just laughed at him.

—Rob DeFrancis, Jr.

The 1996 season is the eighth year KGO has been the official 49ers broadcast station. Before this, we had to knock out the incumbent station and sell ourselves to the 49ers. It was a long and difficult struggle. It's proven to be worth every ounce of energy put forth. The 49ers are the crown jewel of the Bay Area. They are an extraordinary and prestigious team. It's great to be the one chosen for radio.

**—Michael Luckoff,
President and General Manager,
KGO-Radio**

Kezar in the '60s

Kezar Stadium during the late 1960s was kind of a weird place to watch a 49ers game.

First of all, there was absolutely no parking so we'd drive around Golden Gate Park and then the Haight looking for a spot. Once we found someplace to park, which was usually in someone's driveway, we would walk down Haight Street, which was overflowing with hippies then.

It was a strange scene. There were young kids sitting around on the street smoking pot. People would try to sell you drugs as you walked down the street. Other people were asking for money. I guess we looked like we had money because we had coolers with beer and were dressed fairly well.

Sometimes there would be bands playing on the street, even big name groups like the Grateful Dead. And the kids would be dancing around and having fun.

These kids were in their own world, though, and it was like they were oblivious to the fact that 55,000 people were gathering for a football game just a few blocks away.

—Julie Miles

49ERS FANS REMEMBER

Flashers and fumbles

There is one specific game I was at that I will remember for a long time. It was the NFC Championship Game in 1990 against the New York Giants. I went to that game thinking the 49ers had the game in the bag.

I was eating a deli sandwich and enjoying the game. The crowd seemed to have settled down. During a commercial timeout, some lady a couple of rows ahead of me decided to stand up and show everyone her breasts.

It was a tense game. Late in the fourth quarter, the 49ers were trying to run out the clock. I thought there would be no problem and the 49ers would win. Then Roger Craig fumbled and we lost the game. I guess even professionals make mistakes, too.

As everyone was leaving I saw little kids crying and adults cussing out Craig. A couple rows ahead of us was the lady who flashed everybody earlier. Two guys were begging her to do it again.

—Matt Hayes

In March of 1990, the 49ers were invited to the White House after the Super Bowl. President George Bush had invited the team and I was sent back East to cover it. This is one of my biggest interview memories. There I was in the Rose Garden doing a live shot back to San Francisco with Joe Montana. On air, I said, "Well, Joe, it seems the 49ers have been to the White House more often than the Democrats in the past decade." Well, Bush, Montana and Eddie DeBartolo all cracked up and there we were on-air. I don't know what made me say it.
—Dan Lovett, Sportscaster, KGO-TV

Getting a little punchy

There was a game at Kezar Stadium in the mid-1950s (1953) where the 49ers and Philadelphia Eagles got into a big fight. The players had their helmets off swinging them at each other. Hugh McElhenny was in the middle of it, but he was one of the guys who kept his helmet on. He was one of the smart guys.

Once the fight got going, a lot of fans ran onto the field. Some of them were throwing punches at the Eagles players.

I remember running onto the field, too. I thought I was a pretty good-sized guy. But once I got next to a couple of the players I realized how big they were and I ran right back into the stands.

They finally needed the police to go on the field to break up the fight.

—Larry Saros

Monday night at Candlestick

I went to a Monday Night game at Candlestick in 1990 when the 49ers played the New York Giants. Both teams were big rivals and the game had one of the best endings I've ever seen.

The Niners were leading 7-3 and the Giants had the ball on about the 49ers 15-yard line. It was fourth down with about 10 seconds left in the game.

Phil Simms, the Giants quarterback, had been accurate all night. He took the snap out of the shotgun formation. Linemen were being scattered everywhere. Simms looked for an open receiver in the end zone. Just when he saw one, the pocket collapsed. As he tried to escape, he was sacked by Pierce Holt.

The entire crowd jumped to its feet because the clock had run out, too. The 49ers won the crucial game in the closing seconds on an outstanding defensive play.

As I rode home on the bus, everybody talked about it being one of the best 49er games they'd ever seen, even though it was just a regular season game.

—*Bryan Eaton*

My wife Ronni and I have been San Francisco 49er fans and season ticket holders from the beginning and found every game was thrilling but each Super Bowl finish was the ultimate. I was asked by Eddie DeBartolo to design the special 49er Super Bowl watch for each time they won. He gave watches to his players, family and business associates. It has been an honor and pleasure to be a friend of Eddie DeBartolo and his family.

—*Sidney Mobell*

Welcoming home the heroes

A day I'll never forget was the parade after the 49ers beat Cincinnati to win the Super Bowl. Everybody was talking about how Joe Montana had provided one of the greatest Super Bowl endings ever by throwing a touchdown pass to John Taylor in the final seconds of the game.

The parade was special, though, because it brought together people from all over the city. It was a little rowdy, but nobody got hurt. It was like everybody was friends. Everyone was there to worship the Niners.

That's something special when all these people can come together to watch our heroes parade down the street and everyone is cheering them on.

I don't think there is anything else that can bring San Franciscans together like that. We owe it all to the Niners.

—*Tim Weber*

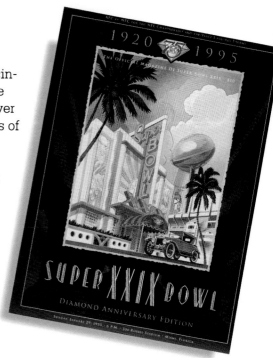

FLASH80

Back in 1987, when I was 11 years old, I found out that Jerry Rice was signing autographs near my home. I told my father, and he got so excited that he immediately drove my brother (who was eight years old) and I out to meet him. When we got to the store where Rice was signing, I noticed a gorgeous red Jaguar in the parking lot that obviously belonged to Jerry Rice, as evidenced by the license plate which read "FLASH80."

Rice was in the middle of a spectacular season, but being a second year player, was signing autographs for free. The line wasn't that long, and when I finally got to meet him, I was in awe. He said some nice things to me and signed a 49ers banner I had brought with me.

What I remember most though is his hands. I got a chance to shake hands with him, and my little 11-year-old hand completely disappeared from sight. His hand was really strong and his fingers seemed a bit longer than normal.

From then on, I believed all those stories about how he developed his catching skills by working with his father, a bricklayer, and catching bricks thrown to him. Rice could have put his hand all the way around a brick without any effort at all. He'd have no problem with a football.

—David Zizmor

Anytime you sit down with (team president) Carmen Policy, it's a pleasure. In the '80s, the team got arrogant and pretty tough to deal with. Policy injected humility back into the team. He knows it's not just about touchdowns, but it's about people, too. The attitude of the entire organization changed when he came in. He understands that just because you're winning, that's not a license to be arrogant.

—Gary Radnich,
Sports Director of KRON-TV and KNBR Radio

Having a ball

Security at Kezar Stadium was pretty lax in the 1960s. One time the 49ers lined up for a field goal attempt. I think the kicker was Tommy Davis. I ran on the field behind the goal post and caught the ball after the field goal. Then I threw it to a group of my friends waiting in the stands and ran off the field before I could get caught. Later I took the ball with me to Santa Clara when I went to college. We used to play touch football with it all the time.

—Larry Bourke

Record breaker

Watching Jerry Rice score touchdown number 127 against the Los Angeles Raiders was a great memory for me. It allowed Rice to break Jim Brown's old touchdown record on Monday Night Football.

I've always thought of Jerry Rice as the greatest wide receiver the NFL has ever seen. Breaking Jim Brown's record proved it. He has a special talent. He works hard and is determined to use his talent to its fullest. He's one of the hardest working players in the game.

The thing that also makes him special is the way he runs after the catch. Many receivers make the catch and are immediately tackled. But Jerry Rice makes the catch, then continues to run through the defense as if it is frozen.

Jerry Rice is a classic example of how hard work can get you to the top.

—*Michael Varni*

I have very vivid memories of the 49ers in 1982 right after their Super Bowl win. I had just moved to San Francisco and my apartment overlooked the entire city. As I looked out, it seemed the entire city was celebrating and everybody was shouting all at once. It's not often a city as diverse as San Francisco agrees on anything, but the 49ers brought everyone together.

—Mike Sugarman, KCBS Radio

49ERS FANS REMEMBER

Oh say, can you see...

We had a bunch of methods for sneaking into 49er games at Kezar when we were teenagers. We had a friend who was a vendor and sometimes we would borrow his vendor shirts and just tell the guy at the gate we were vendors.

Usually we got there early to watch the players warm up. Sometimes we would just pay the 50 cents to get into the east end zone. It was separated from the rest of the stands by a fence. Once the National Anthem started, and all the security guards were standing at attention, we would jump over the fence and find better seats near the 50-yard line.

—Bud Dunn

There's probably not just one memorable 49er moment. I think that the times that most defined the 49ers were the final few moments of any close game when Joe Montana received the snap with the whole field in front of him. Everyone in the stadium knew they were about to see something magical.

**—Joan Ryan, Columnist,
San Francisco Chronicle**

How long have I been a 49er fan? 37 years and climbing!
**—Willie L. Brown, Jr.,
Mayor of San Francisco**

The 49ers have always represented teamwork at its best and a striving for excellence. Both are critical. At our business, we are focusing on both of these, teamwork and excellence. Not only are the 49ers a great team to watch, but because of their example to business, the 49ers have always been a team worth following.

**—Harvey D. Hinman,
Vice President and General Counsel,
Chevron Corporation**

1946–1949

CHAPTER ONE

THE FORMATIVE YEARS

The world was finally at peace in 1946. Harry Truman was president, Joe Louis was the heavyweight champion of the world and Stan Musial was the National League MVP.

In San Francisco, Mayor Roger Lapham ruled City Hall as professional football invaded Kezar Stadium.

The San Francisco 49ers were the dream of a young trucking executive named Tony Morabito who spent six years trying to make his dream a reality. Morabito was a native San Franciscan who attended the University of Santa Clara. After building a trucking empire that spanned the Pacific Northwest, he approached the National Football League in 1941 with a request for a franchise.

The league turned him down, reasoning that the Bay Area was inundated with college football teams. California, Stanford, St. Mary's, Santa Clara and the University of San Francisco were all playing major college schedules. A professional team could never outdraw the college talent in the area, according to NFL management. San Francisco had too much football.

Travel costs were another consideration of the NFL. A round-trip air flight from San Francisco to New York was $270, and all the professional teams were congregated on the Eastern seaboard or in the Midwest. There were no professional teams west of St. Louis. They were not prepared to incur that travel expense for their 32 players and assortment of coaches.

Although rebuffed by the NFL, Morabito did not give up hope of acquiring a franchise. He caught wind of a scheme to start a new football league. It was the brainchild of Arch Ward, sports editor of the *Chicago Tribune*. Eager to join the league, Morabito attended the first meeting of prospective franchise owners. He finally got his wish. The San Francisco 49ers were made charter members of the All-America Football Conference in June 1944 after posting a $25,000 admittance fee. Jim Crowley, one of Notre Dame's legendary Four Horsemen, was appointed the first commissioner. The league began operation in 1946.

Morabito enlisted two partners from his trucking business, Allen Sorrell and Ernest J. Turre, to become partners in the franchise. Victor Morabito, Tony's younger brother, later joined the enterprise as a partner.

Legend has it that Sorrell came up with the name 49ers, although no one knows for sure. It was originally spelled out Forty Niners and was an appropriate reminder of the pioneers who flooded Northern California during the Gold Rush of 1849. Those gold miners eventually helped build the city of San Francisco.

The team's original logo depicted the city's wild beginnings. It consisted of a prospector, clad in boots and a lumberjack shirt, firing a pair of pistols. One shot just misses the miner's head, the other misses his foot. The logo was taken from a design seen on the side of railway freight cars. In that picture, the prospector was in front of a saloon. The 49ers dropped the saloon from the logo.

Morabito recognized that his young team would need an experienced lead

John Colmer of the Brooklyn Dodgers is brought down by the 49ers' Gerry Conlee (22). Don Durdan (93) was in on the stop.

er, so he persuaded Buck Shaw to coach his 'new club before he even had any players.

Shaw came into prominence as a tackle at Notre Dame where he played under the guidance of George Gipp. At Santa Clara, the lean, silver-haired Shaw built a reputation as one of the finest coaches in the nation. His overall won-lost record with the Broncos was 46-10-2, including upset victories over Louisiana State in the 1937 and 1938 Sugar Bowls.

Shaw previously had been approached to coach several professional teams. He turned down the offers, preferring to stay in the Bay Area. During World War II, he served as a temporary coach at the University of California. For Morabito to land a coach of Shaw's caliber was a major coup. His image and national reputation brought instant respectability not only to the 49ers, but to the entire league.

Morabito then focused his attention on the rich supply of college talent in the Bay Area and turned it into an asset. He recruited players whose names were familiar to local football fans. Many of these players were returning from stints in the armed forces during World War II and had played for pow-

erful service teams like the El Toro Marines, St. Mary's Pre-Flight and Fleet City.

Frankie Albert was one of Morabito's first acquisitions. Albert had played his college ball at Stanford, then teamed with Len Eshmont at St. Mary's Pre-Flight. The left-handed Albert stood only 5' 9" and weighed 170 pounds, yet local writers called him the best T-Formation quarterback in the game.

Several other Stanford graduates, including Norm Standlee and Bruno Banducci, joined the 49ers in 1946. Banducci, who played with the Philadelphia Eagles prior to World War II, became an All-Pro guard for the 49ers in 1952, 1953 and 1954.

Standlee, known as Big Chief, starred in the backfield with Albert on Stanford's undefeated team of 1940. He signed with the Chicago Bears in 1941, where he had a spectacular rookie season, leading the Bears to the NFL title. He came to the 49ers after World War II and gave them the tough inside runner needed to complement Albert's aerial game.

Shaw returned to his Santa Clara roots and recruited some of his former players. He signed Alyn Beals, Visco Grgich, Dick Bassi, Eddie Forrest and several other Bronco stars. Beals turned into one of the great receivers of his time and holds the AAFC all-time scoring record.

Many other players with previous NFL experi-

Frankie Albert 1946–1952

He was called "the T-Formation Wizard" and for good reason. Frankie Albert threw 88 touchdown passes in four years of All-America Football Conference play, the league record.

Other than Otto Graham, a member of the Hall of Fame, no one came close to that. Remember, that was the era of three yards and a cloud of dust, a time when throwing the football was akin to witch-

craft. And maybe that's why Frankie Albert was called the wizard. He certainly could throw a football.

In 1948, he led the wildest offense in the nation, throwing 29 touchdown passes in 14 games. That was a 49er single-season record that stood until 1965 when John Brodie threw for 30, the current record.

At 5' 9" and 170 pounds, the southpaw from Stanford didn't look

like a football player. But on the field his wide array of talents took over. He could run, throw, kick and handle the ball like a magician. With Albert in control, the ball disappeared more times than a rabbit in a vaudeville show—now you see it, now you don't.

"I guess my ability to handle the ball made me effective," he said modestly. "I was pretty good on a bootleg. I could hide the ball and run it if I

had to."

But running the football wasn't what made Albert one of the highest paid players in the old league. It was tossing the pigskin. He credits Alyn Beals, a Santa Clara graduate, for helping him set the record for touchdown passes in a season. Beals caught 14 scoring passes in 1948, the AAFC record. The next year he caught 12 touchdown passes. Gene Washington and Dave Parks share the "official" 49er single-season record set in the NFL with 12 touchdown catches.

"Beals was my main receiver," said Albert. "Boy, did he have some great moves. He was a good faker. I can remember several times setting up to pass and watching the defensive back fall down after Alyn put a fake on him. The back would trip over his own feet. I'd look at the defensive man lying on his butt while Alyn was wide open."

Albert was not just an offensive whiz, he mixed it up on defense as well. Against the Cleveland Browns and Otto Graham you could generally find Albert in the defensive secondary.

"I enjoyed playing defense," he said. "I didn't do it as often as I would have liked. I played back there in some of the important games like against the Browns."

Cleveland became the 49ers first great rival. In the AAFC, every game against them was important. Three times between 1946 and 1948, the 49ers finished second to the Browns. In the 1949 AAFC Championship Game, Cleveland beat San Francisco, 21-7.

"When we played Cleveland, it was like the Stanford–Cal game here," Albert said. "It was a real big rivalry. Whenever we beat them, it was a big thrill for me."

Albert had one of the best games of his career against the Browns. The year was 1949. San Francisco was on a roll. They had won four of their first five games and averaged 35 points per contest. When the 49ers battled

Cleveland at Kezar that day, Albert could do no wrong. He threw five touchdown passes as the 49ers whipped the Browns, 56-28.

In 1951, San Francisco acquired Y.A. Tittle from Baltimore. The two quarterbacks alternated for two years before Albert decided to retire in 1952.

"When he arrived there was quite a rivalry for the quarterback position," he said. "Of course, he was already an established star. I guess you could say there was a quarterback controversy. Whenever I see him now, I tell him he sent me to Canada."

Within a year after retiring from the 49ers, Albert went back to work for the Calgary Stampeders of the Canadian Football League.

"I was just getting into the car business," said Albert, "and it was a little slow at first. The Stampeders offered me more money then I ever made in the NFL, so I went up there for a year. We played two games a week, one on a Saturday and one on Monday. That was because the farmers would come to town on the weekends. They'd get drunk, go to the games and raise hell."

Albert returned to the states and was made an assistant coach of the 49ers in 1955 under Head Coach Red Strader. The team floundered under Strader, and Albert was thrown into the fire the next year when he was made the head coach.

"I liked certain aspects of coaching," he said impassively. "I enjoyed teaching the kids."

Albert lasted three years as the 49ers' head coach. His overall record

was 19-17-1. In 1957, he guided the team to an 8-4 season and a playoff spot against Detroit. But that game ended in another agonizing loss when the Lions rallied from a 27-7 deficit, to beat the 49ers, 31-27.

"I still can't believe that game," he said with disgust. "We were ahead and started playing conservative. That's what killed us. They scored once, then they scored twice, and the next thing you know they are ahead. It was embarrassing. It just goes to show you how quickly things can happen on a football field."

Although the 49ers came close to winning a championship several times with Albert at the helm, either as a quarterback or a coach, they never quite made it. That frustration is offset by the camaraderie and friendships Albert established as one of the original 49ers.

"There were some real characters on those teams," he said. "Bob St. Clair was one of them. He used to eat raw meat. We'd go to a nice restaurant and he liked beef so he'd order a steak or something. He'd tell the waiter to just have the chef heat the meat. He didn't want it cooked, just warmed up. A few minutes later the chef would look out from the kitchen to see who was ordering their meat like that.

"He's one of the few guys from the old teams that could be playing today. He was that good. And he had the size (6'9", 265). Besides Bob, Leo Nomellini was a good one on the line. In his

later years, he played only defense, but he was a pretty good offensive lineman too."

Behind those 49er lines were two of the most explosive running backs to ever strap on shoulder pads. Albert cultivated a reputation as an unpredictable gambler on the football field, but he admits that with Hugh McElhenny and Joe Perry in the backfield it was much easier to do the unexpected.

"I had good players to gamble with," he said. "You can't compare many backfields with Mac and Joe Perry. Mac was the best open-field runner from the T that ever played. Perry was a different runner. He was good straight ahead. Mac was always zigging and zagging around the field."

Albert played alongside some of the NFL's biggest stars. Several teammates and opponents are in the Hall of Fame. When he watches the current 49er team, he is reminded of the great quarterbacks of football's past.

"I wasn't bad as a scrambler or ball-handler, but after watching Montana play I don't think I could carry that guy's helmet," said Albert. "I've seen some great quarterbacks—Otto Graham, Bob Waterfield, Norm Van Brocklin—and I'd say Montana ranks with the top two or three to ever play the game. When things break down and people start to scatter, he's at his best. He can get out of trouble and do things no other quarterback can do. He makes plays out of nothing. That's a gift."

ence signed with the 49ers after finishing their military duties. Halfback Len Eshmont, a former New York Giant, Bob Titchenal, an end from the Washington Redskins, and Parker Hall, a halfback who played with the Cleveland Browns, were among those who offered their services to the 49ers in the club's inaugural season.

San Francisco quickly became one of the teams to beat in the AAFC. Unfortunately, they played in the same division as the Cleveland Browns, a perennial powerhouse in the new league. During their four years in the AAFC, the Browns would be a constant thorn in the 49ers' side.

The first professional game played by the 49ers was an exhibition match against the Los Angeles Dons on August 24, 1946, at San Diego's Balboa Park. Only 8,000 fans turned up to watch San Francisco defeat the Dons, 17-7. The first touchdown in the history of the franchise was scored on a 35-yard pass from backup quarterback Parker Hall to Hank Norberg.

A week later, the 49ers played their first home game, a preseason contest, at Kezar Stadium. Despite the sale of only 1,100 season tickets, nearly 40,000 curious fans crowded into Kezar to see the 49ers take on the Chicago Rockets and their spectacular halfback, Elroy "Crazy Legs" Hirsch. They weren't disappointed. Two local boys, quarterback Frankie Albert and receiver Alyn Beals, combined to lead the Niners to a 34-14 win. Albert's accurate passing earned raves in the local press.

The first showing of major league football in San Francisco was hailed as a huge success by local sports writers. Morabito had anticipated losing money in his initial season. Crowds of only 4,000 and 5,000 were expected at the gate. The large turnout at the first contest gave him higher expectations.

The 49ers' successful debut led *Chronicle* Sports Editor Bill Leiser to write, "Their team, we think, is as good as any professional team we ever saw, including the best of the Chicago Bear teams. It is much better than the present National League Champion Los Angeles Rams team." With the fans convinced that San Francisco had a quality football club, they flocked to Kezar on game days.

TOP: Buffalo Bills defensive back Steve Juzwik (88) knocks the ball away from 49er receiver Alyn Beals. Beals was the all-time leading scorer in AAFC history with 278 points. He caught 14 touchdown passes in 1948, a 49er record. BOTTOM: Head Coach Buck Shaw.

The 49ers' John Woudenberg (hidden) and Dick Horne (51) stop Monk Gafford (80), a Brooklyn Dodger running back.

The 49ers now had to tune up for their opening game against the New York Yankees, one of the class teams of the new league. A large crowd was expected at Kezar because of the 49ers' 2-0 preseason record. To avert long waits at Kezar ticket booths, general admission tickets went on sale the week of the game at Roos Brothers clothing stores and at the Crane Box Office.

Kickoff was at 2:30 p.m. The game was rated a tossup by local bookmakers. Experts agreed the game would be decided along the line of scrimmage.

New York's powerful line consisted of Jack Russell, Perry Schwartz, a four-time All-Pro in the NFL, and the intimidating brother combination of George and "Bruiser" Kinard. Schwartz had been an All-American at the University of California as an undergraduate. Ace Parker, Blondy Black and Spec Sanders rounded out the Yankees' offense.

San Francisco's smooth backfield of Albert, Norm Standlee, John Strzykalski and Len Eshmont was expected to carry the team. The line, consisting of

Dick Bassi, Bruno Banducci, John Woudenberg and John Kuzman, was not to be underestimated however. Said Yankee line coach Al Ruffo to the press before the game, "Nobody is going to push this 49er line around."

On game day, 35,700 fans turned out at Kezar despite the thick gray fog that hovered over the stadium most of the day. Things didn't go quite as expected for the 49ers. They were completely dominated by New York, 21-7. San Francisco's only score came in the first quarter on a nifty pass and lateral play. Frankie Albert tossed a 12-yard pass to John Strzykalski, who then lateraled to Len Eshmont. Eshmont took the lateral and romped 54 yards down the sidelines to score. The entire play covered 66 yards. Joe "the Toe" Vetrano added the extra point.

The novelty of professional football apparently wore off quickly because only 17,500 fans turned out at Kezar Stadium the following week to watch the 49ers battle the Miami Seahawks. Prior to the game, it was discovered that running back Norm Standlee had a knee injury that would keep him out of action. Buck Shaw intended to make up for the loss of his star runner by having Albert throw more passes. He did just that, completing passes at will to Alyn Beals, Parker Hall and Nick Susoeff. The 49ers had their first victory in the AAFC, 21-14. All three 49er TDs were scored by fullback Dick Renfro.

The third week of the season, the Niners won big, turning back the Brooklyn Dodgers, 32-13. Albert threw two scoring tosses to Alyn Beals and one to Len Eshmont. Eshmont also threw a 43-yard touchdown pass to Bob Titchenal and scored on an end run.

After the game, Dodgers' assistant coach Mal Stevens told reporters, "San Francisco has a team which its citizens should well be proud of. Either in exhibition or in league, we have played New York, Cleveland, Chicago and Los Angeles, and I can truly say San Francisco was the finest club we met. You have the most imaginative attack and the men to work it. Yes sir, the most imaginative style."

The 49ers continued to play surprisingly good football throughout the season. They beat Cleveland, 34-20, and ended the year with three straight wins over Brooklyn, Chicago and Los Angeles to give themselves a 9-5 record and second place in the Western Division. Most importantly, behind Frankie Albert and Coach Buck Shaw, they had developed the "imaginative style" that would become a 49er trademark for 40 years.

Alyn Beals 1946–1951

In 1948, Alyn Beals caught 14 touchdown passes. No 49er ever scored more in a single season.

The record is an obscure one. It was set while the 49ers were members of the All-America Football Conference. Beals' standard of excellence may be lost on a new generation of 49er fans, but to his peers, he was recognized as one of the best of his time. Three times they selected him to the AAFC All-Star team.

Beals toiled as the 49ers' right end from 1946 to 1951. He was al-ways a reliable receiver. In 1946, his first year in professional football, he tied for the league lead with 40 pass receptions. Ten of those catches were for touchdowns.

He had a knack for finding the end zone. In his four years of AAFC play, he scored 46 touchdowns and was the league's all-time scoring leader with 278 points.

Dante Lavelli is the only receiver to score nearly as many touchdowns and he has been in Pro Football's Hall of Fame since 1975. Yet Lavelli scored only 29 touchdowns in the AAFC.

Beals caught 177 passes in the old league to put him second on the all-time list. Lavelli caught just 142.

Beals played collegiate ball at Santa Clara under Buck Shaw. When Shaw was made coach of the original San Francisco 49ers, he immediately recruited his star pupil. Beals became the first in a long line of great 49er pass catchers.

"I got on the team while I was in Germany," Beals said. "The war had just ended. I was a captain in the Army with a field artillery unit. I was making about $275 a month. Buck Shaw had coached me at Santa Clara, and he sent a contract to Germany asking me to play for the 49ers. The contract was for $5,000. Of course, I signed it immediately. That was good money back then. And I only had to work for six months. I think I was also supposed to get a signing bonus of $50 but I never saw that.

"Buck Shaw was a great innovator," he said. "He was offensive minded. He was one of the first coaches to start spreading the ends out. We used to have the ends spread only about a foot. He kept spreading them off the tackles a little at a time. It opened up the passing game a little more. Playing for Buck was a pleasure. It was just like being back at college."

Beals could not have caught all those passes unless he had a steady quarterback to get the ball to him. Quarterback Frankie Albert was just the man to do it. When Albert was at the helm, he saw to it that Beals got plenty of action.

"Frankie Albert was really something," Beals recalled. "He was a good team leader. What made him so effective as a quarterback was that he could do just about everything. He was a good scrambler. He could pass, run or kick the ball. He was probably the most famous athlete in the area at that time because he'd come from Stanford and got a lot of publicity there."

Like most good passing and receiving combinations Beals and Albert had a special relation-

ship. They were able to predict what the other person would do in certain situations. When the blocking broke down and plays fell apart, Beals knew where to go.

"Whenever Frank was under pressure," Beals said, "I knew what he would try to do. He was left-handed and I knew he would roll out and throw in that direction. Whenever he started to scramble, I would change my pattern and go to his left. He must have known I would because I caught a lot of passes that way."

Beals and Albert put their talents together for six seasons with the 49ers, four years in the AAFC and another two in the NFL. Beals retired in 1951, while Albert played one more season.

In the early years of the franchise, the Cleveland Browns were football's powerhouse. Beals well remembers the awesome talent they had on their offensive unit. Four times the Browns edged out San Francisco for first place in the AAFC.

"The Cleveland Browns were our big nemesis back then," he said. "Just look in the Hall of Fame. A lot of Hall of Famers came from the old Cleveland Browns. There was Marion Motley and Otto Graham in the backfield. They had great receivers like Mac Speedie and Dante Lavelli. Bill Willis was a big lineman. Tom Colella was one of their defensive backs. He gave me a tough time."

Games between the Browns and 49ers drew enormous crowds while they were members of the AAFC. One game in 1948 attracted 82,000

fans. But that wasn't the game that Beals most remembers. A 56-28 trouncing of the Browns in 1949 is his personal favorite. Beals scored one of the touchdowns in that game.

Beals has fond memories of the original San Francisco 49ers during the team's formative years. He is proud of the part he played in the team's birth, like a man who has helped create something special.

"When we started out, we all had to stick together," he said. "We had a lot of things in common. The war was just over and most of us had just gotten out of the service. A large group of us lived out at Parkmerced —it was fairly new then —so we saw one another all the time. We are still good friends. A day doesn't go by when I don't hear from Joe Vetrano. I hear from all those guys.

"We had lots of fun back then. I think we were a lot closer than the guys today. We were a close-knit group. After the games we all went out and drank beer together. It wasn't uncommon to find about 25 of us going out to the same place. You don't see that today.

"When I think back, my biggest thrill wasn't any one game or play, it was just being part of the team. There was plenty of important games in my career, but it was the excitement of being with the 49ers back then. Not many people get a chance to be a part of something like that. We helped get the team started."

Hermen Wedemeyer (94), a halfback with the Los Angeles Dons, has his jaw wrenched by 49er defensive back Paul Crowe. Wedemeyer was a running sensation with St. Mary's College in Moraga before turning pro. Crowe was also a St. Mary's graduate. FOLLOWING SPREAD: Len Eshmont (81) races down the sideline with an intercepted pass against the New York Yankees. Pete Wismann (22) lays a block for his teammate. Eshmont led the club in interceptions in 1947 with six. He also was a running back on offense, rushing for 1,181 yards in his four seasons with the 49ers.

1947 During the off-season, owner Tony Morabito made headlines by trying to sign Glenn Davis and Doc Blanchard, West Point's "Touchdown Twins." The two collegiate stars were entitled to 90-day furloughs. Morabito invited them to play for the 49ers during their break. Army brass quickly put an end to Morabito's plan by prohibiting cadets from participating in activities for personal profit while on furlough.

Although unable to sign the "Touchdown Twins," the 1947 San Francisco club did sign the first Asian-American running back in professional football history. Wally Yonamine was a Japanese halfback from Farrington High School in Hawaii. He never played collegiate football, but Buck Shaw considered him an outstanding breakaway runner. An unexpected development prevented the 49ers from putting his speed to good use.

At Yonamine's first professional game at Kezar Stadium, 43,000 fans were on hand to watch the exhibition contest between the Los Angeles Dons and the 49ers. As the team made its way through the tunnel leading from the locker rooms to the field, Yonamine caught sight of the awesome crowd and froze in his tracks. A fear of large crowds plagued him all season. He played sparingly and never showed the running potential Shaw had hoped for.

The 49ers kicked off the 1947 season with fancy red-and-gold uniforms. The new outfits did little to fool the Los Angeles Dons in their first preseason match. Los Angeles defeated San Francisco, 14-7.

Despite the loss, several returning veterans looked good for the 49ers, particularly quarterback Frankie Albert. Albert sparked the 49ers to their only touchdown on the first possession of the game. Working from the 49ers' 48-yard line, he drove them the length of the field in 12 plays and scored on a three-yard run. The long gain in the drive was a 12-yard pass from Albert to Len Eshmont.

The following week, the 49ers opened regular season play at Kezar against the Brooklyn Dodgers and their star quarterback Glenn Dobbs. Unseasonable San Francisco sunshine greeted the 31,900 fans who watched the 49ers defeat the Dodgers, 23-7, for their first victory of the year.

Dobbs, considered by many to be the premier quarterback of his day, was stymied by a tough 49er defensive line. Ed Balatti, a 22-year-old defensive end from Oakland, led the charge on the line. Balatti teamed with Bruno Banducci and Eddie Forrest to pressure Dobbs into several errant throws. He ended the day completing only eight of 23 passes and had one intercepted.

The 49ers' first score came on a pass from Albert to Alyn Beals. Another Albert pass to Len Eshmont was lateraled to Strzykalski who then ran 17 yards for a touchdown. Reserve quarterback Jesse Freitas also threw a touchdown pass to Beals. Joe Vetrano added a field goal to round out the scoring.

The 49ers had posted a 5-1-1 record when the

Running back Sam Cathcart (86) is tackled by Tom Landry, a defensive back with the New York Yankees. Landry gained fame as the coach of the Dallas Cowboys. PAGE 17: Paul Salata (55), a 49er wide receiver, just misses a pass from quarterback Frankie Albert in a game against the New York Yankees at Yankee Stadium. Defensive back Harmon Rowe (90) stays close.

defending champion Cleveland Browns came to town for the most important game of the season. Paul Brown, head coach of the Browns, had put together one of the most potent offenses in football. The Cleveland scoring machine centered around quarterback Otto Graham, fullback Marion Motley and halfback Dan Greenwood. The previous year the Browns were a 20-point favorite in a game played at Cleveland against the 49ers. The 49ers had soundly defeated them, 34-20. Revenge was in the air.

Cleveland trotted into Kezar Stadium for the 2:30 p.m. kickoff a one-point favorite. A near sellout crowd of 54,500 waited impatiently for the game to begin. At that time, it was the largest attendance at a professional sports function in San Francisco history.

Otto Graham was too much for the 49ers. His pinpoint passes to Dante Lavelli and Mac Speedie led the Cleveland Browns to a 14-7 win. Between sideline tosses to his fleet ends, Graham sent bruising fullback Marion Motley through the middle on slants and trap plays.

San Francisco's only score came after taking the second half kickoff and marching 80 yards in 13 plays. The touchdown came on a one-yard plunge by fullback Norm Standlee. Standlee led the 49er rushing attack, gaining 72 yards on 11 carries for a 6.5-yard average.

Admiral Jonas Ingram, who replaced Crowley as commissioner of the AAFC, raved that the game demonstrated "professional football at its finest."

The 49ers' final game of the season was with the Buffalo Bills. Although the Kezar turf was slippery from rain, Frankie Albert had a fine day, gaining 49 yards on eight carries. He also threw a touchdown pass to Nick Susoeff. Halfback Ned Matthews scored twice for the Niners, once on a two-yard run from scrimmage, and later on an interception he returned 36 yards for the score. But it wasn't enough. The game ended in a 21-21 tie, leaving the 49ers with an 8-4-2 mark and second place behind Cleveland in the Western Division.

1948 In 1948, Buck Shaw was determined to produce the most powerful offense in the league. He unloaded numerous veterans and went after college talent. When final cuts were made, Shaw kept 17 rookies and 16 veterans. It's doubtful that any professional team ever started a season with so many rookies.

Len Eshmont 1946–1949

Len Eshmont was a legend on the East Coast before the San Francisco 49ers were even formed.

He was raised in the coal regions of central Pennsylvania and played high school football at Mt. Carmel Township in Easton, Pennsylvania, just a few miles from his home in Atlas.

At Mt. Carmel, Eshmont set several prep rushing records and was chosen All-State in 1936, his senior year of high school. His outstanding high school play caught the eye of Jim Crowley, one of Notre Dame's Four Horsemen. Crowley, then a recruiter for Fordham University, persuaded

Eshmont to play collegiate ball in New York with the Fordham Rams. At that time, Fordham was one of the most powerful teams on the East Coast.

Eshmont entered Fordham in 1936 and quickly gained recognition as the "Fordham Flash." In his senior year, 1940, he was named to the All-America team.

Eshmont signed with the New York Giants in 1941 where he played for one year before joining the armed forces. In 1942, he was commissioned in the U.S. Navy and served as physical education instructor at Naval pre-flight schools

around the country, including St. Mary's Pre-Flight.

For three years, Eshmont starred with the Navy's football teams and combined with Frankie Albert in 1943 to turn St. Mary's Pre-Flight into a local powerhouse. Eshmont was named to the All-Service football teams in 1942, 1943 and 1944, the only person to be named to the all-star team for three consecutive years.

After leaving the Navy, Eshmont decided to stay in the Bay Area and joined the original San Francisco 49er team of 1946 along with his teammate from

St. Mary's Pre-Flight, Frankie Albert. That year, he combined with Albert, Norm Standlee and John Strzykalski to give the 49ers one of the best running attacks in the AAFC.

Eshmont retired in 1949 as San Francisco prepared to enter the NFL. In his four years with the 49ers, he gained 1,181 yards on 232 carries, an average of five yards per carry.

In 1950, he began a successful coaching career, joining former 49er assistant coach Eddie Erdelatz at the U.S. Naval Academy as a backfield coach. In 1956, he left to coach at the University of Virginia. A year later, in May of 1957, he died of infectious hepatitis in Virginia. He was 39.

Each year the Len Eshmont Award is given to the 49er player who best exemplifies the inspiration and courageous play of Len Eshmont. The recipient is selected by the vote of his teammates. It is the team's highest individual honor.

"Me and Len were roommates for three years. They used to call us Stumble and Fumble. He was a typical Polack, just like me. That's probably why we got along so well. He'd been an All-American at Fordham then played for the New York Giants. When I was back east playing college ball, I remember hearing his name all the time. He was well known back there. When I heard he died, I just couldn't believe it. Bruce Lee, the old *Chronicle* reporter, called to tell me. He was a great

competitor. That's what made him a good football player. He just loved competition."
—John Strzykalski

"Len Eshmont was always the old pro. Most of us had only played college ball or in the service. Len had played with New York (Giants) before the 49ers. That was important to a new team. He had experience. He was a hell of a good guy. He was a quiet leader. He led by example. He did have one funny habit. We called him 'thumbs' for it. Whenever he carried the ball, his thumbs stuck up in the air like he was hitchhiking."
—Alyn Beals

"Len Eshmont was a great guy. He was a dedicated football player. He showed a lot of courage, playing injured and stuff like that. He was one of those born leaders, just a natural leader. Some of the fellows on the 49ers now, I don't think they realize what they are getting when they get the Len Eshmont Award. It's very special, something to be proud of."
—Joe Vetrano

"Len was pretty quiet. He was a team leader but he lead by his example. He was one of those backs who always got the job done. He wasn't flashy or flamboyant. He just did what was necessary to win. I couldn't compare him to anybody playing now."
—Joe Perry

"Eshmont was a great player. I played with him at St. Mary's Pre-Flight

before the 49ers. He led by demonstration and got a lot of respect form his teammates. He wasn't a holler guy. He had desire and was a hell of a competitor.

"He didn't have blinding speed but he knew how to use what he had. He was a smart player more than anything. He was one of those guys you went to in the clutch. I would remember his number in the clutch because he was effective. He was a good receiver. He never fumbled. He wasn't a great open field runner or anything, but when you needed two or three yards, that's who you went to."
—Frankie Albert

WINNERS OF THE LEN ESHMONT AWARD

1957—Y.A. Tittle
1958—Joe Perry
1959—J.D. Smith
1960—Dave Baker
1961—Leo Nomellini
1962—Dan Colchico
1963—Bob St. Clair
1964—Charlie Krueger
1965—John Brodie
1966—John David Crow
1967—Dave Wilcox
1968—Matt Hazeltine
1969—Jimmy Johnson
1970—Roosevelt Taylor
1971—Ed Beard
1972—Tommy Hart
1973—Mel Phillips
1974—Len Rohde
1975—Jimmy Johnson
1976—Tommy Hart
1977—Mel Phillips
1978—Paul Hofer
1979—Paul Hofer
1980—Archie Reese
1981—Charle Young
1982—Dwight Clark
1983—Bill Ring
1984—Keena Turner
1985—Roger Craig
1986—Joe Montana
1987—Jerry Rice
1988—Michael Carter
    —Roger Craig
1989—Joe Montana
1990—Kevin Fagan
    —Charles Haley
1991—John Taylor
1992—Steve Young

A pass intended for 49er receiver Hal Shoener (52) is broken up by Buffalo Bills defensive back Tom Colella (88) in a preseason game at Kezar Stadium in August, 1949.

Verl Lillywhite from the University of Southern California, Joe Perry from Alameda Naval Air Station and Hal Shoener from Iowa, were just a few of the prizes the 49ers added to their roster.

The nucleus of the team was made up of returning veterans Frankie Albert, John Strzykalski, Len Eshmont, Norm Standlee, Joe Vetrano and linemen Bruno Banducci and Alyn Beals. The rookies blended exceptionally well with the established players and the result was one of the most explosive offensive clubs in football history.

The 49ers averaged an incredible five touchdowns a game through the 14-game season and scored 495 points, a record topped only by the 1961 Houston Oilers with 513 points.

The fearsome running attack, led by Perry, Strzykalski, Standlee and Lillywhite gained 3,663 yards rushing, a professional football record. The 49ers averaged 6.5 yards per carry and over 261 rushing yards per game. The 1978 New England Patriots have the second highest rushing total of all-time with 3,165 yards over a 16-game season.

Frankie Albert sparked a 49er passing assault that accounted for another 2,104 yards. He threw 29 touchdown passes. Wide receiver Alyn Beals caught 14 of those scoring tosses, a 49er single-season record.

The 49ers began their scoring show against the Los Angeles Dons in their first preseason game. They whipped the Dons, 42-24, before 58,300 fans at the Rose Bowl. Albert connected on 17 of 21 passes for 222 yards, including three scoring tosses to Beals and one to Eshmont. Lillywhite also scored on a 41-yard run from scrimmage and Albert ran one in from the two-yard line. Joe Vetrano was good on all the conversion attempts.

The game marked the first professional appearance of St. Mary's College standout Herman Wedemeyer. Wedemeyer was drafted by the Dons and reported to the club straight from the College All-Star game. He practiced less than a week and played sparingly against the 49ers.

A week later, the Baltimore Colts came into Kezar for another exhibition game. The 49ers rolled up 42 points for the second successive week. Frankie Albert completed 10 of 13 passes for 190 yards in leading San Francisco to a 42-14 win.

The opening league game against the Buffalo Bills at Kezar Stadium proved the 49ers were a team to be reckoned with. They destroyed Buffalo, 35-14, before 33,950 fans. The 49ers' point total could have been higher but they lost three fumbles deep in Buffalo territory.

Joe Perry flashed his sprinter's speed, when he darted 58 yards for a touchdown. It was the first time he handled the ball in a league game. He gained 65 yards on just three carries for a 21.6-yard average. Strzykalski chipped in a 10.8-yard rushing average with 76 yards on seven carries. He also scored a touchdown on a 48-yard run from scrimmage.

Albert, who completed 13 of 18 passes, suffered a broken nose and rib damage when he was hit hard on a pass attempt. He regained composure and two plays later, scampered 17 yards to set up a 49er touchdown. Albert also threw a touchdown pass to Jim Cason, a rookie halfback out of Louisiana State, and a scoring pass to Hal Shoener.

The following week San Francisco beat the Brooklyn Dodgers, 36-20, putting its league record at 2-0. Interest in the 49ers skyrocketed. Football fans in the Bay Area knew if the team played well against its next opponent, the New York Yankees, they had a real contender on their hands.

In two years of AAFC play, San Francisco had

John Strzykalski 1946–1952

John Strzykalski was the strength of the 49er backfield during the club's first seven years.

At a time when rushing for 1,000 yards per season was considered superhuman, Strzykalski was picking up 900. In both 1947 and 1948, he gained over 900 yards to pace the 49er ground attack. He averaged over six yards a carry in those years and in 1948 was selected to the All-America Football Conference All-Star team.

Strzykalski, or Johnny Strike as he likes to be called, was a small halfback by today's standards. At 5′ 9″ and 190 pounds he wasn't overpowering, but neither was he shy about putting his head down and battling for extra yards.

Like so many of the original 49ers, Strike joined the squad in 1946 after leaving the armed forces. He had been a star with the Fourth Air Corps football team when the 49ers noticed him and signed him to a $50 option contract. When he finished his stint with the Air Corps, he joined the 49ers rather than return to Marquette, where he had two more years of football eligibility.

"In those days we were like one big family," said Strzykalski. "Money didn't mean that much to us. We just wanted to play the game. To be a good football player back then, more than anything you needed guts and heart. And you had to love the game. We had guys playing with the worst injuries. If you had a broken nose you suited up."

Strike knows a few things about playing with injuries. During his seven-year career he suffered broken legs and plenty of broken noses.

In all, his nose was broken eight times playing the game he loves, a testimony to old-time football without facemasks. In fact, in the last game of his career, a day in which he was to be honored at Kezar Stadium for his service to the 49ers, he had to leave the field with a broken nose.

Strike recalls with affection the family-type environment of the original 49er team. In those days it wasn't uncommon for 12 to 15 players and their wives to live in the same apartment complex. The family environment even extended to owner Tony Morabito.

"For a while a bunch of us lived out at Parkmerced," he said." Rent was only $52. When we practiced out at the Polo Fields in Golden Gate Park we'd drop by Tony's house after and get a bite to eat or talk. He lived close by on 36th Avenue. He took good care of us."

Strike played for only one head coach with the 49ers. He remembers Buck Shaw with reverence, saying he was a perfect gentlemen.

"Buck Shaw never cussed," he said. "The worse thing he ever said was 'damn it to hell.' When he said that, you knew he was mad."

Under Shaw, the 49ers employed the T-Formation. The starting backfield consisted of Frankie Albert at quarterback, Norm Standlee at fullback and Len Eshmont and John Strzykalski at halfback. Strike's role in that backfield was as a breakaway threat.

"Norm usually got the short yards," he said. "Len and I caught a lot of passes. We picked up long yardage once in a while. In those days, you have to remember, you could get up and run after you were tackled. The tackler had to hold you until the ref blew the whistle. If he didn't blow it, I was up and running. I was pretty good at that."

Although Strike made his reputation as a running back, he also played defense, as did most of the team. He doubled as a defensive back.

"Back then we all played 60 minutes," he said. "We were young and healthy. After 60 minutes we still felt fresh."

The 49ers' rival in the AAFC was the Cleveland Browns. Their passing attack in those years is still considered one of the best ever produced. Quarterback Otto Graham had two Hall of Fame caliber receivers to throw at—Mac Speedie and

Dante Lavelli. Speedie was an All-Pro twice in the NFL and three times in the AAFC. Lavelli was an All-Pro twice in both leagues. He was selected to the Hall of Fame in 1975. Speedie has yet to be selected.

"Cleveland was easily the toughest team back then, although the New York Yankees were good too," said Strzykalski. "Marion Motley was the best back I ever saw. He was powerful and he was fast. He could also catch the pass.

"I played man-to-man on Dante Lavelli and Mac Speedie. I'll probably put those guys in the Hall of Fame, they caught so many passes over me."

In 1950 San Francisco joined the NFL. Although it was considered a superior league, Strike saw no difference in the competition.

"The NFL was no tougher than the AAFC," he said. "They thought they were King Farouk over there. They had players with a little more experience but they weren't any more talented."

One of the most memorable players of that era was Les Bingaman. Bingaman was a defensive lineman with the Detroit Lions from 1948 to 1954. He was listed at 325 pounds but opponents say that was a conservative figure. According to Strike, Lou Groza of the Cleveland Browns was a tough man to block, but Bingaman was in a class by himself.

"One time, Frankie Albert called an off-tackle play," he said. "Bruno Banducci was supposed to pull out and hit Bingaman. Bruno weighed about 225 and

was strong. He pulled and hit Bingaman as hard as he could and bounced back about five yards. I was right behind Bruno so I hit Bingaman and bounced about five yards, too. The play was a bust. We went back to the huddle and Bruno said, 'Hey Frank, don't call that play anymore.' You just couldn't move that guy. He was too big. He was a blacksmith in the off-season."

Although Strike was the 49ers' leading rusher during their years in the AAFC, he insists the offensive line should receive credit for that total. John Woudenberg, Bruno Banducci, Dick Bassi and Visco Grgich are just a handful of the linemen who opened holes for Strike in the AAFC. And it was in the AAFC that Strike really made his mark. He is fourth on the league's all-time rushing list with 2,454 yards. He averaged 5.7 yards per carry and scored 14 touchdowns during the league's four years of operation.

Before Strike could hang up his cleats, he gained another 960 yards in the NFL, giving him a total of 3,414 yards. His career average was 5.2 yards per carry.

During those later years he knew his days were numbered, he says, especially when a halfback named Hugh McElhenny showed up at the 49er training camp.

"McElhenny was just too good," he said, chuckling at the thought of being replaced by one of the greatest runners to ever handle a pigskin. "He stepped right in and took my place. I knew then it was time to go."

yet to beat New York. The Yankees came to town with two consecutive Eastern Division Championships to boast about. Spec Sanders, the most valuable player in the conference, was their starting tailback.

A paid attendance of 60,927—at that time the largest attendance in the franchise's history—crowded into Kezar Stadium. An additional 10,000 fans had to be turned away at the gates. Those in attendance were not disappointed.

Only 25 seconds into the game, the 49ers put the first score on the board, an omen of things to come. Joe Vetrano booted the opening kickoff to the two-yard line where it was juggled by Yankee Bob Kennedy. John Woudenberg and Bob Bryant promptly tackled Kennedy, the ball squirted into the end zone and Len Eshmont pounced on it for the first 49er touchdown.

After 60 minutes of play, the 49ers had demolished New York, 41-0. Albert completed eight of 13 passes for 135 yards and two touchdowns. He also scored on a one-yard run.

The 49er defense also played well, limiting New York to just 88 yards of total offense. Defensive linemen Paul Maloney, Nick Susoeff, Gail Bruce and Hal Shoener completely shutdown Yankee tailback Spec Sanders. And rookie defensive back Paul Crowe, a graduate of St. Mary's College, rounded out the 49er scoring by returning an intercepted pass 39 yards for a touchdown.

The 49ers continued to pile up lopsided scores against their opponents. They beat the Baltimore Colts, 56-14, and the Chicago Rockets, 44-21, en-route to a 10-0 record. After winning their tenth straight league game, they came up against the formidable Cleveland Browns.

Cleveland also had a 10-0 record and was terrorizing the league with the same lineup that won the 1947 conference championship. However, the 49ers were the only team in the AAFC that continually challenged the Browns. In past meetings, San Francisco had lost twice by identical 14-7 scores and had won once, whipping the Browns, 34-20. The two teams still had to play each other twice in the last four games of the season. A split would mean a playoff to decide the division champion.

A record crowd of 82,769 packed into Cleveland's Municipal Stadium. According to Joe Vetrano and others who were on the field that day, the 49ers were tense. The crowd size, and the importance of the game, played on the nerves of the visiting 49ers.

The tension led to three fumbles that killed San Francisco. Despite playing tough defense, they again lost, 14-7, the third time in three years Cleveland won by that score. It was the Browns' 19th straight win.

San Francisco was confident that a rematch at Kezar Stadium, just two weeks later, would turn things its way. The Browns were on the road those two weeks, and the San Francisco game would be their third during that time. They were tired and rumor had it that star quarterback Otto Graham might miss the game because of an injury. The 61,000 fans at Kezar Stadium were poised for an upset. A win by San Francisco would force a playoff between these two great teams to determine the Western Conference champion.

The 49ers started poorly. In the first nine minutes of play San Francisco mistakes allowed Cleveland to take a quick 10-0 lead. Otto Graham, though reputedly injured, was in the starting backfield. The 49ers fought back gallantly. They scored on a Joe Perry run and a pass from Albert to Beals to go into the locker room at halftime leading, 14-10.

Perry scored again in the second half to give the 49ers a 21-10 advantage, but that was it for San Francisco. Cleveland scored three touchdowns in the third quarter to put the game out of reach. The Browns' 31-28 victory gave them their third straight Western Division title. The 49ers ended the season with a 12-2 record. Despite their sparkling season, they finished in second place for the third straight year.

1949 Prior to the 1949 season, Tony and Victor Morabito bought out their partners, Allen Sorrell and E.J. Turre. Tony got three-fourths of the team stock and Victor got the remaining one-fourth. Then Tony gambled that the franchise would be a success and mortgaged his home to ensure operating capital for the upcoming season.

San Francisco opened the year at Kezar Stadium as 14-point favorites over the Baltimore Colts. Most of the starting lineup that led the 49ers to a 12-2 season in 1948 remained intact. Homer Hobbs, a guard from the University of Georgia, linebacker Pete Wismann out of St. Louis, and Paul Salata, an end who starred with the USC Trojans, were a few of the new names on the roster.

Several 49ers began the year hoping to build on personal records. Alyn Beals had caught at least one pass in 31 consecutive games. Tackle John Woudenberg had started 42 league games in a row—every 49er contest since the team's formation. Joe Vetrano had kicked 41 extra points in succession. And Joe Perry had scored a touchdown in nine straight games. However, Perry sprained his ankle prior to the opener and Coach Shaw vowed to use him only in an emergency.

The season's inaugural game was not broadcast on radio for lack of a sponsor. Loyal fans who became attached to the 49ers in the exciting 1948 season were furious. Radio station KSAN began broadcasting the games the following week with Bud Foster on the microphone.

Forecasts of light showers kept away many fans. Only 29,100 turned out at Kezar to see the opener. The rain never appeared and the game was played under clear skies.

In the first half, the 49ers' line disassembled the Colt attack, allowing just three yards of total offense. The 49ers took a commanding 17-0 lead into the locker room, but the Colts emerged in the second half a completely different team.

Colts quarterback Y.A. Tittle engineered a third-quarter comeback that netted 17 points for Baltimore. The 49ers fumbled the ball twice and Tittle capitalized on the mistakes by scoring two quick touchdowns. A field goal by Rex Grossman tied the game at 17-17 at the end of the third period. The 49ers were in trouble.

Frankie Albert then took matters into his own hands, marching San Francisco 73 yards in 11 plays. Standlee ran eight yards for the score. The 49ers put

Paul Salata (55) came to the 49ers as a wide receiver in 1949 after playing college ball at USC. Here, he stretches for a 50-yard pass from Frankie Albert at Cleveland's Municipal Stadium after slipping in the mud. The pass was just out of his reach. PAGE 25: Joe Perry races 49 yards to score a touchdown against the Cleveland Browns as the 49ers routed Cleveland, 56-28. When he retired in 1963, he had gained the most rushing yardage in NFL history. Jim Brown later broke the record.

Joe Vetrano 1946–1949

Joe "the Toe" Vetrano was with the 49ers in the beginning. He's seen the good teams and the bad. He's played with the all-time greats.

In 1946, the very first year the team came into existence, Vetrano was trying to win a starting backfield spot. The war was over and the 49ers were lucky enough to have the cream of the military crop in the Bay Area. Thousands of servicemen returned to San Francisco from overseas duty. From that talent pool came many of the players that made up the first 49er team, including Vetrano.

"A lot of the players we had on the original team came from the service teams that were around here," Vetrano said. "Some of those teams were almost as good as the pros. Fleet City, the Camp Pendleton Marines and St. Mary's Pre-Flight were all pretty good. Frankie Albert played for St. Mary's Pre-Flight. Johnny Strzykalski and Bruno Banducci came from the service teams too.

"Kezar was packed for some of those games. Even at the Coliseum in Los Angeles they drew big crowds."

Most teams in the newly formed All-America Football Conference lacked players with professional experience. Among the 49ers, Bruno Banducci had played with the Philadelphia Eagles and Len Eshmont had played for the New York Giants before their military days. This gave San Francisco valuable leadership in its initial season, says Vetrano.

Vetrano found himself competing with Len Eshmont and John Strzykalski for a starting backfield spot at the 49ers' first training camp. At 5' 9" and 170 pounds, Vetrano was much smaller than his rivals for the halfback position. He saw limited action behind the two 49er workhorses but he got plenty of playing time as a defensive back and a kicker. He is most noted for his kicking ability.

"In those days everyone played both ways to some extent," he said. "There wasn't a big roster like now. The coaches had to go with what they had. I ended up playing a little offense, a little defense and kicking.

"Being a kicker was a good deal though. You watch these kickers now and as soon as they kick off they run to the sidelines. You would never see that happen back then. We kicked off, then had to go down and help make the tackle."

Vetrano became one of professional football's first place-kicking specialists. He scored 247 points during his four years in the AAFC to rank him third on the all-time scoring list. That's just 12 points behind Lou Groza, Cleveland's noted kicker

who ranks second on the list. All but 12 of Vetrano's points were scored with the toe.

For two consecutive years, Vetrano led the league in extra points. In 1948, he booted 62, and in 1949, he sent 56 through the uprights. At one point, he kicked 107 consecutive extra points, a record at that time. He also led the league in field goal kicking percentage in 1948, making five of eight for a .625 percentage.

Like most of the original 49ers, Vetrano remembers the bitter rivalry San Francisco had with the Cleveland Browns during those AAFC days. San Francisco finished second to the Browns for three straight years. The fourth season, they lost to the Browns in the 1949 AAFC Championship Game. It was the league's last game.

"Cleveland and the New York Yankees were the toughest teams in the All-America Conference," Vetrano said. "The Los Angeles Dons were a rival, too, but Cleveland and the Yankees were excellent teams. To show you how good the Browns were, they went into the NFL and won that league too."

Cleveland had a dynamic backfield that was led by Hall of Famer Otto Graham. Fullback Marion Motley, another member of Pro Football's Hall of Fame, was one of the most punishing runners of his day. Vetrano considers Graham and Motley two of the best football players he faced. But a halfback from the New York Yankees ranks right along with them,

he says.

"Spec Sanders was a tough individual," Vetrano said. "He was very dangerous because he could run and throw. You didn't want him to have the ball."

Indeed, Sanders was named to the AAFC all-star squad in both 1946 and 1947. He led the league in rushing both those years and was first in the league in total offense in 1947. That year he gained 1,432 yards rushing and threw for another 1,442. He also scored 19 touchdowns to lead the league in scoring with 114 points. He's the only running back in the history of the AAFC to gain over 1,000 yards rushing in a season and the only player to score over 100 points in a season.

Professional football has changed quite a bit since Vetrano's days with the original 49ers. But he sees a striking resemblance between the way the 49ers were treated under original owner Tony Morabito and the way the current players are treated by Eddie DeBartolo.

"Tony Morabito was good to us back then," he said. "We were like a little family. It seems that's how the 49ers are today. DeBartolo seems to watch out for his players and take good care of them. Of course, Tony didn't have quite the money that DeBartolo does. He was a kind man though, a real nice guy. DeBartolo reminds me a lot of Morabito.

"I'm glad I had a chance to play with the early teams. I have nothing but good memories of those years."

seven more points on the board when Verl Lilly-white caught a 10-yard pass from Albert to ensure the 31-17 victory.

The 49ers continued their winning streak, running their record to 4-1, by clobbering the Chicago Hornets, 42-7, and the Los Angeles Dons, 42-14, before losing to the Buffalo Bills, 28-17.

The Cleveland Browns, who had not lost a game in over two years, were set to invade Kezar Stadium once again. Their overall record after three years in the AAFC was 42-3-2. The 49ers were 33-12-2 in AAFC play. Cleveland was now San Francisco's most intense rival.

Joe Perry started the day with a dazzling 11.6-yard rushing average. He gained 156 yards in 16 carries against the Browns and scored two touchdowns as the 49ers drubbed Cleveland, 56-28. It was Cleveland's worst beating in four years of AAFC play. The highest previous point total against the Browns was 34 points, and that was by the 1946 San Francisco club.

The 49ers ended the season with a 9-3 record after beating Buffalo, 51-7, and Los Angeles, 41-24. They lost a rematch with Cleveland, 30-28, but their record was good enough for second place in the AAFC and a chance to play the New York Yankees in a divisional playoff. The winner would meet Cleveland in the conference championship.

The week prior to the Yankee game an unexpected obstacle appeared in the playoff picture. The 49ers threatened to strike. The players demanded a $500 bonus to appear in the playoff game against the Yankees.

"We're not asking for a bonus, just extra salary for an extra game," Visco Grgich told the press on behalf of the players. If there was no bonus, there would be no game.

The team members demanded the bonus because they were not paid for the three preseason games they played, and they were not going to be compensated for the playoff game. In effect, they were playing the games for free.

Owner Tony Morabito refused the players' demand and threatened to forfeit the game if they did not show up for practice. An emergency meeting was called between Buck Shaw, line coach Ed Erdelatz and members of the team. Norm Standlee and Len Eshmont negotiated on the part of the players. They agreed to play the game out of loyalty to the fans, but they stood behind the principles put forth in their demands.

The playoff game was the third match of the year between the 49ers and the Yankees. Each team had won one. The Yankees were well rested. They spent a week preparing for the 49ers at the Sonoma Mission Inn in Sonoma County. It didn't help. The Yankees could not stop the passing and ball handling of Frankie Albert, who sparked San Francisco to a 17-7 win.

The 49ers' first championship game, played against the Cleveland Browns, proved to be anticlimactic. Two days before the game was played, the AAFC merged with the the National Football League. Three teams from the AAFC—Cleveland, San Francisco and Baltimore—were to join the new league in 1950.

Horace Stoneham, owner of the New York Giants baseball club (later the San Francisco Giants), was credited with negotiating peace between the two leagues. NFL Commissioner Bert Bell was appointed commissioner of the new circuit. Art Rooney, president of the NFL's Pittsburgh Steelers, summed up the attitude of management by saying the merger would finally end the "absurd" $20,000 salaries being paid to rookies.

The 49ers played their first championship game on a miserable, cold day at Cleveland before only 22,000 fans. Just a year earlier, these two teams drew over 82,000 to Cleveland's Municipal Stadium. The paltry showing was blamed on the merger, which made the championship game of a now-defunct league insignificant.

The Browns put the only points on the board in the first half after quarterback Otto Graham drove them 57 yards in the first quarter. Edgar Jones plunged over from the two-yard line for the score and a 7-0 lead.

In the third period, the Browns' powerful running back, Marion Motley, sprang loose on a 63-yard run to give the Browns a 14-0 advantage.

The 49ers stormed right back, marching 73 yards on 13 plays. Albert capped the drive with a 24-yard scoring pass to Paul Salata. It was the team's last score in the AAFC. Cleveland defeated San Francisco, 21-7.

PAGE 28: Leo Nomellini was the first player drafted by San Francisco in 1950. He started on both offense and defense for five years before settling into the defensive tackle position.

1950–1959

CHAPTER TWO

JOINING THE NATIONAL FOOTBALL LEAGUE

 new era began in 1950. The San Francisco 49ers were now part of the National Football League.

The preseason player draft proved to be a bonanza for the 49ers. With their first pick, they chose Leo Nomellini, a massive tackle from the University of Minnesota. Coach Buck Shaw was in desperate need of linemen since the retirement of John Woudenberg and Bob Bryant, the starting tackles on the 1949 team. Nomellini proved to be more than an adequate replacement. He went on to earn All-Pro honors six times and a place in the Hall of Fame.

Under pressure from other NFL club owners, Tony Morabito reluctantly raised ticket prices at Kezar Stadium. Midfield seats jumped from $3.60 to $3.75, reserved seats went from $2.40 to $3 and general admission tickets were raised from $1.80 to $2. Children were admitted for 50 cents. Even with the price hike the 49ers had the least expensive tickets in the league.

The team held its annual preseason scrimmage in August at Menlo College near Menlo Park. Over 3,000 curious fans showed up to watch the 49ers prepare for their first season in the NFL. Norm Standlee was named team captain for the third straight year.

Herman Wedemeyer was a new addition to the 49er roster after his previous team, the Los Angeles Dons of the AAFC, folded. Although he was a favorite of the fans, he didn't win a spot with the club and was waived prior to the season opener.

Halfback John Strzykalski proudly claimed that this 49er team was the best he'd ever seen and sports writers eagerly picked San Francisco as a contender for the league crown.

In their first exhibition game, the 49ers faced the Washington Redskins. They quickly discovered there was a new level of competition in the NFL.

The Redskins were led by "Slingin" Sammy Baugh. He last appeared in the Bay Area in 1936. That year, Baugh led Texas Christian to an upset win over the Sugar Bowl-bound Santa Clara Broncos. Ironically, the Broncos were coached by Buck Shaw.

Washington was not an NFL powerhouse. The team had finished the 1949 season with a 4-7-1 record. The 49ers had played for the AAFC crown a year earlier and they were confident of a win. Still, Washington was a slight favorite to win the game.

Season ticket sales had been brisk and a sellout crowd was expected at Kezar. In anticipation of a large turnout, San Francisco Mayor Elmer Robinson closed what was then Panhandle Drive, near the edge of Golden Gate Park, to allow public parking.

In his team's first game against the established league, owner Tony Morabito desperately wanted to impress his peers. Prior to the game he implored his troops to "pour it on."

The 49ers were soundly beaten, 31-14. *Chronicle* Sports Editor Bill Leiser wrote, "Frankly, they did not look capable of beating any team in the National Football League."

After the game, local favorite Joe Vetrano was released. Two days later, Gordy Soltau, a receiver and place kicker, was obtained from the Cleveland Browns. Coach Shaw reasoned that Soltau would be more valuable to the team because he was not simply a kicking specialist, as Vetrano had been.

San Francisco met the NFL champion Philadelphia Eagles a week later. They were trounced once again, 28-10. Eagle coach Earle "Greasy" Neale claimed the 49ers had a deceptive offense, but it was not well organized. "Frankie Albert is a wonderful faker, but he's not the passer some of the other

boys are," Neale told the press.

The coach was even less complimentary about the 49er defense. "You've got to have big men in there to handle what they throw at you in this league," he said.

During the exhibition season, the 49ers were able to win only one game. They were defeated by some of the worst teams in the NFL, including the Pittsburgh Steelers and the Chicago Cardinals. Their sole victory was against the Baltimore Colts before only 6,000 fans at Baltimore. Things looked bleak for the 49ers.

San Francisco opened league play against the New York Yankees, a former AAFC rival. Behind 21-17 in the fourth quarter, the 49ers were driving behind the passes of Frankie Albert and the running of Joe Perry. With less than two minutes to play, and the ball at the New York 40-yard line, the 49ers were caught with 12 men on the field. The resulting penalty killed the drive and ended their hope of a victory.

San Francisco continued to have a tough time in the NFL. The 49ers dropped their first five league games before sneaking by Detroit, 28-27. With Baltimore coming to town the next week, the 49ers hoped to put together a two-game winning streak.

In seven exhibition games and five regular season contests, the Colts had yet to win. San Francisco was established as a 20-point favorite by local bookmakers.

Only 15,000 fans showed up at Kezar Stadium. Despite a big day by Joe Perry, who romped for 142 yards on 16 carries, the 49ers needed a field goal by Gordy Soltau with 2:45 to go for a 17-14 win.

After the Baltimore game, San Francisco reverted to its losing ways, dropping four straight games. Entering the season's finale against Green Bay, the club's record was 2-9.

Before the contest, team captain Norm Standlee, who had announced his retirement, was honored for his five years of service to the 49ers as a fullback and linebacker. Mayor Robinson gave him a new 1950 Oldsmobile. It turned out to be a premature gesture. Owner Tony Morabito later convinced Standlee to return to the 49er backfield, and he played for two more seasons before retiring.

San Francisco ended the season on an upbeat note with a 30-14 drubbing of Green Bay. The 49ers were led once again by Joe Perry who scored two touchdowns and gained 146 yards on nine carries.

At the end of the season, the Baltimore Colts folded. Their players were drafted by other NFL

New York Yankee halfback Buddy Young (76) loses his helmet as he is brought down from behind by Lowell Wagner, a 49er defensive back from 1949 to 1955. Wagner had nine interceptions, tops on the club in 1951.

clubs. The 49ers came away with one of the team's prizes, quarterback Y.A. Tittle.

1951 The 1951 college draft considerably strengthened the 49ers. Among the rookies chosen were offensive ends Billy Wilson and Bill Jessup, halfback Joe Arenas and linebacker Hardy Brown, a devastating tackler.

The 49ers rolled through the 1951 preseason schedule with victories over Washington, Pittsburgh, Green Bay and the Chicago Cardinals. They opened the regular season against the Cleveland Browns. Cleveland was the reigning NFL champion, and a seven-point favorite over the 49ers. The Browns entered the game with four victories in exhibition play and a 33-0 win over the College All-Stars.

Frankie Albert edged out Y.A. Tittle for San Francisco's starting quarterback spot. Once again Joe Perry opened at fullback and Verl Lillywhite at left halfback. Rookie Pete Schabarum took over for

the injured John Strzykalski at right half.

San Francisco rallied to score a 24-10 upset of Cleveland. Lillywhite gained 145 yards in 17 carries to lead the club. Talk of a league title once again surfaced in the Bay Area. The victory had its sour side though. Receivers Billy Wilson and Gordy Soltau were lost temporarily due to injuries.

Dissension also began to arise at Kezar Stadium. Y. A. Tittle and Frankie Albert started sharing time behind the center, and San Francisco had its first quarterback controversy. Fans at Kezar were split into different factions, demanding playing time for the quarterback of their choice. Albert had been a local favorite since his playing days at Stanford when he led the Indians to an undefeated season. But Tittle gradually was winning fans with his brilliant passing.

San Francisco defensive backs Sam Cathcart and Jim Powers use the goal post in an unsuccessful attempt to keep Los Angeles Rams running back Paul Barry out of the end zone. Dan Towler (32), Bob Waterfield (7) and Gil Bouley (66) look on.

Joe Perry (74) was inducted into Pro Football's Hall of Fame in 1969 along with Leo Nomellini. They were the first two 49ers to be enshrined at Canton, Ohio.

The 49ers had a 2-2 record when the Los Angeles Rams visited Kezar. The Rams were loaded with superstars in 1951. Bob Waterfield and Norm Van Brocklin shared the quarterbacking duties, while Elroy "Crazy Legs" Hirsch and Tom Fears took care of the pass-catching chores.

The game started slowly with the 49ers taking a 10-3 lead into the second quarter. Suddenly, they caught fire.

Y. A. Tittle hit Gordy Soltau on touchdown passes of 49 yards, 10 yards and 13 yards in the second quarter. The 49ers added another touchdown when Leo Nomellini blocked a punt and pounced on the ball in the end zone. At the half, the score was San Francisco 38, Los Angeles 10.

Los Angeles never rebounded as the 49ers posted a 44-17 win. Soltau scored 26 points—a 49er single-game record—by adding a 23-yard field goal and five extra points to his three touchdowns.

The 49ers played mediocre football the rest of the season, losing to the lowly Chicago Cardinals and playing the New York Yankees to a tie. Going into the final game of the year against Detroit, they had a 6-4-1 record.

Prior to the Detroit game, owner Tony Morabito called the 49ers "the Robin Hoods of football." They took from the rich by beating the good teams, and gave to the poor by losing to the bad teams.

Yet, in the season finale, San Francisco still could salvage a tie for the divisional title. If the 49ers beat Detroit, and Green Bay beat the Rams, the 49ers would end the season deadlocked with the Lions.

With the 49ers behind 17-14, and a little over four minutes to play, Joe Arenas fielded a Detroit punt and raced 53 yards to the Detroit 17-yard line. Tittle and Albert had shared time at quarterback throughout the game, but now it was Tittle's turn. After Joe Perry picked up three yards, Tittle threw a 10-yard pass to Gordy Soltau. From the three-yard line, Tittle bootlegged around right end and ran the ball into the end zone to give San Francisco a 21-17 victory.

Unfortunately, the Rams beat Green Bay leaving the 49ers in second place, behind division champion Los Angeles.

Hugh McElhenny 1952–1960

Hugh McElhenny knew he was breaking a cardinal rule when he fielded a punt on the four-yard line, juked a couple of Chicago Bears, and took off on a 96-yard scamper for a touchdown.

A veteran would have allowed the punt to go into the end zone. But McElhenny wasn't a veteran, he was a rookie playing in his fourth league game in 1952. McElhenny's rookie mistake was ignored, but his running ability wasn't overlooked.

"After the game in the locker room," said McElhenny, "Frankie Albert gave me the game ball and said, 'You're now the King.' Then he turned to Joe Perry and said, 'Joe, you're just the Jet.' "

That's when the legend was born. "The King" was finally coronated. And McElhenny was definitely royalty. In the open field he had no peer, dancing past bruising tacklers with the grace and beauty of Baryshnikov. He was an artist unleashed on a canvas of green grass, sprinting and slashing like no one before him.

McElhenny began to make his presence known barely 24 hours after reporting to the 49er training camp. He played in the College All-Star game on a Friday night, reported to camp on Saturday and was in uniform on Sunday for an exhibition game against the Chicago Cardinals. He hadn't even had time to learn the names of his teammates when he found himself in the 49er backfield.

"Frankie had called a time out and asked Buck Shaw to put me in the game," McElhenny said. "Buck told him I didn't know the plays yet. At that time, Frankie pretty much had his way with Buck, so Buck went along with him. In the huddle, Frankie drew a play on the ground and told everybody what to do. He threw me a pitchout and I ran 42 yards for a touchdown."

It's hard to find a Hugh McElhenny story that doesn't in some way involve Frankie Albert. If not for Albert's acute judgment of talent and character, McElhenny might have played elsewhere. It was at the Hula Bowl in 1952 that Albert first laid his eyes on "the King." The game matched the best college players in the country against top professional talent. Albert happened to be on hand to represent the pros. McElhenny played in two games, made the All-Hula Bowl team and attracted Albert's eye. Frankie immediately got on the phone and told Buck Shaw he had to pick McElhenny in the upcoming draft. The 49ers made him the ninth college player picked in 1952.

When Albert introduced McElhenny to his new teammates for the first time he said, "I'd like you to meet a man who took a cut in pay to become a professional."

McElhenny considers it a curious joke because it was Albert who advised him what kind of contract to ask for when he was bargaining with team owner Vic Morabito. The contract negotiation took place at the Sheraton Hotel on Wilshire Boulevard in Los Angeles.

"Vic Morabito sat down and said to me, 'Well Hugh, what do you want?' I said I wanted $30,000, I was a first-round pick. He told me they were thinking about something in the range of $5,000. I told him I could have signed with the Los Angeles Dons for $10,000 when I got out of high school. At that point he excused himself, got up and never came back. I even had to pick up the check." McElhenny eventually signed for $7,000.

It was a bargain for the 49ers. McElhenny's exceptional running skill earned him *Sport* magazine's Player-of-the-Year award in his rookie season. But his reputation as a game breaker made him a marked man around the league. Everywhere he went defenses devised plans to stop him. Some devised ways to cripple him. They didn't want to just tackle him, they wanted him out of the lineup.

The Chicago Bears had one of those fierce defenses. In 1954, the 49ers and McElhenny were on their way to an exceptional season when he separated his shoulder against the Bears. Joe Perry, John Henry Johnson and Y.A. Tittle, the three other members of that Million Dollar Backfield, couldn't take up the slack. With McElhenny out of action, they lost three straight games and finished 7-4-1.

That year still evokes good memories for McElhenny because it was the first year the Million Dollar Backfield was together. McElhenny rates it the best backfield that ever played.

"That was one hell of a backfield," he said. "Even with all that talent, we could never quite win it. We had an injury here, an injury there. In 1954 we had nine starters injured.

"Perry was an exceptional guy to be with in the backfield," he said. "He was such an outstanding team player. Running backs are only as good as the guys in front of them. I don't know how many times he laid a block that sprang me. I'm just proud to say I was in the same backfield as him.

"Now I keep waiting for John Henry Johnson to go into the Hall of Fame. I don't know why he isn't. That would really be something. We probably would have the only backfield in history to all be in the Hall of Fame.

"Y.A. Tittle used to joke about trying to keep us all happy by giving us the ball. He certainly had his hands full because we all had egos."

One of the disappointments of McElhenny's nine years with San Francisco was the team's inability to win a championship despite having such outstanding individual players as Tittle, Johnson and Perry. Nevertheless, the 49ers were competitive throughout the 1950s. The highlight of that decade was 1957 when San Francisco forced a playoff with Detroit. One of the games that got the team there is etched in McElhenny's memory.

With two games left in the season, the 49ers needed a win against the Baltimore Colts to stay alive in the race for the Western Division title. San Francisco was behind, 13-10, but driving, when Tittle was hurt.

Rookie John Brodie was motioned off the bench and onto the field.

"When Brodie came into the huddle, he looked around and said, 'What do I call?' I told him to throw me the ball. I was going to do a little down and out and he could throw it to the sidelines."

Brodie threw the pass under a heavy rush, McElhenny caught it, and the 49ers won.

McElhenny regards the ability to run with a football as something of a mystery. He had been a prep hurdling champion at George Washington High School in Los Angeles, and that training helped him develop as a running threat. But there is something undefinable that the great backs possess, he says. The intuitive cutbacks and changes of direction that were McElhenny's trademark, are something that can't be programmed.

"Speed is one ingredient," he said. "I had pretty good speed but I couldn't beat Joe Perry in the 50. I could beat him in the 100 though. To be a good running back, well it's just God's gift. It's not something you can teach. I did things by instinct. Running, balance, all of it was instinct. You also have to know where other people are on the field."

He generally doesn't like to compare the modern players with those of his era because he disagrees with the argument that today's players are better athletes.

"We'd probably be just as good as these guys playing today," he said. "They are bigger and faster, but we'd probably have been bigger and faster if we had the same training methods, the vitamins, and all that."

McElhenny remains a 49er faithful to this day. He credits the success of the present team to the system used by Bill Walsh more than the individual players.

"You have to look at Bill Walsh's system," he said. "How do the 49ers evaluate their players? How do they find players that fit into the system that well? If one guy gets hurt, it won't affect the team. They have other talented players that will fit into the system and do just as well.

"The loss of the quarterback might make a difference, but (Matt) Cavanaugh does a good job when he's in there. They have great athletes on that team but the important thing is Walsh knows how to use them. He knows how to get the maximum effort out of his players.

"The organization is great to us. Eddie DeBartolo and Bill Walsh always try to keep in touch and make us part of the organization. They invite us on road trips every year. That's real gratifying to know they want you to still be part of the team. Many teams just forget about us old guys.

"I don't want to be overly sentimental, but I'll always be a 49er."

John Strzykalski (91) was the 49ers' leading ground gainer during their four years in the AAFC. When the league folded in 1949, he was fourth on the all-time rushing list with 2,454 yards. He averaged 5.8 yards per carry in the AAFC.

1952

In 1952, the 49ers had the ninth pick in the draft. It was a year of enormous collegiate talent. Among the players chosen before San Francisco had a chance to pick were Ollie Matson, Les Richter, Bill Wade, Frank Gifford and Babe Parilli. When it was San Francisco's turn to choose, Buck Shaw was astonished to find Hugh McElhenny from the University of Washington still available. He quickly picked McElhenny and never regretted it.

The first time he touched the ball as a 49er, McElhenny ran 42 yards for a touchdown. His shifty runs and elusive moves inspired quarterback Frankie Albert to call him "the King," a name he later would take to Pro Football's Hall of Fame.

San Francisco's third year in the NFL began innocently enough with preseason games against local semi-pro teams. The 49ers demolished the San Francisco Broncos, 79-0, and the San Jose Packers, 76-0. They also dominated the NFL teams, beating the Rams and Cleveland on the way to a 7-0 preseason mark.

They opened the season against the Detroit Lions, a team they knocked out of the playoff picture on the last day of the season a year earlier. Detroit had won all six of its preseason games.

Hugh McElhenny was making his debut as a 49er starter along with rookie tackle Bob Toneff,

defensive end Pat O'Donaghue and J.R. Boone at halfback. Frankie Albert opened the season again as the starting quarterback.

It was Albert who guided the team to its opening game victory. His 47-yard touchdown pass to Boone in the third quarter gave the 49ers a 17-3 lead they never relinquished.

The 49ers continued their winning streak by beating the Dallas Texans, and then Detroit again, before meeting the Chicago Bears in the Windy City.

A standing-room-only crowd of 48,400 gathered at Wrigley Field to see the game. The 49ers had not beaten the Bears since joining the NFL. This time things were different. The 49ers humiliated the Bears, 40-16.

McElhenny was awarded the game ball for his part in the triumph. He broke the game wide open in the second quarter with a 94-yard punt return that put the 49ers in front, 21-9. He also carried from scrimmage 12 times for 103 yards. For his efforts, the

35

Rex Berry, a 14th-round choice in the 1951 draft, stops the New York Giants' Frank Gifford (16) after a short gain.

Chicago fans gave him a standing ovation when he left the field. The 49ers were now the only undefeated team in football, two games ahead of the pack.

The 49ers beat the Dallas Texans the next week, 48-21, to post a 5-0 record, then disaster struck. They lost five of their next six games. Injuries played a big part in the club's decline. Team captain Norm Standlee contracted polio, and Tittle and Perry were in and out of the lineup with less serious ailments. San Francisco finished the year at 7-5, but it was the end of something special.

Three members of the 49ers' original starting backfield retired after the season. Besides Standlee, John Strzykalski, 30, and Frankie Albert, 32, ended their careers.

For Strzykalski, the end wasn't a pleasant one. Just prior to halftime of his final game against the Green Bay Packers—a day when he was to be honored for his achievements—he broke his nose for the eighth time as a professional. He carried the ball only six times for 22 yards that day. His lifetime totals compiled entirely with the 49ers were 3,414 yards on 662 carries.

Albert's final game against the Packers was more satisfying. He completed 16 of 26 passes for 213 yards and a touchdown. His lifetime totals were 631 completions in 1,564 attempts for 10,795 yards and 115 touchdowns.

Gordy Soltau ended the 1952 season as the league's top scorer and Hugh McElhenny was named *Sport* magazine's Player-of-the-Year. He ran for 684 yards on 98 carries, nearly a seven-yard average.

1953 The most memorable part of the 1953 opening game was the bench-clearing brawl that occured near midfield. Tempers began to flare early when 49er linebacker Hardy Brown flattened Philadelphia Eagle halfback Toy Ledbetter with one of his famous shoulder tackles. The jarring tackle left Ledbetter unconscious and crushed his cheekbone.

Minor confrontations continued throughout the game until it finally erupted into a helmet swinging free-for-all. Among the combatants were Hugh McElhenny, who used his helmet to club the Eagles'

Pete Pihos, and Joe Perry, who charged off the sidelines to tangle with Bob Walston. Once the battle was under way, about 150 fans swarmed out of the stands at Kezar Stadium to help their hometown heros. It took the referees nearly 10 minutes to restore order. Even the pleadings of Buck Shaw and Eagle coach Jim Trimble were ignored by the players.

Joe McTique and the 49er band tried to soothe the unruly crowd by playing the national anthem. When that failed, they used their instruments to help break up the fight.

San Francisco won the battle on the field and the scoreboard that day, beating Philadelphia, 31-21. Joe Perry paced the winning club with 145 yards rushing in 16 carries.

The following week the Rams brought their high-flying passing attack to Kezar. Quarterback Norm Van Brocklin led the team to a 20-0 lead in the second quarter. San Francisco battled back and, with three minutes to play, had a 28-27 lead. The Rams quickly regained the lead, 30-28, on a Ben Agajanian field goal.

San Francisco took the ensuing kickoff to the 20-yard line. With less than a minute to play, the Rams' secondary prepared for a long bomb from Tittle. Instead, "the Bald Eagle" tossed a screen pass to Hugh McElhenny, who galloped 71 yards to the nine-yard line. With five seconds on the clock, Gordy Soltau kicked a field goal for a 31-30 win.

A rematch with the Rams at the Los Angeles Coliseum attracted 85,900 fans. The 49ers brought a 4-2 record to town after losing twice to the Detroit Lions. The Rams were 5-1.

Y.A. Tittle was returning to action with a newly designed face mask after his cheekbone was shattered in three places against the Lions. The 49ers trailed the Rams, 27-24, with four minutes to play. Tittle then marched the club 80 yards in 11 plays. Twice on third down and 10 yards to go, he hit receivers for first downs. The winning score came on a Tittle-to-Soltau pass with 1:12 to play. The 49ers won another cliffhanger, 31-27, behind Tittle's 18 completions and 301 yards passing.

The 49ers went into the last game of the season with an 8-3 record. They needed a win over the Colts and a loss by the Detroit Lions to tie Detroit for the league title. The 49ers walloped the Colts, 45-14. But the New York Giants couldn't beat Detroit, and the 49ers again finished in second place, this time with a 9-3 record.

For the second season in a row, Gordy Soltau

led the league in scoring. His 114 points beat runner-up Lou Groza of the Cleveland Browns, who had 108. Receiver Billy Wilson tied Philadelphia's Pete Pihos with 10 touchdown receptions on the season. The team's 372 points topped every other offense in the league. Their 2,230 rushing yards was also the league high.

1954 The 49ers opened the 1954 season as 28-point favorites over the Washington Redskins. For two consecutive seasons, San Francisco had the strongest running attack in the league with Perry and McElhenny. Now, John Henry Johnson, obtained in a trade with Pittsburgh, was added to the backfield.

Hugh McElhenny was nicknamed "the King" by Frankie Albert after he returned a punt 96 yards against the Chicago Bears in his rookie season.

Halfback Jim Cason loses his helmet in a night game against the New York Yankees at Yankee Stadium.

San Francisco's potent offense got rolling immediately. It scored two touchdowns in the first five minutes against Washington and cruised to a 41-7 win. Perry scored two rushing touchdowns.

San Francisco tied the Rams the following week and defeated its next two opponents before meeting Detroit at Kezar Stadium. The 49ers had not been beaten in 15 straight games, including the preseason and the tail end of the 1953 season. Detroit was riding its own streak of 16 straight wins.

The Lions were two-point favorites, largely because Tittle had suffered a broken hand. Midway through the week, it had been announced that 49er rookie Maury Duncan would be starting at quarterback. A capacity crowd of 59,600 was on hand at Kezar Stadium.

Tittle thrilled the crowd by opening the game at quarterback despite the injury. On the second play from scrimmage, Hugh McElhenny set the tone for the day by scampering 60 yards for a touchdown. San Francisco continued to pour it on and jumped out to a 24-7 halftime lead. Detroit fought back and cut the margin to 37-31 in the fourth quarter, but it

was not enough. The 49ers held on to win behind the excellent running of McElhenny, who gained 126 yards on seven carries for an 18-yard average.

The 49ers string of undefeated games came to a halt the next week when the Chicago Bears entered Kezar Stadium and beat the 49ers, 31-27. After that, injuries began to hamper the team. Tittle missed several games with his injured hand. McElhenny separated his shoulder in the sixth game, after piling up 515 yards rushing, and was lost for the season. Gordy Soltau, Don Burke, Jim Cason, Bruno Banducci and Joe Manley all missed games due to injuries. The 49ers finished the season in third place with a 7-4-1 record after beating Baltimore, 10-7, in the season's final game.

Joe Perry gained over 1,000 yards rushing for the second straight year becoming the first man in NFL history to have successive seasons gaining over 1,000 yards.

It was also Buck Shaw's last season as the 49er coach. Tony Morabito was still searching for a championship. He thought a change of coaches might do the trick, so he fired Shaw and hired Norm "Red" Strader. Morabito believed the easy-going Shaw was too lenient with his players and that a different style might rejuvenate the team.

Shaw ended his 49er coaching career with a

Leo Nomellini 1950–1963

Leo Nomellini was a predator. His territory was the line of scrimmage, his prey, opposing ball carriers.

His nickname was "the Lion," an appropriate monicker for a man who pursued and devoured offensive backs. For 14 seasons, Nomellini anchored the 49er defensive line. His presence, like that of a lion, was quickly detected and avoided.

At 6' 3" and 265 pounds, his size, strength and agility were more than most opponents could handle. Nomellini used techniques he learned as an off-season wrestler to manhandle opposing linemen who often double- and triple-teamed him.

On the line of scrimmage he was a picture of intimidation. His crew cut and jutting jaw fit snuggly inside a 49er hel-

met. A frightening scowl revealed missing teeth through which he exhaled grunts and groans. The bestial sounds were designed to strike fear in opposing linemen.

Although Nomellini is noted for his defensive prowess, he was also a stellar offensive tackle. For five years, from 1951 to 1955, he was a starter on both offense and defense for the 49ers.

"I tell you, it was difficult sometimes to stand out there and watch the other 21 players run on and off the field," Nomellini said."I never had much time to rest. In fact, the only rest I got was when the other people were changing over from offense to defense. If I had a choice I would have played just defense. I guess I didn't know any better."

Nomellini should also be known as "the Ironman." When he retired in

1963 at age 39, he had played in 174 consecutive league games. In 60 of those games, he never left the field, playing both offense and defense. In addition, he played in 77 preseason games and 10 Pro Bowls. Incredibly, he never missed a game.

San Francisco made Nomellini its first draft choice in 1950. Luck played a part in his coming to San Francisco.

The Los Angeles Rams originally picked Nomellini in the 1950 NFL draft. After the draft, however, the NFL and All-America Football Conference merged. The draft was held again, and the Rams skipped over Nomellini to choose a fullback named Ralph Pasquariello. The 49ers chose the big lineman from the University of Minnesota.

Nomellini was born in Lucca, Italy. His family immigrated to America when he was an infant and settled in Chicago's West Side. He played no high school sports because he worked after school to help support the family.

During World War II, Nomellini enlisted in the Marine Corps and saw combat in the South Pacific. It was during his Marine Corps days that he began playing football.

Minnesota offered Nomellini a football scholarship based on his performance with the Cherry Point Marine football team. In his first year at college, he won a starting guard position. Ironically, the first college game Nomellini saw was the first one he played in. Later, he was switched to tackle, and for two years he was an All-American. He was also a Big Ten wrestling champion.

Nomellini was a unanimous All-Pro choice six times and played in 10 Pro Bowls. He nostalgically recalls those early 49er days.

"I had some great teammates with the 49ers. There were so many outstanding players—Joe Perry, Y.A. Tittle. I went through 22 roommates on that team. Every one was a joy.

"We considered ourselves pioneers back then. The league was just starting to grow and professional football was gaining popularity. I was just happy to be part of the sport. It's grown quite a bit since those days."

In the early days of football, life on the road was often exhausting. It wasn't uncommon for the 49ers to be on the road for more than three weeks at a time as they swept through the Midwest or the East Coast. Round-trip flights were on propeller-driven planes rather than chartered jets. The trips to a game were often as tough as the contests themselves, Nomellini says.

"We went on road trips back east that lasted 17 to 21 days," he said. "We'd play in Chicago, Detroit, Green Bay and stay back there the whole time. It was tough being away from the family and friends for so long. We'd practice every day, have team meetings and maybe go to a show at night; nothing out of the ordinary. The trips themselves took forever. We flew on props. It would take about 20 hours to fly back from New York."

Nomellini has been honored in many ways for his outstanding play. In addition to his selection to 10 straight Pro Bowls, he was inducted into the Hall of Fame in 1969. His greatest honor, however, is the Len Eshmont Award he received in 1961. The award is given to the 49er who best exemplifies Len Eshmont's spirit and inspiration.

"That award stands out because it was voted by my teammates," he said. "It's special when the people you play with single you out for something like that."

Nomellini played in more than 250 professional football games. He says there is one he will never forget. It stands out for the wrong reason.

"We had some great rivalries back then," said Nomellini. "The Rams were always tough. Of course, we wanted to beat them and be considered the best team in California. Cleveland came over to the NFL with the 49ers so there was a natural rivalry there. Later, the Packers under Vince Lombardi were awfully tough. But I guess the game I most remember was the 1957 playoff game against the Detroit Lions. That game really hurt. We should have done better. Some way or other they just caught us. There was no let down or anything. We were just ahead and we blew it."

The 1957 playoff game against the Detroit Lions was one of the tragic days in 49er history. San Francisco held a 27-7 lead in the third quarter. It seemed certain the 49ers would win the division title. Fans left Kezar Stadium early to celebrate along Haight Street and in Golden Gate Park. But the Lions rallied and won the game, 31-27.

Nomellini remembers Kezar Stadium as a wonderful place to play, a stadium that many teams were happy to see.

"Kezar was a beautiful park," he said. "All the NFL players liked Kezar. The weather was always good for football. It was always cool, which was unlike New York or Chicago where it could be very humid or very cold. Kezar was definitely my favorite place to play.

"The fans were pretty good out there. They could make it hard on some people, the quarterbacks especially, but overall they were pretty knowledgeable. They knew their football."

Hall of Fame cornerback Emlen Tunnell (45), of the New York Giants, intercepts a pass intended for San Francisco's Billy Wilson (84) at the Polo Grounds. Wilson was drafted out of San Jose State on the 22nd round of the 1950 draft.

72-40-4 record. His sparkling .638 winning percentage is still the best among 49er head coaches. He also won more games than any other coach in team history. After leaving the 49ers, "the Silver Fox" coached at the Air Force Academy. In 1958, he moved on to become the head coach of the Philadelphia Eagles. With the Eagles in 1960, he won the NFL championship that had eluded him with the 49ers and promptly retired.

Strader was a local product who had played and coached at St. Mary's College. Later, he became the head coach of the New York Yankees in the AAFC. His methods differed dramatically from Shaw's. He was a strict disciplinarian who prohibited smoking and drinking, while Shaw often looked the other way. Strader recruited Frankie Albert and Red Hickey as assistant coaches.

1955 Prior to training camp for the 1955 season, Bruno Banducci, an All-Pro guard and the 49er team captain, held out for a salary raise. Instead of receiving a raise, Banducci was given his outright release. The team's other starting guard, Nick Feher, was traded prior to the season, leaving a void in the offensive line.

The preseason was a success. The team fin-

ished 5-1, but once the league games got under way the 49ers fell apart.

They opened the regular season with five rookie starters. Dick Moegle, Matt Hazeltine, Carroll Hardy, George Maderos and Lou Palatella all worked their way into the lineup. In their first game against the Rams, they were nine-point favorites.

The oddsmakers had the right point spread but picked the wrong team. Los Angeles walked all over the 49ers, 23-14. Five Y.A. Tittle passes were intercepted. The only 49er highlight was a 42-yard scoring pass from Tittle to McElhenny.

The 49ers struggled along trying to play .500 ball and found themselves in Washington midway through the season. They had a 3-4 record, including wins over Chicago and Detroit. At Washington, the situation grew worse. San Francisco was shutout for the first time in five years.

With little Eddie LeBaron at quarterback, the Redskins downed the 49ers, 7-0. It was a frustrating day for San Francisco. The team had three touch-

Left to right, Hugh McElhenny, Frankie Albert, the injured Gail Bruce and Bruno Banducci watch helplessly as the Chicago Bears' George Blanda kicks a last minute field goal to beat the 49ers, 20-17. PAGE 47: Chicago Bears receiver Bill McColl was unable to hang on to this pass as Rex Berry (23) tries to bat it away. McColl is the father of Milt McColl, a member of the 49ers since 1981.

downs called back due to penalties. Another potential scoring strike of eight yards, from Tittle to Soltau, hit a goal post. The Redskins' sole score came after they recovered a fumble on the 49ers' 33-yard line.

The season turned from gray to black after the Washington game. McElhenny injured a foot and was used sparingly the rest of the season. He gained only 326 yards rushing all year. Joe Perry also missed several games with injured knees. San Francisco closed out the season by losing five of its last six games.

Despite finishing with a 4-8 record, San Francisco set a new single-season home attendance record of 281,780.

1956

Prior to the 1956 season, Red Strader was relieved of his coaching duties, although he had a two-year contract. He was replaced with Frankie Albert. Under Albert's guidance, the 49ers won their first three exhibition games. The optimism soon faded when they lost the next three in a row.

Bruno Banducci tried a comeback. But after playing the exhibition season, he decided his legs had had enough and retired. The Million Dollar Backfield was reduced by half when Perry and McElhenny were injured and started the season opener on the bench.

McElhenny wasn't out of action for long. He came off the bench in the opener to score twice in a 38-21 loss to the New York Giants. Earl Morrall, San Francisco's first-round draft pick in 1956, made his first league appearance as a 49er. He relieved Y.A. Tittle late in the game and completed two passes for 52 yards.

Albert got his first league coaching victory the following week with a 33-30 win over Los Angeles before 57,000 at Kezar Stadium. It was the only win for the 49ers in the first half of the season. After losing six of their first seven games, the 49ers rallied to win three and tie one game, finishing with a 5-6-1 record.

The Baltimore Colts came to town for the season finale with a backfield every bit as potent as San Francisco's. Johnny Unitas was at quarterback with Alan Ameche and Lenny Moore behind him at the running back slots. The star of the day did not start

R.C. Owens 1957–1961

It seemed unlikely that a rookie receiver playing in his sixth NFL game would leap into the stratosphere, grab a 50-yard pass above Detroit's All-Pro secondary and score a winning touchdown with 10 seconds on the clock.

But that's exactly what R.C. Owens did in 1957 when he and Y.A. Tittle made the Alley-Oop pass as much a part of San Francisco as Coit Tower and the Golden Gate Bridge.

Owens' touchdown reception against the Lions that day was not the first time the Alley-Oop was put to use, but it was certainly the most dramatic.

San Francisco trailed Detroit, 31-28, with 1:20 to play. The 49ers had the ball on their own 38-yard line. Three straight pass completions by Tittle moved the ball to the Lions' 42. There was 11 seconds to go. Everyone

at Kezar Stadium knew what was coming. The Lions completely surrounded Owens all the way downfield. Tittle let fly a rocket that sailed about 50 yards in the air. In the end zone, All-Pro Jack Christiansen covered Owens along with Jim David. Owens leapt, grabbed the pigskin over the defenders and scored. San Francisco won, 35-31.

"That Detroit game was probably the most satisfying win for me," Owens said. "Detroit had just scored to go ahead and Abe Woodson made a good kick return. Y.A. went to work after that. Overall, it was a great game played by two great teams."

The Alley-Oop pass was a standard part of the 49ers' offensive plan in 1957. Tittle claims it was developed by accident. Owens says it was an accidental design.

While preparing for the second league game of 1957, the 49er defense was devising ways to stop the Los Angeles Rams. Coach Red Hickey had Y.A. Tittle throw long, high passes into the secondary to prepare it for Bill Wade and Norm Van Brocklin, the Rams' quarterbacks. They gradually realized that R.C. Owens was leaping over the defensive backs and catching the passes.

"It was noticed that I could outjump the defenders," said Owens. "Red Hickey, Frankie Albert and Y.A. Tittle all decided this might be something we could use in a game. Then we wondered what to call it. Somehow we decided on Alley-Oop. In the first game against the Rams, it was used twice for completions, one of those was a touchdown."

Actually, that was not the Alley-Oop's first appearance. It had been used once before in a preseason contest aganst the Chicago Cardinals in Seattle.

"When we used it against Chicago, we had no name for it at the time," he said. "It was still the Alley-Oop but nobody recognized it."

Owens' jumping ability, which he cultivated as a basketball star at College of Idaho, was one of the factors that made the Alley-Oop successful. Tittle's confidence in the unorthodox pass was another.

"Y.A. Tittle believed in it," said Owens. "When a quarterback believes in something he'll use it. The team believed in it so everyone came together when it was called. The line blocked well because they knew it would work.

"I guess you could say the Alley-Oop was the same as a Hail Mary pass, except we didn't pray."

The 1957 San Francisco team was loaded with offensive weapons. No other team in the league could match the backfield of Tittle, Perry and McElhenny. Billy Wilson, Clyde Conner and Owens gave Tittle a trio of excellent pass receivers. But the 49ers rarely demolished their opponent. Virtually every game that year was a cliffhanger.

"It was the best 49er team I played on," said Owens, who spent five years, from 1957 to 1961, in a 49er uniform. "Mac and 'Joe the Jet' were something. The Jet was good on those quick openers. Mac was a zig and zag type runner. He had great peripheral vision.

"Abe Woodson was another weapon. He was a

spectacular kick returner who always got us in good position. He was a Big Ten hurdles champ. You'd always see him hurdling over people. We were always in it with Abe because he would get us good field position."

Since Owens contributed to one of the most exciting seasons in the team's history, one would expect him to choose a heart-stopping Alley-Oop reception as his most thrilling moment that year. Not quite. It was a last-minute reception against the Chicago Bears, but the Alley-Oop was not involved.

With the Bears leading, 17-14, and 20 seconds to play, Chicago went into its prevent defense in an effort to stop the long pass by Tittle.

"The Bears were all set to stop our last-second drive," he said. "I was going downfield and someone knocked me down and out of bounds. I crawled back into the end zone on my knees. Tittle kept pumping the ball looking for someone. Finally, he threw to me. I was still on my knees. It was a touchdown. The refs didn't see me out of bounds or it wouldn't have been allowed. Halas was irate. He was kicking the dirt and kicking at the referees. It was a thrill just to beat George Halas."

Although Tittle and Owens hooked up successfully for several years, it was in 1961, when John Brodie was running the offense, that Owens had his best statistical season. That year, he caught 55 passes for 1,032 yards. He became the first 49er receiver to

gain over 1,000 yards through the air.

As a wide receiver, Owens became intimately familiar with some of the hardest hitting defenses in football.

"The Chicago Bears and Detroit Lions were always tough," he said. "Both teams had tough traditions, tough players and tough defenses. They gave you headaches. When they hit you, they really tattooed you. Bill George from Chicago, for example, was a headhunter. Doug Atkins was another who liked to hit."

Kezar Stadium had a growing reputation in the 1960s as a haven for rowdy fans. At one time city officials considered building a moat around the stadium to keep fans off the field after the game. Owens memories of the fabled stadium on the edge of Golden Gate Park are more peaceful.

"Kezar was a nice stadium," he said. "There's a lot of nostalgia there. One thing I remember about Kezar was the seagulls. There was always seagulls at one end of the stadium and as soon as the play went to that end, they all took off and flew to the other end.

"Another memorable thing about Kezar Stadium was the wrong-way run by Jim Marshall. Bruce Bosley ran after him and shook his hand.

"Fans got a little upset out there once in a while. They threw a few things. One time a guy got upset at a Bears game and ran on the field and kicked Papa Bear—George Halas. Overall the place is full of good memories. I enjoyed it."

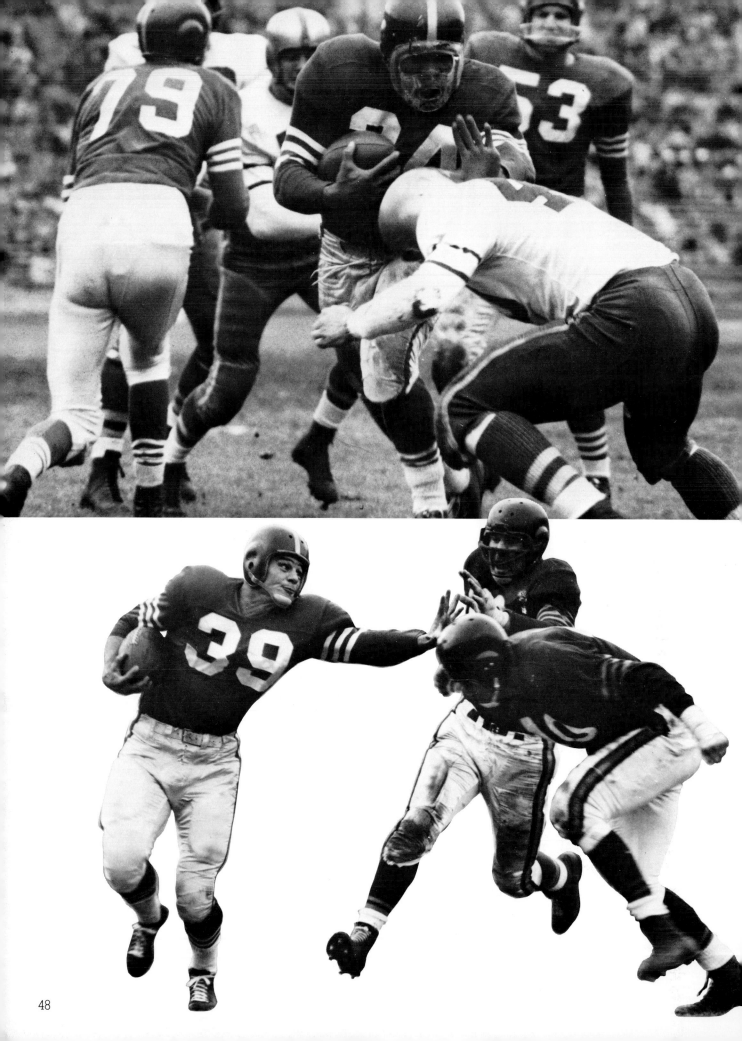

LEFT, TOP: Joe Perry had a facemask designed to protect his jaw after it was broken earlier in the 1953 season. Here, he blasts through the Green Bay Packer line on the way to a touchdown. LEFT, BOTTOM: Hugh McElhenny (39) was named *Sport* magazine's Player-of-the-Year and UPI Rookie-of-the-Year in 1952. Here, he gives the Bears' Stan Wallace a straight-arm as he picks up six yards. RIGHT, TOP TO BOTTOM: John Henry Johnson lunges forward to score before 90,000 fans at the Los Angeles Coliseum in 1954. Johnson was acquired in a trade with the Pittsburgh Steelers prior to the 1954 season.

ABOVE: The opening game of the 1953 season at Kezar Stadium between San Francisco and the Philadelphia Eagles turned into a free-for-all. A shoving match between 49er Clay Matthews (83) and Eagle Ken Farragut quickly escalated as the hometown fans raced onto the field to help the 49ers. Police were needed to break up the brawl. LEFT: San Francisco's Rex Berry tries to unscrew the head of Washington Redskins receiver Ed Barker (87). Berry had seven interceptions for the 1953 49ers, the club high.

in either backfield, however. It was tiny Joe Arenas, a Choctaw Indian from Omaha, Nebraska. The 49er halfback returned a punt 67 yards for a touchdown and ran back a kickoff 96 yards to set up another touchdown as San Francisco defeated the Colts, 30-17.

1957 The year 1957 was both magical and tragic for San Francisco football fans. Heart-stopping finishes became the 49ers' trademark as the team continued its winning ways and innovative tradition.

The 49ers were a box office smash around the league. Average attendance at their games was 60,000. In a game with the Rams, 102,368 fans packed into the Los Angeles Coliseum. It was the largest crowd in professional football history.

Joe Perry 1948–1963

Joe Perry was designed to be a fullback. He carried the ball with the power and grace of a panther, defying tacklers to strike. The first time he touched the ball in a league game, he bolted through a hole in the Buffalo Bills' defense and dashed 58 yards to score.

Y.A. Tittle, the quarterback for most of Perry's years in the 49er backfield, took extra haste when handing the ball to "Joe the Jet." He was so quick off the snap, he often shot past Tittle before the quarterback could turn to make the handoff.

His playing weight was 195 pounds and that was distributed over a six-foot frame. Opponents claimed he was bigger. He could run to daylight, or create his own running room by bowling over potential tacklers. He made a habit of carrying opposing players for extra yards.

Perry gained 8,378 yards in the National Football League and another 1,345 in the All-America Football Conference. He averaged over five yards per carry. After 16 years of professional football, "Joe the Jet" retired in 1963 with more rushing yards than any player in NFL history. That record stood until someone named Jim Brown came along to break it.

In the mid-1950s, Perry teamed with Y.A. Tittle, Hugh McElhenny and John Henry Johnson to form the most famous backfield in football. With three great running backs hungry to carry the ball, Tittle's chore was to keep them all happy.

"Tittle would try to divide the ball between us back there as much as possible," Perry said with a laugh. "He kept me satisfied anyway."

Indeed, Perry's 1,929 lifetime carries has been surpassed by only seven other running backs in NFL history.

Perry was discovered playing football when he was a running sensation for the Alameda Naval Air Station Hell Cats.

John Woudenberg, an offensive tackle for the 49ers at the time, is credited with the find that became a 49er gold mine.

After playing two years with the 49ers in the All-America Football Conference, Perry and the club moved to the NFL. Although the established league was reputed to have fiercer competition, Perry saw little difference between the two leagues.

"The first year in the NFL we weren't too successful," he said. "We were 3-9. The next two years we almost won the thing. There wasn't a real big difference. There was one game, though, when we played the Bears that I noticed it. They won, 13-7. But they beat the hell out of us physically. We were beat up pretty good. I guess that was the only game where I noticed a difference in the leagues.

"They could play good defense in the old league, too. I remember one game in the AAFC against the New York

Yankees. They had a middle linebacker who followed me everywhere.

"There is quite a difference between my era and football now. The game is more scientific now. There are more specialists. In my day we had 33 players and 22 of them went both ways. As far as I am concerned football is football, just get out there and play."

Perry has nothing but praise for the quarterbacks he worked with in the 49er backfields. Frankie Albert and Y.A. Tittle had different styles but they excelled in their own way, he said. They were quarterbacks that reflected their separate eras.

"Frankie Albert was like a riverboat gambler," Perry said. "He had a sharp mind and did the unexpected. He was unpredictable. But if you gave him something he would run the same play 20 times until you stopped it. He used to throw a quick pass to Strzykalski. One game he threw the same pass over and over for about five yards. We marched right down the field and scored.

"Y.A. Tittle was a brainy quarterback. He was a thinker and he had a strong arm. He would stay in that pocket and wait for the man to get open. He'd wait until he got done what he had to do."

Perry is diplomatic about praising his peers on the gridiron. All the running backs he saw had something that made them professionals. But he is not shy about praising his fellow running back, Hugh McElhenny.

"Mac was the best open field runner of our era. He was a will o' the wisp out there. Sayers was a great open field runner, too, but he was different than Mac. It's hard to pinpoint what it was."

Not all of Perry's memories of life in the NFL are rosy. He was one of the first black men in professional football, joining the 49ers just a year after Jackie Robinson broke the color line in professional baseball. He encountered racism both on the field and off. His teammates were very supportive, he says, as was the club management.

"I was the first black to play football here," he said. "It was rough as hell. There were a lot of unpleasant things that happened. Lots of things were said on the field. You could imagine what they were. It was probably worse playing football instead of baseball, like Jackie Robinson did, because football is such a physical game.

"The 49ers were great though. If one person was in a fight, the whole team was in a fight. We were like a big family. That was part of the Morabito influence. Italians always do things family-style. We always had meals family-style. In training camp, the food was on the table and you just served yourself."

Like most former 49ers who played in the 1950s, the year 1957 is one that stands out. Many players recall the playoff loss to Detroit that year. Others remember the 49ers' powerful offense and the Alley-Oop Pass. Perry remembers the game against the Chicago

Bears at Kezar Stadium.

"That game stands out for me because it is the game when Tony Morabito died," Perry said. "I had been hurt for several weeks. At halftime, Chicago was ahead, 17-3. We got word that Tony had died. The mood turned pretty somber. You could hear people crying, that's how much people loved the guy. I played the second half and we all made a great comeback. We ended up winning, 21-17."

Perry played 14 years with the 49ers and another two for the Baltimore Colts. He was the first man in NFL history to rush for over 1,000 yards in two consecutive years. In 1953, he rushed for 1,018 yards, a feat that inspired owner Tony Morabito to reward Perry with a $5,090 bonus, $5 for every yard. In 1954, he ran for 1,049 and was named the NFL's Player-of-the-Year. He is also the 49ers' all-time leading rusher. Although proud of his accomplishments, there is one award that tops them all.

"The biggest thrill for me has to be making the Hall of Fame," he said. "There is no way anything could surpass that."

Since retiring, Perry has not missed the game. He doesn't miss the long flights in propeller-driven planes or the games on frozen fields in Green Bay and Cleveland. He has remained a devoted 49er fan, however, and the new version of the 49ers is a sight to behold, he says.

"I think they'll be there for years to come. They have depth and talent at every position. That's what it's all about."

ABOVE: Clyde Conner was the 49ers' leading receiver in 1958 when he caught 49 passes. Here, he reaches back for a Y.A. Tittle pass that is picked off by Yale Lary (28) of the Detroit Lions.

They drafted consensus All-America quarterback John Brodie out of Stanford and were blessed with three of the finest signal callers in the game. Brodie competed with Earl Morrall and Y.A. Tittle for the starting job. However, before the start of the regular season, Morrall was traded to Pittsburgh for linebacker Marv Matuszak.

In the league opener, the 49ers were soundly defeated by the Chicago Cardinals, 20-10. Former University of San Francisco star Ollie Matson returned to Kezar Stadium and ran through the 49er defense. After the game, local writers said there was no reason to believe the 49ers would be contenders. In 12 weeks they would eat their words.

In the second week of the season, the Los Angeles Rams met the 49ers at Kezar Stadium. The Rams had mauled San Francisco in a preseason game, 58-27. They were favored to win the league championship.

The Rams held a 20-16 lead late in the fourth quarter. But just as the 59,700 fans at Kezar were preparing to head for home, Tittle got the team untracked. With short passes to his receivers, and several fine runs by McElhenny, he drove the team 50 yards to the Rams' 11-yard line. With four minutes to play, Tittle dropped back and threw a high arching pass to the corner of the end zone. R.C. Owens, a rookie from College of Idaho, leaped into the sky. He outjumped Los Angeles defensive back Jesse Castete and came down with the football. The Alley-Oop pass was born. San Francisco had itself a 23-20 win.

Spectacular finishes eventually became commonplace. The following week in Chicago, the Bears were in the driver's seat with a 17-14 lead and four minutes to play. Tittle dropped back and looked for Owens again but the receiver had been knocked to the turf by a Chicago defender. Undaunted, Tittle threw a low pass to the squatting Owens and he caught it on his knees to give San Francisco a 21-17 win.

Two weeks later they played Chicago at Kezar. Behind at the half, 17-7, the team received word in the locker room that owner Tony Morabito had suffered a heart attack while in the stands. He died a short time later. The inspired 49ers battled back and defeated Chicago, 21-17.

Dick Moegle (47) was the 49ers' top pass defender in the mid-1950s. He was the team's first draft choice in 1955 and led the club in interceptions for three straight years from 1956 to 1958. Here, he deflects a pass intended for Green Bay's Max McGee. PAGE 57: Abe Woodson (40) breaks up a pass from Baltimore's Johnny Unitas to receiver Raymond Berry. Woodson thrilled 49er fans with his spectacular kick returns. He ranks second on the NFL's all-time kickoff return list with 5,538 yards.

The next week they were behind Detroit, 31-28, with less than a minute to play. Tittle valiantly worked the ball downfield. With 11 seconds to play, he launched a rocket into the end zone. R.C. Owens came down with the pigskin. The Alley-Oop had done it again. The 49ers won it, 35-31.

With two weeks left in the season, San Francisco was 6-4. They needed wins in the last two games to tie for the league title.

Baltimore was the first hurdle. The Colts were a pass-oriented team with Johnny Unitas at the helm. The day before the game, a crowd formed at the Kezar Stadium ticket booths to buy tickets. When the booths finally opened, a near riot ensued and thousands of fans had to be turned away.

The game was a defensive battle most of the way. With less than two minutes remaining in the game, Baltimore held a precarious 13-10 lead. But the 49ers had the ball and Tittle was moving the

club. A pass to Hugh McElhenny picked up 28 yards and put the ball on the Colts' 15-yard line.

On the next play, Tittle was belted by Baltimore's defensive line as he tried to get off a pass. Afterward, he lay motionless on the field. His teammates carried him to the sideline while rookie John Brodie quickly warmed up. With precious seconds remaining on the stadium clock, Brodie took the field. Then, with 46 seconds to play, Brodie found McElhenny wide open. He drilled a pass to "the King" and San Francisco won, 17-13.

The Green Bay Packers were next. A win would leave the 49ers tied for the league crown with Detroit.

Before the game Tittle was still hobbling on pulled leg muscles suffered in the collision against the Colts. Brodie got the starting assignment. Rain soaked Kezar Stadium throughout the day but 59,530 paying customers remained in their seats.

Green Bay took a 20-10 lead into the locker room at halftime. Coach Frankie Albert decided to go with the old master, Y.A. Tittle, in the second half. On the 49ers first offensive possession in the third quarter, the fans roared their approval at the sight of Tittle leading the team onto the field. He didn't let them down.

The 30-year-old Tittle completed 10 of his 14 passes for 94 yards and Joe Perry gained 130 yards

Y.A. Tittle 1951–1960

When Y.A. Tittle joined the 49ers in 1951, he found himself in a new role. Frankie Albert was still in command of San Francisco's offense and he wasn't about to give up the controls. For the first time in his life, Tittle was a backup quarterback. It was a role he did not enjoy.

Tittle became a 49er after the Baltimore Colts folded in their first NFL season. Baltimore was originally a member of the All-America Football Conference and joined the NFL with Cleveland and San Francisco in 1950.

Near the end of the 1951 season, Coach Buck Shaw began to take notice of Tittle's strong throwing arm and started alternating his two quarterbacks. Albert would play the first and third quarters of a game, while Tittle played the second and fourth. The 49ers' first quarterback controversy began to brew. By 1952, Tittle and Albert were alternating full time.

"Frank was more of a roll-out type quarterback," said Tittle. "He used a lot of play action. There was more running than passing when he was in there. His whole style of play was built off the run. I was more of a drop-back quarterback, so defenses had to shift according to our styles.

"Frankie Albert was a big influence on me. Of course, we were intense rivals for the quarterback position, but I learned a lot just watching him play. His leadership qualities were unparalleled.

"He gave me another dimension. I never had been around someone who was such a loose quarterback and had so much freedom. I was more of a coach's quarterback. I did what I thought the coach wanted done. Frank was unpredictable. I learned from him that being unpredictable can be a good quality, that nutty things sometimes will work.

"The bootleg is another thing I got from him. After I left the 49ers, it helped me win a championship at New York."

Tittle got the freedom he wanted under Coach Buck Shaw. Shaw allowed Tittle to call his own plays or improvise when necessary. Such independence instilled Tittle with confidence. For that reason, he considers Shaw one of the best coaches he played under.

"Buck Shaw was probably the easiest coach to play for," he said. "As a quarterback, he let you be yourself. He had respect for your ability. He would never second guess you. If I called a long pass on third down and two, he wouldn't say, 'What did you call that for?' He let me play the way I wanted."

The 49er backfield of the 1950s was among the best of all time. Tittle played alongside Joe Perry, Hugh McElhenny and John Henry Johnson. All but Johnson are in the Hall of Fame.

"I was lucky to play with the greatest running backs in history," Tittle said. "Joe Perry and Hugh McElhenny were probably the best running combination ever together on one team. McElhenny was the greatest broken field runner I ever saw play. There's no doubt about that. Perry was great because he was so quick to hit the hole. He was fast and powerful."

The first time they played together Perry's quickness startled Tittle. On several handoff attempts, Perry was past the quarterback and into the hole before Tittle could hand him the football.

"I told him he was jumping offsides," Tittle said jokingly. "He just wanted to beat the handoff and make me look bad."

The 1957 season was one of triumph and agony for Tittle. Last-second victories became a 49er trademark. The Alley-Oop pass became their most potent weapon.

"The Alley-Oop was developed by accident," Tittle recalled. "R.C. (Owens) wanted to try it out. We practiced it a few times, but I never thought we would use it in a game. In 1957, we won five games in the last couple minutes using the Alley-Oop. What made it work was timing and R.C.'s jumping ability. The defenses knew it was coming. They would put extra defensive backs on R.C. It didn't help though. They just got in the way of each other."

The Alley-Oop couldn't help the 49ers on Dec. 22, 1957. It was the 49ers' first playoff appearance in the NFL. They jumped out to a commanding 24-7 halftime lead over the Detroit Lions. On their first series of plays in the second half, Hugh McElhenny raced 71 yards with a pitchout, only to be dragged down at the nine-yard line. The 49ers had to settle for a field goal, but a berth in the championship game looked secure. Suddenly, the team fell apart. De-

troit came back to win, 31-27. Tittle sighs painfully as he recalled the game in his Texas drawl.

"We watched the clock too much," he said. "Once we had that 20-point lead, I thought we could wait it out. We tried to kill the clock by running the football. It was the pass that got us the lead and we should have stayed with the pass. We should have been more aggressive and continued to throw the ball."

Throwing the football is a passion for Tittle. He believes it is the game's ultimate weapon. In his prime, he could toss the pigskin 60 yards with the same ease as Ray Wersching kicking an extra point. His strong throwing arm kept defensive coaches scribbling X's and O's that would stop him.

"I'd like to play now," Tittle said. "The new rules make it easier for the passing game to succeed. It's much more wide open. You can't put your hands on receivers like you could before. I'd love to play against the zone defense. A strong arm can succeed against the zone. Marino has shown that. The field is still 53 yards wide so it's only a matter of time before someone gets open. You just have to be patient.

"Don't get me wrong. I'd prefer to play during my era. I'm not saying we were better or anything, I just liked our rules better. I liked the individual matchups, players going man-to-man. You knew who your opponent was going to be. You knew what defensive back was going to be watching which receiver. With the

zones you don't know who is watching who. In our day, you had a four- or five-man rush. Now they use stunts and turns and all kinds of funny games on the line. You don't know what's going on."

Not all the teams of Tittle's era played conventional defense. The Chicago Bears were one team that was always a thorn in Tittle's side.

"I hated to play the Bears," he said. "They were the one team that didn't do anything normal. They made you look bad even when you played good. For some reason, you felt like you played a sloppy game. Chicago always did crazy things on defense. They used safety and corner blitzes. They did things to screw up the blocking. Now the Bears are doing all this stuff again under Ditka.

"Cleveland was another tough team when I played. Paul Brown was the coach. But they were a very disciplined team. Unlike the Bears, they were an orthodox team. Brown had them well trained."

Tittle was traded to the New York Giants prior to the 1961 season and it was there that he had his greatest success. He led the Giants to three straight appearances in the NFL Championship Game, which he considers his greatest thrill as a player. He never forgot his ties to the Bay Area, however, and relished his return trips to Kezar Stadium.

"Kezar Stadium was one of the unique stadiums in football," he said. "The fans were so close to you. It seemed like

they were right on top of you. In my day it was a great place to play. It was really something just driving there because of the surroundings in Golden Gate Park. You had all these people walking through the park to the stadium. Driving to the games I just felt it was a beautiful place to play."

Ask Tittle about the most fearsome defensive players of his day and he'll tell you about his 49er roommate. He was Hardy Brown and he was a legend around the NFL. He was small for a linebacker, weighing in at 190 pounds, but rumor has it he knocked out more teeth than a country club full of oral surgeons.

"We called him Hardy the Hatchet," said Tittle. "He may be the hardest hitter that ever played the game. Butkus would maul you when he made a tackle, and Nitschke, too. They were strong and would bring you to the ground with arm strength. Hardy just exploded. He popped you. In 1951, we played the Washington Redskins and he knocked out the entire backfield. He knocked the running backs out cold."

Tittle was honored for his outstanding ability when he was selected to the Hall of Fame in 1971. It was a thrill unsurpassed by anything he ever achieved.

"Well that's got to be my most cherished memory," he said. "I'm in great company. You can't get much better than the Hall of Fame."

on 27 carries. There was no need for magical Alley-Oop passes this day. Perry scored two second-half touchdowns on runs of nine yards and two yards. That was all the scoring the 49ers needed to take a 27-20 win. They had gained a first-place tie with Detroit. A playoff was needed to determine who would face Cleveland in the NFL Championship Game.

The playoff was held at Kezar. Frenzied fans scrambled to get tickets. People began lining up at Kezar ticket booths on Friday night in hopes of purchasing a ticket on Saturday. The game was blacked out on local television. Busloads of fans unable to obtain tickets went to Reno to see the game on television.

The 49ers found themselves 3½-point favorites at game time. The favorable odds were due in part to the broken leg suffered by Detroit quarterback Bobby Layne. He was replaced by Tobin Rote.

In the first quarter, Tittle connnected on a 34-yard Alley-Oop pass to R.C. Owens to put the 49ers in front 7-0. A 47-yard pass to McElhenny made the score 14-0. Before the half, Tittle threw another touchdown pass, this one a 12-yarder to Billy Wilson. Gordy Soltau added a 25-yard field goal and the 49ers looked unbeatable. The halftime score read 24-7.

McElhenny opened the second half by taking a pitchout and racing 71 yards to the nine. The 49ers couldn't push it in and had to settle for a field goal. Their 27-7 lead looked insurmountable.

Suddenly, the Lions came to life. Three interceptions and two lost fumbles contributed to the Detroit cause. When it was all over the 49ers had lost a heartbreaker, 31-27.

1958

The 49ers hobbled through a mediocre 1958 exhibition season with a 3-3 record. Quarterback John Brodie showed flashes of brilliance, however, and Albert named him the starting quarterback. Brodie had taken the starting position from the 1957 Player-of-the-Year, Y.A. Tittle.

Several other newcomers worked their way into the starting lineup. Among them were John Thomas, who began the year at left tackle, and John Wittenborn, who opened at right guard.

The opening game was against the Pittsburgh Steelers. Former 49er Earl Morrall was the quarterback.

Brodie played brilliantly in his first game as a starter. Down 20-7 in the closing minutes of the third quarter, he marched the club 73 yards in eight plays cutting the margin to 20-13. On the next possession, he took the 49ers 30 yards to tie the game at 20-20. Finally, with 2:30 remaining, he set up the winning field goal by throwing three passes to Owens for gains of 12, 15 and eight yards. Overall, Brodie completed 19 of 28 passes for 244 yards.

The game proved to be one of the highlights of a lackluster year. Brodie and Tittle alternated at quarterback much of the season. Tittle completed 120 of 208 passes for 1,467 yards over the course of the season. Brodie hit on 103 of 172 for 1,224 yards.

The 49ers suffered some drastic defeats in 1958, including the worst loss in the history of the franchise when Los Angeles embarrassed them, 56-7, before 96,000 at the Coliseum.

San Francisco salvaged some respect by defeating the Baltimore Colts, champions of the Western Division, 21-12, on Albert's last day as coach. He resigned after the season with a 6-6 record. He had a three-year coaching record of 19-17-1.

After the victory, a riot broke out at Kezar as young fans attempted to tear down the goal posts. When police tried to disperse the mob, the largely young crowd threw cans, seat cushions and dirt at police.

1959

Howard "Red" Hickey took charge in 1959. Under their new coach the 49ers jumped off to their best start since joining the NFL by winning six of their first seven games. They beat Los Angeles twice, 34-0 and 24-16. They also defeated Detroit twice, 33-7 and 34-13. Their only loss was a 21-20 squeaker at the hands of Green Bay.

But things went bad in a hurry. The 49ers dropped four of their next five games. They still had a shot at first place on the last weekend of the season, but a victory by Baltimore, coupled with San Francisco's 36-14 loss to the Packers, knocked them out of contention. The 49ers ended the year with a 7-5 record and tied for third place.

PAGE 60: Defensive back Elbert Kimbrough (45) receives a straightarm that looks more like a right cross from Green Bay halfback Elijah Pitts. Kimbrough played in the 49er secondary from 1962 to 1966.

1960–1969

CHAPTER THREE

THE LEAN YEARS

Coach Red Hickey began to reshape the team in 1960 by adding two draft picks that had an immediate impact. Monty Stickles, a tight end from Notre Dame, was used as a spot starter and caught 22 passes in his first season. Mike Magac, a guard from Missouri, helped strengthen the offensive line.

San Francisco opened the 1960 season with a 21-19 loss to New York. Kicker Tommy Davis missed four field goal attempts in the game, including a 37 yarder with 30 seconds to play.

Tittle won the starting quarterback position over John Brodie and completed 21 of 34 passes in the opener. As the season wore on, Tittle saw less action, and it became clear John Brodie was the quarterback of the future.

The 49ers unveiled a new offense on Nov. 27, 1960, when they surprised the Baltimore Colts with the Shotgun Formation. The 49ers had been struggling all season and had a 4-4 record. The Colts were two-time NFL champions and 21-point favorites. San Francisco did not look capable of an upset.

The week prior to the game, Coach Red Hickey decided to try the Shotgun Formation because it would allow his quarterbacks to run, pass, pitch out, handoff, or kick. The new weapon helped the 49ers defeat the Colts, 30-22.

Using the formation, the 49ers won four of their last five games in 1960 and finished in second place with a 7-5 record.

In the off-season, Hickey drafted UCLA's Billy Kilmer, a skillful passer and runner. Kilmer was the ideal man for the Shotgun Formation. To make room for his new quarterback, Hickey traded veteran Y.A. Tittle to the New York Giants. Tittle, a drop-back passer, was uncomfortable with the Shotgun.

Tittle wasn't the only veteran to go after the 1960 season. Two other members of the Million Dollar Backfield departed as well. McElhenny was picked up by Minnesota in the expansion draft, and Joe Perry was traded to the Colts for a third-round draft pick. In addition, Ed Henke was traded to the St. Louis Cardinals.

1961 In the 1961 season opener, Brodie got the starting call and immediately made the 45,000 fans at Kezar forget about Y.A. Tittle. He threw four touchdown passes as the 49ers defeated the Washington Redskins, 35-3.

After a 30-10 loss to the Green Bay Packers, the 49ers were set to play the Detroit Lions. The Lions were 10-point favorites. Their defense, rated the best in football, was led by All-Pro linebacker Joe Schmidt.

To counter the Lions' defense, Hickey used the Shotgun, but with an additional twist. He rotated his three quarterbacks—Brodie, Kilmer and Bob Waters—on every down and sent in plays from the bench. San Francisco walloped the Lions, 49-0, the most overwhelming win in the team's history.

San Francisco's rotating quarterbacks were devastating against the

Lions. Kilmer ran for 103 yards out of the Shotgun and scored two touchdowns. Waters ran for another 38 yards and Brodie, who did most of the passing, completed five of 12 for 108 yards.

The victory set several team standards. It was the highest number of points scored by the 49ers in NFL play. It established the largest margin of victory in team history. And it handed the Lions their first shutout in 10 years.

The Los Angeles Rams were the 49ers' next opponent. Before 59,000 paying customers at Kezar Stadium, San Francisco accumulated 521 yards of total offense and scored a 34-0 win. It was the second consecutive shutout for the 49ers and only the second time Los Angeles had been held scoreless in 140 games.

Dave Wilcox (64) pulls Frank Nunley (57) away from the referees as Nunley argues a pass interference call. PAGE: 65 R.C. Owens goes high in the air to grab an Alley-Oop Pass. Owens became the first 49er receiver to gain over 1,000 yards through the air in 1961.

Once again, Hickey rotated his quarterbacks and they responded with an even better performance than the one against the Lions. They combined for 201 rushing yards and another 261 yards passing to account for all but 58 yards of San Francisco's total offensive output.

Kilmer gained 131 yards in 19 carries and scored two touchdowns. Brodie threw for 151 yards, completing 12 of 17 passes. Waters completed seven of eight passes for 53 yards and one touchdown.

After five games, the 49ers led the league in points scored, passing yardage and running yardage. They looked invincible.

Two weeks after routing Los Angeles, the 49ers were matched with the Chicago Bears. Clark Shaughnessy, the man who perfected the T-Formation, had been scouting the 49ers for Chicago. He detected a slight flaw in the Shotgun. To snap the ball, the center had to look between his legs to see the backs. Shaughnessy thought it would be easy for the Bears' middle linebacker, Bill George, to shoot past the center before he had a chance to look up and block.

The adjustment worked. San Francisco netted only six first downs and 132 yards of total offense all day. Hickey used the formation sparingly the rest of the year and ended up with a 7-6-1 record. His experiment with the Shotgun ended as abruptly as it began.

1962 In the 1962 college draft, the 49ers made Lance Alworth their first-round choice. Alworth was a spectacular runner and pass catcher out of the University of Arkansas. The 49ers were unable to sign him after a bidding war with the San Diego Chargers of the American Football League. Instead, second-year man Jimmy Johnson started the season in the flanker position. Johnson later became an All-Pro defensive back. Alworth went on to become one of the greatest deep threats in history, averaging 19 yards per reception. He was selected to the Hall of Fame in 1978. Long-time fans still marvel at the thought of Alworth and Dave Parks, a first-round selection in 1964, catching passes together for the 49ers.

When the 1962 season started, most of the Bay Area's attention was riveted on the San Francisco Giants, who were in the midst of a tight pennant race. Later that year, they would appear in their only World Series.

Bruce Bosley 1956–1968

Ask Bruce Bosley who his toughest opponent was and he'll recite a virtual who's who of the Hall of Fame.

Imagine bumping heads with Dick Butkus, Ray Nitschke, Joe Schmidt, Sam Huff and Bill George. Or trap blocking Roger Brown, Rosey Grier, Bob Lilly, Alex Karras and Merlin Olsen. Bosley's played against them all. To rate one of those stars over the rest is impossible, he says. They all stood out in their own way.

Bosley came to the 49ers as a second-round pick in the 1956 college draft. At 6′ 3″ and 245 pounds, the 49ers originally planned to use the West Virgina graduate as a defensive end.

"I remember my first game with the 49ers," Bosley said. "I just got in from the College All-Star Game. It was a pre-season game against Cleveland and I'd been in camp for three days.

Leo Nomellini, the old pro, was going to be playing next to me. He said, 'Don't worry rook, I'll take care of you.' We ended up beating Cleveland. I played the whole game and did pretty good. Nomellini gave me the game ball afterward. It was the only one I ever got."

In 1957, Bosley was switched to the offensive line where he made his home for the next 12 years. Four times he was selected to play in the Pro Bowl, once as a guard and three times as a center. It was from his offensive line position that he encountered the game's greats.

"Butkus wasn't really mean like everyone said he was," Bosley recalled. "He wouldn't deliberately try to twist your leg off. He was just rough. He liked to hit. In fact, he loved to hit. But I'd hit him back as hard as he hit me. I wanted him to respect me."

Eugene "Big Daddy" Lipscomb was a massive defensive tackle who terrorized ball carriers in the 1950s and early 1960s while playing with Los Angeles, Baltimore and Pittsburgh. He stood 6′ 6″ and weighed 300 pounds. He was more than most linemen could handle. Bosley tried to neutralize him by holding him when the referees weren't looking. Finally, Lipscomb had had enough.

"He turned around and started yelling and screaming at me," Bosley said. "Saliva was coming out of his mouth. He said to me, 'Bosley, if you hold me one more time, I'll kill you.' "

Not wanting to lose his starting center to penalty or injury, John Brodie grabbed Bosley and pulled him back to the huddle. On the way, Bosley could not refrain from adding one more retort.

"I didn't want anyone to think I was afraid so I

yelled back and told him we were going to run right over him. I guess Brodie thought I was serious because in the huddle he asked me if I wanted to run a 31 trap on him. I said, 'Hell no, that guy's going to kill me.' But Brodie called it anyway.

"As I walked up to the line, Lipscomb was snorting and digging his feet in. He's all set to tee off. At the last minute, Brodie calls an audible so the play would be going the other way. I look up and Lipscomb is grinning at me. He says, 'Boz, I was just kidding you.'

"Later we got to be good friends. I'd see him in the off-season and tell him I voted for him for All-Pro. That was just a little psychology to butter him up so he'd take it easy when we played."

One of Bosley's teammates at West Virginia was Sam Huff, a Hall of Fame linebacker who was the leader of the New York Giants fabled defense in the 1950s and 1960s. When they faced each other, they never allowed their friendship to surface.

"Sam always tried to distract me," he said. "Dick Modzelewski was a defensive lineman for the Giants. Huff would yell out for everyone to hear, 'Boz, Modzelewski is going to tear you up.' Then he'd smile at me.

"Huff had a reputation for piling on. Once a referee was getting everyone off a pileup. I heard someone in the pile say, 'We can't, Huff isn't here yet.' I guess he figured the play wasn't over until Huff jumped on the pile.

"Bill George was another nasty linebacker—

tough as nails. He used to call me a snake eater because I was from West Virginia. I had to laugh at that."

During Bosley's tenure with San Francisco, he had the priviledge of blocking for some of the game's most talented backs. Joe Perry, Hugh McElhenny, Ken Willard and John David Crow all owe thanks to Bosley for the holes he opened for them.

"McElhenny was the best to block for," Bosley said. "He wasn't the fastest, but he was very elusive. It was easy to throw a block for Hugh because he set the block up himself with his moves and great running ability. He made us look good. A lot of backs tend to outrun their blockers. McElhenny's greatness was his ability to use blockers, to set the block up for his linemen."

The 49er teams of 1965 and 1966 were exciting, according to Bosley. Although the team record was only 7-6-1 in 1965, they had a potent offense that averaged 30 points a game. They scored over 40 points four times.

"Brodie was really on the stick then," said Bosley. "He was hitting long passes, short passes, everything. And Ken Willard was grinding out yardage. It really pumped you up when Brodie completed those 50-yard passes."

On the receiving end of many of Brodie's tosses was Dave Parks. Parks was the first college player chosen in the 1964 draft. He led the league in receptions in 1965 with 80. Bosley has fond memories of the Texas

Tech star.

"That Parks was a great competitor," he said. "I hated to see him go. A lot of receivers are prima donnas. They don't like to get in there and block. Dave wasn't like that at all. He was a tough nut. He liked to get in there and mix it up."

The starting running backs in the mid-1960s were characters in their own right. Ken Willard was a hard-running fullback who was well known as a prankster. John David Crow, a former Heisman Trophy winner, was a respected team leader.

"Ken had a poker face," recalled Bosley. "But don't let that fool you, he was always up to something."

The mere mention of the name John David Crow stirs Bosley's memory. The 49ers obtained him in a trade with the St. Louis Cardinals in 1965.

"I always heard about John when he played for St. Louis," Bosley said. "I was real excited when he came to the 49ers. First of all, he was a great guy. He was also a heck of a competitor. He always wanted to run with the ball. It jacks you up when you have a guy come into the huddle and say, 'Give me the ball.' That's what he did."

Bosley made four trips to the Pro Bowl but he'd gladly trade those games for the chance to have played in a championship game, the one goal that eluded him.

"A championship is what every professional plays for," he said. "It's something I never attained. I wish I had gotten just one shot."

The 49ers never really got going in 1962. Green Bay, led by Vince Lombardi, continued to dominate the NFL and the 49ers were no exception. The Packers beat up on the 49ers in both their meetings, and San Francisco finished with an uneventful 6-8 record. It was the club's first losing season under Red Hickey.

1963 Hickey's troubles continued into the 1963 season. Injuries to key players hampered the 49ers. The club's first- and second-team quarterbacks were injured in separate car accidents. Brodie walked away with a broken arm that kept him out of several games. Kilmer broke a leg and was out for the season.

The team got off to its worst start since joining the NFL, dropping five exhibition games and its first three league contests. Hickey decided he'd had enough. He called it quits, ending his career with a 27-27-1 record as the 49er head coach.

Assistant coach Jack Christiansen took over the controls after the third league game, but he fared no better. He directed the team to just two victories in 1963. The 49ers ended their worst season in professional football with a 2-12 record.

1964 Prior to the 1964 season, tragedy struck the 49er front office when team owner Victor Morabito died of a heart attack. The wives of Victor and Tony Morabito retained control of the team but hired Lou Spadia as team president. Spadia had been with the team since its inception, and had worked in virtually every job imaginable from ticket salesman to equipment manager.

In the 1964 college draft, the 49ers selected Texas Tech receiver Dave Parks on the first round. Parks teamed up with Bernie Casey and Monty Stickles to give the 49ers one of the best pass-catching trios in football.

In mid season, knee injuries to the 49ers' two top running backs, J.D. Smith and Don Lisbon, prompted the team to recall Gary Lewis, one of the draftees they had released in training camp. Lewis was a pounding fullback who played his high school football at San Francisco's Polytechnic, located directly across the street from Kezar Stadium. Lewis lasted six seasons with the 49ers and gained over 1,400 yards

Jim Marshall, a defensive end with the Minne-

Running back J.D. Smith (24) rushed for 4,370 yards with the 49ers between 1956 and 1964, an average of 4.3 yards per carry. Here, he hurdles over the Chicago Bears' line for a touchdown. He also played defensive back. PAGE 68: The 49ers made Dave Parks the first player chosen in the 1964 draft. He caught 208 passes in just four seasons with the team and was the league's leading receiver in 1965 when he caught 80 balls. Parks was an excellent runner after making the catch, averaging 16 years per reception. PAGE 71 Bernie Casey (30) caught 277 passes for the 49ers from 1961 to 1966. He led the club in receptions three times. Casey teamed with Dave Parks and Monty Stickles in the mid-1960s to give the 49ers one of the best pass-catching trios in football. He was sent to the Atlanta Falcons in 1967 in a trade that gave the 49ers the draft rights to Steve Spurrier.

sota Vikings, made the 1964 season memorable in the seventh week when he scooped up a Billy Kilmer fumble and rambled 60 yards—the wrong way. Thinking he'd scored a touchdown for the Vikes, he threw the ball into the air and ensured the 49ers a two-point safety. The safety didn't help the 49ers though, they lost to Minnesota, 27-22.

A quarterback controversy that would rage on and off for five years got under way in the Minnesota game when Brodie had four passes intercepted. The fans booed him steadily in the second half until rookie quarterback George Mira entered the contest. Mira was unable to get the offense moving either and before the game was over, he also was showered with boos. Although Brodie continued to start regularly during the next five years, there was always a contingent of fans at Kezar anxious to see Mira play. The quarterback debate lasted among fans until Mira was traded to Philadelphia in 1969.

Outstanding rookie performances by Parks, Mira and linebacker Dave Wilcox helped take some of the bitterness out of the 4-10 season.

1965 In 1965, the 49ers molded their most explosive offense since the record-setting 1948 season. Ken Willard, a 220-pound fullback from North Carolina, was the team's number-one choice. He stepped into the starting slot and held it for eight seasons. Halfback John David Crow, a former Heisman Trophy winner, was acquired from the St. Louis Cardinals for Abe Woodson. Crow solidified the 49ers' weak running game. They now had a pair of running backs to complement an already potent passing attack. Up front, Bruce Bosley, Howard Mudd and John Thomas anchored one of the best offensive lines in the league.

Charlie Krueger 1959–1973

Charlie Krueger vividly recalls his start in pro football. He'd been with the 49ers only a couple of weeks when he found himself on the defensive line in a game against the Chicago Bears.

"Willie Galimore carried the ball about six times against us in that game and three of those were touchdown runs," he said. "I thought to myself, 'Jesus what am I up against here.' This is quite an introduction."

Krueger was selected by the 49ers on the first round of the 1958 college draft. He'd been a standout at Texas A&M, where he played under Paul "Bear" Bryant. He began his career with the 49ers as a defensive end. When Leo Nomellini retired, Krueger was moved into "the Lion's" defensive tackle position. He became a fixture there until his own retirement in 1973.

"I tell you, we saw some great runners," he said with a hint of a Texas drawl. "Jimmy Taylor was in his own league as far as toughness. He was a physical animal. He pre-

ferred running right over you instead of around you. He was not a polished runner like Jim Brown, but he was fierce. Taylor would demolish defensive backs. He loved that contact. He was a great blocker, too."

The Chicago Bears have had their share of outstanding runners. In addition to Galimore, Krueger spent some time chasing after Gale Sayers. He ranks Sayers as one of the greatest backs of all time. Krueger was on the field on Dec. 12, 1965, when Sayers put on a one-man show, scoring six touchdowns against the 49ers.

"It was cold and wet that day, just miserable," he said. "We were playing in the mud at Chicago. I looked at the scoreboard near the end of the game and saw the 61 points the Bears scored and thought, 'This is a hell of a way to treat visitors.' "

Krueger, a two-time Pro Bowl participant, was a nightmare for offensive linemen. He was often double- or triple-

teamed. But there was one lineman who didn't need any help, according to Krueger. He played for the Green Bay Packers and was in a class by himself.

"The Green Bay line was always one of the best," he said. "Some others came close but were never quite as good. On the Packers' line, Forrest Gregg was the one who stood out. He was 6' 4" and about 245 pounds, not a real big lineman. He was smart, agile and he had a lot of guts and stamina. That's what made him good."

Dick Nolan built the 49ers into a solid defensive team in the 1970s. Krueger anchored the defensive line with Tommy Hart, Roland Lakes, Cedrick Hardman and Bill Belk. Although Krueger was one of the senior members of the team, he says he wasn't the leader of that unit. That distinction belonged to a hard-hitting linebacker.

"You want to talk about a stud," Krueger said. "Dave Wilcox, now he was a stud. He had a lot of physical ability. He was strong, fast, he set a good example. He was the leader.

"Tommy Hart was another one. He had a lot of ability too, but he didn't get the recognition he deserved back then."

The 49er defense had 46 quarterback sacks in 1972 to lead the NFC. In 1971, they were second with 38 sacks. As good as that defensive unit was, Krueger insists the teams of 1960 and 1961 were better.

Official records for quarterback sacks were not kept then, but the defense gave up only 205 points in 1960, lowest in the NFL. The same year, quarterbacks completed just 47 percent of their passes against the 49ers.

"That defensive backfield was just outstanding," he said of the teams of the early 1960s. "There was Dave Baker and Eddie Dove and Abe Woodson and Jerry Mertens back there. They did a damn good job."

Defensive linemen are paid to harass quarterbacks, and Krueger did his share of annoying. But with certain quarterbacks, that harassment often turned into long-term chases. The elusive Fran Tarkenton was one quarterback that gave fits to the 6' 4", 250-pound Krueger. Tarkenton's scrambling ability exhausted defensive lineman. Krueger remembers one game in 1965 that Minnesota won, 42-41.

"Tarkenton just got going in that one and ran us to death," he said. "His line really knew how to block for him. Once he started moving around

back there, you'd run from one end of the field to the other chasing him. His linemen would wait and just pick you off as you ran across the field. It's hard on you chasing those guys around. Staubach was a scrambler, too, but nothing like Tarkenton."

Krueger has more pleasant memories of two Hall of Fame quarterbacks. "Johnny Unitas was my hero," he said. "Sammy Baugh, too, but I never played against him. Johnny was a fine guy on and off the field. On the field, he'd talk to you like you were friends. I'd think, 'Geez, he's a nice guy. He remembers who I am.'"

According to his teammates, Krueger never got the recognition in the NFL he deserved. He was selected for two Pro Bowls, but his teammates say he consistently was one of the top defensive linemen in the league.

Bruce Bosley, a former Pro Bowl center with the 49ers, was Krueger's teammate for 10 years. In practice, they lined up on the opposite side of the line of scrimmage and battled each other daily.

"Charlie was a real hard knocker," Bosley said. "They always had two or three guys blocking on him in a game. That enabled the other linemen to do their job. He got a lot of respect. With the 49ers, he was a quiet leader. He was like E.F. Hutton. When he said something, people listened."

Every Sunday was a challenge for Krueger. Despite playing for 15 seasons, he never had trouble getting

motivated.

"Every game was a big game for me," he said. "I didn't want to get my butt whipped out there. I didn't want to embarrass myself. I think a lot of jocks work in that way. Every game was important to me from that respect."

Krueger was honored by his teammates in 1964 when they voted him the Len Eshmont award. He was also honored when he became one of only six 49ers to have his uniform number retired. Yet one simple moment stands out as Krueger's biggest football thrill.

"The first game ball I ever got is something I won't forget," he said. "We were playing Cleveland at Cleveland. There was snow flurries blowing across the field and about five-foot snow banks. I was playing against Lou Groza, who must have been about 34 at the time, and I was about 21. I made a few tackles and stopped Jim Brown for a couple of losses. The team captains, Bob St. Clair and Y.A. Tittle, gave me the game ball."

With his playing days over, Krueger is content to watch football on television or make an occasional trip to Candlestick Park. He does not miss the Sunday hoopla.

"Missing football is like missing a car wreck," he said. "I'm older now. I don't miss it. I'm proud I played for the 49ers though. I'm sure happy for them and proud of them now. Eddie De-Bartolo and Bill Walsh sure turned things around. It's that combination that made them successful."

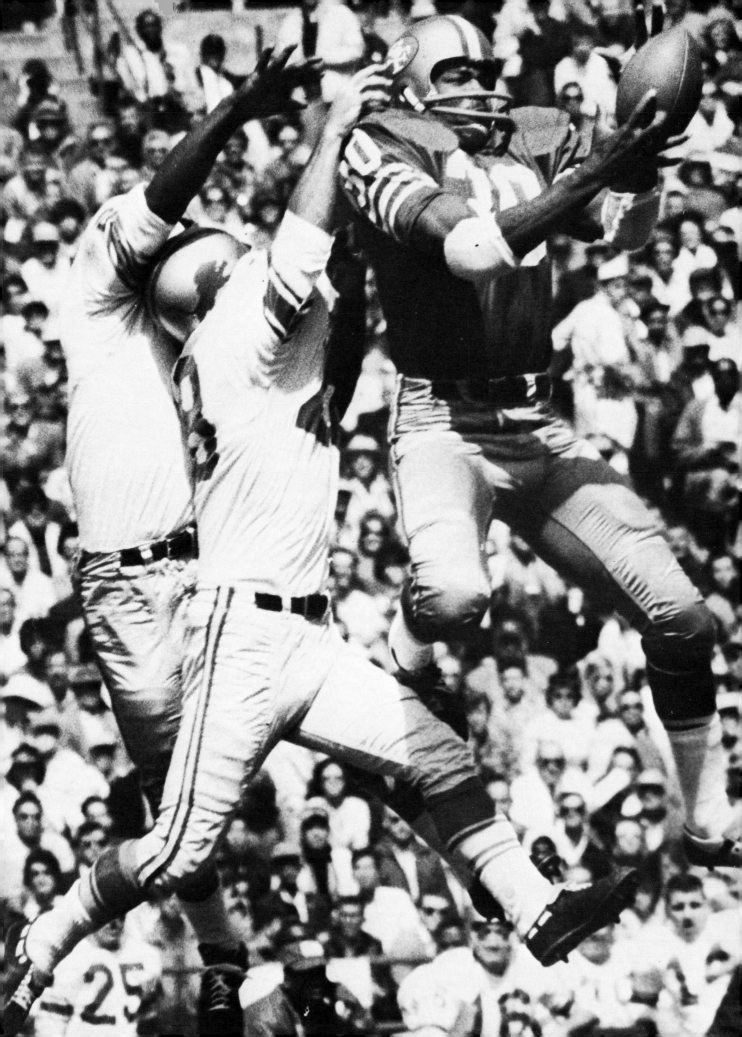

Doug Cunningham was a reliable running back for seven seasons. His best year was 1969 when he gained 541 yards. He added 51 receptions that year to tie for the team lead with Gene Washington. Cunningham started alongside Ken Willard when the team played for the 1970 NFC Championship.

The 49ers exhibited the effectiveness of their new offensive combination when they mauled the Chicago Bears, 52-24, in the season opener. It was the most points ever scored by the 49ers in the NFL. Brodie was on target, completing 14 of 20 passes for 259 yards and four touchdowns. Gary Lewis gained 91 yards on seven carries and scored one touchdown. Crow added 39 yards on six carries. Parks caught five passes from Brodie for 90 yards. And defensive tackle Charlie Krueger scored the first touchdown of his career when he picked up a fumble and plowed six yards into the end zone.

In the Chicago game, the 49ers got their first peek at a running back named Gale Sayers. The defense held Sayers to just 44 yards in 12 carries. It wouldn't be so lucky the next time. Sayers ran circles around the 49ers in the second game of the season, scoring six touchdowns.

San Francisco's offense almost burned out the scoreboard lights in 1965. The 49ers scored 421 points, an average of more than 30 points a game. They beat Minnesota, 45-24, and the Rams twice, by scores of 45-21 and 30-27. Dave Parks' 80 receptions led the league, and Brodie's 30 touchdown passes set a club record. Brodie also was voted the Len Eshmont award by his teammates for his outstanding play.

But San Francisco's defense was giving up points faster than the offense could score. The team lost to Minnesota, 42-41, Dallas, 39-31, and Chicago, 61-20, on the way to a 7-6-1 season. Obviously, defensive help was needed.

1966 Part of the problem was solved when Stan Hindman, a number-one pick in 1966, was signed. Hindman, from the University of Mississippi, was regarded as the best interior lineman in the nation. The 49ers planned to use him as a defensive end. Alvin Randolph and Mel Phillips were also selected in the player draft. They reinforced a weak defensive backfield.

The bidding war between the AFL and NFL got nasty prior to the 1966 season. Brodie came close to signing a contract with the Houston Oilers of the AFL. After deciding to continue his career with the 49ers, he missed the first two weeks of training camp

Jerry Mertens 1958–1965

Jerry Mertens was a 20th-round draft choice out of tiny Drake University in 1958. He was a long shot to make the team. Six months after reporting to the 49ers' rookie camp, he was playing in the Pro Bowl.

Mertens was drafted as a receiver and was paid a $10 signing bonus. When he showed up at training camp he ran into Billy Wilson, Gordy Soltau and R.C. Owens, the 49ers' established receivers. He had to win a spot from one of the veterans to make the team and get a $4,500 salary.

Mertens figured he had a better shot at that $4,500 if he was playing another position. He tried the defensive backfield. Because he was an excellent athlete, he was

able to make the adjustment from offense to defense. In his rookie season, he became a starter. By year's end he was playing in the Pro Bowl.

For eight seasons, from 1958 to 1965, he quietly roamed the secondary, earning the respect of his teammates and opponents with his steady play. Abe Woodson, the team's other cornerback, gained the headlines with his spectacular kick returns, while Mertens remained unheralded. A fractured neck in the last game of the 1965 season ended his playing days.

"Playing for the 49ers was like a dream come true," he said. "When I joined the 49ers they had just come off the 1957 season when they were in the playoffs against

Detroit. I grew up back east and was a fan of the Bears, but it was exciting coming out here. This was when they had the Million Dollar Backfield of Perry, McElhenny and Tittle. When I got here from Wisconsin I was in awe of these guys. Here I was with some of the greatest players in the game."

From his cornerback position, Mertens confronted the legends of football. Paul Hornung, Jim Brown, Lenny Moore and Ollie Matson all came his way at one time or another. But there is one fullback who was in a class by himself. Mertens will never forget him.

"Jim Taylor of the Packers was the toughest back I ever faced," Mertens said. "He was a punishing runner." It was a collision with Taylor that ended Mertens' career.

"I remember Taylor was sweeping around end," Mertens said. "There were a couple of blockers out in front, the usual Packer sweep. I was coming up to make the play. I hit him behind the line of scrimmage for about a four- or five-yard loss. I went down and he went down. For some reason my neck didn't feel right. I thought maybe I'd torn something. After about 70 X-rays, the doctors found a fractured Atlas vertebra. Luckily, I wasn't paralyzed or anything. Those things happen in football though."

The passing game reached new heights in the late 1950s, and Mertens, from his cornerback position, was right in the middle of it. Johnny Unitas, Sonny Jurgensen and Bart Starr revolutionized football with their aerial shows, changing the responsibilities of the defensive secondary. The long pass became a standard part of every offensive arsenal, and defensive backs were matched against bigger and faster receivers.

Mertens was tested repeatedly by Johnny Unitas when Baltimore was in town. And the Colts' stable of fine receivers were a constant challenge to the entire San Francisco secondary. Mertens' usual chore was to cover elusive Raymond Berry, a dangerous assignment. Baltimore quarterback Johnny Unitas was probably the best in the game at that time, Mertens says. The combination of Unitas and Berry, both now in the Hall of Fame, was often overwhelming.

During Mertens' tenure with San Francisco, he was party to numerous memorable games. The old rivalry with the Cleveland Browns began to fade and the intrastate rivalry with the Los Angeles Rams grew intense. Enormous crowds packed the Los Angeles Coliseum and Kezar Stadium every time the two teams battled.

"The crowds we got against the Rams were incredible," Mertens said. "In L.A. we'd draw nearly 100,000 people. Kezar was pretty well packed, too. That place was a different story, though. Going onto the field at Kezar reminded me of going into the Roman Coliseum. (Coach) Frankie Albert used to remind us to keep our helmets on when we went through the tunnel. If we didn't play well, we could expect a few beer cans to come our way. Of course, as tough as the fans could be at Kezar, it was always more comfortable playing here than on the road."

One of the interesting developments Mertens witnessed with the 49ers was the birth of the Shotgun Formation in 1960. It really wasn't new at all but a variation of the old short-punt formation, he says. It was the Shotgun that led to one of Mertens' most satisfying wins.

"We didn't beat the Rams much when I was playing so when we did, it was something special," he said. "They just seemed to be tough every year. Early in the 1961 season, *Sports Illustrated* had written a story on the Rams and their offense. About a week after the story came out, we played them at Kezar. They were favored. We went out and shut them out. It was one of the few times we beat them convincingly."

The 49ers beat the Rams that day, 35-0. A week prior to that, they beat Detroit, 49-0. A lot has been said about the use of the Shotgun Formation in those victories, but it wasn't the Shotgun that stopped two powerful offenses in consecutive weeks. Indeed, the 49er defense of the early 1960s was better than it was generally given credit for. And most of that credit should go to the defensive backfield of Mertens, Eddie Dove, Dave Baker and Abe Woodson. All of them made at least one Pro Bowl appearance between 1959 and 1962.

A year after the bone-cracking collision that ended Mertens' playing days, the AFL and NFL merged. The merger was a ticket to riches for many players. The average NFL salary nearly doubled. Mertens missed out on the big money. In his last season with the 49ers, the former All-Pro was paid $22,000. But the money meant little to Mertens.

"I was just thrilled to play with the 49ers," he said. "Playing pro football was a tremendous opportunity. It was a dream come true. I'm just happy to say I made it."

Monty Stickles (85), a first-round draft choice from Notre Dame in 1960, was a sure-handed tight end. He caught 207 passes with the club from 1960 to 1967.

while negotiating a contract. It took several weeks for him to regain his form.

As Brodie worked his way into shape, the 49ers dropped two of their first three games and tied the other. Then they got hot, beating the World Champion Green Bay Packers while registering four wins in five games. Going into the final game of the 1966 season, the 49ers were 6-5-2 and in position to make the Playoff Bowl which was held each year for the league's runner-ups. A berth in the bowl could mean an additional $3,000 for each player.

Apparently the monetary incentive was not enough for the 49ers. The Baltimore Colts routed them, 30-14. The game closed out another wild season at Kezar Stadium. But most of the excitement was generated by the fans.

During the Baltimore game, the 40,000 people in attendance at Kezar grew irritable after several questionable calls went against the 49ers. Late in the fourth quarter, after a penalty was marched off against San Francisco, one woman sprinted onto the field, picked up an official's penalty flag and threw it at him.

The crowd grew even more restless when the game was over. As head linesman Gerard Bergman made his way to the tunnel leading to the Kezar dressing room, a drunken fan heaved a whisky

bottle that caught Bergman in the head. Bergman had to be helped off the field. Meanwhile, fans stormed out of the stands to rip down the goal posts.

After the contest, George Mira voiced his desire to be traded. An irritated Coach Christiansen said there would be big changes before the 1967 season got under way. He was right.

1967 Among Christiansen's changes was the trade of Bernie Casey, guard Jim Wilson and defensive end Jim Norton to the Atlanta Falcons for their first-round draft pick in 1967. With Atlanta's pick, San Francisco selected Heisman Trophy winning quarterback Steve Spurrier.

Besides Spurrier, the 49ers chose a host of future stars in the college draft including Cas Banaszek, Frank Nunley and Doug Cunningham.

Just two days prior to the start of the regular season, the 49ers acquired flanker Sonny Randle from the St. Louis Cardinals for a future draft pick. Randle, a four-time All-Pro, was needed to take the

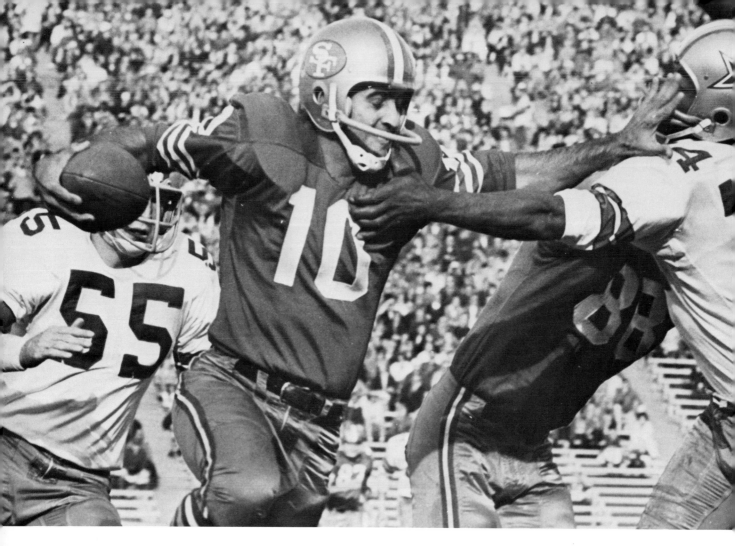

San Francisco quarterback George Mira (10) was an excellent scrambler. Here, he takes off on a 20-yard run and gives Cornell Green (34) of Dallas a stiff-arm along the way. Mira played five seasons with the 49ers behind starter John Brodie.

pressure off Dave Parks. After three spectacular seasons, Parks was a prime target for head-hunting defensive backs.

Randle was put to work immediately. In the league opener, against Minnesota, Parks and flanker Kay McFarland were injured. Despite less than an hour of practice with his new club, Randle was pressed into service. He responded admirably by catching three passes, including a 41-yarder.

The 49ers beat Minnesota and got off to an excellent start winning five of their first six games. At midseason they went into a slump and lost six consecutive games. Backup quarterback George Mira got the starting call for the last four games of the season and rumors began to circulate that Brodie was about to be traded to the Detroit Lions.

The rumors began to look more credible when Mira led the team to convincing wins over Atlanta and Dallas in the last two games of the season to give San Francisco a 7-7 record. Once again, Mira said he would not return to the 49ers unless he was guaranteed a starting role.

Mira played one more season with the 49ers before he was traded to the Philadelphia Eagles in 1969, but several other familiar faces did not return for the 1968 season.

1968 Jack Christiansen was relieved of the head coaching chores and replaced with Dick Nolan. Nolan brought with him a reputation as an excellent defensive coordinator. The 49er offense was always able to score points. Now it was up to Nolan to prevent the other team from getting into the end zone.

Several veterans were traded during the off-season, including Dan Colchico, Monty Stickles, Walter Rock and Dave Kopay. In addition, Dave Parks left the club after a contract squabble to play with the New Orleans Saints. Draft picks Forrest Blue, Skip Vanderbundt and Tommy Hart joined the team as Nolan prepared to shape a winner.

Brodie firmly established himself as the starting quarterback in the opening game of the 1968 season by connecting on 23 of 42 passes for 200 yards. Fumbles and miscues hampered the team, however, and Baltimore soundly beat the 49ers, 27-10.

Bolstered by Nolan's confidence in him, Brodie had a banner year in 1968, throwing for 3,020 yards

Dave Parks 1964–1967

It didn't take long for Dave Parks to become John Brodie's favorite receiver.

Just six games into Parks' rookie season, he established a 49er record when he caught an 83-yard touchdown pass against the Los Angeles Rams. It was the longest reception in team history. A week later, he caught an 80-yard touchdown pass against the Minnesota Vikings, the second longest in team history. And two weeks after that, he caught a 79-yard touchdown pass.

Dave Parks, the first player chosen in the 1964 college draft, had clearly established himself as the premier deep threat in the NFL. His records for the longest receptions in team history stood for 13 years.

"After that first season, the defenses tightened up on me," he said. "I didn't have any more 80-yard receptions. They covered me pretty good."

Opposing defenses may have stopped the long bomb but they didn't stop Dave Parks. In 1965, he caught 80 passes for 1,344 yards and 12 touchdowns. He led the league in all three categories.

That was the year the 49ers lit up the scoreboard everywhere they went. They led the league in scoring in 1965 with 421 points, an average of 31 points a game. Unfortunately, the defense was giving up points faster than the offense could score them. They lost games with final scores of 42-41, 61-20, and 39-31.

"My feeling was, if we had the ball last, we would score and win," he said. "Brodie could always get the ball into the end zone.

"The number of balls I caught was never really a big factor. I didn't think about the statistics. Neither did John Brodie. I re-member a game against Pittsburgh where I could have caught 20 balls. No one could cover me effectively. John only threw me three passes. We just did what we had to do to win."

The offensive line of Walter Rock, Len Rohde, Bruce Bosley, Howard Mudd and John Thomas played a big part in the 49er scoring show of 1965. Each of them played in at least one Pro Bowl.

"We had the best line in football at the time and the best quarterback," he said. "All they had to do was give Brodie a little time and that was it. As a receiver it was simple. John just had to throw it to me.

"I don't know how they choose people for the Hall of Fame, but John Brodie was the best quarterback I was ever around," he said. "I don't think anyone even came close. I know I wanted him in there at quarterback. There may have been others that were just as good, like Bart Starr, but I was more than satisfied with the man I had."

Like so many good passing combinations, Brodie and Parks were able to detect what defenses were doing and react to it. They were able to spontaneously adjust to each other on the field. Despite facing double coverage for most of his career, Parks had an uncanny ability to find the open area in a secondary. And Brodie had the talent to find him. Good communication played a vital part in their relationship.

"Me and John always thought along the same lines," he said. "If we saw something with the defense that we could take advantage of, we were able to adjust accordingly. If I saw something that I thought would work, I told him about it and if he wanted to use it, he did. He had a great knack for adjusting and getting me the ball."

During his 10 years of professional football, Parks caught 360 passes for 5,619 yards and 44 touchdowns. His ability to catch the ball is well chronicled but his blocking ability stands out as well. It is a rare receiver that combines both of those talents.

"I always liked to block," said Parks. "The way I figure it, the back had to pick up a linebacker and throw a block while I was catching a ball, so it's just as important for me to block for the running back when he has the ball. The point is, we were a real close team back then. That's

how we got it done. We didn't have the individual player that could break open the game. We had to count on each other."

Although San Francisco had some potent offensive teams with Dave Parks at wide receiver, the team's best finish while he was on the roster was 7-6-1 in 1965. The mediocre records are a reflection on the 49ers' porous defense at the time.

"People scored a lot of points against us, but they never went over to Jimmy Johnson's side," he said. "He was the best damn cornerback in the game but nobody ever heard of him until the end of his career. The reason nobody heard of him was that nobody challenged him."

Parks played out his option during the 1967 season and left for New Orleans. With the Saints he wasn't as successful statistically, but he says he was just as effective.

"At New Orleans we didn't have Brodie at quarterback or the great line they had at San Francisco," he said. "I was open just as much but they didn't have the time to get me the ball.

"I get together down here (Dallas) with some friends that played with the Dallas Cowboys and they get to talking about big games they played in. When they do that, I really don't have anything to talk about. In New Orleans, we were just another team on everybody's schedule. I didn't like it but that's the way it was."

Although Parks ended his career at New Orleans, it was his days at San Francisco that were

the highlight of his 10-year career. Three times he played in the Pro Bowl from 1965 through 1967. He recalls with laughter some of the memories of his days in San Francisco.

"I remember going to Kezar on game days," he said. "That was when the hippies were coming around. Sunday was the big day for them out there by Kezar. We'd go down Haight Street on the way to the game looking at all the hippies. That's kind of a funny thing to remember, but that's what I remember most about the place."

Like almost all of Ken Willard's teammates, Parks has a favorite story about the talented fullback. This one occurred at the 49ers' training camp.

"Someone, I won't say who, ran a garden hose up the side of the building to Willard's room. It was on the second floor. He stuck the hose at the head of the bed so when it was turned on it would spray on Willard's head. When the water was turned on, Willard came running out and knocked on my door. He thought I did it. He was mad because he just bought some new shoes and they were floating around in his room. To this day he still thinks I did it.

"I think about those years with the 49ers a lot. That was the best bunch of guys I played with. That's what I hated most about leaving the team. There was a lot of comradeship. New Orleans was fun too, but San Francisco, well, they were a class bunch of guys."

and 22 touchdowns. He led the team to a 7-6-1 record, including upset wins over the New York Giants and the Green Bay Packers. Receiver Clifton McNeil was Brodie's primary target, catching 71 passes. McNeil was obtained in the off-season from the Cleveland Browns and in his first year with the 49ers was selected All-Pro.

John David Crow ended a magnificent career when he retired after the season. He gained 4,963 yards in his 11 years of pro ball for a 4.3-yard rushing average.

1969 The passing game went from good to great in 1969 when receivers Gene Washington from Stanford, and Ted Kwalick from Penn State, both were selected on the first round of the college draft.

Although the 49ers looked good on paper, the league standings revealed something different. They went winless through their first five games. Injuries to several key starters caused the team to nose dive.

Defensive ends Kevin Hardy and Stan Hindman were lost for most of the season and John Brodie injured a knee that hampered him for several games. The linebacker position was decimated when Matt Hazeltine retired, and Ed Beard was hurt midway through the season.

The team wound up a disappointing season with a hobbling John Brodie coming off the bench to spark the 49ers to a 14-13 win over Philadelphia. The Eagles were quarterbacked by Brodie's old nemesis, George Mira. The win gave San Francisco a 4-8-2 record in 1969.

The 1970s brought the merger of the American and National Football Leagues. It also brought about a new winning tradition for the 49ers. Finally, a championship was on the horizon.

The 49ers' left defensive tackle spot was anchored by Charlie Krueger for 15 seasons. He was drafted on the first round in 1958 after starring at Texas A&M under coach Bear Bryant. The 49ers honored Krueger by retiring number 70 at the end of his career. Only five other 49ers have had their numbers retired—Leo Nomellini, Joe Perry, Hugh McElhenny, Jimmy Johnson and John Brodie. PAGE 80: Running back Gary Lewis (22), a graduate from San Francisco's Poly High School, shakes off the Cowboys' Cornell Green (34). Lewis gained 573 yards in 1968, his most productive as a 49er. PAGE 84: Coach Dick Nolan gets a ride from the field on the shoulders of Skip Vanderbundt (52) and an unidentified teammate, after the 49ers clinched the NFC Western Division Crown in 1971 with a win over Detroit. Jim Sniadecki (58) unwraps the tape from his hand.

Abe Woodson 1958–1964

The longest kickoff return in 49er history was a 105-yard run by Abe Woodson. The second longest return in team history was also by Woodson, and so was the fourth longest and the fifth longest.

In fact, Woodson has five of the longest kickoff returns in 49er history. All of them were touchdowns. In nine years of NFL service, he brought back 193 kickoffs for 5,538 yards, ranking him second on the all-time yardage list. His average of 29 yards per return is topped only by Gale Sayers with a 30.5-yard average.

"You have to remember we did a lot of losing back then," he said. "The other teams scored a lot so I got a lot of kicks to return. The odds were with me to break one once in a while."

In a more serious vein, the former Big Ten hurdles champ credits Red Hickey, the 49ers' head coach from 1959 to 1963, for the emphasis he placed on kick returns. It was Hickey's belief that good returns led to good field position and good field position enabled a team to score points. To get good returns, Hickey used his best linemen in punt and kickoff situations.

"Red Hickey used to put the All-Pros out there like Bob St. Clair," Woodson said. "He wanted his best blockers out there. Good blocking had a lot to do with our success returning kicks."

Woodson is proud of his 105-yard return against Los Angeles that set the 49er record, but he is more satisfied with a 99-yard touchdown run against the New York Giants.

The Giants took the 49ers apart that day in 1963, winning 48-14, but they were wary of Woodson's running skill. After each touchdown, they sent squib kicks bouncing down the field, making it hard for Woodson to return them. After the Giants' fourth touchdown of the day, Woodson fielded one of the squibbling kicks, followed a couple of good blocks and took off on his 99-yard touchdown run.

That return was satisfying because he scored despite the Giants persistent effort to keep the ball away from him.

The 49er defensive secondary in the early 1960s consisted of Jerry Mertens, Eddie Dove, Dave Baker and Woodson. It was considered one of the best of its time. Jack Christiansen, an All-Pro safety with the Detroit Lions, and a member of the Hall of Fame, was the coach of that unit. It was Christiansen who helped the backfield develop its aggressive style.

"We were one of the first teams to use the bump-and-run," said Woodson. "The man-to-man competition was something I enjoyed. It was with the bump-and-run that we were able to defense people like Raymond Berry. He was good because of his moves and precise patterns. The bump-and-run took that away. That 1961 team was probably our best defensive team."

Woodson was selected All-Pro four times between 1959 and 1963, but even All-Pros had certain receivers that gave them trouble.

"I always seemed to have problems with Max McGee," said Woodson. "The Packers had good timing and Bart Starr was very accurate on those kinds of passes. No matter what I did against McGee, it was wrong."

Returning kicks and preventing pass completions was just part of Woodson's job. From his cornerback position, he had a unique perspective from which to judge the great runners of his time. And as a gifted runner himself, he knew what to look for.

"Well, Jim Brown was probably the best," he said. "He was powerful, he had that great stiff-arm and he was also a very shifty runner. He was damn fast for a man his size. I remember chasing him 70 yards and just barely catching him on about the one-yard line.

"Gale Sayers was the most elusive runner I faced. He was probably the most difficult to tackle, especially in the open field.

"Jim Taylor was a harder runner than anybody. When he carried the ball, he went after defensive backs. Most people ran away from a tackler. Not Taylor. Even if he had a clear path to the goal line, he'd look for a defensive back to run over on the way."

Woodson's memories of the 49ers are laced with comical moments. He recalls one game against Green Bay in Milwaukee in late November of 1958. Vince Lombardi was in his first year as the Packers' coach. The 49ers won the game, 33-12, in

ice-cold conditions.

"In Milwaukee, the stands were real close to the bench," he said. "In those days when you were thirsty there was just a water bucket and dipper. Well, somehow one of the fans got on the field and poured scotch into our water bucket. It was a real cold day so you really didn't need a lot of water, but people kept getting water. Players would run off the field and take a big swig. The coaches started wondering why the players were having such a good time over at the water bucket.

"One game I'll always remember was against the Los Angeles Rams in 1961. What is funny is what happened after the game. I remember it because we were using the Shotgun and we beat them, 34-0. After the game there was a call to the locker room to see who won. Whoever answered gave out the score. The person on the other end said, 'Young man, this is the commissioner. I want to know the score of that game.' He didn't believe that we could beat the Rams."

One of the characters of the 1959-1960 49er teams was a tackle who played at USC and Trinity College named Henry Schmidt. He was affectionately known to his teammates as "wedge buster." On kickoffs, Schmidt's assignment was to run downfield and hurl himself at the wedge set up by the kick-return team.

"We used to get a per diem allowance for our meals," recalled Woodson. "To save money, Henry would come down to the hotel kitchen,

order a bowl of hot water and pour ketchup in it to make himself some soup. Then he'd pocket the money. One time he even pitched a tent out at training camp and lived in a tent right on the field."

Whenever the Chicago Bears were in town, strange things happened. Rumor had it that Bears coach George Halas regularly sent spies to the 49er practices to diagram the team's plays. The 49er coaches solved that problem by placing large pieces of canvas along the fence so nobody could see the team practice, said Woodson.

"One Bears' game at Kezar, a strange thing happened," he said. "Willie Galimore was carrying the ball and he fumbled. We recovered, but Halas started arguing with the referees and they changed their call. It was right before the half and as we were leaving to go to the locker room, some guy came running out of the stands and kicked Halas right in the butt. It was one of the funniest things I've ever seen."

Woodson sees quite a difference from the players of his era and the present day stars. Although the current crop is more talented, that does not make the game more interesting.

"Today's guys are bigger and stronger and faster," he said. "Especially on the artificial turf people are faster. The defenses are more complex. There's more substitution. But I think all the substitution takes away from the man-to-man competition. To me it makes the game less of a challenge."

1970–1979

CHAPTER FOUR

FROM CHAMPIONSHIP TO THE CELLAR

In 1970, the club's 25th year of operation, the 49ers finally put it all together. Coach Dick Nolan, the NFC's Coach-of-the-Year, assembled a solid defensive team led by All-Pro's Dave Wilcox at linebacker and Jimmy Johnson at defensive back. The defensive line of Cedrick Hardman, Tommy Hart, Charlie Krueger and Roland Lakes intimidated opposing quarterbacks. And defensive back Bruce Taylor was selected Rookie-of-the-Year, due in part to his 12-yard punt return average, which ranked him first in the NFC.

The 49ers' offense played well also. In the first game against Washington, Brodie completed 17 of 20 passes, including one for a touchdown. San Francisco came out on top, 26-17.

The offense continued to chalk up points, beating Chicago, 37-16, and Green Bay, 26-10, enroute to a 7-1-1 record at midseason. Ironically, the one tie came against the New Orleans Saints when two 49er castoffs, Bill Kilmer and Dave Parks, teamed up for a touchdown in the closing seconds of the game.

The team suffered consecutive losses to Detroit and Los Angeles before it got back to its winning style. In the final game of the season, the 49ers needed a win or a tie against the rival Oakland Raiders to secure the NFC Western Division title.

Going into the game, Brodie had been sacked only eight times behind a fine offensive line consisting of Len Rohde, Woody Peoples, Forrest Blue, Randy Beisler and Cas Banaszek. Oakland defensive end Ben Davidson predicted to the media he would personally tear apart the line and get to Brodie at least twice.

The Oakland Coliseum was packed with 55,000 Raider fans who sat through a steady drizzle. San Francisco got off to a quick 10-7 lead after a Bruce Gossett field goal and a 26-yard touchdown pass from Brodie to Ted Kwalick. An intercepted pass, returned 34 yards for a touchdown by Jimmy Johnson, and a three-yard touchdown pass to Gene Washington, put the 49ers well in front at the intermission, 24-7.

Many veteran San Francisco fans had a frightening recollection at halftime. The 24-7 score was the same margin the 49ers held at the half of the 1957 playoff game against Detroit. Of course, the 49ers went on to lose that one, 31-27.

The 49ers came out and played another half of solid football. Ben Davidson and the rest of the Raider defense were unable to get to Brodie, ensuring the 49er offensive line of an NFL record for allowing the least sacks in a season. Behind the line, Brodie threw three touchdown passes and San Francisco beat Oakland, 38-7. The 49ers' next opponent was the dangerous Minnesota Vikings.

The week of the Minnesota game, Brodie was honored as the NFC Player-of-the-Year, but his mind was on the Vikings. Minnesota was rated a seven-point favorite.

The temperature in Minnesota at game time was 10 degrees and the field

was in danger of freezing over. San Francisco was given little chance to beat the Vikes on their icy turf.

The frozen terrain worked to the 49ers' advantage. The Vikings' fearsome pass rush, consisting of Alan Page, Carl Eller, Gary Larsen and Jim Marshall, was unable to get any footing. The "Purple People Eaters," as they were called, had terrified opposing quarterbacks all year and went into the game with 49 sacks for the season. Against the 49ers they managed only one and that was due to a confused blocking assignment.

With the defensive line unable to operate effectively, Brodie took to the air and completed 16 of 32 passes for 201 yards. Several other passes were dropped due to the cold. Fullback Ken Willard complemented the passing game by gaining 85 yards on the ground to lead all rushers.

The 49ers scored on a 24-yard pass from Brodie to Dick Witcher and a one-yard plunge by Brodie. Gossett rounded out the point total with a 40-yard field goal in the 17-14 win.

The 49ers were established as 3½-point favorites to defeat the Dallas Cowboys in the NFC Championship Game at Kezar Stadium. At City Hall, San Francisco Mayor Joe Alioto boldly predicted the 49ers would demolish Dallas on the way to the Super Bowl. The winner of the championship game would not only go to the Super Bowl but would pocket $8,500. The loser's share was $5,500.

Long lines of faithful fans waited at the Cow Palace to purchase the $12 game tickets. They were anxious to see the 49ers in their first championship game. The contest also would mark the 49ers' last appearance at Kezar Stadium before moving to Candlestick Park.

The Cowboy offense was led by moody running back Duane Thomas. The Dallas defense had not given up a touchdown in 21 quarters prior to the game.

San Francisco got on the scoreboard first. Gene Washington hauled in a 42-yard Brodie pass and was downed at the 10-yard line. The 49ers had to

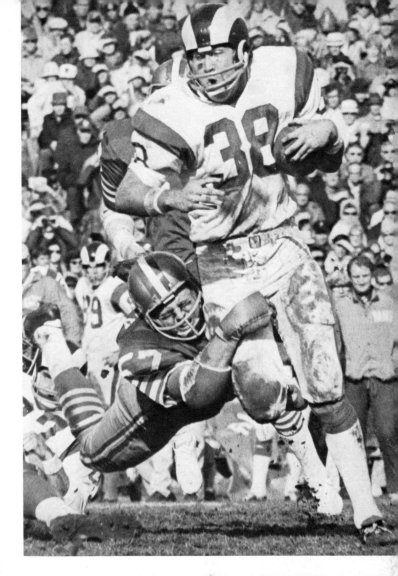

LEFT: Receiver Gene Washington (18) goes high in the air to make a spectacular catch against the Rams. Defending Washington is Kermit Alexander (39). Alexander was a 49er defensive back from 1963 to 1969. He led the team in interceptions in six of those seven years. RIGHT, TOP: Frank Nunley (57) grimaces as he grabs the legs of Rams running back Larry Smith (38). Nunley, nicknamed "fudge hammer" was a 49er linebacker from 1967 to 1976. RIGHT, BOTTOM: John Brodie.

Ben Davidson (83) and Tom Keating (74) of the Oakland Raiders charged through the 49er offensive line to grab John Brodie (12). The play was disallowed because of a penalty. The 49ers beat Oakland, 38-7, in 1970 to clinch their first division title.

settle for a Bruce Gossett field goal. The first half remained a defensive game and both teams went into the locker room tied at 3-3.

Two interceptions by Dallas in the third quarter gave the Cowboys excellent field position. They capitalized on the mistakes, scoring touchdowns both times and building a 17-3 lead. Late in the third quarter the 49ers began to battle back. Brodie drove the team 77 yards and capped the drive with a 10-yard scoring strike to Dick Witcher.

With a 17-10 lead, the Dallas running game ate up the clock in the fourth period. With 12 seconds left in the game, San Francisco finally got the ball back but was 72 yards from the goal line. Brodie quickly completed a 30-yard pass to Bob Windsor. He was dragged down as time ran out.

1971 After their appearance in the championship game, the 49ers no longer were a team to be taken lightly. They were made over-whelming favorites to win the division title in 1971. They were also favorites to appear in the Super Bowl.

In the league opener against Atlanta, San Francisco didn't look like a Super Bowl team. The Falcons beat the 49ers, 20-17. They intercepted four Brodie passes and recovered three fumbles. With 30 seconds on the clock, and the 49ers within range to tie the game with a field goal, Brodie tried one more time to pass the ball into the end zone. As he dropped back to pass, he was sacked and fumbled away the ball.

The fumble sparked a bench-clearing brawl. After picking up the loose ball, Falcon Tom Hayes rambled about 10 yards ending the game. He then threw the ball toward the 49er bench where it hit Cas Banaszek. Bedlam broke loose.

The team settled down after that initial loss and won six of their next seven games. Late season losses to New Orleans, Los Angeles and Kansas City seemed to end the 49ers' championship hopes. But several losses by the Rams put them right back in it. Going into the final game of the season, they had an 8-5 record and could still win the Western Division title with a win over the Detroit Lions.

Several key players had injuries in that game including Mel Phillips, Bill Belk and Jim Sniadecki.

John Brodie 1957–1973

When John Brodie retired in 1973, he had passed the football 31,548 yards, or about the equivalent of one long pass from Kezar Stadium to Half Moon Bay.

And that's how Brodie made his living really, by throwing the long ball. For 17 years he wore the red-and-gold uniform of the San Francisco 49ers. He was the one constant in a sea of changing football faces. Among them were some of the best receivers to set foot on NFL turf. Brodie remembers them all. Billy Wilson, Gordy Soltau, Dave Parks, Bernie Casey, Ted Kwalick, Monty Stickles and Gene Washington were just a few of the men that contributed to those 31,548 yards.

"I can't pick out one as my favorite receiver," he said. "I had a good relationship with all the receivers I played with. Most of them fit in with what I liked to do, throw the ball."

During his tenure, Brodie guided the 49ers to two NFL Championship Games and one playoff appearance. He played in two Pro Bowls and was the NFL Player-of-the-Year in 1970. But none of that seems to impress Brodie. He stresses the fun he had playing the game and the friendships he made as a member of the 49ers.

"Football was a great experience," he said. "I was fortunate to be a part of it. I met some great people playing here. I was lucky to be able to play in my hometown and stay here for 17 years as a professional.

I was able to play in the same place that I grew up and went to college. All I can say is I enjoyed the hell out of it."

Brodie was picked by the 49ers in the first round of the 1957 college draft. He had been an All-American at Stanford. The 49ers already had Y.A. Tittle at quarterback so Brodie saw little action that first year. But in one game, late in the 1957 season, he was forced to take over in a tense situation. It was a game the 49ers needed to win in their drive for the playoffs. It was Brodie's first test as a professional.

Baltimore had a 13-10 lead over San Francisco. With less than a minute to play and the ball on the Colts' 15-yard line, Tittle was injured trying to pass. Brodie was quickly summoned and sent into the game. He looked around and asked if anybody had a play they wanted to run. Hugh McElhenny, the old pro, told Brodie to throw him a pass out toward the sideline. The play worked, the 49ers scored, and eventually they made the playoffs.

"I never even saw the pass," Brodie said. "I got buried by Art Donovan as soon as I threw. I heard the crowd respond, that was about it."

It was ironic that 16 years later in the twilight of his career, Brodie would be called off the bench again to save the 49ers' playoff hopes. This time Brodie was the old pro.

He had been sidelined most of the 1972 season with an ankle injury, but backup quarterback Steve Spurrier had filled in admirably. In the last game of the season, San Francisco needed a win over Minnesota to propel itself into the NFL playoffs. Spurrier had been struggling against the Vikings for three quarters. In the fourth period, with Minnesota leading, 17-6, Brodie got his chance. In just eight minutes, Brodie led the team to two touchdowns and another playoff appearance.

Under Brodie's guidance the 49ers were a perennial playoff team for three years from 1970 through 1972. But the year that stood out for him was 1965. That year he threw 30 touchdown passes, a 49er record, and completed 62 percent of his 391 tosses. Dave Parks caught 80 passes to lead the league

and had 12 touchdown catches. The 49ers averaged over 30 points a game.

"I think that year turned everything around for me offensively," he said. "That was the start of our best offensive years. We had excellent running backs with Ken Willard, John David Crow and Doug Cunningham. Our line was very good too. I don't like to compare athletes, but we had some outstanding players on that team."

Y.A. Tittle returned to San Francisco as an assistant coach in 1965. Under his tutelage, Brodie began to blossom.

"I learned a hell of a lot from him as a coach," Brodie said. "When we played together, it was a little different. The most important thing I learned then was that there was only room for one quarterback."

The 49ers really have had only four starting quarterbacks in the history of the franchise. Frankie Albert was the quarterback from 1946 to 1951, Y.A. Tittle from 1952 to 1959, John Brodie from 1960 to 1973, and then a string of journeymen ran the show until Joe Montana popped onto the scene in 1980.

Brodie commanded the 49er offense longer than anyone. He completed 2,469 of 4,491 career passes to put him fourth on the all-time list for pass completions. His 214 career touchdown passes ranks him eighth among the all-time leaders.

So what is it that made Brodie a consistently effective quarterback, one that Dave Parks believes

should be in the Hall of Fame?

"Well that's not for me to say," Brodie said. "That's not my nature to talk about my skills. I just played the game and had a lot of fun doing it. I will say I was persistent. That about sums it up, persistence."

Brodie is not one to dwell on the past and his prior accomplishments, but the mention of Kezar Stadium is one thing that raises nostalgic feelings about his prior team.

"My most vivid recollections of the 49ers were those days at Kezar Stadium," he said. "That was the place that best represented where football should be played. That was a real football stadium. The conditions were generally good. The weather was usually workable. The field was nice until it got sloppy near the end of the season.

"It was at Kezar that the 49er spirit really began. They had a great following back then. Those were the 49er faithful. The 49er spirit you see now didn't just get started. It's been around for a while."

Brodie senses that 49er fans may be getting spoiled by the recent success of the team.

"I would say that the 49ers are the best team playing in the 1980s," he said. "It's one of the few teams I have seen that is so good people would be surprised if it didn't win."

Brodie finds it difficult to sum up his 17 years of NFL competition. "There's nothing real deep I can say about my career," he said. "The most important thing is that I survived."

In the fourth period, Detroit held a 27-24 lead and was driving. San Francisco's defense stopped the Lions at their own 40-yard line on fourth-and-one and the offense went to work.

Larry Schreiber gained 10 yards on the ground and another 10 on a Brodie pass. With third-and-eight from the 10-yard line, the Lions sent everyone after Brodie. He spotted a hole through the middle of the blitzing line and ran 10 yards for the score that put San Francisco in front for good, 31-27.

Willard finished the day with 81 yards rushing while Schreiber added another 42 yards on seven carries. Brodie completed 14 of 20 passes for 186 yards.

The win insured San Francisco of a 9-5 record and a match with the Washington Redskins in the NFC playoffs. Former 49er Billy Kilmer would be the starting quarterback for Washington in place of the injured Sonny Jurgensen.

Thunderstorms before the game made the artificial turf at Candlestick hopelessly slick. Winds in excess of 30 mph played havoc with the passing attack of both teams. Nevertheless, the game was a classic cliffhanger.

Washington held a 10-3 lead at the half after both teams spent 30 minutes testing each other. Brodie got things started in the third quarter with a 78-yard scoring pass to Gene Washington that tied the game at 10-10.

Both teams traded points until San Francisco added another touchdown when Washington punter Mike Bragg muffed a punt snap in the end zone and Bob Hoskins pounced on it to put the 49ers in front, 24-13.

But Kilmer still wanted to play. He came right back, moving the Redskins 45 yards for a touchdown that made it 24-20.

Washington got the ball again with only 46 seconds on the clock. That was plenty of time for

TOP: Fullback Ken Willard (40) was the 49ers' first-round pick in 1965 out of the University of North Carolina. In nine seasons with the club, he gained 5,930 yards to rank second behind Joe Perry on the team's all-time rushing list. His best year was 1968 when he was the NFL's second leading rusher with 967 yards. Willard played in four Pro Bowls between 1966 and 1970. BOTTOM: Jimmy Johnson was recognized by his peers as one of the premier defensive backs in the game. For 16 seasons he was the 49ers' left cornerback until his retirement in 1976. He was a unanimous All-Pro selection every year from 1969 to 1973 and holds the team record with 47 interceptions. Johnson was used as a wide receiver in 1962 and caught 34 passes for 627 yards.

LEFT, TOP: Quarterback Tom Owen (14) prepares to take the field with running backs Delvin Williams (24) and Larry Schrieber (35) prior to the start of a 1974 game with Green Bay.
LEFT, BOTTOM, LEFT: Gene Washington writhes in agony after injuring his ankle in a 1973 game against the New Orleans Saints. Washington ended his 49er career with a total of 6,664 receiving yards.
LEFT, BOTTOM, RIGHT: Center Forrest Blue played in every Pro Bowl from 1972 to 1975. He was the 49ers' first-round pick in 1968 and spent seven years with the club.
RIGHT, TOP: Frank Nunley questions a referee's wisdom from the 49er bench. RIGHT, BOTTOM: Cas Banaszek was drafted in the first round of the 1967 draft as a linebacker. The Northwestern graduate was converted to tackle in 1968 and was a reliable blocker for 10 seasons with the 49ers.

Len Rohde 1960–1974

Len Rohde had a frightening thought on the way to his first 49er training camp. It was 1960, and Rohde, a star tackle at Utah State, had been selected on the fifth round of the college draft.

"Before I left for camp I had read up on the team," he recalled. "I was driving cross country to St. Mary's and I kept thinking about Leo Nomellini, who was a pro wrestler in the off-season and was supposed to have wrestled a bear. Then I started thinking about Bob St. Clair, who was 6' 9" and 270 pounds. I remember reading that he liked to eat raw meat. As I got closer to St. Mary's these guys kept getting bigger and bigger in my mind. I kept wondering how I was going to take a job from them."

It didn't happen over-

night. The 6' 4", 240-pound Rohde payed his dues, waiting for two years in a reserve role before getting a starting assignment at tackle. Those two seasons were spent in the shadow of Bob St. Clair. The waiting period enabled Rohde to learn technique from the veteran linemen on the squad. And it wasn't all related to football.

"Bob St. Clair taught me a few things," Rohde said jokingly. "Most of the technique I learned from Bob couldn't be used on the field though —like how to sneak out of the dorms."

Rohde developed into a solid starter at tackle. He was selected to play in the Pro Bowl in 1971 after anchoring one of the superior lines in football. That line blossomed in 1970 when it allowed only eight quarterback sacks all season, a league

record. In addition to Rohde, the offensive line consisted of Elmer Collett, Cas Banaszek, Woody Peoples, Forrest Blue, Randy Beisler and Bob Hoskins. They became minor celebrities in the area and were nicknamed "The Protectors."

Although Rohde was the veteran in that group, with 11 years of playing experience, he denies that he was their leader.

"We were just good," he said more with honesty than braggadocio. "We were a hard-working bunch of guys. We'd all been together for a while and that helped us. I was the vet of the group, but I don't think that meant anything. It would have been a tough bunch to lead. Everyone was self-motivated.

"Brodie was a big help in getting that sack record. He got rid of the ball quickly. He didn't hang onto it."

The offensive line helped forge the 49ers into near champions in the early 1970s. The teams of 1970, 1971 and 1972 were the best that Rohde played with in his 15 years with the organization. But those years bring mixed emotions to Rohde. Mention "THE" Dallas game and he turns silent. For prior to 1981, when Dwight Clark made "the Catch" that beat Dallas and sent the 49ers to their first Super Bowl, there was only one Dallas game that mattered to 49er fans.

"I don't want to talk about that," he said remembering the team's bitter loss in the 1972 playoffs. But then, as if seeking to purge his feelings, he begins to speak about it.

"That game is still painful to think about. The pain went away and I hadn't thought about it for a while until I saw the team in the Super Bowl the last couple years. Then it came back. I realized how close we had been and what we had missed and it hurt all over again. It was a shock when we lost. All I can say is give credit to Roger Staubach. He brought the Cowboys back."

The near championships of the 1970s offer more than just agony for Rohde. It was particularly sweet for him to play in his first playoff game after suffering through 10 lackluster seasons with the team.

"I remember we had to beat Oakland in 1970 to get into our first playoff game," he said. "We did that. We beat them pretty good (38-7). Then we played against Min-

nesota in the playoffs. That was my biggest thrill from a team standpoint. I remember that game well. We played in the snow back there and were underdogs." San Francisco won, 17-14.

The 49er backfield in those years consisted of two of the team's all-time greats. It was fullback Ken Willard and quarterback John Brodie that made the offense click.

"In the huddle, Brodie was able to communicate just what he wanted to do," Rohde said. "You could tell when we were going to score and when we weren't by the way things were communicated. Brodie knew what he was doing out there. He had a lot of experience. So if he said to the line, 'Give me an extra second here and we'll have six points,' you believed it.

"Willard had a good sense of humor. He was great around the goal line and when a first down was needed, but we used to kid him anyway. We had a saying about him. If we needed two yards, Willard was sure to get us one."

Football in the 1980s has evolved into a highly specialized game. But up front on the offensive line, things have basically remained the same, according to Rohde. The offensive linemen still use brute srength to move their opponents out of position.

"The only difference in the linemen today is they are getting bigger," Rohde said. "It doesn't take much to get bigger —just eat. I don't see them as any better than we were. If anything, the

liberal holding rules make it easier for offensive linemen now. You don't have to be as mobile as you used to be."

After 15 years in football, Rohde retired in 1974. He played in the trenches against some of the league's toughest customers. He laughs and scoffs at the generally accepted notion that linebackers are the hatchet men of football.

"The linebackers were nothing," he said with a laugh. "They were little guys who were vocal. They liked to talk to you, but that's about it. They just got in my way."

The defensive linemen were a different story.

"They switched guys around on me quite a bit because I was around 15 years," he said. "But there was a few linemen that were pretty tough to play against. Doug Atkins of the Bears was no fun. He could be devastating."

To round out his top three, Rohde rates Deacon Jones and Coy Bacon, two former Los Angeles Rams, among the defensive linemen he least enjoyed facing.

In 1974, his last season in professional football, Rohde was awarded the Len Eshmont award, the team's most prestigous annual honor.

"That was the biggest personal award I ever received," he said. "As a lineman you don't get many individual awards. That was one of the times I was singled out. It was also voted by the team so it was special. Making the Pro Bowl was a thrill too, but nothing like getting the Len Eshmont Award."

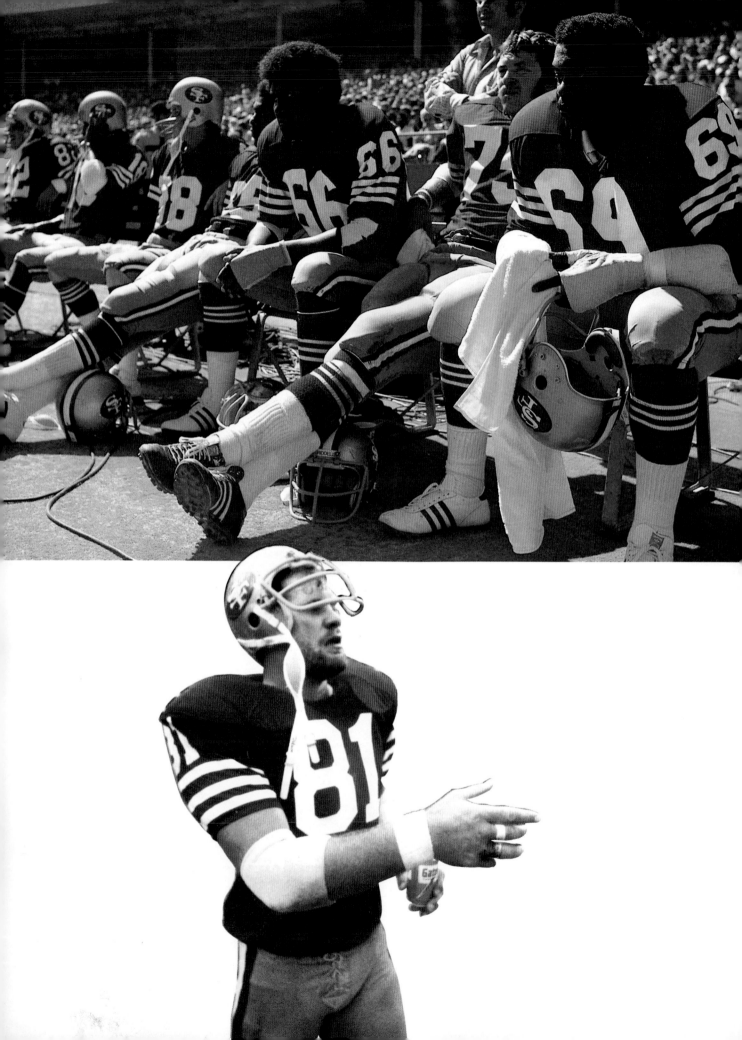

PRECEDING SPREAD: Paul Hofer (36) prepares to hurdle over the Atlanta line on the way to the winning touchdown in a 20-15 win in 1979.

OPPOSITE, TOP: The 49er bench includes, from left to right, Ted Kwalick (82), Gene Washington, Terry Beasley, Bob Penchion, Forrest Blue and Woody Peoples. OPPOSITE, BOTTOM: Ken MacAfee had four touchdown catches in 1979, the ex-Notre Dame star's best year as a professional. LEFT, TOP: Joe Montana in training camp as a rookie in 1979. LEFT, BOTTOM: Keith Fahnhorst, a second-round pick from Minnesota in the 1974 draft, played in his first Pro Bowl in 1985. RIGHT, TOP: Dwaine Board recovered five fumbles and had 13 sacks in 1983 as he helped the 49ers gain a spot in the NFC Championship Game. RIGHT, MIDDLE: Charlie Krueger anchored the 49er defensive line for 15 seasons before retiring in 1973. RIGHT, BOTTOM: John Ayers was an eighth-round draft choice out of West Texas State in 1976, who, prior to the start of the 1985 season, had started 102 of the 49ers' last 105 games.

ABOVE: Delvin Williams (24) bursts through the Miami Dolphins line on the way to a big gain. He set a team single-game record by rushing for 194 yards against the St. Louis Cardinals in 1976. RIGHT, TOP: Dwight Clark races down the sideline on his way to a 41-yard touchdown against the Rams in 1981. RIGHT, BOTTOM: Team owner Edward DeBartolo suffered through four miserable seasons before the 49ers won their first Super Bowl after the 1981 season. OPPOSITE: Roger Craig plows through the Miami Dolphins on the way to one of the three touchdowns he scored in Super Bowl XIX.

FOLLOWING PAGE: Ted Kwalick hauls in a touchdown pass against the Denver Broncos, one of 19 touchdown passes he caught for the 49ers between 1971 and 1973. He led the team in receiving in 1971 with 52 catches and in 1973 with 47.

Kilmer. He moved the ball to midfield with 14 seconds left. Then, with six seconds on the clock, and no time outs left, Kilmer dropped back to pass from his 48-yard line. End Cedrick Hardman burst through the line and dropped Kilmer from the blind side to end the game and preserve a 24-20 San Francisco victory.

The Dallas Cowboys were San Francisco's next opponent. The 49ers had not forgotten the championship game of the previous season. Once again rain was to be a factor, but this time it was at Texas Stadium instead of Candlestick Park. The Cowboys were listed as eight-point favorites.

The 49er offense, which was spectacular all season, fizzled in the championship game. It gained just one first down in the first half. A Brodie screen pass that was picked off by lineman George Andrie killed San Francisco. He returned it to the two-yard line and two plays later, Calvin Hill plunged into the end zone for the only touchdown that Dallas needed. The Cowboys' "Doomsday Defense" controlled San Francisco's offense the rest of the way and led Dallas to a 14-3 win.

1972 The quest for a third consecutive Western Division title got underway in 1972 with a 34-3 drubbing of the San Diego Chargers on opening day. Gene Washington had eight receptions, including scoring catches of 13, 23 and 45 yards. Brodie completed 11 of 19 for 156 yards.

Brodie sprained his wrist in the second game of the season against Buffalo and missed part of the action as the Bills won, 27-20.

The 49ers got right back on track the next week as they clubbed New Orleans, 37-2. Brodie returned to form hitting on 18 of 26 passes for 156 yards and two touchdowns.

The offense scored easily in wins over Atlanta, 49-14, Chicago, 34-21, and Dallas, 31-10. Going into

RIGHT, TOP: Steve Spurrier (11), college football's Heisman Trophy winner in 1966, played nine seasons with the 49ers before being traded to Tampa Bay after the 1975 season. He played behind John Brodie most of his career, but saw action as a starter in 1972 after Brodie was injured. He helped guide the team to an 8-5-1 record that year and a spot in the NFC Championship Game. RIGHT, BOTTOM: Wilbur Jackson (40) was the heart of the 49er backfield from 1974 to 1979 gaining 2,955 yards. He averaged 3.9 yards per carry in a 49er uniform.

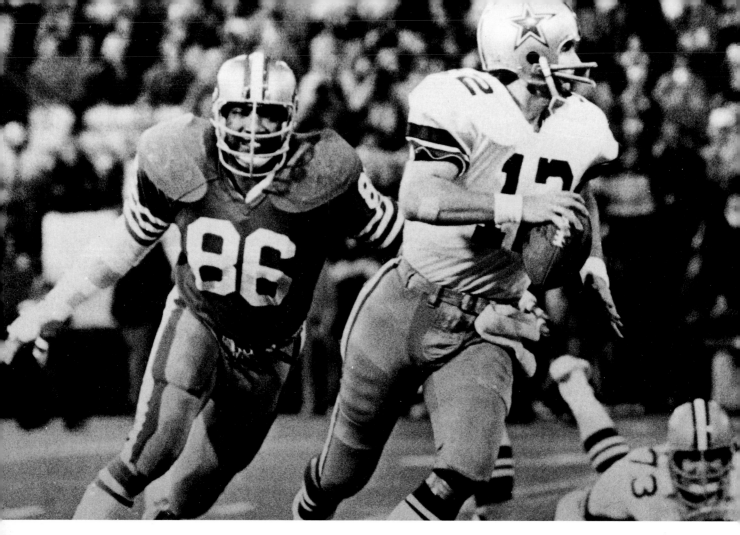

Cedrick Hardman (86) was the 49ers' first-round draft pick in 1970. The 250-pound defensive end made a living terrorizing quarterbacks and appeared in three Pro Bowls. He's the 49ers' career leader in sacks with 111.5. Here, he puts a scare in Dallas quarterback Roger Staubach.

the final game of the season, the 49ers were 7-5-1. Their opponent at Candlestick was the Minnesota Vikings with a 7-6 record. Once again, a victory was needed on the final day of the season to secure a playoff spot.

San Francisco was a six-point favorite to win it despite the absence of John Brodie who had been sidelined for 10 weeks with a badly injured ankle. Steve Spurrier, who played magnificently in place of Brodie, opened the game at quarterback.

Minnesota jumped out to a 17-6 lead and held it as the fourth quarter began. Under Spurrier, the 49ers were unable to launch any offense. Nolan decided it was time for a change. He motioned to Brodie to begin warming up on the sidelines. The 61,214 fans at Candlestick, who had resigned themselves to defeat, roared their approval as Brodie trotted on the field to begin the last period of play. It was his first appearance for the 49ers in over two months.

It took Brodie nearly half of the fourth quarter to regain his bearings. His first two possessions ended

in interceptions. With eight minutes left in the game, he went to work from his own one-yard line. He hit John Isenbarger for 12 yards, and Gene Washington for 53. Then he found Washington in the end zone on a 24-yard toss. The 99-yard drive brought the 49ers to within four points, at 17-13. They needed one more touchdown.

Minnesota wasn't about to give up the ball. The Vikes worked the clock down to 1:39 and punted. San Francisco took over at its own 35-yard line. But 65 yards of Candlestick turf stood between the 49ers and a playoff spot.

Schreiber picked up nine yards and Vic Washington got eight on two consecutive running plays to move the 49ers past midfield. With a minute to play, Vikes' linebacker Jeff Siemon interfered with Ted Kwalick on a pass play. The 49ers got the ball on the 27-yard line as a result of the penalty. After two running plays picked up six yards, Brodie tossed to Vic Washington who scampered 18 yards to the two with 39 seconds on the clock.

Brodie threw two incomplete passes leaving only 25 seconds to go and the 49ers two yards from the end zone. On third down, Brodie rolled to his right. Several times he pumped the football and motioned to Dick Witcher in the end zone. Witcher broke free, Brodie fired a perfect pass and San

Gene Washington (1969–1977)

He could run like a deer and had hands that were soft as cotton. As a former quarterback, he could read the field as well as any offensive co-ordinator. He had all the physical and mental attributes needed to become an All-Pro wide receiver in the National Football League.

And Gene Washington did just that. A first round pick of the 49ers in the 1969 draft, he broke into the league with a flurry. As a rookie, Washington caught 51 passes for 711 yards and averaged 14 yards per catch. At the end of his initial NFL season, he was selected to play in the first of four consecutive Pro Bowls.

It was no accident that the arrival of Washington coincides with some of the greatest offensive teams in 49er history. From 1969 to 1973, Washington teamed with John Brodie to give the 49ers one of the best passing combinations in football. San Francisco consistently ranked at the top of the NFL in passing offense. And for the first time, San

Francisco was a legitimate playoff contender.

"John Brodie was a fantastic quarterback," Washington said. "He was a much better quarterback than he ever got credit for. Of course, he had an excellent arm, but he was like a coach on the field. I had tremendous respect for him. He called all his own plays. He was fantastic at picking up defenses and then calling plays according to how the defense was set up."

The year 1970 was Brodie's signature season. He led the NFL in passing and was named the league's MVP. Washington was the team's top receiver that season with 53 catches. He led the league with 1,100 receiving yards and averaged 21 yards per catch. Most importantly, the 49ers won the Western Division Championship and found themselves in the playoffs for the first time in 14 seasons.

"He had a phenomenal year (in 1970)," Washington said. "The recognition he finally got was a long time in coming."

The Brodie-to-Washington connection depended on more than pure athletic ability. To a certain degree, they played a thinking man's game, which could be expected from a pair of Stanford graduates. Both Washington and Brodie had a unique insight into the workings of a defense, and they used that knowledge to their advantage.

"It helped that I had been a quarterback in high school and for two years in college," Washington said. "It allowed me to think along the same lines as John. Often a receiver will come back to the huddle and tell the quarterback he's open when he's not because he can't see the defense properly. Because I was a quarterback, I could see the field in the same way John could. I would recommend plays to him, things that I thought would work. There was a lot of give and take between us."

Together they matched wits and muscle with some of the NFL's great defenses. More often than not they were successful.

"There were some outstanding defensive teams back then," Washington said. "The Rams' pass rush, when they had the Fearsome Foursome, was one of the best ever. They made it extremely hard on the passing game because they were so big you couldn't see over them. The Steelers in the mid- to late-1970s were tough. The best secondary we played against was the Oakland Raiders' with Willie Brown, Jack Tatum and that group."

Beating the Raiders was always special to Washington, but one victory over the 49ers' cross-bay rivals stands out. It occurred in 1970 when San Francisco was battling the Rams for the NFC Western Division title. On the last day of the season, the 49ers needed a win over Oakland to clinch the first division championship in team history. But the Raiders had other ideas, and Oakland defensive end Ben Davidson guaranteed the East Bay fans a victory.

"We had to beat Oakland in the Oakland Coliseum to get into the playoffs," Washington said. "They had a terrific defense, and the fans over there were absolutely wild."

Before 56,000 Raider rooters, Brodie threw three touchdown passes, including a three-yard scoring toss to Washington, to lead San Francisco to a 38-7 win.

Washington also suffered his share of disappointments with the 49ers. None was bigger than San Francisco's 1972 playoff loss to the Dallas Cowboys.

"Anytime you beat Dallas it was an accomplishment," said Washington. "They consistently had great teams. But in 1972 they had one of their weaker teams. We were better than them; there was no doubt about it. We had scored easily on them in the first half, so maybe we got a little overconfident and let up. I don't know. But that was a fluke. We should have won that game."

Instead, Roger Staubach came off the bench to rally the Cowboys to two touchdowns with less than two minutes to play. The coup de grace for the 49ers was an onside kick that was fumbled by San Francisco's Preston Riley with 1:10 left to play. The Cowboys recovered, and Staubach needed just three plays to guide Dallas to the winning score.

"You can't blame anyone in a game like that," Washington said. "You certainly can't blame Preston Riley. We were in a state of disbelief when it was over. Disbelief is the only way to describe it."

Washington's prime production years matched Brodie's best seasons with San Francisco. Between 1969 and 1973, Washington averaged 50 receptions a season and nearly 20 yards per catch. He was the NFL's consummate deep threat. When the veteran quarterback finally retired from the 49ers after the 1973 season, some of the club's offensive firepower went with him.

Washington's production gradually tapered off as well. And the 49ers went into a tailspin that would take nearly a decade to correct.

Although Washington has a soft spot in his heart for Brodie, he credits a number of other players for the 49ers' success in the early 1970s, when San Francisco had a brief reign at the top of the Western Division. Many of the stars were overlooked.

"Dick Nolan was a defensive coach, so defensively the 49ers had some excellent people," Washington said. "Jimmy Johnson was one of those players who didn't get the credit he deserved. He was one of the greatest defensive backs to play the game. He didn't get the recognition because there may have been an eastern bias. The media favored players from the East Coast. Dave Wilcox was another one. He was a phenomenal player, just an outstanding linebacker."

Washington looks all the way back to his high school years when trying to recall an important mentor. He came out of Poly High School in Long Beach, California, a cradle of athletic talent which has sent more players to the professional ranks than any other high school in America. There, Washington's physical prowess on the field, and academic achievements in the classroom, attracted the attention of numerous collegiate scouts. Washington chose Stanford University, where he was recruited as a quarterback.

"One of the biggest influences on me as an athlete was a coach named Bill Mulligan at Poly High School," Washington said. "He was the basketball and football coach. He was a very positive guy who took an interest in me. I probably owe more to him than any other coach."

When Washington's 49er career came to an end in 1977, he had racked up 6,664 receiving yards, a club record until Dwight Clark and Jerry Rice came along to surpass it. He still holds the team record of 17.9 yards per catch. But it's not the records that are important to him.

"I met a great bunch of guys playing for the 49ers," Washington said. "The best things were the great friendships. I'm probably most close with John Brodie—he's a good friend. Those are the things that I'll remember."

Francisco had a dramatic 20-17 win.

In his one quarter of play, Brodie connected on 10 of 15 passes for 165 yards and two touchdowns.

The drama continued the following week as San Francisco faced Dallas in the playoffs. It was a game that still elicits emotion from 49er fans and players.

Vic Washington started the day off right by returning the opening kickoff 97 yards for a touchdown. With only 17 seconds gone, San Francisco had a 7-0 advantage. They gradually padded that lead as Larry Schreiber scored two touchdowns before the half on runs of one and eight yards. In the third period, Schreiber added another touchdown on a one-yard plunge to put San Franciso in front, 28-13.

The Dallas offense was stagnant throughout the third period and coach Tom Landry decided to replace quarterback Craig Morton with Roger Staubach to begin the fourth quarter.

With nine minutes left in the game, Staubach guided the Cowboys into field goal range. Toni Fritsch hit on the three-pointer, cutting the score to 28-16. At the two-minute warning, the score was still 28-16. It looked like the 49ers had shaken the Cowboy jinx that had kept them from the Super Bowl in 1970 and 1971.

With 1:53 to go, the Cowboys took over at their own 45-yard line. Working quickly, Staubach hit Bill Parks on two consecutive passes, the last one a 20-yard scoring strike to make it 28-23 with 1:30 on the clock.

Everyone in Candlestick Park knew that an onside kick was coming. All the 49ers had to do was cover the ball and run out the clock. Fritsch kicked a hard bounder at Preston Riley. The ball bounced off his hands and Mel Renfro recovered on the 50. With just over one minute to play, Staubach was back in business. It took him only three plays to put the Cowboys in the end zone again and give them a 30-28 win. The Cowboys had risen from the dead, scoring two touchdowns in less than a minute. It was a shocking end to an otherwise successful season for the 49ers.

TOP: Delvin Williams (24), receiver Mike Holmes (20) and running back Kermit Johnson rejoice after a 31-3 win over the Chicago Bears in 1975. BOTTOM: Monte Clark guided the 49ers to an 8-6 mark in 1976, his one season as head coach. The following season he resigned after a power struggle with new general manager Joe Thomas. Here, Clark discusses strategy with tackle Keith Fahnhorst.

1973

The 49ers had a difficult time in 1973 trying to rebound from the bitter playoff loss to Dallas. Early in the season, John Brodie announced it would be his final year with the 49ers.

In their first game, the 49ers faced the Super Bowl Champion Miami Dolphins. Miami was coming off the best season in football history winning 17 straight games in 1972 enroute to a perfect season.

The winning streak continued against the 49ers. Brodie had a marvelous first half completing 11 of 14 passes as the 49ers got off to a 10-6 lead, but the heat and humidity, which was over 100 degrees on the field, finally caught up with him. He was replaced by Spurrier in the second half. Spurrier was able to complete only six of his 18 passes and the Dolphins rallied back to win, 21-13.

The 49ers continued to play .500 ball the first

half of the season and appeared to be on the right track after beating New Orleans, 40-0. But nothing went right for the 49ers after that. They lost three consecutive games and were 3-6 when they faced Los Angeles in the Coliseum. Joe Reed, who occasionally sang the national anthem prior to the games, was given the starting nod at quarterback for the 49ers. The Rams won easily, 31-13, ending any remote hope of a playoff spot.

It was John Brodie Day at Candlestick on the last day of the season against the Pittsburgh Steelers. Brodie wanted to go out in style. Despite suffering arm problems most of the year, he got the starting call. But there were no miracles this day. His arm obviously was still sore. He completed six of 12 passes, then removed himself in the second period. Pittsburgh won, 37-14. San Francisco finished with a 5-9 record and a tie for last place in the Western Division.

Brodie ended his career with 2,469 completions in 4,491 attempts and 31,548 yards. He threw for 214 touchdown passes. It was also the last season for Ken Willard and Charlie Krueger. Willard gained

The offensive line discusses its game plan. Clockwise are John Watson (67), Cas Banaszek, Bill Reid, Woody Peoples, Jeff Hart, Bob Penchion and Keith Fahnhorst.

Dave Wilcox 1964–1974

Dave Wilcox's best memories of the 49ers involve the crazy pranks they used to play on one another.

"Charlie Krueger was one of the best," Wilcox said. "He liked to pull little tricks on people. He got Howard Mudd good one time.

"Howard used to chew Copenhagen. Somehow, Charlie Krueger found a little tree frog and put it in Howard's Copenhagen before practice. Everyone knew about it but Howard, so we were all wait-ing to see him put it in his mouth. As soon as he did, he knew something was up. But he wouldn't let on. He wouldn't spit the frog out. He didn't want to give everyone the satisfaction of seeing that.

"Ken Willard was an-other one. One time—I think it was after he had a bad game—he showed up at practice wearing those fake glasses with the big nose and mus-tache. That really cracked up (Dick) Nolan.

"We were all little kids at heart. But it was the guys that played the hardest that were usually the biggest pranksters."

By all accounts, Dave Wilcox was one of the guys that played the hardest. For 11 years he terrorized opponents from his left side line-backer position. He was a fixture in the Pro Bowl from 1967 to 1974.

"It's hard to say what it takes to become a good linebacker," he said. "I guess the first thing is you have to be a little crazy. You have to be aggressive. You can't be overly aggressive, though, because you have to be able to react to things as they happen."

Mental preparation is also important for a line-backer and it was one of the traits that made Wil-cox a stand out. He con-stantly reviewed his defensive assignments to ready himself for an upcoming game.

"I didn't like to make mental mistakes," he said. "Once the game started I'd go like hell.

I did everything 100 percent. Even if I made a mistake, I did it at 100 percent.

"I was a perfectionist I guess. I hated to lose. When I went on the field, I thought I could beat anybody. That's the way you have to be when you go out there."

From the outside linebacker spot, Wilcox was often called on to cover running backs on pass patterns. He laughs as he recalls his 235-pound frame trying to keep up with swift backs like Gale Sayers and Jim Brown.

"I was lucky to be in the same neighborhood as those guys," he said. "I saw Gale Sayers at a banquet recently and when I shook his hand I said, 'Geez, its nice to get a hold of you for a change.'"

Sayers tied an NFL record in a 1965 game against the 49ers when he scored six touchdowns. Wilcox was one of the members of the defensive unit that seemed to be constantly chasing Sayers that day.

"I thought that poor guy was going to die of exhaustion," he said jokingly of Sayers' performance. "If he could have gotten some oxygen, he would have scored six more touchdowns. I tell you, that guy was just fantastic."

The 49er defense was molded into a solid outfit in the early 1970s under Coach Dick Nolan. Wilcox teamed up on the left side with All-Pro defensive back Jimmy Johnson, safety Mel Phillips, and linemen Tommy Hart and Charlie Krueger. He says the entire left side worked well together, and as a result,

opposing teams stayed away from them as much as possible.

"That defensive team was a good mix of old and new players," he said. "Cedrick Hardman and Bruce Taylor were rookies in 1970 and Roosevelt Taylor joined us from Chicago. He added a lot of experience."

"From a defensive standpoint, Nolan was good as a coach," Wilcox said. "He was an ex-player. He knew what players thought and how they would react. He had a good feel for defense. If Nolan had a fault, although I wouldn't really call it a fault, it was that he would always talk about Dallas because he had coached there. We got tired of hearing him talk about how Dallas did things. We were the 49ers. We didn't care what Dallas did."

Although Wilcox was part of the 49er teams that lost two NFC championships to Dallas and one playoff game, he feels no animosity toward them. He admits, however, he was crushed when they lost in the 1972 playoff.

"I'll remember that for the rest of my life," he said mournfully. "I remember at halftime someone saying, 'We're doing great.' I thought, this guy must be crazy. We have another half to play. We really hadn't done anything up to that point. We scored on Dallas mistakes.

"I could feel the game slipping away in the second half. The intensity level had dropped off. There was a feeling that we could screw around in the second half and win anyway. Well, we didn't win because we didn't do

our jobs. We had the gates wide open and couldn't get them shut."

One of the most satisfying wins in Wilcox's career came in the 1970 playoff game against the Minnesota Vikings. The 49ers were appearing in their first playoff in 13 years and only the second as a member of the NFL. It was played at Bloomington Stadium in Minneapolis in weather only an Eskimo could enjoy. Temperature at game time was 10 degrees.

"Nobody gave us a chance in that game," he said. "Roman Gabriel was a television announcer at the time and he told Brodie we didn't have a chance. Before the game, we went out there in short sleeves and started jumping around like we were crazy, like we were enjoying the weather. Then we went out and beat them. It was gratifying to go back to Minnesota and win. It shocked everybody."

Minnesota was a tough place to play in the winter due to the nasty weather conditions, but San Francisco's Kezar Stadium had a reputation as a tough park on any given Sunday. Wilcox remembers it as a symbol of history and nostalgia.

"Me and Matt Hazeltine used to drive down Haight Street on the way to the park on Sundays," he said. "That's when all the hippies were hanging around. That was interesting.

"I had some friends who used to come to the games and they always went to the Kezar Club. They didn't think they could drink beer in the stadium, so they did it at the Kezar Club. After-

ward, they would walk right into the locker room and socialize. Nobody stopped them. In fact, a lot of people used to walk in off the street and socialize. They let anybody in the locker room. You couldn't move in there it was so small."

Wilcox finally retired after the 1974 season. He went out in fine fashion playing in the Pro Bowl for his seventh time. Before he retired though, he was party to one of the classic pranks in 49er history, one that is retold by veterans of the team whenever they congregate.

"In 1974, the streakers were going pretty good," he recalled. "We were in training camp going through two-a-day practices. You need something to break up the monotony. We had two go-go dancers come down to practice. We gave them cleats and helmets. It was supposed to be secret but everybody knew what was going to happen. Everybody but Dick Nolan. We were lined up running plays, but no one could concentrate because we were waiting. People were jumping offsides and forgetting the snap count. Finally, they came running across the field with nothing but their helmets on. One of the girls picked up the ball and threw it at Nolan. It hit him right in the chest. We had a cameraman there to film the whole thing."

"That's what I miss the most about football, the crazy things we used to do. I miss some of the other guys. The paycheck wasn't bad either."

6,105 yards in his career and scored 45 touchdowns. Krueger was a fixture on the defensive line for 15 seasons.

1974 The 49ers were fortunate to have four choices in the first two rounds of the 1974 college draft. They used them wisely. Among their picks were Keith Fahnhorst, Wilbur Jackson, Bill Sandifer and Delvin Williams. In addition to the first four choices, Sammy Johnson, Manfred Moore, Tom Owen and Mike Holmes also made the roster, giving the club eight rookies.

In an obvious rebuilding year, Joe Reed and Steve Spurrier battled it out in the preseason for the number-one quarterback position. Spurrier appeared to have the job won until he separated his shoulder in the last exhibition game against the Rams.

In his debut against the New Orleans Saints, Reed didn't remind any fans of John Brodie. He completed seven of 15 passes for only 56 yards. Larry Schreiber was the big gainer for San Francisco, rushing for 75 yards. It was enough to help the 49ers to a 17-13 win.

After beating Atlanta in the second game of the season, the 49ers lack of an experienced signal caller became a serious problem. They dropped seven straight games. During that span they tried five different quarterbacks. In addition to Spurrier and Reed, veteran Norm Snead and rookies Tom Owen, a 13th-round pick from Wichita State, and Dennis Morrison, a free agent from Kansas State, tried their hand at quarterback.

After losing seven in a row, the unexpected happened. San Francisco shutout its opponent in two straight games, beating Chicago, 34-0, and Atlanta, 27-0. It was the first time the 49er defense had shutout two consecutive opponents in 13 years.

The 49ers stumbled to a 6-8 record by beating New Orleans, 35-21, in the final game of the year. Several veterans retired after the 1974 season, including Dave Wilcox and Len Rohde. Tight end Ted Kwalick left the 49ers to play in the World Football League.

1975 Training camp was like a revolving door for quarterbacks in 1975. Norm Snead won the starting job after beating out both Tom Owen and Steve Spurrier.

San Francisco acquired from Dallas a slightly aged Bob Hayes. The former Olympic sprinter was obtained for a third-round draft choice and was intended to give Norm Snead a long ball target.

The 49ers beefed up the defensive line by drafting Jimmy Webb, a tackle from Mississippi, and Cleveland Elam, a defensive end from Tennessee State.

Despite the changes, San Francisco started the 1975 season right where it ended the last one, fumbling away another game. In the opener against Minnesota, Norm Snead completed 10 of 18 but lost the ball twice on fumbles. Minnesota took advantage of the miscues and turned them into touchdowns, winning 27-17.

All season the coaching staff searched for a starting quarterback. Snead, Steve Spurrier and Tom Owen alternated at the position but none of them had much success. The team struggled all year with the high point a 24-23 win over the Rams. They finished the season with four straight defeats.

San Francisco's 5-9 record was good enough for second place in the horribly weak NFC Western Division. There was little room for optimism outside of the 49er running game, which consisted of Delvin Williams, Larry Schreiber and Wilbur Jackson. Williams was the team's leading ground gainer with 631 yards. Schreiber retired at the end of the season having gained 1,734 yards in his five seasons with the 49ers.

1976 The head coaching job was handed to Monte Clark before the start of the 1976 campaign. Clark, formerly a defensive end with the 49ers, was the youngest head coach in the league at 39. He tried to solve the quarterback problem that had plagued the 49ers since John Brodie's retirement by acquiring Jim Plunkett from New England. In what proved to be a costly trade, San Francisco gave up Tom Owen, two number-one picks in 1976, and its first-round and second-round picks in 1977.

Clark and Plunkett made their 49er debuts a memorable one by defeating the Green Bay Packers, 26-14, on opening day of the 1976 season. Plunkett hit on eight of 12 passes for 120 yards. Running back Delvin Williams also showed flashes of brilliance, gaining 121 yards on the ground.

The 49ers staged a remarkable turnaround from the previous season by whipping Los Angeles, 16-0, New Orleans, 33-3, and Atlanta, 15-0. The de-

fense, led by Tommy Hart and Cedrick Hardman, blended into one of the premier outfits in football. In those three games, the defense sacked the quarterback 25 times as the team went on to win six of its first seven games.

The next week, the 49ers lost to St. Louis in overtime, 23-20, and began a four-game slide in which they also lost to Washington, Atlanta and Los Angeles. The possibility of an outstanding season finally ended when they lost to San Diego, 13-7, in their second overtime loss of the year.

Jim Plunkett was benched in the last game of the season and Scott Bull tried his hand at quarterback against New Orleans. Bull guided the team to a 27-7 win and appeared to be the quarterback of the future.

The 8-6 record was the team's first winning season since 1972. The high point of the year was the outstanding work of the defense, which allowed an average of just 13 points per game. Delvin Williams finished the season with a club record 1,203 yards rushing. Jimmy Johnson, a fixture in the 49ers' defensive backfield for 16 seasons, and a five-time Pro Bowl player, retired at the end of the year.

1977 During the off-season there was an unusual amount of activity in the 49er offices. Prior to the start of the season, Edward De-Bartolo Jr. became the new owner of the team. It was the first change of ownership in the franchise's history. Joe Thomas was hired as general manager and the popular Monte Clark resigned after a power squabble with Thomas. Thomas hired Ken Meyer to coach the club.

The team got off to a disastrous start. After losing five of six exhibition games, they were routed in the season opener at Pittsburgh, 27-0. They managed just 101 yards of total offense. For the fourth straight game, including exhibitions, the 49ers failed to score a touchdown. Plunkett completed just three of 13 passes for 30 yards, all to running back Delvin

TOP: Quarterback Steve DeBerg set NFL records in 1979 with 578 pass attempts and 347 completions. The record was broken a year later by San Diego's Dan Fouts. BOTTOM: Coach Bill Walsh considered running back Paul Hofer (36) one of the best all-purpose backs in football. In 1979, he led the 49ers in rushing with 615 yards and averaged five yards a carry. He also topped the club with 58 receptions. Hofer is the only 49er to receive the Len Eshmont Award two consecutive years. An injury cut short his career in 1981.

Delvin Williams 1974–1977

Delvin Williams didn't know what to expect at the start of the 1976 season. The 49ers had finished the previous year with a miserable 5-9 record. In two seasons, they had gone through five quarterbacks. Now there was a new coach in town by the name of Monte Clark and still another quarterback named Jim Plunkett.

It turned out to be quite a year for Williams. His uncertainty was quickly alleviated when he gained 121 yards in the season opening win over Green Bay. It was the first in a series of outstanding games that eventually netted him a club record 1,203 rushing yards.

"We had a lot more fun under Clark," he said. "It was the most fun I had playing football since my senior year in high school. 1976 was prob-

ably the peak of my career."

Williams' single-season rushing record was broken in 1984 when Wendell Tyler picked up 1,262 yards rushing. Prior to 1976 the last time a 49er running back had gained over 1,000 yards was in 1959 when J.D. Smith ran for 1,036 yards. Only five times in the team's history has a back gained over 1,000 yards.

"That's definitely a reflection on the coach," Williams said. "There was a noticeable turn around in the team when he took over. The thing about Clark was that he was able to come in, see where the talent was, and put it to use. He put people in the right position. Me and Wilbur Jackson had both been playing halfback up until then. He put Wilbur at fullback and me at halfback. It just made for a

better atmosphere. Plus, I was coming of age as a player."

The highlight of the season for Williams was a game against the St. Louis Cardinals when he set the 49er single-game rushing record with 194 yards on 34 carries.

"We lost that game in overtime but it was a good one for me personally," he said. "After that game I was just beat but you don't feel it during the game. I was young and I guess I didn't know any better. It sure didn't feel like I had 34 carries, though."

Just one week later, Williams had another big day. He gained 180 yards on 23 carries in a tough 24-21 loss to Washington. His total offensive output running and receiving that day amounted to 279 yards.

"I liked to think of myself as a complete

player," Williams said. "I ran, blocked and caught the ball. I always tried to play intelligently. I always tried to be a student of the game. It's not just athletic skill that is needed in pro football."

The 1976 season was a curious one. The 49ers finished with an 8-6 record but could easily have won 10 or 11 games. They lost twice in overtime and also had a three-point loss to Washington and a five-point loss to Atlanta.

The quarterback situation was unsteady throughout the year, which makes Williams' running achievement even more remarkable. Plunkett was hurt midway through the season, and Clark was forced to use the untested Scott Bull and Marty Domres at quarterback. Wide receiver Willie McGee was also injured, so defensive backfields could double-team Gene Washington, the 49ers' only other deep threat. The passing game was virtually helpless. San Francisco finished the year 11th in the NFC in passing yardage with 1,963 yards. They were second in rushing yardage with 2,447 yards.

Credit for that rushing total obviously goes to the offensive line—which included Randy Cross, Keith Fahnhorst and Cas Banaszek—for its ability to open holes for Williams and Wilbur Jackson. Williams says the ends deserve special mention because it was on sweeps that Williams gained many of his yards.

"Tom Mitchell, our tight end, was a very effective blocker on the run," he said. "He was the one that made it pos-sible to turn the corner. He was underrated."

Williams and Jackson had one of the biggest collective days ever for two running backs on a nationally televised Monday Night Football game. In that contest, against the Minnesota Vikings, they both rushed for more than 150 yards, a rare feat. Williams had 153 yards, while Jackson gained 156.

Things weren't always so good for Williams. In his rookie year with the 49ers, he broke his wrist in a preseason game and wondered if he'd stick with the team. He made the club, but didn't return to action until halfway through the regular season.

It wasn't until his second year with the 49ers that he began to become an effective part of the team's offensive unit. In 1975, he led the team in rushing with 631 yards, averaging 5.4 yards per carry. He caught an additional 34 passes.

"In the second year, I started to become acclimated to pro ball," he said. "The first year did a lot of good though, because I got to play through the pain and the injuries. I got to be part of the team and didn't have to go through the process of being new all over again the next year."

Leaving the relative security of college football for the professional game is often a traumatic experience for a rookie. During his initial season, Williams often looked to backfield coach Doug Scovil or veteran running back Vic Washington for advice.

"It is always a big adjustment for athletes to go from college to pro ball," he said. "In college they take care of everything for you. Suddenly you get to the pros and you have to take care of yourself. The social life is different and, of course, the physical dimension is much more intense on the pro level. They are much bigger and faster than anything you saw in college. You see these guys on TV and now all of a sudden you are playing with them.

"Vic Washington was pretty helpful to me as a rookie," he said. "He was always willing to talk to you. He'd tell you things that made sense. Basically though, it's something you just have to go through. You have to experience it."

Williams had a fruitful career with the 49ers from 1974 to 1977. He ranks fifth on the 49er all-time rushing list with 2,966 yards. He was traded to the Miami Dolphins in 1978 for wide receiver Freddie Solomon and a number-one draft pick. The 49ers used the draft choice to select Dan Bunz. The two players acquired for Williams were instrumental in the 49ers' two Super Bowl victories.

"I'm real happy for the 49ers now," he said. "They have good fans and good people here. They deserve a championship.

"I just wish I could have ended my career here. I enjoyed the time I was with the 49ers. Even when I left for Miami my heart was still in San Francisco."

Tony Bennett couldn't have said it better.

Williams. He also had two passes intercepted.

In the continuing search for an effective quarterback, Scott Bull was sent in to replace Plunkett late in the fourth quarter. He completed just one pass for 26 yards. Prior to that 26-yard pick up, the 49ers biggest gain of the day had been a 15-yard personal foul penalty marched off against Pittsburgh.

The 49ers' ineptitude continued as they lost five straight games. The offense was unable to put together any kind of attack and they were shutout for the second time of the season, 7-0, by Atlanta. In five games they scored 46 points, an average of just nine points per game.

Near midseason, kicker Ray Wersching was signed to replace Steve Mike-Meyer. Wersching immediately made his presence known when he kicked a 50-yard field goal in his first game against the New York Giants. Three weeks later, he kicked a field goal to beat New Orleans, 10-7, in overtime.

At midseason, the 49ers put together a four-game winning streak, mostly through outstanding defensive efforts. Besides the 10-7 overtime win at New Orleans, they won, 10-3, at Atlanta. Although they were winning, the offense was still unable to score consistently.

Before the season was over, Jim Plunkett gave fans hope for the future when he flashed his old form against Dallas on Monday Night Football. He threw four touchdown passes in a 42-35 loss.

It was still a disappointing season. The 49ers finished 5-9. The highlights of the year were the development of a strong defensive line and the improved running game. Delvin Williams had another fine season gaining 934 yards, while fullback Wilbur Jackson added 780.

1978 Something obviously had to be done to rebuild the 49ers. General manager Joe Thomas got started by firing Ken Meyer and the rest of the coaching staff and hiring Pete McCulley. Then,

TOP: Tight end Ken MacAfee (81),dejectedly buries his head as the 49ers lose another game in the miserable 1979 season. They finished the year with a 2-14 record. MacAfee was a first-round choice from Notre Dame in 1978. BOTTOM: Bill Walsh started the 1985 season with a record of 56-41 as head coach of the 49ers. The only San Francisco coach to win more games was Buck Shaw. Shaw had a 72-40-4 record and a .638 winning percentage. Walsh has a .577 winning percentage. PAGES 118-119: Bill Walsh reviews strategy with his troops prior to a game with the Los Angeles Rams in 1979, his first year as head coach.

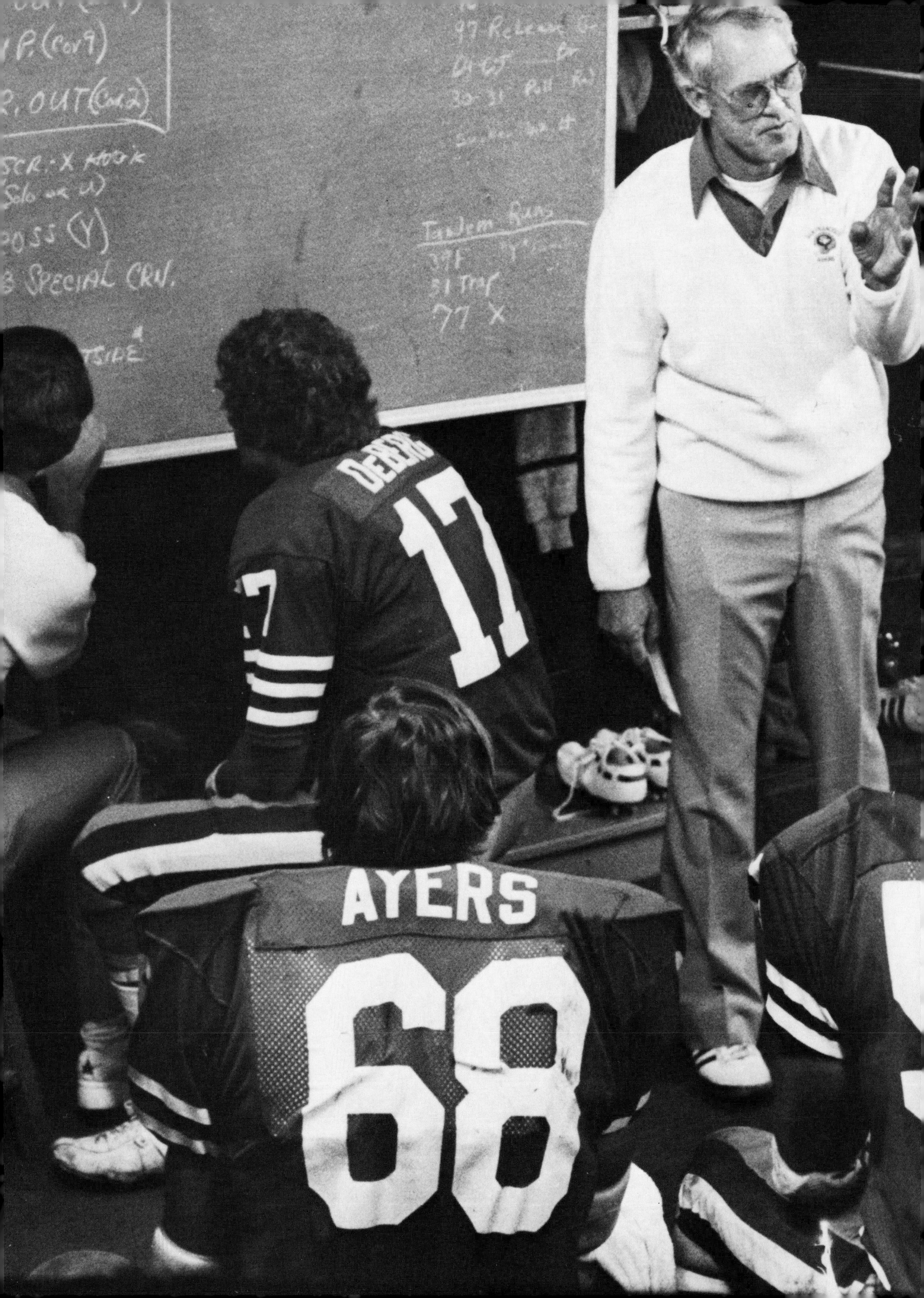
17
AYERS
68

in a bold move, Jim Plunkett was released and the quarterback job was handed to the untested Steve DeBerg. Several other popular veterans were unceremoniously released or traded, including Gene Washington, Bruce Taylor, Skip Vanderbundt, Tommy Hart, Delvin Williams and Woody Peoples.

In the backfield with DeBerg on the opening day of the 1978 season was O.J. Simpson, who was obtained from the Buffalo Bills. The 49ers gambled their future on Simpson, giving up second- and third-round picks in the 1978 draft, first- and fourth-round picks in 1979, and a second-round choice in 1980.

In 1978, the schedule was extended to 16 games. The extra two weeks just added frustration to the longest season in 49er history. The opening game was an indication of things to come when the 49ers turned the ball over six times to Cleveland and were beaten by the Browns, 24-7. DeBerg completed 16 of 32 passes for 174 yards. Simpson gained 78 yards on 22 carries. Ironically, it proved to be one of O.J.'s most fruitful days in a 49er uniform. Before the season was over, he would be sidelined with a separated shoulder.

There wasn't much to cheer about as the team floundered along losing eight of its first nine games. The club's sole win came at the hands of the Cincinnati Bengals. In the ninth week, after suffering a 38-20 beating at the hands of the Washington Redskins, McCulley was fired and Fred O'Connor took over.

O'Connor couldn't do much to change the 49ers' luck in his coaching debut, but then, it's doubtful that Knute Rockne could have redirected the team either. Atlanta beat the 49ers, 21-10, and once again it was turnovers that killed San Francisco.

The 49ers were able to win just one more game all year, a 6-3 yawner over Tampa Bay. But it was the team's final game at Detroit that epitomized the entire frustrating season.

The Lions won the game, 33-14, but it was a comedy of errors from the start as San Francisco fumbled 10 times. Quarterbacks Steve DeBerg and Scott Bull were both injured and wide receiver Freddie Solomon had to be inserted at quarterback.

Solomon never had played the position in the pro ranks. He turned out to be more effective than the regular quarterbacks, completing five of nine passes for 85 yards. He also ran for another 42 yards and a touchdown.

The 49ers finished 2-14 and had the dubious distinction of being only the third team in NFL history to lose 14 games in a season.

1979 Once again there was considerable activity in the front office during the off-season. Eddie DeBartolo fired Joe Thomas and Fred O'Connor, and hired Bill Walsh as head coach and general manager. The most successful era in the team's history was about to begin.

Walsh got to work immediately, choosing Joe Montana, an unheralded quarterback from Notre Dame, in the third round of the 1979 college draft. With his 10th-round pick, he went after Clemson receiver Dwight Clark. Walsh had set the framework for the 49ers' future success.

Walsh's first season did not go as anticipated, but the 49ers played noticeably better football. The offense moved the ball well as Walsh turned loose DeBerg and put the passing game in high gear.

The losses continued to pile up though, as San Francisco dropped its first seven games. Several were heartbreaking losses including a 28-22 defeat at Minnesota on a disputed touchdown in the last 10 seconds of the game, and a 27-24 loss to the Rams.

Finally, in the eighth week of the season, Walsh got his first 49er victory when the club downed Atlanta, 20-15. The only other win that year came against Tampa Bay. San Francisco's second consecutive 2-14 record placed it in the record books as the losingest team in NFL history over a two-year span.

There were some bright spots. The 49er offense became one of the most productive in football after being virtually last in every offensive category the previous season. Steve DeBerg set new NFL records in pass attempts and completions. He connected on 347 of 578 passes for 3,652 yards to better Fran Tarkenton's single-season marks.

Paul Hofer came into his own as a running back. He gained 615 yards on the ground for a five-yard average and was also the team's leading receiver with 58 catches. He was awarded the Len Eshmont award for the second straight year.

It was also the final time around for the great O.J. Simpson. "The Juice" carried one last time in the season finale against the Atlanta Falcons and picked up 10 yards. It was an insignificant addition to the 11,236 yards he gained in his career.

PAGE 122: Dwight Clark's catch gave the 49ers their first NFC Championship. "It was a perfect pass," Clark said.

1980–1989

CHAPTER FIVE

THE SUPER BOWL YEARS

Walsh continued his rebuilding program in 1980 by trading away veterans Cedrick Hardman and Wilbur Jackson and concentrating on young talent. In the college draft, he selected running back Earl Cooper and defensive end Jim Stuckey in the first round, and linebacker Keena Turner in the second round. By the end of the 1980 season, just 16 of the players that Walsh inherited from Joe Thomas remained with the club.

In pre-season, the 49ers looked promising by beating Oakland, San Diego and Kansas City, and losing to Seattle by only three points. They opened the regular season against the New Orleans Saints in the Superdome and carried with them an NFL-record 18-game losing streak on the road.

San Francisco broke the road jinx with the help of New Orleans kicker Russell Erxleben, who missed a 34-yard field goal at the gun. The 49ers held on to win, 26-23. Earl Cooper was the workhorse for San Francisco, picking up 77 yards on the ground and catching 10 passes for another 71 yards. He also scored two touchdowns. Paul Hofer added 68 yards on 12 carries and 114 yards with seven receptions. Steve DeBerg also had an outstanding day, completing 21 of 29 passes for 223 yards.

On defense, the club was led by linebacker Scott Hilton, who had made his living as a carpenter just a year earlier. Hilton had a game-high 15 tackles aganst the Saints, nine of them unassisted.

San Francisco continued its surprising start by beating St. Louis in overtime the following week and then the New York Jets. But after posting a 3-0 record, reality set in. The 49ers were blown out by the Rams 48-26 and Dallas, 59-14. Then they lost four consecutive heartbreakers, to Tampa Bay 24-23, Detroit 17-13, Green Bay 23-16, and Miami 17-13, dropping their record to 3-8.

Midway through the season, Paul Hofer, who was off to an outstanding start with a 4.9-yard rushing average, was lost to the club with a knee injury. At quarterback, Joe Montana began alternating with Steve DeBerg and gradually worked his way into the starting lineup.

With three games left to play, the 49ers entertained New Orleans at Candlestick. The Saints were 0-13, but they were able to make the 49ers look pathetic in the first half, jumping out to a 35-7 lead. The 49er offense had gained just 21 yards. As the 49ers left the field at intermission, 37,000 fans at Candlestick booed them unmercifully.

In the second half, Montana caught fire. He threw touchdown passes to Solomon and Clark and scored another on a one-yard run. Suddenly, the 49ers were back in the game. With 1:50 to play, Lenvil Elliott's seven-yard run tied it up. San Francisco won in overtime on a Ray Wersching field goal, and the most remarkable comeback in NFL history was complete.

San Francisco closed out the season with a 6-10 record, but there was evidence that the club had a good nucleus upon which to rebuild. Rookie Earl Cooper led the league in receiving with 83 catches and Clark was second with 82 receptions. Montana won the starting quarterback job in the second half of the season with his intelligent play. He completed 65 percent of his 273 passes for 1,795 yards and 15 touchdowns.

1981 In the 1981 college draft, the 49ers hoped to improve the porous pass defense that plagued them throughout the 1980 season. They selected Ronnie Lott in the first round, Eric Wright in the second round and Carlton Williamson in the third round. The three defensive backs stepped into immediate starting roles. By the end of the 1981 season, the 49ers had the best secondary in football.

To further improve the defense, they obtained linebacker Jack Reynolds from the Rams. He brought leadership and experience to the young defensive unit. Midway through the season, quarterback terrorist Fred Dean was obtained from the Chargers for a second-round draft pick, a trade that was the equivalent of highway robbery.

The start of the 1981 season was less than spectacular. The 49ers lost two of their first three games and seemed headed for a mediocre year. But then things began to happen.

San Francisco squeaked by New Orleans, 21-14, and beat Washington, 30-17, in the nation's capital. They returned home to play the Dallas Cowboys at Candlestick. Just a year earlier, Dallas had humiliated San Francisco, 59-14. This time it would be different.

The 49ers jumped off to a 21-0 lead in the first quarter behind the passing of Joe Montana, who sparked the club on touchdown drives of 61 and 68 yards. At the half, San Francisco held a 24-7 advantage.

In the third quarter, Montana hit Clark on a 78-yard scoring pass. Then Lott intercepted a pass and returned it four yards for a touchdown. The 49ers were in the driver's seat. But Montana was not finished. He took the 49ers on an 89-yard march to

TOP: Archie Reese was an instrumental part of the 49er defense during the 1981 Super Bowl season. The defensive end from Grambling played from 1978 to 1981 with the 49ers. BOTTOM: Linebacker Bobby Leopold (52) returns to the huddle after the 49er defense knocked Cardinal running back Ottis Anderson out of the game in 1980 with a separated shoulder.

Dwight Clark 1979–1987

The image of Dwight Clark leaping into a darkening sky and snagging a pass to send the 49ers to their first Super Bowl is indelibly etched in the memory of every 49er fan.

No one will forget "the Catch." It is a play that will live on forever. It set the 49ers free from a jinx they had not been able to shake. On three previous occasions in the 1970s, the Dallas Cowboys terminated 49er drives to the Super Bowl. But Clark ended that hex in one electrifying moment when he returned to earth with the pigskin and six points.

"When Joe threw that ball, I thought at first it was a little high," Clark said. "Later, Irv Cross was interviewing me and after I thought about it, I said it was a perfect pass. He started laughing because he thought I was joking,

but it was a perfect pass. There's no other place Joe could have thrown the ball. If it had been anywhere else, Everson Walls would have made a play on it.

"That catch was a big thrill, but what made it exciting was the whole drive and coming back to beat Dallas. Dallas was usually the team that made the comebacks."

Dwight Clark is painfully modest. He is a master of understatement. He caught 297 passes from 1980 to 1983, more than any other receiver in the NFL, and was Sports Illustrated's Player of the Year in 1982. But Clark says it was Bill Walsh's offensive system and Joe Montana's pinpoint passing that made him successful.

And he may have a point. He was a 10th-round draft pick out of

Clemson in 1979. He caught only 33 passes in his three years of varsity action. He hardly could have expected to be in the NFL Pro Bowl two years into his professional career.

"I don't think I would have had this success if I had played anywhere else," he said. "When I first got there, Sam Wyche (the 49ers' former quarterback and receiver coach) took me aside and worked with me. That helped a lot. But it was Bill's system that made everything work, not any individual skill of mine.

"Joe made me play better," he added. "He's good at reading what will happen. He knows what his receivers will do. He can tell by the way a guy runs downfield which way he will cut."

What was it about Montana and Clark? They had an undefinable mystique, an ability to complement one another in a way that set them apart from other passing combinations. They may have been the most productive aerial duo since Johnny Unitas and Raymond Berry.

In nine seasons with San Francisco, Clark caught 506 passes for 6,750 yards and 48 touchdowns. When he retired in 1987 he was the 49ers all-time leader in catches and receiving yards. But those records were soon eclipsed by a dynamic young receiver named Jerry Rice.

"Joe and I did have something going that was different," Clark said about their on-field relationship. "But after awhile Joe had that with every receiver on the team."

Clark and Montana figured prominently in the 49ers' development into an NFL power. When Clark joined the team in 1979, it was coming off a 2-14 season, the worst in its history. In his rookie year, the team did no better, struggling along and finishing again at 2-14. But the pieces were slowly being put into place, Clark said. It took one more season of refinement before San Francisco finally won a championship.

"That first Super Bowl was the culmination of two years of putting the Bill Walsh system into place," Clark said. "I knew we were going to win eventually, but I didn't think we'd win so soon. In 1981, the team wasn't deep. But we were lucky, we didn't have any injuries so things worked out."

Defense became a potent weapon for the 49ers in 1981. The acquisition of Fred Dean solidified the defensive line. But it was in the 1981 college draft that San Francisco boosted itself into a Super Bowl contender, Clark said. When Ronnie Lott, Eric Wright and Carlton Williamson joined the club, there was a noticeable change in attitude.

"One of the big things that season was all the rookie defensive backs we drafted," he said. "They were not only good, they infected the rest of the team with their college enthusiasm. That really helped spark things."

After the 1984 season, the 49ers' entire defensive backfield was selected to play in the Pro Bowl. Practicing against the best in the business on a daily basis could only be a help, Clark said. "You'd know if something worked against them it would work against anybody.

"I'm lucky we didn't have to play against our defensive backs in a real situation. After watching some of the hits Ronnie Lott put on people, especially in the preseason of 1985 when he belted Wes Chandler, I'm glad he was on my side.

"If I was to single out one guy other than our defense that I preferred not to play against, it would be Mike Haynes from the Raiders. He gave me trouble."

One defensive unit that sticks out in Clark's mind belonged to the Atlanta Falcons. Over the years, the Falcons and the 49ers have engaged in physical warfare. Cuts and bruises were the norm after any game that matched the two Western Division rivals.

"Atlanta had a very intense defense," Clark said. "They were like bees. Everyone swarmed to the ball. It cost them though because they got a lot of people hurt."

One of the most memorable games in Clark's career was played against the San Diego Chargers in the strike-shortened 1982 season. He caught 12 passes, a personal high. The game stands out because it contained the type of football Clark liked to play: lots of passing and plenty of scoring. The Chargers eventually won, 41-37.

Clark had an idyllic life as a San Francisco 49er. He cannot envision himself having played for anyone else. The combination of Walsh's offensive system, Montana's throwing ability, and the team's camaraderie and spirit, would have made it hard for him to play with any other team. When he was drafted, he had no idea San Francisco would be so good to him.

"I remember when I got drafted by the 49ers, I was really happy and everything, but I didn't know that much about them," he said. "I knew John Brodie had been the quarterback for a while, but that's about it. When I got there, I found out O.J. Simpson was on the team. I was real excited about that. I couldn't wait to meet him. He was my hero as a kid.

"If I played anywhere else I don't think I'd have had all those good things happen to me. I was in the right place at the right time. I'm fortunate I was drafted by the 49ers."

make it 45-7. The rout was complete. Dallas added another touchdown on a fumble recovery to make the final score 45-14, but the damage was done. It became apparent that something special was happening in San Francisco.

Two weeks later, the Los Angeles Rams came to town. The 49ers had a four-game winning streak on the line, their longest in four years, but they had not beaten the Rams at home since 1966. They had never beaten them at Candlestick Park.

Montana moved the club early, connecting with Dwight Clark on a 41-yard touchdown pass and Freddie Solomon on a 14-yard scoring pass. When the Rams had the ball, they advanced at will, but mistakes and tough defense when it counted kept them out of the end zone. The Rams still managed to put 17 points on the board. Two Wersching field goals gave the 49ers a 20-17 edge in the fourth quarter, but a game between the 49ers and Rams rarely ends without drama, and this was no exception.

With six minutes to play, Rams' kicker Frank Corral tried a 32-yard field goal that would tie up the game. The ball hit the right goal post, then the cross bar, and bounced right back at Corral.

With 2:03 to play, the Rams got the ball again. Quarterback Pat Haden was sacked twice, but on third down he completed a 33-yard pass for a first down at the San Francisco 31-yard line. The Rams moved the ball to the 28 with three more plays. With 17 seconds left on the clock, Corral tried a 45-yard field goal. This one was wide to the left. The 20-17 lead held.

The 49ers were tested again the following week against the Pittsburgh Steelers. The Steelers

TOP: Defensive end Lawrence Pillers was an instrumental part of both 49er Super Bowl teams.
CENTER: "Hacksaw was one of the guys that helped turn the team around in 1981," Ronnie Lott says. The 49ers signed Jack Reynolds (64) as a free agent in 1981. He instilled confidence into a young defensive unit and helped guide the 49ers to two Super Bowl appearances. Here, he discusses strategy with linebacker coach Norm Hecker. BOTTOM: From left to right, Charles Johnson, Charles Cornelius and Charle Young await pre-game taping. Young has a muscle stimulator taped to his thigh.

PAGES 128-129: Joe Montana gives encouragement to members of the offense in the closing minutes of a game against the Pittsburgh Steelers in 1981. Clockwise are Montana (16), Eason Ramson (80), Freddie Solomon (88), Randy Cross (51), Charle Young (86), Fred Quillan (56) and Dwight Clark (87).

In 1984, kicker Ray Wersching became the first 49er to lead the NFL in scoring since Gordy Soltau in 1953.

were the most feared team in football during the 1970s, when they won four Super Bowls. The game was played in the hostile environment of Pittsburgh. San Francisco was given scant chance of beating the AFC powerhouse. But nobody told Joe Montana.

For Montana it was a homecoming of sorts. He grew up in nearby Monangahela, about 20 miles south of Pittsburgh. He was forced to play the game with a flak jacket because of bruised ribs. The injury did not hamper his performance. He completed 16 of 23 passes in the first half as the 49ers took a 10-0 advantage.

Pittsburgh scored two quick touchdowns in the third period to go in front 14-10. The 49er offense was unable to generate any momentum after that, but an interception by Carlton Williamson, who ran the ball 28 yards to the Pittsburgh 43, set up their final scoring march. Montana moved the ball into the end zone in nine plays with Walt Easley covering the last yard for the score that made it 17-14. The 49ers had survived another test. They were now 7-2 and had to be considered a legitimate contender.

After beating Atlanta, San Francisco took a seven-game winning streak into Cleveland. The 49ers

could put only 12 points on the scoreboard with four Wersching field goals and they lost to the Browns, 15-12.

They rebounded against the Rams, beating them 33-31, when Wersching kicked a 37-yard field goal with no time on the clock. Then, in the 13th game of the season, the 49ers clinched the NFC Western Division title with a 17-10 win over the New York Giants.

The last three games of the season were anti-climactic. The 49ers beat Cincinnati in a Super Bowl preview, 21-3, eased by Houston, 28-6, and defeated New Orleans, 21-17. San Francisco finished the season 13-3, the best record in the NFL. The 49ers' first opponent in the playoffs would be the New York Giants.

The week before the game, a wild storm made practice at the 49ers' Redwood City training facility impossible. Bill Walsh arranged for the team to practice indoors at a local high school. The rain didn't dampen the 49ers' spirit or effectiveness against the Giants.

San Francisco struck first against New York on an eight-yard pass to tight end Charle Young and

Archie Reese celebrates a goal line stand in Super Bowl XVI.

never looked back. The 49ers beat the Giants 38-24. Montana completed 21 of 30 passes for 304 yards, including another touchdown pass of 58 yards to Freddie Solomon.

Dallas was next. The Cowboys had finished the year with a 12-4 record and were aching for a rematch after their embarrassing defeat at the hands of the 49ers earlier in the season. For the 49ers, it was their first appearance in an NFC Championship Game since 1971 when they played Dallas. The Cowboys were posted as a 2 1/2-point favorite.

Rain pelted the Bay Area the week before the championship game. The Golden Gate Bridge was closed due to high winds for only the third time since its opening. Walsh searched the Peninsula for dry fields to practice on and finally moved the entire organization to Anaheim to practice on the Los Angeles Rams' field.

The 1981 NFC Championship Game was one of the most exciting games in football history. San Francisco scored first on an eight-yard pass from Montana to Solomon, but the two teams exchanged the lead six times before the game was over. The 49ers scored a second quarter touchdown on a 20-yard Montana pass to Dwight Clark. At the intermission, Dallas went into the locker room with a 17-14 lead.

Defense dominated the third quarter. An interception by 49er linebacker Bobby Leopold set up a two-yard touchdown run by Johnny Davis to give the 49ers a 21-17 lead. The Cowboys went back in front, 27-21, in the fourth quarter after Rafael Septien kicked a 22-yard field goal and Danny White connected with Doug Cosbie on a 21-yard scoring toss.

The best was yet to come. San Francisco's offense took over again on its own 10-yard line with just under five minutes to play. It was do-or-die for the 49ers and they knew it.

Montana moved the ball downfield on short passes to Solomon and Cooper, while Lenvil Elliott picked up yardage on several shifty runs. At the two-minute warning, with the 49ers at midfield, Montana went to the sideline to discuss the situation with Walsh. On the next play, Solomon picked up 14 yards on a reverse, moving the ball to the 35. Montana then threw a 10-yard pass to Clark and a 13-yard pass to Solomon. San Francisco called time out again with 1:13 left to play and the ball on the 12-yard line. Again Walsh and Montana conferred. When play resumed, Montana missed Solomon on a pass to the end zone. Then Elliott

131

rushed for seven more yards to the six.

With 58 seconds to play, Montana dropped back to pass and was pursued by Ed "Too Tall" Jones and Larry Bethea. As he was about to be sacked, he lofted a soaring pass that appeared to be going out of the end zone. Dwight Clark had other thoughts. He made a straining leap, grabbed hold of the football and came down near the back of the end zone. The 49ers were going to the Super Bowl. Their opponent would be the Cincinnati Bengals.

The week before the Super Bowl, Coach Bill Walsh was honored for transforming the 49ers from the worst team in the NFL to the top of the heap in just two years. He received the NFC Coach of the Year Award at a ceremony in Washington, D.C.

Arriving in Pontiac, Michigan, site of Super Bowl XVI, Walsh found the temperature to be 15 degrees below zero. The wind chill factor made it 51 below zero. His only consolation was the knowledge that the game was to be played indoors at the Silverdome.

The 49ers were one-point favorites at game time. The coaches of the two playoff teams San Francisco beat to get to the Super Bowl thought differently. Dallas coach Tom Landry picked the Bengals to win by seven points. Ray Perkins, coach of the New York Giants, picked the Bengals by 10 points.

San Francisco won the coin flip and elected to receive. On the opening kickoff, Amos Lawrence fumbled the ball and the Bengals recovered on the 26-yard line. It was not the kind of start Walsh had expected.

Cincinnati immediately drove to the San Francisco five-yard line. On third down, Ken Anderson's pass to Issac Curtis was intercepted by Dwight Hicks who returned it to the 32.

Montana didn't waste any time. He drove the 49ers 68 yards in 11 plays and scored the first touchdown himself on a one-yard dive. The big plays in the drive were a Montana pass to Charle Young for 14 yards and a 14-yard completion to Freddie Solomon.

In the second quarter, with the 49ers still in front 7-0, Cincinnati threatened again. The Bengals were on the 49ers' 27-yard line when Anderson completed a 20-yard pass to Cris Collinsworth to the seven-yard line. As he was hit by Eric Wright, Collinsworth fumbled. The 49ers recovered and stifled another Bengal scoring opportunity.

Montana went back to work from the eight-yard line. He completed a 20-yard pass to Solomon and a 12-yarder to Clark. Cooper picked up 14 yards on a sweep. Then, from the 11-yard line, Montana completed a pass to Cooper for the touchdown that gave San Francisco a 14-0 lead. The 92-yard drive was the longest in Super Bowl history.

On their next possession, the Bengals were unable to move the ball and were forced to punt. San Francisco took the ball on its own 34 and drove to the Bengals' five-yard line. With 18 seconds left in the half, Wersching kicked a 22-yard field goal and the score was 17-0.

On the ensuing kickoff, Wersching booted a deliberate squib kick that bounced into the arms of Archie Griffin. He promptly fumbled and the ball rolled toward the goal line. The 49ers' Milt McColl covered it on the four. The Bengals were stunned. With five seconds left before intermission, Wersching kicked another field goal and the 49ers had a 20-0 halftime lead.

The second half took on a different tone. The Bengals came out charging and scored on their first possession when Anderson ran five yards to cap an 83-yard drive. The two sides exchanged punts before Cincinnati regained the ball with 6:53 in the third quarter. Anderson completed a 49-yard pass to Collinsworth, and several running plays moved the ball to the three-yard line.

The Bengals had two of football's toughest short-yardage runners in Pete Johnson and Charles Alexander. Johnson, a 250-pound fullback, was considered unstoppable on the goal line. It seemed an impossible task to keep them out of the end zone.

On first down, Johnson gained two yards up the middle. The Bengals had three more downs to pick up one yard and a touchdown that would move them to within six points of San Francisco. On second down, linebacker Dan Bunz plugged a hole over left guard and stopped Johnson for no gain. On third down, Anderson threw a quick swing pass to Alexander. Bunz was ready for it. He flattened Alexander less than a yard from the goal line.

The Bengals were confused. Nobody had stopped Johnson and Alexander on short yardage plays like the 49ers had done. Anderson called a time out to talk things over with Forrest Gregg. The Bengal coach decided to go for the touchdown rather than a certain field goal. They agreed to use the Bengals' best goal-line play, a fullback plunge over right guard, behind Alexander's lead block. Bunz was there again. He

Bill Walsh fires up his troops during the halftime of the 1981 NFC Championship Game against the Dallas Cowboys.
PAGE 132: Guard Randy Cross was named to the Pro Bowl following the 1981, 1982 and 1984 seasons.
He was the team's top choice in 1976 for the center position.

stuffed the hole, slowing down Johnson so that Jack Reynolds and the rest of the defense could make the stop.

The dramatic goal-line stand changed the complexion of the game. The momentum swung back to the 49ers. Now the game was clearly in their hands. Ray Wersching added two more field goals and the 49ers held on to win their first Super Bowl, 26-21.

1982 In the offseason, Walsh strengthened his Super Bowl team by coaxing Russ Francis out of retirement. Francis was a former All-Pro tight end with the New England Patriots. He also signed Renaldo Nehemiah, holder of the world record in the 110-meter hurdles, to give the 49ers a deep threat at wide receiver. With the 49ers' first pick in the college draft, Walsh selected Bubba Paris, a massive offensive tackle from the University of Michigan.

The 49ers opened the 1982 season against the Los Angeles Raiders. They needed a victory to validate their Super Bowl victory. Many people still believed it was a fluke. They didn't get it. Sloppy

play, turnovers and blown assignments led to a 23-17 loss. More importantly, Dwaine Board, one of the team's best defensive linemen, went down with a knee injury. The loss of Board was noticed immediately as Raiders' running back Marcus Allen ran through the 49er defense for 116 yards.

The 49ers lost their second game of the season at Denver, 24-21, and then the NFL players went on strike. When they returned to action in November, the 49ers won their first game of the year over St. Louis, 31-20. They stumbled through the rest of the season and had a 3-5 record going into their final game against Los Angeles. It was a game the 49ers had to win to gain a playoff spot.

Los Angeles was one of the worst teams in the league with a 1-7 record. The Ram defense was as solid as a wet soda cracker. The 49ers were favored to beat them by 9 1/2 points.

Somehow the 49ers managed to lose. With 1:50 to go, Ray Wersching could have put San Francisco ahead with an easy 24-yard field goal. The kick was blocked by Ivory Sully, giving the Rams a 21-20 win and capping a dreadful season for San Francisco.

Roger Craig 1983–1990

Roger Craig is one of those physical specimens football coaches dream about. He is built like a thoroughbred, sleek and muscular, with the power and stamina of a Clydesdale.

The former San Francisco 49er running back used that compact efficiency to have the best year of his National Football League career in 1988. He rambled for 1,502 yards on 310 carries, both career highs for him, and averaged 4.8 yards every time he was handed the ball.

But for Craig, individual statistics pale in comparison to team accomplishments. The 49ers did the ultimate in 1988, taking their third Super Bowl title. That was what mattered. Victory is the true

measure of success, according to Craig.

Craig was a major cog in the 49er wheel that rolled to Super Bowl wins after the 1984, 1988 and 1989 seasons. Team historians would have to return to the time of the Million Dollar Backfield to remember when San Francisco had such a dominant running back in its lineup.

Craig shattered the team's rushing record in 1988. His 1,502-yard season was the finest ever had by a 49er running back, eclipsing Wendell Tyler's old rushing mark of 1,262 yards.

Only Eric Dickerson, the Rams' Greg Bell and Herschel Walker of the Dallas Cowboys claimed more rushing yardage in 1988. But those three weren't in the same league with Craig when it came to catching passes. Craig ended the

season with 76 receptions for 534 yards.

That was where Craig's value lay. He was much more than a ball carrier. He was also an integral part of the 49ers' passing attack, one of the main links in a refined offensive machine. He's the only player in NFL history to rush for over 1,000 yards and gain 1,000 yards receiving in the same season. Craig established that record in 1985. And he holds the NFL single-season record for most receptions by a running back with 92. In 1989, he led all 49er receivers with 76 catches totaling 534 yards.

To put Craig's 1988 season into better perspective, he gained 2,036 total yards in 1988, nearly 35 percent of the 49ers' 5,900 yards of total offense. He might not have been a one-man show, not on a team that also showcased Joe Montana and Jerry Rice. But no one else in the NFL was responsible for such a huge chunk of a team's offense.

Craig's durability and stamina did not develop overnight. He came into training camp in 1988, 15 pounds lighter than the 227 pounds he carried in 1987. He also made use of a personal masseuse who helped prepare the running back's body for its Sunday beatings.

"The off-season conditioning program I was on helped out," Craig said. "I felt sluggish near the end of the 1987 season. The lost weight gave me more stamina over the length of the season."

Craig could afford to lose the weight. During his first four seasons with the 49ers, Craig was used as a fullback and needed the added bulk to stand up to enemy linebackers. In 1987, that job was turned over to fellow Nebraska Cornhusker alumnus Tom Rathman, a guy who would rather run over linebackers with a good lead block, than score the winning touchdown in the Super Bowl.

Attention to health served Craig well. During his eight seasons with the 49ers, he was rarely out of the lineup with injuries. And his former teammates claim he actually got better as he aged.

"There's no doubt that Roger had a little extra step as the season progressed," said ex-49er center Randy Cross. "Most backs lose a step after a couple years in the NFL. Roger seemed to gain one."

"That's something I'm proud of," Craig said. "Everyone thought I wouldn't be durable in the NFL. But I love winning and I'll do what it takes to win. I look at taking care of my body just as a business man would attend to taking care of his business. It's my bread and butter."

Surprisingly, when Craig was selected by the 49ers in the 1983 draft, his pass-catching abilities were in question, as well as his stamina. He was hurt much of his senior year at Nebraska, and therefore lasted well into the second round of the draft. He turned out to be the sixth running back chosen that year, behind Eric Dickerson, Curt Warner, Michael Haddix, James Jones and Gary Anderson. Surely, some coaches and general managers are now cursing their short-sightedness.

The claim that Craig was not a good receiver was a knock that had no basis in fact. The truth is, at Nebraska the forward pass has always been as rare as a snow storm in June. A running back could end up collecting social security before he saw a pass thrown his way.

With San Francisco, Craig proved he had excellent hands. And in one of football's great ironies Craig teamed up with Rathman, another former Cornhusker, to give the 49ers the NFL's best pass-catching duo out of the backfield.

Craig's last game with the 49ers came in the 1990 NFC Championship against the New York Giants. It is a game he would rather forget. His fumble with time running out gave the Giants the opportunity they needed to kick the winning field goal.

During his eight seasons with San Francisco, Craig became the standard by which other NFL running backs were judged. He led the club in rushing five times and ran for over 1,000 yards on three occasions. His 7,064 career rushing yards are on the club's all-time list, second only to Joe Perry. He was also the 49ers' leading receiver in four different seasons. Only Jerry Rice has caught more passes in a 49er uniform than Roger Craig's 508 receptions.

Craig has come a long way from his days as a track, football and wrestling star in his hometown of Davenport, Iowa. Despite life in the big time, he clings to his small town values. Success comes only through hard work, he says, and that attitude paid off when he finally made it to the NFL.

"My father died of cancer when I was a senior in high school," he said. "He was a mechanic and a hard worker. I think that's where my work ethic comes from. He impressed on me that no amount of hard work is too much when you're reaching for a goal. I was lucky to be in San Francisco in a system that used me in a lot of ways."

Craig's dedication and determination did not go unnoticed by his teammates. In 1985 he received the club's Len Eshmont Award which is given annually to the 49ers' most courageous and inspirational player. It was an award that Craig relished because it came from the players, he says. For a player who is concerned with team goals rather than personal achievement, there can be no higher award.

After playing in the Pro Bowl for three straight seasons as a member of the New England Patriots, Russ Francis (81) suddenly retired in 1980. He came out of retirement in 1982 to play for the 49ers. An excellent all-around athlete, Francis was drafted by the Kansas City Royals baseball team out of high school. He also set an American prep record by throwing the javelin 259' 9".

1983 The 49ers had lived and died by the pass for too long. They needed a running game to complement the passing of Joe Montana if they wanted to be successful in the NFL. In 1983 they did just that by selecting Roger Craig, a fullback from Nebraska, in the second round of the college draft, and obtaining halfback Wendell Tyler from the Rams for a second- and fourth-round pick.

Tyler did not endear himself to 49er fans in the 1983 season opener against Philadelphia. With the Eagles leading 22-17, and 1:19 to play, the 49ers were driving. They had the ball on Philadelphia's 10-yard line when Tyler fumbled it into the end zone, killing the 49ers' scoring chance.

The game was not over yet. Miraculously, the 49ers got another chance when they recovered an Eagle fumble on their 28-yard line. Less than a minute remained when Montana was knocked out of the game on a ferocious hit by linebacker Jerry Robinson. Backup quarterback Guy Benjamin replaced Montana. With 11 seconds to go, he threw a 17-yard touchdown pass to Dwight Clark, but it was negated due to a holding penalty. San Francisco had run out of time.

The 49ers turned things around, winning six of their next seven games. Their only loss was to Los Angeles, 10-7, at Candlestick. A home-field jinx began to haunt them. In addition to the home losses to Philadelphia and Los Angeles, they lost to the New York Jets and Miami Dolphins at Candlestick.

The 49ers ended the season on a Monday night at Candlestick against the Dallas Cowboys. It was their first appearance on Monday Night Football in five years. The 49ers entered the game with a 9-6 record. Dallas was 12-3. The last time the two teams had met was in the 1981 Championship Game.

San Francisco needed a win to clinch the NFC Western Division title. They got it by ripping the Cowboys, 42-17. There was bad news to go with the win, however. Star receiver Dwight Clark was lost for the playoffs with a torn knee ligament.

The Detroit Lions were the 49ers' opponent in the opening round of the NFC playoffs at Candlestick. San Francisco squeezed by the Lions, 24-23, when Eddie Murray missed a 43-yard field goal attempt with just seconds remaining. The next stop for San Francisco was RFK Stadium, where they would take on the 1982 Super Bowl Champion Washington Redskins for the NFC title.

The first half of the game proved to be a defensive battle. The only scoring came after Washington drove 64 yards and went ahead 7-0 on a four-yard run by John Riggins.

In the third quarter, Washington began to open things up. Joe Theismann directed the Redskins on a 36-yard touchdown drive. On their next possession, he threw a 70-yard scoring pass to Charlie Brown. At the end of the third quarter, Washington had a 21-0 lead.

Joe Montana likes exciting finishes. He earned the nickname "Comeback Kid" at Notre Dame for just that reason. He began another one against Washington by moving the 49ers 79 yards in nine plays. Early in the fourth quarter, he hit Mike Wilson with a five-yard pass to put San Francisco on the scoreboard, 21-7.

After Mark Mosley missed a 41-yard field goal attempt, San Francisco took over on its own 24-yard line. On the first play from scrimmage, Montana hit Freddie Solomon with a 76-yard pass to put San Francisco right back in the game at 21-14. There was still nearly 10 minutes to play.

Equipment manager Bronco Hinek applies shadow under the eyes of Wendell Tyler prior to the game.

After the ensuing kickoff, the 49ers held the Redskins and took over at their own 47-yard line. San Francisco again scored quickly. It took the offense just four plays to go 53 yards for a touchdown. Montana was the difference, hitting on passes of 16 yards to Eason Ramson, 22 yards to Mike Wilson and 12 yards to Wilson again for the score.

The 49ers had scored 21 points in seven minutes to tie the game. The momentum was clearly with them. Their biggest enemy now was the clock and, as it turned out, the officials.

There were seven minutes to play after Washington returned the ensuing kickoff to its own 14-yard line. The Redskins used John Riggins and a ball control offense to march down the field. The big plays, however, were two penalties called against the 49er secondary.

With four minutes to play, and the Redskins facing a second and 10, Eric Wright was called for pass interference on Art Monk. The call was questionable, since it did not appear that Monk could have caught the ball anyway. The penalty gave the Redskins a first down and a 27-yard gain.

Three plays later, the Redskins had a third-and-five situation from the 13-yard line. A pass to Alvin Garrett was incomplete. It would have given the Redskins no choice but to try a field goal on fourth down.

However, Ronnie Lott was called for holding on the play. He was covering a man away from the ball and not involved with the pass. Washington had another first down.

The Redskins used three plays to run the clock down to 40 seconds before Mosley attempted his fifth field goal of the day. He already had missed four attempts. This one, from 25 yards, was good.

The 49ers had 36 seconds left after the ensuing kickoff. A desperate pass by Joe Montana was intercepted and San Francisco's Super Bowl dreams were over.

1984 The 49ers put together the most successful single season in NFL history in 1984. They won 15 games in the regular season and three in post-season play. Their 18-1 record, including a Super Bowl victory, left little doubt around the league that they were the best team in football.

The 49ers started the year off right in the 1984 college draft. Of the nine players chosen, six made

138

Keith Fahnhorst 1974–1987

After spending 14 seasons in the grueling world of professional football, former San Francisco 49er All-Pro tackle Keith Fahnhorst sums up his successful career with one word of understatement—luck.

He doesn't stop to consider his enormous physical talent or the fact that he regularly pushed around barbarians on the defensive line each Sunday from September to January. None of that occurs to the overly modest Fahnhorst. It was plain old luck.

"I never really felt I was a natural athlete," said Fahnhorst, who announced his retirement after the 1987 season. "I worked hard and fortunately I stayed healthy. I always felt that as soon as the team

started losing, the 49ers would let me go."

The 49ers did lose, but Fahnhorst never left. He survived the dreadful 1970s, when the 49ers' annual highlight film could have been featured on television's "Bloopers and Blunders." And he was there in the 1980s, when the 49ers were resurrected from the NFL trash pile and became Super Bowl champions. From 1974, when the Minnesota graduate was drafted in the second round, until 1986, Fahnhorst played in all but five games. In 1987, the pounding finally caught up with him and he was sidelined with injuries.

Luck may have played a role in keeping Fahnhorst injury-free, but it didn't help him

develop into one of the most solid offensive linemen in the 49ers history. He acknowledges several men for the influence they had on his career. Monte Clark, the 49ers' head coach in 1976, was a natural teacher. Clark, a former offensive lineman, was a talented line coach who worked extensively with Fahnhorst on technique and mental preparation. But another man who influenced Fahnhorst's career rarely even talked to him. He was former 49er tight end Tom Mitchell.

"Mitch was one of those grizzly old vets," Fahnhorst said.

"He would sit in the locker room before the games, shot up with novocaine and chain smoking cigarettes. He

looked like he was sick, like he'd been up drinking all night or something. You'd never think he was going to get the job done. But then we'd get on the field and he was ready to go. All of a sudden he was tough as hell.

"I was a rookie when Mitchell was here in the mid-1970s and he never talked to rookies. He wouldn't even recognize your presence. It was like you weren't there. He felt that if you didn't have at least three or four years in the NFL, you had no clue what was going on out there on the field. I didn't appreciate that kind of thinking until later when I realized he was right. Lots of rookies come into the league thinking they know all they need to know about football. But they don't understand a thing about the NFL. You try to teach them, but they don't listen. I later realized it takes several years to find out what's really going on."

When Fahnhorst says it takes years to learn to play in the NFL, he means learning to deal with the awesome athletic talents of men like Claude Humphrey and Jack Youngblood. He claims the two former All-Pro defensive ends were the toughest men he played against in 14 years.

"I was younger when Humphrey was at Atlanta," Fahnhorst said. "But he was still a mean, ornery presence. He'd line up across from you and do a lot of talking about how he was going to kick your butt. Then he'd go out and do it. To top it off, on the way back to the huddle he'd step on you.

"Youngblood was a different type of player. I had a kind of a mental block about him because he was already a superstar when I came in. You'd go a whole game without getting a good lick on him because he was so active. I judged my whole season on how well I played against him."

Fahnhorst has a unique perspective from which to view the 49ers. When he joined the club in 1974, it was in a state of decline. Between 1974 and 1980, San Francisco had just one winning season, posting an 8-6 record in 1976 under Coach Monte Clark. The team changed coaches continually, going

through six men in five years. Then, in 1981, the 49ers shocked the NFL by winning their first Super Bowl.

"Things started to change for us when Eddie DeBartolo hired Bill (Walsh) as head coach," Fahnhorst said. "Everyone finally knew who was in charge. They weren't going to undermine him. He provided a lot of stability.

"Bill made some good moves in the draft, picking up Dwight Clark and Joe Montana. The 1981 draft was probably the big one, when we picked up Ronnie Lott, Carlton Williamson and Eric Wright. So it was a combination of a good administrative situation and good draft picks that helped mold the team into a winner.

"We set a tradition as a winner. Once you start believing in yourself and your ability to win, it continues to grow and you keep on winning. You look around the NFL and you'll see teams loaded with talent that can't win. Unless you're the last team standing at the end of the season, you're nothing."

Fahnhorst played on a club that was the last one standing on two different occasions— 1981 and 1984. He sees distinct differences in those two Super Bowl champions.

"The Super Bowl seasons were obviously the highlight of my career," Fahnhorst said. "Winning it in 1981 was probably more gratifying because no one expected us to win. The newness of winning was a great experience for us. We

had a lot of guys together that year who had gone through the losing seasons and suddenly we were on top.

"The 1984 team was different. It had the most talent of any 49er team I played on. We expected to win and we just dominated people that year. The other clubs were prepared for us, but we overwhelmed them with talent.

"The 1986 season was also satisfying for me even though we lost to New York in the playoffs. We had lots of injuries that season. Joe Montana was out with his back injury and everyone had given up on us. It's satisfying to win after everyone writes you off."

Besides being a rock on the 49ers offensive line for 14 seasons, Fahnhorst was also one of the club's most dependable people off the field, serving as the club's NFL player representative. During the 1987 players' strike Fahnhorst was a central figure in the players union's decision-making process.

"I'm glad I was a player rep," he said. "It was a good learning experience for me dealing with these political entities. Even though it was very frustrating at times, I liked it. I remember during the early days of the 1987 strike, I was pacing in the kitchen, sweat pouring off my face and I was on the phone to Washington. My wife looked at me and said, 'You really like these types of situations.' I guess I really did. There was a lot of

satisfaction in doing it. That high pressure situation is what I'm looking for to replace the emotional high of football."

Fahnhorst returned to his Minnesota home after retiring, to work with a brokerage firm. He also assists his attorney as a player's agent.

"During the season, it's tough not being on the field," he said. "But I don't feel my career was cut short or anything. I was lucky to have 14 years in the NFL."

The 49ers may have lost one of the most solid linemen in team history, but Fahnhorst doesn't think they will collapse without him.

"The 49ers have the talent to be good for many, many years," he said. "The thing that people don't realize is that you can't win the Super Bowl every year. There is a fine line between a team that goes to the Super Bowl and one that makes the playoffs. You need some luck along the way. As long as they have Joe (Montana) they will be there. On the other hand, I'd hate to see the 49ers become a team on the edge of winning every season and not do it. But I don't really see that happening."

the club. Among those who found a place on the roster were linebacker Todd Shell, tight end John Frank, guard Guy McIntyre, defensive tackle Michael Carter, linebacker/safety Jeff Fuller and running back Derrick Harmon.

San Francisco opened the season at Detroit. It was a good omen. When the 49ers went to the Super Bowl in 1981, they opened the season at Detroit as well. But the Lions were motivated this time. They had been knocked out of the 1983 Super Bowl hunt in the first round of the playoffs by the 49ers.

At the half, San Francisco held a 14-13 lead. The Lions went ahead, 20-14, in the third quarter on a two-yard pass from quarterback Gary Danielson to James Jones. San Francisco came back with two Ray Wersching field goals, and Wendell Tyler added a nine-yard run to even up the score at 27-27. With five minutes remaining, Joe Montana started a drive from his own 29-yard line. He worked the ball down to the Detroit 22, and Ray Wersching came on to kick the winning field goal with four seconds remaining.

In the second week of the season, San Francisco had a rematch with the Washington Redskins, runners-up in Super Bowl XVIII. It was the Redskins who prevented San Francisco from playing in the Super Bowl by beating the 49ers in the NFC Championship Game.

The 49ers started with a vengeance. They built up a 27-0 first-half lead before Joe Theismann could spell M-O-N-T-A-N-A. Tyler scored twice in the first quarter on runs of one and five yards. Clark caught a 15-yard touchdown pass from Montana. And Wersching added field goals of 19 and 46 yards.

In the second half the tide changed, but never enough to seriously put the game in doubt. The Redskins scored 14 unanswered points in the third quarter to bring them within 10 points at 27-17. But the 49ers coolly exchanged scores with Washington in the fourth period and walked away with a 37-31 victory.

Montana completed 24 passes for 381 yards, and Tyler gained 96 yards rushing against the Redskins.

The 49ers looked like they were in for an easy one in the third game of 1984, when they jumped out to a 17-0 lead against the New Orleans Saints. But then a snake got loose at Candlestick as Ken Stabler replaced Saints' starting quarterback Richard Todd in the second quarter. In one of his last

games, "the Snake" rallied New Orleans to four straight scores, putting the Saints in front, 20-17, at the start of the fourth period. He threw touchdown passes of eight and 26 yards, and connected on 14 passes for 157 yards. Just two weeks later, Stabler retired from football.

In the last period, San Francisco took over. Matt Cavanaugh replaced an injured Joe Montana and threw a 23-yard touchdown pass to Earl Cooper. Tyler picked up 82 yards rushing and the 49ers came out on top, 30-20.

The 49ers' next opponent was the Philadelphia Eagles. This was to be a test of the 49ers' offensive capability without Montana, who was still sidelined. Cavanaugh performed admirably, completing 17 of 34 passes for 252 yards and three touchdowns. Tyler gained 113 yards rushing as San Francisco defeated the Eagles, 21-9.

The 49ers beat Atlanta, 14-5, and the New York Giants, 31-10, before the Pittsburgh Steelers showed up at Candlestick to play football. The 49ers suffered their only defeat of the season against the Steelers, 20-17. Gary Anderson's 21-yard field goal with 1:42 to go proved to be the winning margin.

The 49ers got revenge on the Houston Oilers. They jumped off to a 10-0 lead after the first quarter on an 11-yard Montana pass to Russ Francis and a Wersching field goal. They upped the total to 17-7 at the half on a 26-yard pass from Montana to Tyler.

In all, San Francisco compiled 517 yards of offense as they defeated Houston, 34-21. Wendell Tyler had another 100-yard day, picking up 108 yards on 23 carries.

The highlight of a 35-year rivalry between the Rams and the 49ers was reached on October 28, when the 49ers destroyed Los Angeles, 33-0. Montana completed 21 of 31 passes for 365 yards and three touchdowns. Roger Craig caught a touchdown pass of 64 yards and ran in another from the six.

San Francisco continued its winning streak, rolling up big scores against Cleveland, 41-7, New Orleans, 35-3, and Minnesota, 51-7. The 49ers ended the season five games in front of the second place Rams. Their offense scored 475 points, the most as a member of the NFL, and an average of nearly 30 points a game. On defense, they gave up a league-low 227 points, an average of 14 points per game. In four games the defense didn't allow a touchdown.

The 49ers' first opponent in the NFC playoffs was the New York Giants. Once again the 49ers' defense prevented a critical touchdown as San Francisco beat the Giants, 21-10. New York's sole touchdown came on a 14-yard interception return by linebacker Harry Carson.

Montana completed 25 passes for 309 yards and three touchdowns. He also had three passes picked off by the Giants' tough defense. Dwight Clark was the receiving leader with nine catches for 112 yards and one touchdown.

The 49ers now had to prepare for the Chicago Bears, their opponent in the NFC Championship Game. It was the 49ers' third appearance in the championship game in four years.

The week of the game, Chicago's unconventional defense was the subject of the media's attention. Many predicted that the Bears' All-Pro pass rushers, Richard Dent and Dan Hampton, would chase Montana out of Candlestick Park.

The largest crowd in Candlestick history, a screaming throng of 61,050, jammed into the stadium. But it wasn't the Bears' defense that was overwhelming, it was the 49ers' pass rushers. The defense sacked Chicago quarterback Steve Fuller

nine times, intercepted one of his passes and allowed just 83 yards passing. Walter Payton, the NFL's all-time leading rusher, was held to a harmless 92 yards. The defense prevented a touchdown for the second week in a row, shutting out the Bears, 23-0.

The 49ers scored just six points in the first half on field goals of 21 and 22 yards. In the second half, Montana tossed a 10-yard scoring pass to Freddie Solomon, and Tyler ran nine yards for another touchdown to round out the 49ers' scoring.

The Miami Dolphins were all that stood in the way of the San Francisco 49ers' second Super Bowl championship. They were a formidable opponent. They finished the season with a 14-2 record. Quarterback Dan Marino seemed to set new passing records every time he stepped onto the field. The pre-game hype centered on Marino, who was said to be unstoppable. In the AFC Championship Game against the Pittsburgh Steelers, Marino completed 21 passes for 421 yards and four touchdowns. The Steelers, the only team to beat San Francisco in the regular season, were picking the Dolphins to win.

San Francisco had the unique advantage of playing the game in its backyard at nearby Stanford University. The overwhelming demand for tickets among 49er fans drove the price of 50-yard-line seats from scalpers above $1,000. A capacity crowd of 84,059 was on hand to witness the event.

The 49ers won the coin toss by President Ronald Reagan but were unable to move the ball on their first possession. Kicker Uwe Von Schamann started the scoring for the Dolphins when he split the uprights with a 37-yard field goal.

San Francisco took the kickoff and drove 78 yards. Montana completed all four of his passes for 50 yards, including a 33-yard touchdown pass to Carl Monroe that put San Francisco in front, 7-3.

When he regained the football, Marino showed millions of television viewers why he was considered the premier quarterback in the game. He completed all five of his pass attempts and the Dolphins scored in just six plays to go in front, 10-7. The pre-game hype appeared to be correct. Marino looked superb.

Then the 49ers scrapped their three-man defensive line and went to a nickel defense with four down linemen. The defensive line had a field day after that. Dwaine Board, Fred Dean and Gary "Big

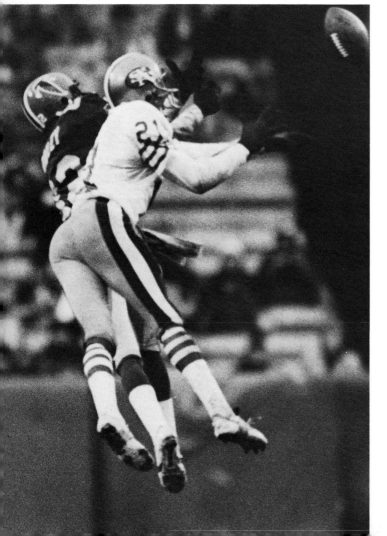

Eric Wright (21) was considered one of the best coverage men in football by head coach George Seifert. In 1983, he intercepted seven passes and returned them 164 yards. He was selected to play in his first Pro Bowl after the 1984 season.

Ronnie Lott 1981–1990

Pride has always been the ultimate motivator for Ronnie Lott. On the field, nothing is more insulting to the former 49er safety than getting beat on a long pass. To embarrass him is to infuriate him.

But the challenge of stopping the best receivers in football week after week is what makes Lott tick. He loves the competition.

"There is no way to describe the feeling of getting beat on a pattern," he said. "It makes you want to come off the field and hide. The only person that can understand that feeling is another defensive back."

Lott is everything you want in a football player. He is a hard-hitting team player who disregards individual awards in favor of collective success.

Despite Lott's absence in the 49ers' secondary since 1990, such teamwork is still evident. He instilled in his teammates the idea that working together often means the difference between success and failure. Lott always considered himself a member of a unit rather than an individual cornerback.

"We always had a lot of confidence in one another back there," he said. "One person can't do it by himself and we all knew that. You can't keep everybody from scoring, but still we always competed as best we could at all times. One of the things that made us good as a unit was that we tried to get the best out of each other whenever we were on the field."

In 1979 and 1980, the 49ers had the worst pass defense in football. There was more action in the foggy Candlestick air than over San Francisco International Airport. Opposing quarterbacks completed 66 percent of their passes against the 49ers, the highest in the NFL. The secondary gave up 29 scoring passes, a figure topped only by New Orleans with 30. And they allowed 3,958 yards through the sky. Only the Atlanta Falcons gave up more aerial yardage with 3,990.

The 49ers could see they had a problem so they rectified it by selecting defensive backs Lott, Eric Wright and Carlton Williamson with their first three picks in the 1981 college draft. With Dwight Hicks and three rookie starters in the defensive backfield, the 49ers drastically cut those numbers from the previous years. Dwight Hicks and the Hot Licks, as the secondary was called, allowed only 53 percent of the opposing teams' passes to be completed. They gave up just 16 touchdown passes and 3,135 total passing yards.

The drastic improvement in the defense is a reflection on the talented athletes in the secondary, but Lott thinks credit for the success should go to other people as well.

"In pre-season that first year, I remember someone saying it looked like a three-ring circus back there," Lott said. "We were having a tough time because we knew that everyone was watching us. We were concentrating too hard, trying to make the transition to the pros. It was like being under a microscope. George Seifert, the 49ers' secondary coach at the time, took us aside and told us to just relax and have fun. That helped a lot. He wanted us to play hard but have a good time while we were doing it."

The three rookies were looking for an on-field mentor when they reported to the team in 1981, and they got it when the 49ers acquired linebacker Jack Reynolds from the Los Angeles Rams. He instilled a winner's attitude into the entire defense.

"One of the things that turned the team around was the addition of Hacksaw," Lott said. "He knew defense and showed us the little things that made us successful.

"The overall chemistry of that team was good. Everyone started to believe that we could win. There were a lot of fresh people that year who didn't know about the 49ers' past and didn't want to know.

"Bill Walsh was the biggest factor. He was the mainstay of the organization. I'd compare him to Lee Iaccoca. Here's a guy that took over an organization that was down, turned it completely around and made it into a winner."

The turning point for the 49ers in 1981 was a game against the Dallas Cowboys in the sixth week of the season. Lott intercepted two passes, including one he returned 41 yards for a touchdown. The 49ers came away with a 45-14 win and a 4-2 record. More importantly, the victory gave the team confidence in its ability and proved the 49ers were a competitive team.

"That was a big game for me because I had a lot of admiration for some people on the Dallas team," said Lott. "Not admiration for the team, just some of the players on the team. I was able to pick off a couple of passes and make some tackles. When you play against people you admire, you want to play well against them.

"Whenever I go out on the field, I know there are a lot of people out there watching. I know my family, the fans and people I care about are watching me and counting on me to play up to their expectations. If I can play up to their expectations, that's what makes it all worthwhile."

Nagging injuries caused by his ferocious style of play have hampered Lott at various times in his career. Rarely have injuries kept him out of the lineup. But in 1984 a twisted ankle caused a position change for Lott. At various times Lott has played strong safety, free safety and cornerback. This time, he switched positions with free safety Dwight Hicks. Lott says he has no preference between safety and cornerback but hints that the one-on-one challenge of the cornerback position is something he enjoys.

"I prefer playing wherever they put me," he said. "Right now it's at safety so I prefer safety."

And when he was at the corner, his biggest challenge was always Green Bay Packer receiver James Lofton.

"He is such a gifted athlete," said Lott. "He's got good speed and moves, I have to think that was helped by being coached by Bill Walsh at Stanford.

"At this rank everyone is tough though. Every team gives us some type of problem. One week you think you can relax and the next week you find a receiver that is outstanding."

Lott was a perennial Pro Bowl selection during his 10 years with the 49ers. But personal awards mean very little to him. He says his biggest thrill as a player is contributing to a winning team.

"When I retire, I'll be able to look back and say I played with a great bunch of guys," he said, "that I was able to enjoy the game and that I played well with some of the best players around.

"What makes football a thrill for me is that I meet such great people. When people stop me on the street and tell me they enjoy the 49ers, that gives me a big thrill. It's exciting to know that people enjoy watching us play and really care how we do. I know that these people are counting on us to perform our best. The only thing that I can promise them is we're going to play our butts off."

Hands" Johnson were on top of Marino the rest of the afternoon. He was sacked four times, threw two interceptions and hurried countless passes. Miami didn't score another touchdown.

Meanwhile, Roger Craig was busy crossing the goal line three times as the 49ers routed Miami, 38-16. He scored on an eight-yard pass from Montana, a 16-yard pass and a two-yard run. Craig caught eight passes in all for 82 yards.

Montana was putting on quite a show himself and was named the game's most valuable player. He set Super Bowl records for passing, with 331 yards on 24 completions, and rushing by a quarterback, with 59 yards. It marked the second time he had been honored as the Super Bowl MVP, a distinction held by only two other players, Green Bay's Bart Starr and Pittsburgh's Terry Bradshaw. Bradshaw led the Steelers to four Super Bowl victories. Montana was on this way to doing the same.

1985 The 49ers opened training camp in 1985 with another Super Bowl victory under their belt. The nucleus of the team was virtually unchanged except for a rookie wide receiver named Jerry Rice, the club's first-round draft pick from Mississippi Valley State. Coach Bill Walsh picked Rice in the first round after trading a first- and second-round pick to New England to move up in the draft.

San Francisco opened the season at the Metrodome against the Minnesota Vikings. The Minneapolis crowd was emotionally charged because head coach Bud Grant was returning to the sideline after a year away from the game. The emotion seemed to get to the 49ers. They looked nothing like the Super Bowl squad of a year earlier. They fumbled seven times, losing five of them, as the Vikes beat San Francisco, 28-21.

Running back Roger Craig got the 49ers on the board first, scoring on a 10-yard run just two minutes into the first quarter. The touchdown was made possible when Viking quarterback Tommy Kramer fumbled a snap from center. From there, it took San Francisco just two plays to go 24 yards. Roger Craig picked up all the necessary yardage on

a 14-yard pass from Montana and a 10-yard run.

The rest of the first half was nothing more than a punting duel, as neither team mounted any offensive threat. At the end of the half, San Francisco held a slim 7-0 lead.

The second half was a study in frustration for the 49ers. They began by driving 59 yards on 10 plays only to have wide receiver Freddie Solomon fumble the ball away on the eight-yard line. It was an omen of the bad things to come.

Minnesota took over and drove 78 yards in seven plays to tie the score. San Francisco responded with its own 70-yard scoring march. Craig ended the drive by catching an 18-yard touchdown pass from Montana.

On the ensuing possession, Minnesota tied the score again when receiver Mike Jones burned cornerback Ronnie Lott for a 44-yard score. The wheels seemed to fall off the 49ers' wagon at that point.

After Craig put the 49ers in front again, 21-14, on a 19-yard scoring pass, the rest of the game began to look to the 49ers like a "Nightmare on Elm Street."

Super Bowl XIX put Roger Craig (33) into the national spotlight when he set a Super Bowl record with three touchdowns. He led the team in receptions in 1984 with 71 catches good for 675 yards. He also gained 649 yards rushing.

Running back Wendell Tyler fumbled on the 49ers' next possession and the ball was returned to the one-yard line. Minnesota scored on the next play to tie the game, 21-21. On the ensuing kickoff, Ronnie Harmon fumbled and it was recovered by Joey Browner, his third fumble recovery of the day. The Vikings took over at the 34 and needed just three plays to go in front, 28-21.

The 49ers had one last chance with 1:30 left in the game, but their offense looked as effective as a Pop Warner team without a coach. Montana fumbled the snap from center Fred Quillan on the second play of the drive, then tight end Earl Cooper dropped two consecutive passes, and tackle Keith Fahnhorst was called for a false start. Finally, receiver Dwight Clark was called for offensive pass interference, ending any hope for a 49er win.

After the game Walsh said, "We have to go back to the dark ages, maybe as far back as 1980, to find a game where we played this poorly. We have 15 games left and we'll just have to deal with it."

Despite the loss, there were some good signs. The backfield looked particularly solid. Tyler gained 125 yards on the ground and Craig added 78. Montana was 24 of 39 for 265 yards.

San Francisco got untracked the next week by beating the Atlanta Falcons in the home opener, 35-16, and following up with a win over the Los Angeles Raiders, 34-10, before running into a buzzsaw in the form of the New Orleans Saints. In that game, New Orleans quarterback Dave Wilson, working behind a patched-up line, threw a 44-yard touchdown pass to Eugene Goodlow early in the fourth quarter to give the Saints the win.

The New Orleans defense sacked Montana six times and intercepted him twice as the Super Bowl MVP completed just 12 of 26 passes for 119 yards. In addition, the 49ers were plagued by fumbles again. Tyler lost his fourth fumble of the young season, giving New Orleans good field position in the second period, which led to a touchdown.

San Francisco had its first big test of the year two weeks later with the Chicago Bears. The game tested the patience of Coach Bill Walsh. San Francisco had 13 penalties and two fumbles as Chicago humbled the 49ers, 26-10. The loss prompted Walsh to say, "We have to be considered a very average football team that is not playing well, and it's our job to do something about it."

Several milestones were set in this game. The 49ers gained just 183 yards on offense, the fewest ever by a Walsh team and failed to score a touchdown on offense for the first time under Walsh. Montana was also sacked a career-high seven times.

Despite the loss, the low point of the season was still a week away when San Francisco fell to the Detroit Lions 23-21. With a 3-4 record, San Francisco's playoff chances looked dimmer than a 60-watt light bulb. The 49ers were four games behind the undefeated, division-leading Los Angeles Rams and were traveling to Anaheim for a showdown.

Joe Montana has always fared well at Anaheim Stadium, and this game proved to be no different. San Francisco ripped the NFL's number two ranked defense, scoring four first-half touchdowns en route to a 28-14 win. Montana quieted the critics who said he had lost his edge by completing 22 of 30 passes for

Wide receiver Freddie Solomon spent eight years with the 49ers, catching 310 passes. He also filled in as a quarterback and kick returner.

Joe Montana 1979–1992

It's probably safe to say that Joe Montana means more to the people of Northern California than any politician, religious leader or fancy San Francisco landmark. He is an icon; a symbol of hope, victory and leadership. He's the patron saint of lost causes.

Montana's importance to the Bay Area is simple. He made the 49ers a winner and by proxy gave Northern Californians a sense of pride. With Montana at the helm, the 49ers won respect around the league and the citizens rallied around his leadership. They could finally walk with the winners. San Francisco was no longer a second-rate sports town and it was all because of Montana. He will always

be viewed as a savior.

Before Montana's appearance, San Francisco never had a winner it could call its own. Not a single major league sports franchise from San Francisco had ever won a championship.

The 49ers were the worst of the local sports franchises. When Montana reported to the 49ers as a third-round draft pick in 1979, the club was stinking up Candlestick Park on a weekly basis and setting new lows for ineptitude. Every Sunday was a laugh riot and the 49ers were the top comedians. Rookie Coach Bill Walsh anticipated Montana would be little more than a backup in his early years and fan expectations were no higher.

Followers of the 49ers

had developed thick skins after watching three decades of football at Kezar Stadium and Candlestick Park. It was this healthy skepticism that enabled fans to survive when the 49ers inevitably choked in the clutch, as they had done so many times in the past. There was no reason for them to suspect Montana would make life any different.

But Coach Walsh had plans for the former Notre Dame signal caller. He brought Montana along slowly and stroked his ego. In his second year with the club, Montana started seven games. He showed his magnificent gifts in two of them. Early in the season, he entered a game against the New York Jets as a substitute for Steve DeBerg and completed four of six passes for two touchdowns. He also ran for a score as he guided the club to a 37-27 victory.

Montana flashed his magic again later in 1980 when he helped the 49ers pull off the biggest comeback in NFL regular season history. Montana threw for 285 yards and two touchdowns as he led the 49ers from a 35-7 halftime deficit to a 38-35 overtime victory over the New Orleans Saints. With Montana's help, the 49ers improved their record to 6-10.

The Candlestick crowd began to sit up and take notice. Something special was happening. In 1981 they saw it evolve before their very eyes. It started slowly and began to build, like a snowball careening down a mountainside.

Montana was firmly entrenched as the starting quarterback in 1981 and he guided the club to an early 4-1 record. Then the 49ers met their first big test, a showdown with America's Team, the Dallas Cowboys. Montana was brilliant, passing for 279 yards and two touchdowns as San Francisco destroyed the Cowboys 45-14. The skepticism began to turn to optimism.

The 49ers finished the 1981 season 13-3 and won a spot in the playoffs for the first time in nine years, and it took one shining moment to change that optimism to euphoria. It happened when the 49ers met Dallas in the 1981 NFC Championship Game. In

an electrifying instant, Montana set the 49ers free from a 36-year jinx when he connected with Dwight Clark on a touchdown pass that shot the 49ers into their first Super Bowl. The play transformed a legion of San Francisco cynics into believers. They worshipped a miracle-worker named Joe Montana.

Longtime 49er fans descended on Pontiac, Michigan for Super Bowl XVI keenly aware that their team would win the big one as long as this kid named Montana was around. He gave San Franciscans more than hope. For the first time in the history of the franchise, they had confidence.

Montana didn't let them down. He did what everyone expected he would do. He led the 49ers to victory, won MVP honors and gave San Francisco its first championship. As the final seconds ticked away at Super Bowl XVI, grown men stood on their end zone seats with tears streaming down their cheeks. They were tears of joy and tears of pride.

That was just the beginning. As the years wore on, new players came and went but Montana was always there. Like a real-life Superman, Montana was invariably around to save the day when the situation looked bleak and hopeless. Montana was the guy who made the big play when it had to be made. He was the man who would engineer a comeback when it seemed impossible. The

fans believed in him, the players believed in him and the coaches believed in him. On 26 occasions over 13 seasons he led his team from fourth quarter deficits to victory.

Montana brought four Super Bowl trophies to San Francisco, but it was more than just victories that made 49er fans so proud to have him on their side. It was the way he went about his work. Hemingway called it "grace under pressure." Where others saw chaos, Montana saw order. When the passing pocket broke down, receivers were covered and mammoth defensive linemen were breathing down his neck, Montana calmly searched for his second, third or fourth receiver. He usually found one without breaking a sweat.

Even more impressive than his cool under pressure was the style and humility Montana brought to his victories. There was no taunting or showboating from Joe Montana. He won with class and dignity.

During his 13 years with San Francisco, Montana compiled a 100-39 record as the starting quarterback. Twice he was the league's Most Valuable Player, and he has the highest career quarterback rating of all time. But the ultimate test of any player is his performance in the big games, and in that regard, Montana has no peer. In four Super Bowl games, he threw 11 touchdown passes and not a single interception. He completed 68 percent of his

passes. On three occasions he was named Super Bowl MVP. He holds numerous Super Bowl passing records. And the 49ers won all four games.

Montana's career is over now, but the memories will always linger. He's a legend, a certain Hall of Famer. San Francisco 49er fans were lucky to have him on their side for 13 years. They will never see anybody like him again.

306 yards and three touchdowns. Roger Craig had one of his best days of the season, grabbing six passes for 132 yards and rushing for another 63. Meanwhile, the defense shut down the Rams' star running back Eric Dickerson, holding him to just 61 yards on 12 attempts and forcing three interceptions by quarterback Dieter Brock.

The victory over Los Angeles sparked the 49ers and they went on to win five of their next seven games. They did it in part without Montana, who suffered a shoulder injury against the Rams. Backup quarterback Matt Cavanaugh filled in against his former teammates, the Philadelphia Eagles, and led the 49ers to a 24-13 win.

Montana returned to play in time to see action against the Rams again in the 13th week of the season. San Francisco entered the game with an 8-5 record, one game behind the Rams at 9-4. A victory over the Rams would put the 49ers in the driver's seat for at least a wild card berth in the playoffs.

Instead, the 49ers did their best Santa Claus impression, handing Los Angeles one gift after another and losing, 27-20. Among them was a fourth-quarter touchdown pass that could have been intercepted by either Ronnie Lott or Dwight Hicks. They bumped into each other and the ball fell into Rams receiver Henry Ellard's hands for a touchdown. There was also a holding penalty by tight end John Frank that nullified a 42-yard field goal by Ray Wersching, a blocked PAT by the Rams, an 86-yard kickoff return by Rams speedster Ron Brown, and two interceptions from Joe Montana, one of which was returned for a touchdown.

On the positive side, Jerry Rice showed why he was a first-round pick, catching 10 passes for a team record 241 yards. Montana completed 26 of 36 passes for 328 yards.

With two games left on the schedule, San Francisco needed a pair of victories to clinch a wild card playoff spot and that's just what it got. The 49ers demolished the New Orleans Saints, 31-19, then met the Dallas Cowboys on the final day of the season. Dallas had already clinched a division title, so the 49ers were installed as nine-point favorites in the game. They routed the Cowboys, 31-16, earning a wild card spot and a chance to face the New York Giants in the playoffs at Meadowlands.

The Dallas game marked the end of Freddie Solomon's playing days at Candlestick Park, and he went out in style. Coach Walsh sent Solomon in at quarterback for the last play of the game, a position

Solomon had played in college and on several occasions for San Francisco. Despite loud cheers from the fans for him to run with the ball, Solomon took the snap and cradled the ball to end the game.

Roger Craig made football history in 1985 by becoming the first player ever to gain 1,000 yards rushing and 1,000 yards receiving. But the brutal physical pounding that he suffered during the season became obvious during the playoffs.

San Francisco went into the Giants game beat up and run down. Wendell Tyler vowed to play despite having undergone arthroscopic knee surgery two weeks earlier. Roger Craig, weary from the poundings he took as the club's leading receiver and rusher, played with one hyperextended knee, then injured the other during the playoff game. Joe Montana needed six pain-killing shots for his sore ribs. Ronnie Lott took the field with a cast on his fractured left hand. Michael Walter played despite a dislocated thumb. And All-Pro nose tackle Michael Carter hobbled on and off the field with a sprained ankle.

On the sideline, the 49ers looked more like a MASH unit than a football team. New York scored on its first possession of the day, a 47-yard field goal, and coasted to a 17-3 win. The only bright spot for San Francisco was Dwight Clark who caught eight passes for 120 yards.

Injuries had clearly gotten to San Francisco during the 1985 season. Bill Walsh summed up the status of his club after the New York game, saying, "Even if we got by the Giants, I don't know who I would have suited up next week."

1986

There were a number of changes in the 49er roster before the 1986 season began. Running back Joe Cribbs was obtained from the Buffalo Bills for a future draft choice, Jeff Kemp replaced Matt Cavanaugh as Joe Montana's backup, and All-Pro defensive end Fred Dean retired after six productive seasons as a 49er.

San Francisco had an outstanding draft, picking up Larry Roberts in the second round, Tom Rathman, Tim McKyer and John Taylor in the third, Charles Haley, Kevin Fagan and Steve Wallace in the fourth and Don Griffin in the sixth. Griffin and McKyer found an immediate home in the starting defensive backfield, while Haley and Roberts played important parts in the 49er defensive scheme.

In the opening game, San Francisco took on

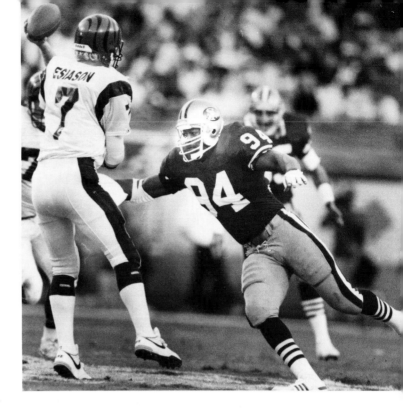

Charles Haley puts pressure on the Bengals' Boomer Esiason.

Tampa Bay, led by Steve DeBerg, a former 49er quarterback. DeBerg was treated rudely by his former teammates. He was intercepted seven times as the 49ers stomped the Bucs, 31-7. The seven interceptions set a 49er club record and provided some relief for Coach Walsh who was concerned about starting two rookies at the corners.

On the other side of the line was Joe Montana. Montana had missed three exhibition games because of various injuries, but they didn't show as he picked apart the Tampa Bay defense, completing 32 of 46 for 356 yards. Later in the week, however, it was revealed that Montana had suffered a herniated disk and would need surgery to repair it. Walsh speculated that his star quarterback would be out for the season and that his playing days could be over. Dr. Robert Gamburd said Montana would never play again without the surgery. He also ruled out the possibility of Montana returning during the 1986 season. With Montana in the hospital, the starting job was handed to Jeff Kemp. His first assignment was against the division rival Los Angeles Rams.

San Francisco lost to Los Angeles 16-13 when the Rams marched 92 yards in the fourth quarter. Mike Lansford kicked the winning field goal with two seconds remaining. In his first start, Kemp played admirably, completing 19 of 24 for 252 yards. He had two passes intercepted.

Kemp settled into the quarterback slot the next week, beating New Orleans 26-17, and guiding the 49ers to three consecutive wins. The streak ended when Minnesota defeated San Francisco in overtime, 27-24. It was a frustrating loss for the 49ers. Kicker Ray Wersching had a chance to win the game as time expired, but hooked the 36-yard field goal attempt and hit the upright.

Poor special team's play was a major reason for the 49ers' loss. Max Runager had a punt blocked and Issac Holt recovered it in the end zone for a touchdown. But what made the outcome tougher to digest was how easily quarterback Tommy Kramer was able to engineer a 58-yard, 10-play drive in overtime to set up Chuck Nelson's game-winning 26-yard field goal.

Montana's replacement, Jeff Kemp, played well, throwing for 358 yards and three touchdowns. Wendell Tyler, injured since training camp, was reactivated for the game, but he was unable to liven up the 49ers' anemic running game.

The loss at Minnesota was followed by a 10-10 tie against the Atlanta Falcons in one of the most boring football games in recent memory. It also marked a time when the 49ers went through a puzzling period of inconsistency. Injuries contributed to the slump. Jeff Kemp was injured during the Atlanta game and replaced by Mike Moroski the following week at Green Bay. In that game, the 49ers dropped behind early at 14-0, but Moroski rallied the club with the help of some fine defensive play by the Niners. Moroski ended the day 17 of 29 for 147 yards and scored one touchdown on a quarterback sneak. Meanwhile, Ronnie Lott and Tory Nixon combined for three interceptions for 161 yards in returns. Each defender returned one for a touchdown, as San Francisco beat Green Bay, 31-17.

Moroski didn't have as much luck the following week at New Orleans. Among the players out of uniform due to injuries were Montana, Lott, Kemp, Wright and Paris. In addition, Michael Carter went down early in the first quarter with an ankle sprain and spent the entire afternoon on crutches. Once again the 49ers fell behind in the first quarter 14-3, but against the Saints swarming defense they couldn't rebound. Injuries completely decimated the 49ers' running game, despite the presence of the reactivated Wendell Tyler. Tyler gained 18 yards on three carries, but lost a crucial fumble on the Saints 20-yard line. Craig, playing with a bad hip and severe knee bruises, gained just nine yards on the ground and Cribbs ran for eight. Moroski was forced to throw the ball often and completed 23 passes for 332 yards. Two of his passes were intercepted. New Orleans won the game handily, 23-10.

After the disaster at New Orleans, San Francisco needed a spiritual lift and got it in the form of Joe Montana. Montana defied the doctors and critics who said he would never play again by announcing he was ready to play in the upcoming game against the St. Louis Cardinals. Just seven weeks earlier he had disk surgery, which threatened to end his career.

Montana's return sparked the 49ers to a 43-17 win. Except for a second-quarter interception, Montana was nearly flawless. He displayed his usual poise and completed 13 of 19 passes for 270 yards and three touchdowns. Halfback Joe Cribbs had his best game as a 49er, gaining 105 yards on 21 carries. And Jerry Rice caught four Montana passes for 156 yards.

The victory gave the 49ers the lift they needed to jump back into the playoff race. Still on the horizon were games with the Washington Redskins and the New York Giants.

Against Washington, Montana completed 33 of 60 passes for 441 yards but suffered three interceptions. Jerry Rice caught a dozen passes. And the defense played inspired football. Still, it wasn't enough. Washington defeated the 49ers 14-6, but San Francisco was still only a half game behind the Los Angeles Rams, with five games left to play.

San Francisco put together its most complete game of the season against Atlanta a week later, winning 20-0. Craig had 101 yards rushing, his season high. Meanwhile, the defensive line sacked Turk Schonert eight times, with rookie Charles Haley getting three.

The 49ers playoff chances took a nosedive when the New York Giants came from behind to beat San Francisco on a Monday Night Football game at Candlestick, 21-17.

San Francisco took a 17-0 lead into the locker room at halftime, then watched as New York quarterback Phil Simms came out throwing. He connected on two long touchdown passes early in the third quarter as New York rallied for three touchdowns in the third quarter.

San Francisco played steady football the rest of the regular season. They beat the New York Jets 24-10 and the New England Patriots 29-24. They also received help from the Miami Dolphins, who beat the Los Angeles Rams to set up a showdown for the NFC West title on the final day of the season.

Montana wasted no time against Los Angeles. He threw early and often, leading the 49ers to a 24-14 win over the Rams at Candlestick. It was easily the best game played by the 49ers all season. Montana connected on short passes and a long 44-yard scoring strike to Jerry Rice that allowed the 49ers to clinch the Western Division title and set up a rematch with the New York Giants in the playoffs.

The rematch quickly turned into one of the ugliest games in 49er history. New York scored first, but San Francisco was driving midway through the first quarter when Montana hit Jerry Rice over the middle with a 20-yard pass. Rice had clear sailing to the end zone and raced past the last New York defender when he suddenly dropped the ball. New York recovered the fumble, wiping out a sure 49er touchdown. The game rapidly went downhill from there. Montana took a vicious hit from nose tackle Jim Burt and had to leave the game and the team fell apart as the Giants destroyed San Francisco 49-3.

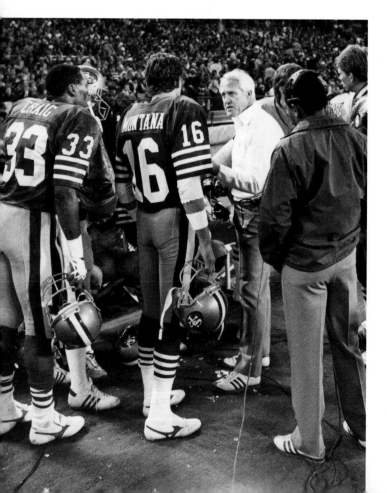

Bill Walsh goes over offensive strategy with quarterback Joe Montana and running back Roger Craig. Walsh retired after Super Bowl XXIII as the winningest coach in 49er history. He led the team to a 102-62-1 record and three Super Bowl titles.

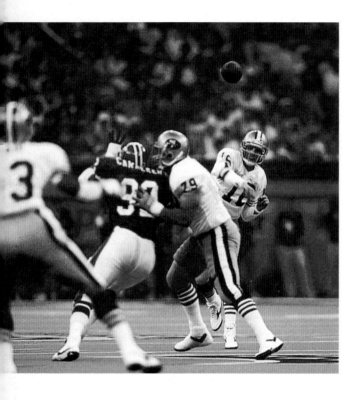

PRECEDING SPREAD: Matt Cavanaugh drops back to pass while his offensive linemen search for someone to hit. ABOVE, TOP: Ray Wersching (14) kicks off. Wersching retired in 1987 as the 49ers all-time scoring leader. ABOVE: Joe Montana throws a pass to Roger Craig while tackle Harris Barton lends a hand. BOTTOM: Kicker Mike Cofer put this kick through the uprights at Super Bowl XXIII. OPPOSITE: Roger Craig goes over the top for a touchdown against Atlanta.

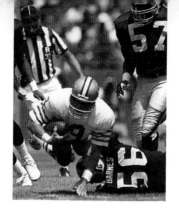

PRECEDING SPREAD
Joe Montana turns to hand
off to Roger Craig during a
game against the Atlanta
Falcons. RIGHT: Joe Mon-
tana calls a play in the
49er huddle. DIRECTLY
ABOVE: Eddie DeBartolo
and George Seifert pre-
pare to receive the Vince
Lombardi trophy for win-
ning Super Bowl XXIV.

OPPOSITE PAGE, CLOCK-
WISE FROM TOP, LEFT:
Steve Young drops back to
pass, while Randy Cross
awaits the oncoming Car-
dinal linemen. TOP, MID-
DLE: Jeff Kemp dives for
extra yardage against the
Los Angeles Raiders. TOP,
RIGHT: Dwight Clark con-
gratulates John Frank after
a touchdown during the
1985 season. MIDDLE,
RIGHT: Offensive linemen
Fred Quillan and John
Ayers block against New
Orleans. BOTTOM,
RIGHT: Head coach
George Seifert took over
for Bill Walsh in 1989 and
led the 49ers to a Super
Bowl title in his first sea-
son. Seifert is a native San
Franciscan who attended
Poly High School.

RIGHT: Roger Craig high-
steps downfield in an effort
to break a tackle. BELOW:
Bill Walsh and Joe Mon-
tana consult during Super
Bowl XXXIII. FOLLOWING
PAGE: Jerry Rice goes
high to make a reception
against the Los Angeles
Raiders.

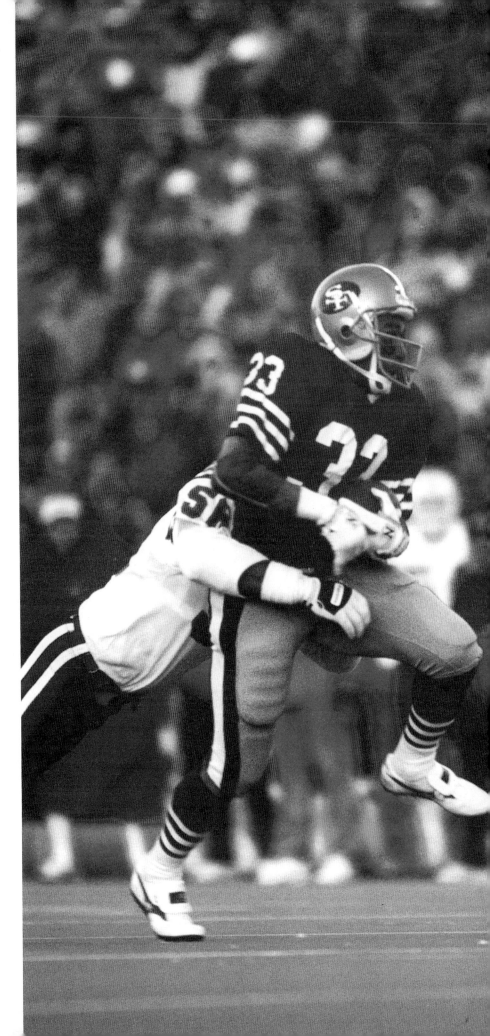

Bubba Paris 1982–1990

For seven years, William "Bubba" Paris was the most important man on the 49ers' offensive line. It wasn't because he was the biggest man on the field or because San Francisco ran behind him in short yardage situations. As the left tackle, Paris was the 49ers' version of a Secret Service agent. It was his job to sacrifice his body and ensure the safety of the team's leader.

The 49ers' field commander during the 1980s was more valuable than the Hope diamond. Quarterback Joe Montana has been acknowledged as the greatest quarterback in NFL history. If Paris missed a pass block from his left tackle position, it would be magnified 100 times because Montana would be flattened from the blind side. He would never know what hit him.

Paris understood the role he played in keeping Montana healthy. And when Montana was healthy, so was the 49er offense.

Paris joined the 49ers in 1982 after being drafted in the second round. As an undergraduate at the University of Michigan, Paris was an overpowering, straight-ahead blocker in the Wolverine's running attack. When he moved to San Francisco he got a quick lesson in pass-blocking skills.

At 6'6" and 300 pounds, Paris had been a machine who man-handled defensive linemen with his straight-ahead, run-blocking technique. Pass blocking was a different story. The pass was not stressed in the Bo

Schembechler system of football. At Michigan, Paris was more likely to spot Halley's Comet than a forward pass.

With the 49ers his role was much different. The pass has always been one of San Francisco's most effective weapons. Paris had to work on his pass-blocking technique from the start. Still, contributing to an efficient running game gave him great satisfaction.

"I've had a history of being able to play with great backs and San Francisco was no exception," he said. "Roger Craig was one of the greats in the game. He gave 150 percent on every play. I know if I gave him an avenue, he'd just take off.

"Wendell (Tyler) was just naturally blessed. He was an outstanding back, too. He might not have had to work as hard as Roger to produce, but he sure got results.

"Joe (Montana) could make you look good. If you gave him an inch, he'd take five miles. If you missed a block, he could still dodge tacklers and make the play."

The improvement in Paris' pass-blocking ability was evident in the 1984 NFC Championship Game when he faced Chicago's Richard Dent. Dent led the NFC with 17.5 quarterback sacks during the regular season. Against Paris, Dent made only four tackles and had no sacks.

"We were truly tested in that Chicago game," Paris said candidly. "Going into the game, there was a lot of talk about their defense. I didn't know if we could stop them. I knew it was up to me to stop Dent. It turned out I did, and the team played well, and we won.

"As a team, the Chicago Bears had about the toughest defense I faced," he said. "I knew whenever we played them, I had to really buckle on my chin strap. They had a good defensive scheme and some big hitters. Whenever we played them, they wanted to show us that they should have been the ones in the 1984 Super Bowl."

Paris got off to a rocky start with the 49ers. In the last preseason game of his rookie year, he injured a knee and was out for the season. Paris came back to play all 16 regular season games in 1983, as well as the playoffs. He had a string of 28 consecutive starts until a bruised knee forced him to miss a game against Cleveland in 1984.

The injury that sidelined Paris for his rookie season had a profound effect on him. He thought his professional career was over before it even began.

"I would prepare myself mentally as well as I could," Paris said. "I know as long as my body functioned, my mind would take care of the rest. As long as I was close to God I felt I could perform on the field. When I received that injury my rookie season, I thought I'd never get another chance to perform. I thought it was over."

Paris is a deeply religious man who claims he found time to do some preaching while on the field.

"One of my goals was to expand my witness on the field," he said. "I talked to people on the line about letting God into their life. I had 20 games in which to witness each year. I had nobody particular that I singled out, but that was one of my goals for the season—to expand my witness."

And what was the reaction of brutes like Richard Dent and Lyle Alzado to Paris' sermons?

"Some people were shocked," he said. "They don't expect that on the line of scrimmage. Some people got irritated and hit you. Others ignored you altogether. But once in a while someone would say, 'Yeah, maybe you're right.'"

The first year he was in the league, Paris heard rumors about Tampa Bay's Lee Roy Selmon. He was miffed when his fellow linemen voted Selmon to the Pro Bowl. The 49ers had not even played Tampa Bay that year. After facing Selmon for the first time in the 1983 season, Paris was convinced.

"There's no doubt that Lee Roy Selmon is the best I ever played against," he said. "In practice, I played against Fred Dean, who was probably in the same league, but I've never had to go against Fred in a game. Lee Roy was big, quick and strong. He had a good arm-over. I would vote for him to be All-World."

In the 1984 Super Bowl season, a game against the Pittsburgh Steelers, which the 49ers lost 20-17, was the turning point for Paris.

"It was probably good for us," he said. "After that, we knew we couldn't just show up at the stadium and walk away winners. We knew we had to pull together. It put us all back on earth."

Paris gives thanks for the natural ability with which he was born.

"So far in my life and my football career I've been blessed," he said. "First of all, there is my size. I'm bigger than people say I should be. I'm an example of what God can do with life. I was able to come back from an injury after I thought I'd never play again. On top of that, I came to a Super Bowl team right out of college. You can't ask for much more than that."

1987 Offensive linemen were the 49ers' priority in the preseason draft and they got a pair of good ones in first-round pick Harris Barton from North Carolina and second-round choice Jeff Bregel of USC. They also selected running back Terrence Flagler with their other first-round pick. Barton and Bregel were expected to replace aging linemen John Ayers and Keith Fahnhorst.

San Francisco started off the season with four consecutive road games. The first was at Pittsburgh, where poor defensive play and offensive mistakes combined to doom the 49ers.

The Steelers built a 14-0 lead behind much-maligned quarterback Mark Malone. Malone completed just 9 of 33 for the day, but he connected when he had to, including two touchdown passes.

The 49ers were unable to establish any running game. Craig gained just 16 yards on 10 carries and Montana was forced to throw often. He completed 34 of 49 passes for 316 yards, but had three interceptions as Pittsburgh sent San Francisco down to defeat, 30-17.

The 49ers were still looking for their first regular season win when they experienced a minor miracle at Cincinnati. The Bengals completely dominated the 49ers in the first half, staking a 20-7 halftime lead behind the accurate arm of Boomer Esiason. San Francisco bounced back in the second half when Montana connected on a 34-yard scoring toss to Jerry Rice. Wersching added two field goals and after three quarters the game was tied, 20-20.

In the fourth quarter the game turned into a nightmare for Cincinnati coach Sam Wyche, a former assistant to Bill Walsh with the 49ers. The Bengals had posted a 26-20 lead late in the game and had the ball with less than one minute to play at their own 25 yard-line. San Francisco stopped the Bengals in three plays, bringing on a punting situation. Instead, on fourth down, Wyche had his quarterback fall on the ball in hopes of running out the clock. The 49ers were able to get on the field and run one more play before time expired and Montana used that time to hit Jerry Rice in the end zone as the clock ran out, beating the Bengals 27-26.

After the Bengals game, the NFL Players Association went on strike. Most of the 49er veterans walked out of camp and San Francisco was

forced to line up the next week against the New York Giants with names like Gagliano, Varajon and Cherry in the starting backfield. They were enough to beat the Giants, 41-21.

The 49ers finished out the strike games with wins over the Atlanta Falcons and St. Louis Cardinals. With the strike settled, New Orleans was next on the schedule.

Saints running back Ruben Mayes gained 144 yards rushing and Morton Andersen kicked five field goals to beat the 49ers almost single-handedly. A last minute field goal try by Andersen missed preserving a 24-22 San Francisco win.

San Francisco traveled to Anaheim next, where quarterback Joe Montana seems to live in his own fantasyland. He did it to the Rams again, completing 21 of 30 passes for 294 yards and three touchdowns, including a 51-yard scoring toss to Jerry Rice. Tight end Russ Francis was the leading receiver with six catches. Roger Craig also had his best day of the season, rushing for 104 yards on 23 carries, as the 49ers whipped the Rams, 31-10.

Jerry Rice was named the National Football League Player of the Year in 1987 after scoring 23 touchdowns, a single-season record.

Two weeks later, the 49ers' seven-game winning streak came to a halt at Candlestick Park, when the Saints' Morton Andersen kicked a 40-yard field goal with 1:02 to play, providing a 26-24 win.

San Francisco trailed through most of the game but took the lead with three minutes to play, when Montana led the Niners on an 11-play, 63-yard drive. He capped the march with a 28-yard touchdown pass to tight end Ron Heller, putting the 49ers briefly in front before Andersen spoiled the comeback.

San Francisco got back in the win column against Tampa Bay the next week and followed that up with wins over Cleveland and Green Bay. After 13 weeks, the 49ers looked like the class of the NFL with an 11-2 record. They were ready to take on the always dangerous Chicago Bears at Candlestick.

While Montana rested up for the playoffs, Steve Young went most of the way at quarterback for San Francisco. Young completed nine passes for 100 yards and four touchdowns as San Francisco dismantled the Bears, 41-0. Jerry Rice caught three scoring passes and Roger Craig ran for 51 yards to help pace the offense.

The 49ers' defense did its share against the Bears, recovering two fumbles and intercepting four passes. Dana McLemore also returned a punt 83 yards for a touchdown.

San Francisco continued to roll with wins over Atlanta, 35-7, and Los Angeles, 48-0. In their final three games, the 49ers looked virtually unstoppable. Jerry Rice scored eight touchdowns in those three games, and the defense intercepted nine passes. More importantly, the defensive unit did not allow a touchdown or field goal in those three games.

San Francisco was matched with the Minnesota Vikings in the first round of the playoffs and was considered a 10-point favorite. But Minnesota was not intimidated by the 49ers and was prepared to play.

The game quickly turned into a horror show for Coach Bill Walsh. Montana never got the 49er offense untracked and the 49ers' tough defense was taken apart by quarterback Wade Wilson and elusive wide receiver Anthony Carter. Wilson completed 20 of 34 passes for 298 yards and two touchdowns. Carter caught 10 passes for 227 yards.

The Vikings put together a 20-3 halftime lead and never looked back. Steve Young replaced Montana at quarterback in the third quarter and almost got the 49ers back into the game. He scored on a five-yard run late in the third period to make the score, 27-17, but the Vikings continued to chip away at the 49ers defense and posted a 36-24 win.

It was a disappointing loss for the 49ers, and Young's appearance in place of Montana raised speculation that the two-time Super Bowl MVP had lost his luster. Throughout the off-season, a quarterback controversy raged over whether the younger, quicker, more mobile Steve Young should replace the wily veteran, Joe Montana. The controversy wouldn't be settled until nearly a year later.

1988 When training camp opened in 1988, the question most asked of Coach Bill Walsh was: "Who will be your starting quarterback?"

Steve Young and Joe Montana had equal opportunities to display their talents during the preseason, but on opening day it was Montana who lined up behind center Randy Cross.

Dallas Cowboys' Gary Hogeboom finds himself face to face with a fierce 49er rush from Riki Ellison.

Jerry Rice 1985–

Just four days before Super Bowl XXIII, San Francisco 49er wide receiver Jerry Rice dutifully told the press that he had doubts about playing in the biggest game of his life.

Rice, who had just reinjured his oft-sprained ankle said, "I could limp out there, I guess. I have four days to go so I don't know if my ankle will get any stronger. It's up to Bill Walsh if I play."

Four days later, Rice jubilantly wondered what he would do with the new Subaru sedan he won as the Most Valuable Player in the 49ers' 20-16 victory over the Cincinnati Bengals in Super Bowl XXIII. Despite the sprained ankle, Rice caught 11 passes for 215 yards, a Super Bowl record.

Rice's performance should come as no surprise to anyone familiar with his wide range of talents. Catching 11 passes is a good day's work for Rice. But it wasn't the quantity of his catches that was so impressive, it was the quality. Nine of his 11 receptions were for first downs. Most importantly, he saved his best for last, snaring five passes for 109 yards in the final quarter. Three receptions came as the 49ers marched downfield on their final, game-winning drive.

Rice also showed a flair for the dramatic. He made believers out of the most hardened skeptics when he made a leaping, falling 44-yard catch in the fourth quarter of Super Bowl XXIII. It happened with 11:05 minutes left in the game, when Rice ran a streak and Montana put the ball up for grabs. Sensing that cornerback Lewis Billups had him covered, Rice slowed down, felt Billups with his left arm, then leapt over him to make the catch. He appeared to have mistimed his jump, but readjusted in midair and grabbed the ball as he fell to the ground. The reception brought to mind former Pittsburgh Steeler star Lynn Swann's great, juggling catch in Super Bowl X against Dallas. Swann said Rice's grab was one of the finest catches he has ever seen.

Super Bowl XXIII capped a marvelous post-season effort for Rice. During that three-game stretch, he grabbed 21 passes for 409 yards and six touchdowns. And, of course, he was the Super Bowl MVP.

Like good French Bordeaux, Rice continues to improve with age. During the 1989 season, a year after his Super Bowl MVP performance, he hauled in 82 passes and added another 17 touchdowns to his collection. In 1990 he was Sports Illustrated's NFL Player of the Year when he caught 100 passes. In one game against Atlanta that season, he tied an NFL record with five touchdown receptions. In 1991 he caught 80 more passes and scored 14 times. And in 1992 he had 80 receptions for 10 touchdowns.

Super Bowls have become a personal playground for Rice. He caught seven passes for 148 yards and three touchdowns in Super Bowl XXIV and had 10 receptions for 149 yards and three touchdowns in Super Bowl XXIX. In just about any other season Rice would have been named Super Bowl MVP but both times he was upstaged by a teammate's remarkable quarterbacking skills, first Joe Montana and later, Steve Young.

To understand Rice's importance to the 49ers and his impact on the game of football, one must look at the statistics. Only one other receiver in the history of the game comes close to matching his accomplishments. That man is Don Hutson, and he did his damage nearly half a century ago for the Green Bay Packers. In 11 seasons, from 1935 to 1945, when the NFL was playing only 10- to 12-game seasons, Hutson caught 99 touchdown passes. He led the league in receptions eight times and retired with 488 career catches.

Rice has eclipsed the records of the game's most prolific receivers and continues to add to his NFL touchdown record in virtually every game he plays. He now overshadows such pass catching legends as Hutson, Largent, Lance Alworth, Don Maynard, Paul Warfield and Charley Taylor. He is clearly in a league all his own, sitting at the top of the NFL record book after just 10 years as a pro.

But there is more to Rice's game than statistics. He has natural instincts and abilities that can't be measured with numbers. He also has physical tools that few others can claim.

Rice was born with receiver's hands—long fingers and strong wrists—but it was years of manual labor, working as a bricklayer with his father, that helped him to develop the strength and work ethic he needs to stay at the top of his game.

"Believe me, when it's 100 degrees outside and your brothers are tossing you bricks," he said, "you get used to using your hands. The hands develop strength pretty fast."

He also owes a debt to Hutson, who is generally credited with having invented pass patterns. Rice has refined and developed those patterns into an art form, making two and three defenders aware of his every move on each play.

"I like the defender to think the opposite from what I'm going to do," Rice says. "I know how to do that."

Prior to the start of his NFL career, Rice's speed was questioned by many NFL insiders. He's silenced the critics and developed into the league's premier deep threat.

"There are probably 20 receivers in the league faster than Jerry," says former 49er teammate Mike Wilson. "But when a football is in the air, he can outrun anyone. One of Jerry's great attributes is his burst of speed to the football. He can make the adjustment that says 'that ball's mine, it belongs to me.'"

Once Rice has the ball in his hands, he is always a scoring threat. Just ask the Minnesota Vikings. In the 1989 NFC playoffs, they saw Rice catch a 10-yard pass under the secondary, then sidestep a linebacker and outrun everyone en route to a 70-yard touchdown.

Rice joined the 49ers in 1985 after a bit of draft-day maneuvering on the part of Bill Walsh. The All-American from Mississippi Valley State was set to be taken by the Dallas Cowboys as the 17th pick in the 1985 college draft. But Walsh cooked up a deal with the New England Patriots, sending them San Francisco's first and second choice in exchange for the Pats' first- rounder, which was the 16th pick. Walsh then selected Rice, causing Cowboys' Head Coach Tom Landry to nearly choke on his coffee.

Rice started slowly with the 49ers, dropping an occasional pass in his inaugural season. He showed his potential late in his rookie year against the Los Angeles Rams. On Monday Night Football, he set a team single-game yardage mark when he caught 10 passes for 241 yards. He ended the year with 49 catches for 927 yards, averaged 18.9 yards per catch and was named UPI Rookie of the Year. More importantly, he won the praise of teammates and opponents. Just two years later, he was being compared to the all-time greats.

"I would say Jerry Rice is probably the most dangerous receiver in the NFL," says Cincinnati safety Lewis Billups. "(In Super Bowl XXIII) they kept going to him. I was right on him, but he made a couple of super catches. I don't know what else I could have done. He was in another world."

Before he's done, Jerry Rice should have records that no one from this world will touch.

The opener between the 49ers and the up-and-coming New Orleans Saints was an old-fashioned barn burner. Both quarterbacks lit up the sky. The Saints' Bobby Hebert threw four touchdown passes, and Joe Montana tossed three, as the 49ers beat the Saints, 34-33, at the Superdome.

Although the 49ers allowed more points than in any game since 1983 they showed a strong pass rush. Nose tackle Michael Carter led the way, finishing with two sacks and an interception.

It wasn't an easy win for San Francisco. The Saints went into the locker room at halftime with a 17-10 lead, but Montana came out firing in the third quarter. He connected on touchdown passes of nine and 17 yards to John Frank, and 71 yards to Mike Wilson. But it was Mike Cofer's 32-yard field goal with 1:48 left that iced the game for San Francisco.

The 49ers traveled to the Meadowlands for their next contest. It was the site of one of the worst defeats in club history, occurring in the 1986 playoffs. Coach Walsh made a surprise announcement earlier in the week, saying Steve Young would start at quarterback against New York because Montana wasn't completely healthy. As a result Young had most of the practice time during the week. The announcement added fuel to the already raging quarterback controversy.

New York took a quick 7-0 lead on a 12-yard pass from Phil Simms to Lionel Manuel, but the Niners came back on a 35-yard Cofer field goal and a one-yard touchdown run by Doug Dubose. The 49ers kept the lead until later in the fourth quarter when the Giants struck. With 1:25 to play Simms connected with Manuel again on a 15-yard touchdown pass to give New York a 17-13 lead.

Young had been ineffective in the first half and was replaced by Montana. The veteran quarterback had little time, but it was a situation he had found himself in plenty of times before. With 53 seconds to go Montana launched a 78-yard scoring toss to Jerry Rice to win the game. In addition to the heroics of Rice and Montana, Craig rushed for 110 yards and added 69 on pass receptions.

The 49ers went into week three of the season as 14-point favorites against the hideous Atlanta Falcons. Montana got the starting call after his exciting performance in relief of Young at New York. He couldn't duplicate his success of a week earlier. San Francisco scored first on a Cofer field goal, then it was all downhill. Atlanta scored 24

unanswered points enroute to a 34-17 win.

San Francisco bounced back to beat Seattle and Detroit before blowing another one at home against the Denver Broncos. That game will be remembered for two things: the fierce winds blowing out of the north and the hellacious officiating. Those two elements combined to stymie the offense of both clubs.

Each team could muster just one touchdown in what turned into a kicking contest. Denver's Rich Karlis won it in overtime with a 22-yard field goal. The winning points came just two plays after a Steve Young pass went through Rice's hands and into the arms of cornerback Steve Wilson. Wilson returned it to the 49ers' five-yard line to set up the winning field goal.

Against Los Angeles a week later, Roger Craig put on a running show unseen by 49er fans since the days of Hugh McElhenny. He gained 190 yards on the ground, four shy of the team single-game record, and scored on runs of 46, 16 and 2 yards. His 46-yard run in

Tackle Bubba Paris eyes a Los Angeles Ram defensive lineman.

the first period was one of the great individual efforts of the season, as he high-stepped through six tackles on his way to the end zone. His three touchdowns paced a 24-21 San Francisco win.

San Francisco hit a slump after the Rams game, losing three of four. The one victory during that stretch came on a miraculous fourth quarter run by Steve Young. It was a gallop worthy of NFL highlight films.

Minnesota held the lead at 21-17 with 1:50 to go when Young dropped back to pass. The Vikings defensive line chased him out of the pocket and ended up pursuing him all the way to the end zone. Seven different Vikings had a shot at Young before he half-dived, half-collapsed into the end zone to give the 49ers a 24-21 win.

After 11 games the 49ers record stood at 6-5. The team's chance for a post-season game looked slim, as the Saints and Rams continued to win and the 49ers languished in third place. But against the defending Super Bowl champion Washington Redskins, the 49ers rose from the dead. John Taylor uncorked the longest punt return in team history at 95 yards in what was the pivotal play of the game. The score gave the 49ers a 17-7 lead and San Francisco never looked back. The 49ers went on to win, 37-21, starting a four-game winning streak.

San Francisco rolled over San Diego, Atlanta and New Orleans before facing the Los Angeles Rams in its final game. During that time, New Orleans and Los Angeles went through slumps of their own. Before taking the field for their final game, the 49ers found they had clinched the NFC West title by virtue of a Saints' win over Atlanta and the complicated tie-breaking formula. The game was meaningless and the 49ers played like it, losing to Los Angeles, 36-16.

San Francisco was faced with the task of preparing for the Minnesota Vikings in the first round of the playoffs. Minnesota had handed the 49ers a heartbreaking defeat in the first round of the 1987 playoffs, and Bill Walsh had not forgotten.

The Vikes scored first, marching to the 49ers 47-yard line where Chuck Nelson booted a field goal, then Montana and Rice went to work. In the next 20 minutes, Montana threw three touchdown passes to Rice and suddenly San Francisco had a 21-3 lead.

The game turned shockingly one-sided in the second half as Roger Craig got in the act with scoring runs of 4 and 80 yards to secure a 34-9 win. Craig's second touchdown run set a playoff record for the longest ever from scrimmage.

San Francisco's next stop was windy Soldier Field in Chicago. At game time, the wind-chill factor was a numbing 26-degrees below zero. All week the talk was of how "Bear weather" would destroy the 49ers, but it was the California club that looked at home. The 49ers' defense, ranked number three in the NFL, chased Jim McMahon from sideline to sideline, while Montana hooked up with Rice for two first-half touchdowns. At the half, the 49ers led 14-3.

San Francisco poured it on in the second half as Montana added a five-yard scoring pass to tight end John Frank, and Tom Rathman scored on a four-yard run. That was all the offense San Francisco needed. The defense did the rest of the work, and San Francisco skipped town with a 28-3 win and one more game to play.

After the contest, head coach Bill Walsh said, "This is one of the greatest games Joe Montana has played, considering the situation, the climate and everything that goes with it."

Now, only one team stood in the way of a third

Harris Barton, the 49ers' number one draft pick in 1987, pulls in front of the ball carrier to lead the blocking.

Bill Romanowski
1988–1993

Bill Romanowski thought he might be dreaming when he saw a Boomer Esiason pass float into his hands in Super Bowl XXIII. It was the first interception of his NFL career and it happened in the biggest game of his life.

"It's one of those things you dream about," Romanowski said. "All of a sudden the ball was just there."

Romanowski made a habit of being in the right place at the right time after joining the 49ers in 1988. In the first game of his NFL career against the New Orleans Saints, he was awarded the game ball after making six unassisted tackles.

The following week, Romanowski teamed with fellow linebackers Riki Ellison, Mike Walter and Charles Haley to cool off the New York Giants' always dangerous running game. New York was held to only 112 rushing yards. All-Pro running back Joe Morris collected just 67 yards in 22 carries. And quarterback Phil Simms was under more pressure than General Custer at Little Big Horn.

The 6'4", 235-pound Romanowski finished the game with 7 1/2 tackles, third in the club behind Haley's nine tackles and Ellison's eight. Most significantly, Romanowski was there when it counted. In a critical short-yardage situation in the fourth quarter, Romanowski took on Morris at the line of scrimmage, stopping him for no gain and killing an important Giants' drive.

"Really, there have been no surprises since I've been in the league," Romanowski said. "I came to camp in shape and with the intention of making the starting team. I've been a starter ever since I began playing football, including

161

four years at Boston College. I'm at a different position than I played in college. That adjustment was tough at first, but it's starting to become second nature now."

Romanowski is not intimidated by 280-pound maniacs, or "linemen" as they are referred to in the National Football League. He has the attitude of a big league linebacker. He's confident to the point of brashness—a Joe Namath on defense. He knows he can play with the best.

If Romanowski sounds cocky, he can afford to be. In his rookie season, he established himself as a force at weak outside linebacker. What had been considered a missing link in the 49ers' defense, had suddenly become a major asset. He became a fixture in the starting lineup.

After joining the 49ers as a third-round draft choice in 1988, the 80th player selected overall, Romanowski found himself at his new position. An inside linebacker at Boston College, he suddenly had to learn the outside spot with San Francisco. The adjustment wasn't easy.

"The big difference is I need more discipline at the outside spot," Romanowski said. "I have to hold my leverage more. At the inside spot, I could just look at the backs and fly to the ball. At the outside spot, I have to watch my balance and what's happening around me. I can't let anyone get outside me and around the ends."

While the 49ers' blitzing linebacker usually lines up on the strong side, Romanowski lined up on the weak side, a spot where a linebacker's deficiencies can quickly be exposed. It's not a position for the faint-hearted, yet it was a challenge Romanowski relished.

For a linebacker, sometimes ignorance is bliss. That could have been Romanowski's excuse when he said he wasn't intimidated by the New York Giants' formidable offensive line in just his second NFL game in 1988. On running plays, he was often matched against Giants tackle Karl Nelson, who was returning to the club after a bout with Hodgkins disease. Nelson, a former All-Pro, was considered one of the premier drive blockers in the game. Other times, Romanowski lined up opposite 305-pound behemoth John Elliot. Neither of the Giants tackles are known for their gentle demeanor.

"I wasn't really worried about their offensive line," he said. "I was prepared. Sure, I had read about the Giants and how good their running game is, but then every team we play has someone I've been reading about. Once I get on the field I'm just playing football. It doesn't matter who I line up against."

Romanowski's versatility was a boon to the 49ers. He was often shuttled between inside linebacker and the outside linebacker spot, depending on the situation. Always a hard worker, Romanowski began preparing for his role with San Francisco immediately after the 1988 college draft, when he was contacted by 49ers' strength coach Jerry Attaway, who put Romanowski on a strength and conditioning routine. Before training camp opened, Romanowski moved to the San Francisco Bay Area to work personally with Attaway.

"We got a lot of football stuff in during the summer of my rookie season," Romanowski said. "We worked a lot on agility and different drills to improve quickness for the outside spot. I spent a lot of time on balance and leverage drills."

Romanowski's strong work ethic and competitive spirit caught the eye of the 49ers' coaches before he was selected in the college draft. As a senior at Boston College, he led the team in tackles with 156, including a 19-tackle game against Pittsburgh, and 18 tackles against Army. He also made the All-East and All-East Coast Athletic Conference teams and was a finalist for the Dick Butkus Award, given annually to the top college linebacker. As a sophomore, he led the team in tackles with 150.

Consistently among the 49er leaders in tackles, Romanowski improved with each season. He was named to the All-Rookie team in 1988 and by 1990 was the team's leading tackler with 79, including 68 solo tackles. In 1991, he became a one-man wrecking crew who was able to dismantle the Los Angeles Rams one Sunday with 10 solo tackles.

Romanowski signed with the Philadelphia Eagles in 1993, where he immediately won a starting linebacker spot.

"Football is a game where you have to prove yourself before you are accepted," Romanowski said. "You're just another body until you show you can play."

Most observers would concur that Romanowski was not just another body.

Super Bowl title for San Francisco. That team was the Cincinnati Bengals and their coach, former 49er assistant Sam Wyche.

After a series of blowouts in the Super Bowl, there finally was a game that exhibited high drama. It started off slowly. The game was tied at the half, 3-3, and then 6-6 in the third quarter. But Cincinnati's Stanford Jennings broke loose on a 93-yard kickoff return and the excitement started.

Montana got that one back, marching 85 yards on four plays and connecting with Jerry Rice on a 14-yard touchdown pass. When Cincinnati's Jim Breech made a 40-yard field goal with 3:20 to play, many people thought the game was over. They hadn't seen Joe Montana.

After the kickoff, the San Francisco 49ers huddled at their own eight-yard line trailing 16-13 with 3:08 to play. Montana had pulled off miracle finishes before. Could he do it again? Cincinnati wide receiver Cris Collinsworth was one man on the Bengals sideline who knew what Montana could do.

"Montana is not human," Collinsworth said. "I don't want to call him a god, but he's definitely somewhere in between. I've never seen a guy who, every time the chips are down and people are counting him out, is able to come back."

Montana's task was to solve a puzzling defense. The Bengals had given up lots of yards, but had kept the 49ers out of the end zone. When he trotted onto the field, he thought briefly to that game seven years ago when Dwight Clark made "the Catch" after another memorable 49er drive.

As Montana came out of the huddle on first down, he saw that Cincinnati continued to play zone defense, as he had hoped. He passed quickly down the middle to Roger Craig for nine yards, then to tight end John Frank for five more and a first down. After Rice caught a seven-yard pass in the flat, Craig was tripped up after a one-yard gain, bringing up third and two at the 31.

Montana went back to Craig, who followed a Guy McIntyre block to pick up four yards and a first down. Montana then called timeout with 1:54 left to talk strategy with Bill Walsh. After the timeout, Montana caught the Bengals in man-to-man again and connected with Rice for 17 yards. Then he found Craig over the middle for 13 yards.

With the ball at the Bengals' 35 and the clock showing 1:22, Montana threw a pass over Rice's head and out of bounds to slow things down. By

this time he was so excited he thought he was hyperventilating.

"I was having a hard time breathing," Montana said. "That had never happened before."

A penalty moved the ball back to the 45 and out of field goal range, but Montana looked for Rice again. Although he was being double-covered, Montana connected for a 27-yard pickup to the 18-yard line.

"That's when I started thinking touchdown," Montana said. Montana hit Craig again with an eight-yard pass to the 10. The clock showed 39 seconds when the 49ers called another timeout.

The play called was "20 halfback curl x-up." Craig was the primary target over the middle, with Rice in motion to freeze the defense. When Rice drew double coverage, Montana looked to John Taylor and fired a strike.

Montana had done it again, marching the 49ers 92 yards in 11 plays and consuming 2:36. It was a fabulous ending to a frustrating season. It was also the last game for Coach Bill Walsh and center Randy Cross. Both men took their three Super Bowl rings and moved into the broadcast booth. Jerry Rice, who ended the game with 11 receptions for 211 yards, was the MVP. Montana finished with 23 completions in 36 attempts for 357 yards.

Ronnie Lott summed up the feelings of millions of Super Bowl viewers when he said, "I've seen Joe do this time and time again. You can't question his heart. Without a doubt, he has to be one of the greatest quarterbacks to ever play."

1989 They say it's nearly impossible for a NFL team to repeat as champion. Tell that to Eddie DeBartolo, George Seifert or any member of the San Francisco 49ers. The 49er team is not your average NFL franchise.

The 1989 season was one of surprises and memorable moments. There was a second consecutive Super Bowl win, Joe Montana establishing himself as pro football's all-time premier quarterback, John Taylor taking his place alongside Jerry Rice as a true game-breaker and George Seifert quieting critics who questioned his ability to follow Bill Walsh.

But there was also tragedy. Jeff Fuller was lost with a career-ending spinal injury that left one arm partially paralyzed.

The season started innocently enough for San Francisco, with a close win over the Indianapolis Colts 30-24. But this game proved to be an omen of things to

Offensive line coach Bobb McKittrick reviews blocking assignments with his troops at halftime.

come. What should have been a cakewalk turned into a photo-finish when San Francisco needed Joe Montana to hook up with Jerry Rice in the last six minutes of the game to supply the margin of victory. Rice ran a short slant pattern over the middle, took a pass from Montana, then outran the Indianapolis secondary, en route to a 58-yard touchdown. It was a pattern that would be repeated several times during the season— Joe Montana riding his stallion to the rescue in the closing minutes of a tight game.

Rice and Montana were aided by Roger Craig who scored two touchdowns and outgained the Colts' Eric Dickerson 131 to 106.

Game three against the Philadelphia Eagles was vintage Montana. In perhaps his best individual performance of the season, Montana threw four touchdown passes in the final quarter and 428 total yards, to bring the 49ers back from what seemed to be certain defeat.

The Eagles sacked Montana eight times and forced him out of the game briefly in the second period. Down 28-17 with seven minutes to play, Montana fired three touchdown passes to three different receivers to give San Francisco a dramatic 38-28 win.

John Taylor opened the fourth quarter scoring spree by taking a 12-yard pass from Montana and racing past everyone for a 70-yard touchdown. Tom Rathman got into the act with an eight-yard touch-

down reception. Tight end Brent Jones added a 25-yard scoring catch. And Rice took Montana's final touchdown pass 33 yards to score.

The 49ers returned to Candlestick Park for the season's home opener against the Los Angeles Rams. After building a 12-10 lead late in the fourth quarter, San Francisco was driving and eating away the final minutes on the game clock. But then the sure-handed Tom Rathman fumbled. It was only the second time in four years Rathman coughed up the football, but this time it was particularly costly. It gave Los Angeles possession at its own 20-yard line. Rams quarterback Jim Everett made the most of it with three big pass plays, to move the Rams within field goal range for the reliable Mike Lansford. His 26-yard field goal with two seconds showing gave the 49ers their first loss of the season.

The bad luck looked like it was going to follow the 49ers to New Orleans in week five, but some last minute heroics and questionable officiating combined to save the 49ers.

New Orleans built an early 17-3 lead, but once again Montana rescued the 49ers in the second half by throwing three scoring passes. The defense also played a big role in this win. Michael Carter and Keena Turner made crucial plays. And defensive back Eric Wright broke up a potential game-winning touchdown pass to Saints' receiver Brett Perriman late in the fourth quarter to save the day. Replays

Ray Wersching 1977–1987

It's not easy being a placekicker. The typical kicker plays less than one minute per game, but often, it's his foot that provides the margin between victory and defeat.

Ray Wersching relished that role with the San Francisco 49ers. His ability to perform in the clutch was taken for granted. When Wersching retired in 1987, he was the 49ers all-time leading scorer with 979 points. His field goal accuracy of .739 was far better than any kicker in team history. Bruce Gosset is next with a .641 percentage.

Wersching signed with the 49ers midway through the 1977 season after being released by the San Diego Chargers. He suffered through four dismal years with the 49ers before they won Super Bowl XVI in 1981. Wersching played a major role in the club's turnaround. He led the team in scoring for nine straight seasons from 1978 to 1986. In 1984, he was the leading scorer in the NFL with 131 points.

"I went through those 2-14 seasons, and believe me, they were no fun," Wersching said.

"Actually, there was a lot of spirit on the team when I got there. There were a lot of older vets still around that made you feel comfortable. People like Cedrick Hardman and Jimmy Webb made it easy on newcomers. And it seemed like the 49ers were acquiring a lot of players at that time. The vets were friendly and that filtered down to the rookies, too. We just kept rolling along. Those losing years were no fun though."

Wersching made an immediate impact with the 49ers. In his first game with the club, he made good on a 50-yard field goal attempt against the New York Giants. Just three weeks later, his 33-yard field goal in overtime beat the New Orleans Saints, 10-7.

Wersching was born in Mondsee, Austria, but grew up in Downey, California, where he became a Los Angeles Rams fan. That affinity quickly changed when Wersching joined the San Francisco 49ers. The intense rivalry between the two clubs helped alter his opinion.

"I was a Rams fan as a kid," Wersching said. "I dislike them a little bit now, but when I lived there I used to follow them closely."

Wersching was particularly delighted by a 33-31 win the 49ers scored over the Rams during the 1981 season. He kicked four field goals that day, including the game-winning 37-yard field goal with two seconds to play.

"What happened was the Rams had just scored to go ahead," Wersching said. "They were jumping around thinking they had won the game. There was less than two minutes to play, but Joe (Montana) got hold of the ball and moved us into field goal range. Beating them that day was a pleasure because I'd grown up there."

Super Bowl XVI against the Cincinnati Bengals was another big game for Wersching. In the 49ers' first Super Bowl appearance, Wersching connected on all four of his field goal attempts and scored 14 of the team's 26 points.

His deliberate squib kicks also played an instrumental role in the game's outcome. The Bengals were unable to return any of his kickoffs for sizable gains. One squib kick was fumbled by Bengal return man Archie Griffin just before the first half ended. San Francisco recovered, and Wersching kicked another field goal to give the 49ers a 20-0 lead at halftime. The Bengals never regained momentum.

In Super Bowl XIX against the Miami Dolphins, Wersching connected on his only field goal attempt from 27 yards. He added five extra points to give him a total of 22 points scored in his two Super Bowl games. He is ranked second on the Super Bowl scoring list behind Franco Harris, who has 24 points.

The kicker's job has become as much a mental chore as a physical one, Wersching says. Distractions can alter the kicker's timing or affect his confidence. Wersching relied on his holder to take care of the mechanical adjustments that must be made prior to a field goal attempt. As he trotted onto the field before an attempt, he never looked at the goal posts. It was the holder's job to guide Wersching to the spot from which he kicked.

Wersching says that his reluctance to look up at the goal posts was not a conscious action.

"I did that because that's the way I had always done it," he said. "I tried to relax as much as possible and just tried to remember to keep my head down and follow through.

"Holding is a lot more important than people think. Joe Montana was a great holder. He gave me a sense of security out there. He'd been on the field and he knew the flow of the game. He wasn't nervous or anything.

"Joe was very fluid. The ball was always there. It gave me one less thing to worry about. All that stuff—style and rhythm of the holder—is important and Joe did it well. I wasn't distracted by anything."

A common ploy used by opposing coaches is to call a time out prior to a field goal attempt. The added seconds of anticipation are enough to break the concentration of some kickers. Wersching said he wasn't bothered by such tricks during the course of a game.

"It got to the point where I expected a time out," he said. "If they didn't call one, it was likely to distract me."

Wersching believes the 49ers will continue as champions. The team is loaded with talent, he says, and has a good nucleus of veterans.

"Playing together for the last couple of years helped them develop into a solid team," he said.

"I just wanted to contribute to the team as much as I could. The 49ers changed my career. They gave me a chance. I owe the 49ers."

showed that Wright may have interfered with Perriman, but the officials let the play stand.

Officials also missed a more obvious miscue when Jerry Rice spiked the football on the one-yard line as he was on his way to a third-quarter score. San Francisco was credited with a touchdown that eventually proved to be the winning margin in the 24-20 victory.

San Francisco rolled through the next five weeks, beating the hapless Dallas Cowboys, the New England Patriots, the New York Jets, the New Orleans Saints and the Atlanta Falcons to build an insurmountable 9-1 record.

The New England game took on added significance, coming less than a week after a massive earthquake that devastated northern California and caused billions of dollars in property damage and dozens of deaths. Candlestick Park was in the process of being inspected for structural damage, so the game was relocated to Stanford Stadium.

The game itself proved unsettling for other reasons. Safety Jeff Fuller, considered by many to be the best athlete on the talented 49er squad, suffered a career-ending injury on the second play of the game while making a tackle. Joe Montana also went

down midway through the game and was lost for two weeks. And Jim Fahnhorst and Harry Sydney met with season-ending injuries.

San Francisco met its match for only the second time of the season against its next opponent, the surprising Green Bay Packers. The 49ers turned the ball over four times against Green Bay and committed 10 penalties. Meanwhile, Packer quarterback Don Majkowski kept his club close, then scored the winning touchdown on an eight-yard quarterback draw in the fourth quarter.

There were few positives from the 49er side. Chet Brooks' interception was one of the few bright spots. He raced 94 yards for a touchdown, but it was called back because of a penalty. The 49er running game also was ineffective and the passing game out of sync.

San Francisco got back on track the next week with a 34-24 win over the New York Giants. The game was billed as a preview of the NFL Championship. The 49ers struck early, as Montana completed 15 of 16 passes and threw three touchdown passes to help the 49ers build a 24-7 lead. But Phil Simms brought the Giants back to tie the score with 7:54 left when he completed a seven-yard touchdown pass to Odessa Turner.

Montana went to work and moved San Francisco to the Giants' 32. The big play was Montana's 17-yard scramble. Then Cofer came in to try a field goal and missed. But the Giants were called for being offsides. Cofer got a second chance and nailed the kick to put San Francisco in front for good.

The 49ers glided through the next four games, beating Atlanta, Los Angeles, Buffalo and Chicago to wrap up another Western Division championship. But the second part of the season—the playoffs—was about to begin.

San Francisco was matched with Minnesota in the divisional playoff game. Head coach George Seifert had vivid memories of a Minnesota team that had annihilated the 49ers in the playoffs just two years earlier. The Vikings fabled pass rush was set to tee off at Candlestick Park, but this time Seifert had his team prepared.

PREVIOUS PAGE: Fullback Tom Rathman steamrolls into the secondary. Rathman was also an overpowering blocker and is credited with helping Roger Craig break the 49ers single season rushing record in 1988.

Guard Guy McIntyre (62) and center Randy Cross (51) set up pass-blocking protection for Joe Montana.

The pass rush never materialized, and Montana threw four touchdown passes in the first half, as the 49ers walked all over the Vikings, 41-13. Montana started early with a 72-yard scoring strike to Rice just five minutes into the game. He followed that with an eight-yard scoring pass to Jones, an eight-yard pass to Taylor and a 13-yard pass to Rice.

Roger Craig helped the offense along with 125 yards on the ground, the most rushing yards allowed by the Vikings all season.

The game was best summed up in the half-time statistics. San Francisco had 320 total yards against a defense that usually allowed just 260 per game.

San Francisco advanced to the NFC Championship Game to face its nemesis and arch rival from the south, the Los Angeles Rams, one of two teams that defeated the 49ers in 1989.

Los Angeles took the early lead, 3-0, and threatened to increase it to 10-0 as Jim Everett coolly led the Rams downfield. On third down inside the 50-yard line, Everett spotted a hole in the 49er secondary. He fired a long pass to receiver Flipper Anderson, who was wide open at the 10-yard line. But safety Ronnie Lott came out of nowhere to knock the pass away. Lott's play changed the complexion of the game. The 49ers took over and rolled through the Rams' defense, scoring three times in the second quarter and building up a 21-3 halftime lead. Los Angeles never recovered.

The shell-shocked Rams retreated to the locker room, but they'd already played their best hand. They never again marched beyond the San Francisco 40-yard line. Meanwhile, the San Francisco 49ers tripled the Rams' offensive output, tripled their number of first downs and nearly doubled their time of possession, posting a 30-3 win. The next stop was New Orleans.

The Denver Broncos showed up at the Superdome with an 11-5 regular season record, intent on winning their first Super Bowl in four tries. They made it a game for about three minutes, until Joe Montana was able to hook up with Jerry Rice on a 20-yard scoring strike.

The 49ers completely dominated Super Bowl XXIV in one of the most lopsided championship games ever played. By halftime, the 49ers had a 27-3 lead and Denver quarterback John Elway was trying to hide his head in the sand. The second half was even worse.

The 49ers were favored by 12 points but won by a staggering 45. The final score of 55-10 had historians looking for comparisons. They had to reach back to Chicago's infamous 73-0 thrashing of Washington in the 1940 NFL Championship Game to find anything comparable.

Montana, who has a habit of playing the game of his life at Super Bowl time, once again had the game of his life. He completed 22 of 29 passes for 297 yards and a Super Bowl record five touchdown passes. He was named Super Bowl MVP for the third time—another record.

The 49ers pounded the Broncos with 461 yards of offense and limited Denver to just 167 yards. San Francisco held the ball for nearly 40 minutes, while Denver had possession for just 20. In short, it was downright ugly for Bronco fans, players and management.

"They could have lined up in the single wing, and we could have had nine men on the line and they'd still have beaten us the way they played," said Denver defensive coordinator Wade Phillips.

Even the 49ers began to feel compassion for their hapless opponents. "I felt sorry for Elway at one point," said linebacker Matt Millen. "Believe me, I haven't felt sorry for many quarterbacks."

Indeed, as the lead continued to grow, the 49er defense had a field day with Elway. There's no point in running when you're down by 24 points at halftime or 31 in the third quarter, so Elway was forced to pass on virtually every play. Two of his passes were intercepted and he completed just 10 of 26 for 108 yards. He was sacked four times and pressured throughout the game.

The victory enabled San Francisco to join elite company. The 49ers became the first team since the 1978-79 Pittsburgh Steelers to repeat as champions, and one of the only two teams to win four Super Bowls.

1990–1995

CHAPTER SIX

ERA OF EXCELLENCE

The San Francisco 49ers closed out the 1980s as the "Team of the Decade." As the 1990s opened, Coach George Seifert was determined to keep the franchise at the top of the NFL.

"Three-peat" was the phrase most often heard as the 49ers congregated in Rocklin, California, to open training camp for the 1990 season. With two consecutive Super Bowl victories under its belt, San Francisco was determined to become the first team in NFL history to win three straight league championships.

Looking for a breakaway player to team with Roger Craig, San Francisco used its first pick in the draft to select Florida State running back Dexter Carter. With two picks in the second round, the 49ers chose Washington's mammoth defensive lineman Dennis Brown and cornerback Eric Davis from Jacksonville State.

San Francisco rolled through the first 10 weeks of the season, getting off to the best start in team history. Behind quarterback Joe Montana, who threw for 300 yards in four of the first five games, the 49ers won 10 in a row in their quest for a third straight Super Bowl title. The highlight of that winning streak was a 476-yard passing performance against Atlanta, when Jerry Rice tied a league record with five touchdown receptions.

After running up a 5-0 record, San Francisco had its hands full with the Pittsburgh Steelers. Rookie running back Dexter Carter had his best game of the season, rushing 17 times against Pittsburgh for 90 yards. It turned out to be a season high for 49er ball carriers. Carter also caught seven passes for 57 yards. He combined with Tom Rathman, who scored two touchdowns, to lead San Francisco to a 27-7 win. Mike Sherrard contributed a third touchdown on a five-yard pass from Joe Montana.

The 49ers continued their winning streak against Cleveland the following week despite a rare sub-par day by Montana, who completed less than 50 percent of his passes for only the sixth time in 130 starts as a 49er quarterback. He threw a 15-yard touchdown pass to Rice, and Rathman added another score, as San Francisco built a comfortable 14-point margin with one quarter left to play. Then the game took an ugly turn. Montana threw a pair of interceptions in the fourth quarter, giving Cleveland good field position and enabling the Browns to tie the game.

The 49ers were able to salvage a 20-17 win when Mike Cofer kicked a 45-yard field goal with five seconds remaining in the game. The win was bittersweet, however, because receiver Mike Sherrard suffered a broken ankle while making a third-down catch with 38 seconds left. Sherrard's clutch reception set up the winning field goal.

In week 11, the 49ers suffered their first loss of the season at the hands of the Los Angeles Rams. The mid-season letdown came at a time when the 49ers were looking over the horizon to their next opponent, the New York Giants.

The showdown between the 49ers and the Giants the following week matched

the two best teams in football. It was a classic confrontation that turned into one of the best defensive struggles in NFL history. All the scoring came in the second quarter when Matt Bahr kicked a 20-yard field goal for New York and Montana hit John Taylor on a 23-yard scoring pass. Taylor's touchdown was enough offense for the 49ers because it was the defense that won this game for San Francisco.

The 49ers' defense came up with a number of big plays, including a pair of emotional goal-line stands, some clutch pass deflections and a multitude of thunderous hits. Appropriately, the game ended when 49ers' defensive linemen Pierce Holt and Kevin Fagan teamed up to sack New York quarterback Phil Simms on the last play of the game to preserve a 7-3 San Francisco win.

Crunch time came late in the fourth quarter, however, when the Giants had a first and goal at the 49ers' nine-yard line. New York tried to pass on four straight plays and each time San Francisco made the right move. On the first down, Michael Carter chased Simms out of the pocket and forced an errant throw. Don Griffin broke up a pass on the second down. Ronnie Lott deflected a pass on the third down. Then, on the fourth down, Darryl Pollard made one of the most important defensive plays of the season when he slipped in front of Giants receiver Lionel Manuel to tip the ball away in the end zone and preserve the 49ers' win.

The New York defense was equally tough. Montana was able to complete just 12 of 29 passes for 152 yards, his lowest total in over five years. Dexter Carter was the leading ground gainer for San Francisco with just 29 yards. Jerry Rice was held to one reception for 13 yards, a season low for the NFL's premier receiver.

San Francisco finished the season with an NFL-best 14-2 record. The 49ers met the Washington Redskins in the first round of the playoffs and beat them handily, 28-10, as Montana hit on 22 of 31 passes for 274 yards and a pair of touchdowns. The victory set up a rematch with the New York Giants.

TOP: Pierce Holt (78) was the anchor of the 49ers defensive line from 1989 to 1992.

LEFT: Charles Haley (94) was a ferocious pass rusher for the 49ers and was named NFC Defensive Player of the Year in 1990.

Harris Barton 1987–

Offensive tackle Harris Barton was seated on a stool in front of his locker when the doors swung open and his worst fears were realized.

It was Super Bowl Sunday, four-and-a-half hours before the 49ers would take on the San Diego Chargers, and quarterback Steve Young was already strolling in.

"I don't know why he got there (so early)," Barton would admit later. "It's not like he has to tape his ankles or his pads."

Barton knew that everything was in place for the 49ers to win Super Bowl XXIX. The defense played well throughout the playoffs, and was prepared to cage running back Natrone Means. The secondary could easily handle the Charger wide receivers. Even the special teams, traditionally a 49er weakness, had an advantage over San Diego. In Barton's mind, the only way the 49ers could lose was if Young got nervous.

Barton figured a half empty locker room four hours before game time was the devil's workshop. It was the perfect place for Young's mind to become clouded with doubt and worry.

Earlier in their 49er careers, Barton and Young had lived the bachelor life together and Barton probably knew Young better than anyone on the team. He realized that this game meant everything to his former roommate. Winning the Super Bowl was the only way for Young to lend meaning to a season in which he set the NFL all-time quarterback rating mark. If Young was to establish his own identity in the minds of 49ers fans, he had to win a championship, something his legendary predecessor, Joe Montana, did four times.

Barton realized Young had every right to be nervous. He took it upon himself to keep Young occupied so the 49ers quarterback wouldn't be overcome by worry.

"How did you sleep?" Barton asked.

"Fine, I got up at

about nine," Young said.

"I don't want you just sitting around and sipping coffee," Barton said. "It'll make you edgy."

"I'm Mormon," Young said. "I don't drink coffee."

As team photographer Michael Zagaris strolled by, both players remarked on the resemblance between Zagaris and Young's father. They chatted for about 20 minutes, and then Barton walked Young over to safety Tim McDonald. McDonald talked to Young for about 20 minutes, then Barton escorted Young to quarterback Bill Musgrave's locker for another 20-minute bull session.

Barton kept a close eye on Young during the discussions. He looked for signs of tightness, particularly a clenching of the jaw. A few times he went over to tight end Brent Jones, another close friend of Young, and asked if the quarterback's jaw looked like it was tightening up.

"Brent's kind of the judge," Barton said.

Jones assured Barton that Young was fine. Then Young tried to show everybody he was already loose by demonstrating a newly learned dance he claimed he was going to perform during pregame introductions. Barton laughed at Young's antics. Soon, he realized Young was the calmest guy in the entire locker room, and it was Barton himself who was worried sick.

But Barton was born to worry. He left Young and went back to his own concerns, mainly

the huge Chargers defensive line that some football insiders claimed would derail the 49ers mighty offense.

And that is Barton's forte. He is the offensive line's detail man, the guy who calls linemen-only meetings during the week to review additional game film.

Barton's also the man who nervously called his cohorts together at 9:30 on Super Bowl Sunday morning for an extra film session. All this despite the fact that the game plan had been in place for 10 days, and everyone could practically recite it in their sleep.

"We meet every night at 7:30, without coaches, before a game," Barton said of the tradition he helped establish. "If you're not there, you're fined. We go over short yardage. We go over goal line. We go over certain blitzes. We go over every possible situation."

But the meetings have also been therapeutic for Barton. Last year, he flew home to Georgia nearly every Monday and Tuesday to be with his father, Paul Barton, who was dying of brain cancer. The disease began to rob him of his short-term memory, and slowly the only thing that remained was Paul's dry sense of humor. Paul died in the spring of 1994.

Barton couldn't wait for the 1994 season to begin, figuring a return to his job would ease his grief. He was in great shape, and made it through training camp without a scratch. Barton was ready for another Pro Bowl season.

Then, in the first quarter of the 1994 season opener against the Los Angeles Raiders, the unthinkable happened. Barton heard a pop in his upper right arm. X-rays revealed a torn triceps muscle. Surgery followed and Barton spent the next eight weeks on the bench. While he was unable to play, he continued to lead the film study meetings. They kept Barton connected to the team. Without them, he would have felt like a complete outsider.

Barton returned to action in the ninth game of the season against the Washington Redskins. He wore a cumbersome brace on his right arm and felt he may have rushed back before being entirely ready. Nevertheless, he returned to form and began to play well toward the end of season. But the injury, and his father's death, left lasting marks.

Even in the elation of the 49ers' Super Bowl victory, Barton couldn't let go of one regret. He wished the game had been played a year earlier, when the Super Bowl was in Atlanta, minutes away from his childhood home. Even in his weakened condition, his father could have made the game. Barton knew it would have provided his father with some priceless moments.

"1994 was a miserable year for me," Barton said after Super Bowl XXIX. "It just was. The only thing that could really save me was playing in this game. It was difficult for me to play in it, diffi-

cult for me to enjoy it."

Before the Super Bowl, when the 49ers went through their pregame warm up, Barton noticed the packed stadium, the fire work silos and the large floats that would be a part of the celebration. He knew his father would have loved the pomp and circumstance of it all.

When the team went back into the locker room right before the introductions, Harris wrote "Paul C. Barton" on the palm of his glove. When he was introduced, he opened his hand for the television camera. It was his own way of dedicating the game to his dad.

The NFC Championship Game between New York and San Francisco turned into another defensive struggle. The 49ers' offense was shut down again by New York gaining just 39 yards rushing. In a more telling statistic, San Francisco had possession of the football for only 21 minutes in the game.

In the first half, the two clubs matched field goals as Mike Cofer connected from 47 and 35 yards and New York's Matt Bahr made field goals of 28 and 42 yards. The score remained tied at 6-6 as the clubs went into the locker rooms at halftime.

Joe Montana got the 49ers rolling in the second half when he connected with John Taylor on a 61-yard touchdown pass to give the 49ers a 13-6 lead. The Giants pecked away at the 49ers lead as Bahr added two more field goals to bring the Giants to within a point at 13-12.

Then with nearly 10 minutes left to play came one of the turning points not only in the game, but in the history of the 49er franchise. New York defensive lineman Leonard Marshall crushed Montana on a blind-side hit, leaving the 49er quarterback with a broken bone in his right hand, a bruised sternum and a concussion. Montana was forced to leave the game, finishing with 18 completions in 26 attempts for 190 yards and one touchdown. He would not appear in another game for San Francisco for nearly two years.

New York still trailed 13-12 as time ticked away. But with Steve Young replacing the injured Montana, the 49ers went to a ball-control offense in an effort to run out the clock. San Francisco was marching down the field with 2:36 to play when disaster struck. Roger Craig took a handoff from Steve Young and lost the football. New York linebacker Lawrence Taylor recovered, giving the Giants one last chance at victory. Quarterback Jeff Hoestetler made the most of it. He drove New York 33 yards and as time expired Matt Bahr kicked a 42-yard field goal to send the Giants on to Super Bowl XXV. The loss ended the 49ers quest for an unprecedented third consecutive Super Bowl championship.

Several 49ers had outstanding years in 1990. In his last season as the 49ers' starting quarterback, Joe Montana was named the NFL's Most Valuable Player and Sports Illustrated's "Sportsman of the Year." Jerry Rice ended the season with 100 pass receptions for 1,502 yards and 13 touchdowns.

Charles Haley led the defensive charge throughout the season. He finished with 58 tackles and an NFC-leading 16 sacks. Linebacker Bill Romanowski had 79 tackles, a team high.

Representing the 49ers in the Pro Bowl were Charles Haley, Jerry Rice, Ronnie Lott and Guy McIntyre. Joe Montana was selected but unable to play because of the hand injury suffered in the championship game.

1991

San Francisco began the 1991 season with a new look. Joe Montana was placed on injured reserve after undergoing surgery to repair a torn tendon in his throwing elbow, and was inactive for the entire season. Steve Young took over as the 49ers' starting quarterback after waiting in the wings behind Montana for four years.

Among the new faces on the roster were 300-pound defensive lineman Ted Washington, a first-round draft pick from Louisville, and running back Ricky Watters, a second-round pick from Notre Dame.

The 49ers got off to one of their worst starts in memory, losing three of their first five games. After dropping the opener to the New York Giants 16-14, San Francisco beat San Diego, 34-14. San Francisco was then defeated 17-14 at Minnesota and also lost to the Raiders, 12-6.

In need of defensive help, the 49ers signed Green Bay's pass rushing specialist Tim Harris five games into the season. It wasn't enough to help the floundering 49ers. The worst was yet to come.

The Atlanta Falcons strutted into town under the direction of Coach Jerry Glanville and whipped San Francisco 39-34, to drop the 49ers into last place in the NFC West with a 2-4 record, four games behind the undefeated New Orleans Saints.

Against the Falcons, the 49ers broke down in all phases of the game, playing miserably on defense and misfiring at key times on offense. But it was the special team's play which put the 49ers out of this one, allowing a blocked punt, a blocked extra point and a 100-yard kickoff return by Deion Sanders.

Atlanta quarterback Chris Miller looked like the reincarnation of Sammy Baugh during the first five minutes of the game, hitting four of five passes for 114 yards and two touchdowns. Before San Francisco could jump-start its offense, it trailed 17-0.

Steve Young rallied San Francisco in a losing effort, throwing two long touchdown passes of 54 and 57 yards and running for two more scores. He

NEXT PAGE: Steve Young (8) pulls down the football and scampers away from a New Orleans Saints defender.

William Floyd 1994–

Fullback William Floyd added a new dimension to the 49ers when he reported to the club as a first-round draft pick in 1994. For one, he already had a fancy nickname. Secondly, he seemed to be on a personal mission to add flash and emotion to the 49ers' business-like approach to football.

Floyd was known as "Bar None" from his first day in a San Francisco uniform. That was the handle Floyd's agent hung on his client before the former Florida State star ever stepped onto a 49er practice field. The agent considered Floyd to be the best fullback in the NFL, bar none, hence the nickname. After the 1994 season, players around the league began to believe it.

"William did some things that you don't really expect from a rookie running back," said coach George Seifert. "He's an excellent blocker, one of the best in the league at his position, whether it be as a pass blocker or as a lead blocker. He's not afraid to take on people."

At 6'1" and 240 pounds, with 4.6 speed in the 40-yard dash, Floyd has uncommon physical gifts for a fullback. He carried the ball 87 times for 305 yards and six touchdowns in 1994. Although the numbers are not overwhelming, they don't reveal his true value to the team. It was during the postseason that Floyd really made his worth known.

In two playoff games and the Super Bowl, Floyd carried the football 26 times for 77 yards and four scores. Against the Chicago Bears in the first round of the playoffs, he scored three of those touchdowns. All of them came on pounding runs against goal-line defenses. But Floyd's reputation was made as much off the field against Chicago as on it.

Just before halftime, 49ers quarterback Steve Young scored on a six-yard run, giving the 49ers a 30-3 advantage. After Young crossed the goal line, Chicago defensive back Shaun Gayle popped him with a shoulder and sent him sprawling to the turf. Young jumped up and spiked the ball at Gayle's feet.

But the late hit infuriated several 49ers. Brent Jones, Bart Oates, Jerry Rice and Floyd were among the players who took exception. They quickly came to Young's defense, wrestling Gayle to the turf and giving him a pummeling.

Soon Floyd found himself in a shoving match with Chicago's 290-pound defensive end Alonzo Spellman. Floyd didn't back down. Instead, he picked up Spellman and tossed him about 10 feet through the air, knocking him to the ground. The show of strength impressed several 49er veterans.

"I've got to admit," Young said, "I kind of enjoyed getting protection like that."

"You can't mess with our quarterback," Floyd said. "Steve's the guy who makes it all click. He's the one who got us here. We'll go out of our way to protect him."

Floyd didn't become an enforcer overnight. In fact, it wasn't until the sixth week of the regular season against the Detroit Lions that Floyd got his first start. It came a week after the 49ers were hammered mercilessly by the Philadelphia Eagles 40-8. San Francisco was in desperate need of pass protection that day, having lost four starting offensive linemen since the season began. Seifert watched in horror as his franchise quarterback, Steve Young, was regularly grinded into the turf by

the sack-happy Eagles. He decided to give Floyd the nod the following week against the Lions, more for his blocking skill than his running ability. Floyd provided both against Detroit.

In his first pro start, Floyd led the 49ers with 78 yards rushing and receiving. More importantly, he gave the team the emotional spark it needed after San Francisco fell behind 14-0 early in the game and appeared lethargic.

Floyd's first career touchdown came midway through the second quarter and seemed to turn the game around. Minutes later he supplied the lead block on Ricky Watters' touchdown run that tied the game. Floyd added another touchdown on a one-yard run in the third quarter, putting the 49ers ahead for the first time. The second touchdown was the most impressive. After being stopped short of the goal line, Floyd twisted away from a tackler then surged forward again with a great second effort to score.

"That was an awesome effort," center Bart Oates said. "I thought he was stopped, but he refused to go backwards. Then he surged forward again and pushed the whole pile into the end zone."

During the Detroit game, a new style also began to emerge from the 49ers. Floyd is one of the players credited with bringing a looser atmosphere to the team's formerly stoic approach to football.

"When I got here, I saw a bunch of guys

who were like robots," Floyd said. "They went to practice, watched film, went to meetings, then went home. There was no joking around. It didn't look like some guys were having fun. But some new people came in like Deion, Ken Norton, Richard Dent, and they were veterans with a little different attitude. Things loosened up a little and everybody started to play better and have more fun."

Floyd's infectious enthusiasm began to rub off on other players and coaches. By midseason, end zone dancing and high stepping became accepted parts of the 49er routine.

"I have to be excited and emotional to play well," Floyd said. "If I'm tense and tight, I won't play well."

The Super Bowl at Miami's Joe Robbie Stadium was the highlight of Floyd's rookie season. It was like a homecoming for Floyd, who grew up nearby in St. Petersburg, Florida. In high school, he was an all-county running back and rated the second best back in the nation, according to Super Prep Magazine.

Floyd attended Florida State University, where he was named to the All-America team in 1992 and 1993. With the Seminoles, he demonstrated a knack for finding the end zone, scoring 21 touchdowns and averaging 4.4 yards per carry. He also developed into a reliable receiver out of the backfield.

In 1993, Floyd was one of the main cogs on a Florida State team that

thumped Nebraska in the Orange Bowl to win the National Championship. In the title showdown, Floyd rushed seven times for 53 yards and scored one touchdown.

"I have to admit there were times during the season I was thinking about getting back to Miami for the Super Bowl," Floyd said. "I thought it would be great to return to the same place where we won the National Championship."

To get there, the 49ers had to beat the Dallas Cowboys. Floyd didn't realize the significance of the victory until afterward in the locker room.

"I was kind of surprised at the emotion," Floyd said. "There were some guys crying. There were some guys yelling because they were happy. Everyone from the owner to the coaches to the players were emotional. I wasn't used to seeing guys crying after a win."

And Floyd is no stranger to big games.

"I got used to playing in big games with Florida State," Floyd said. "The Miami-Florida State game is one of the biggest rivalries going. We always played before a packed house. The Super Bowl is a little like playing for a National Championship, except maybe on a bigger scale."

San Francisco 49ers President Carmen Policy shares a light moment with linebacker Mike Walter (99), after the 49ers destroyed the Chicago Bears 55-14 on Monday Night Football in 1991.

ended the day completing 22 of 38 passes for 348 yards.

San Francisco rebounded with two straight impressive wins, a 35-3 dismantling of the Detroit Lions, and a 23-7 defeat of Philadelphia. Then the 49ers returned to Atlanta for a rematch.

San Francisco completely dominated Atlanta in the first half, gaining 275 yards to the Falcons' 35. Yet the 49ers put only seven points on the scoreboard. Three times the 49ers were within the Falcons 15-yard line and failed to score. Mike Cofer missed four field goal attempts in the half, one of which was blocked. The 49ers' only points came on a 97-yard bomb from Steve Young to John Taylor, the longest pass in team history. Instead of having a four touchdown advantage at halftime, San Francisco led just 7-0.

Steve Bono started the second half at quarterback, as Young nursed a sprained knee which he suffered late in the first half. Both men watched as Atlanta took a 10-7 lead. Then Bono got the offense moving late in the game as he guided San Francisco to a touchdown with 59 seconds left. On the scoring play, Bono hit John Taylor in the corner of the end zone with a 30-yard pass to give the 49ers a 14-10 lead.

With time running out, Atlanta needed divine intervention to win this game. It got the miracle it needed—and broke the 49ers' hearts—as Billy Joe Tolliver hit Michael Haynes on a desperate 44-yard touchdown pass with one second left.

The 17-14 loss dropped the 49ers to 4-5, the first time they found themselves under .500 in the second half of a 16-game season since 1980. It also allowed New Orleans to hold a four-game lead over San Francisco.

The 49ers faced a desperate situation against New Orleans the following week. It was a game San

Francisco needed to win in order to get back on track. But the 49ers' season got bleaker as they failed to score a single touchdown in a 10-3 loss to New Orleans.

The Saints' only touchdown came in the second quarter after Tom Rathman fumbled at the Saints' 32-yard line. From there, New Orleans needed just five plays to get into the end zone.

With their backs to the wall and the playoffs now a long shot, San Francisco regrouped and won its final six games of the year. The 49ers thrashed Phoenix and Los Angeles and eagerly awaited a rematch with New Orleans. Steve Bono played the game of his life against the Saints' top-rated defense, completing 27 of 41 passes for 347 yards, three touchdowns and no interceptions. He completed 12 of 15 passes in the fourth quarter as the 49ers scored three touchdowns in the final five minutes to beat the Saints 38-24.

The fireworks began with just five minutes to play as Bono hit Dexter Carter on an 11-yard scoring pass to tie the game at 24-24. The deciding touchdown came with just over a minute left, when Jerry Rice hauled in a Bono pass at the 35-yard line and outraced three Saints to the end zone.

Dexter Carter supplied some special team punch in the first half, returning a kickoff 98 yards for a touchdown. It was San Francisco's third straight win and gave the 49ers a 7-6 record, putting them over the .500 mark for the first time in 1991. With three weeks to go in the season, a wild card spot in the playoffs was beginning to look like a faint possibility.

The 49ers continued to string wins together down the stretch, beating Seattle 24-22 and Kansas City 28-14. But despite their wins, San Francisco's wild card dreams were eliminated on the last Sunday of the season by the successes of other teams vying for a position in the playoffs.

Although shut out of the playoffs, San Francisco had one final game to play, a Monday Night Football affair against the playoff-bound Chicago Bears. The 49ers put on an awesome display, destroying the Bears 52-14, and matching the franchise record for points scored in a regular season game.

Steve Young was the hero in San Francisco's effort. Returning to the lineup after missing five weeks with a knee injury, Young threw three touchdown passes in the 49ers first three possessions and was 21 for 32 overall for 338 yards. He finished the year as the NFL's top-rated passer.

In the opening drive, Young directed San Francisco 76 yards, scoring on a roll-out pass to tight end Jamie Williams. On its second possession, San Francisco went 98 yards in 10 plays, capping the drive with a three-yard pass from Young to Rice. On the third possession, the 49ers took just one play when Young hit Rice with a 69-yard scoring pass.

Cornerback Don Griffin recovered two fumbles, returning one 99 yards for a touchdown, a team record.

The 49ers finished with a 10-6 record for third place in the NFC West and the knowledge that they were the best team in the NFL not to make the playoffs.

Steve Young won the passing title, despite missing six games, finishing with a 101.8 rating. Jerry Rice, Guy McIntyre and Charles Haley were selected to play in the Pro Bowl. And John Taylor was selected by his teammates as the recipient of the Len Eshmont Award.

Steve Bono (13) laughs at a Joe Montana joke prior to the start of a game in 1991.

1992 San Francisco bolstered its offensive and defensive backfields in the college draft by selecting hard-hitting Washington safety Dana Hall with its first-round pick and Florida State running back Amp Lee in the second round. Hall eventually won a starting job alongside strong safety David Whitmore, who was acquired from the New York Giants during the off-season.

With the departure of defensive end Charles Haley, Tim Harris became the team's new pass-rushing specialist.

Quarterback Joe Montana, who was still recovering from elbow surgery, was placed on injured reserve to start the season. Coach George Seifert did his best to defuse a quarterback controversy by naming Steve Young as his starter and appointing Steve Bono as Young's backup.

The 49ers opened the season impressively by throttling the New York Giants, 31-14. The defending AFC Champion Buffalo Bills then beat San Francisco, 34-31. The loss didn't seem to faze San Francisco as it rebounded to beat the New York Jets and New Orleans Saints before returning to the friendly confines of Candlestick with a 3-1 record.

Los Angeles Rams quarterback Jim Everett had fallen on hard times in recent years, but at Candlestick Park he shredded the 49ers' young secondary early in the game. Using his tight ends effectively, he marched the Rams downfield to a first-quarter touchdown and a 7-3 lead.

Everett blistered the 49ers' defense most of the day, but in the fourth quarter the defense stiffened and forced two Rams' turnovers. Steve Young took advantage of the miscues as he directed the 49ers to 17 points in the last six minutes of the game. Young capped two of the drives with touchdown runs of eight and 39 yards. The second score gave the 49ers a 24-17 lead.

There was plenty of time left and Everett continued to have his way with the 49ers' secondary. He drove the Rams 69 yards in two minutes, throwing a nine-yard scoring pass to Flipper Anderson to tie the game at 24-24 with 1:50 remaining.

Steve Young continued to have his own brilliant day, hitting Brent Jones for 43 yards and Jerry Rice for 26 yards to set up Mike Cofer's game-winning 21-yard field goal as time ran out. The win improved the 49ers' record to 4-1 and gave them a one-game lead over the New Orleans Saints in the NFC West.

After defeating New England 24-12, the 49ers unleashed a scoring flurry against the visiting Atlanta Falcons. San Francisco set a new regular season scoring record against Deion Sanders and friends as it posted a 56-17 win.

The following week, San Francisco scored its biggest victory of the season, overcoming a 13-point fourth-quarter deficit to beat the New Orleans Saints, 21-20, at Candlestick Park.

Utilizing a no-huddle offense and a steady diet of blitzes on defense, the 49ers defeated the Saints for the second time of the season. Steve Young scored the team's first touchdown on a 10-yard run, then brought them from behind with two late-scoring passes to tight end Brent Jones. Jones' final catch came on an eight-yard pass from Young with just 46 seconds remaining. It capped a 74-yard drive.

This victory improved the 49ers' record to 8-2, giving them a one-game lead over New Orleans in the West.

San Francisco waltzed through the rest of the schedule beating three playoff contenders, Philadelphia, Miami and Minnesota, before meeting Detroit in the final game of the regular season on Monday Night Football. The 49ers had already clinched the home-field advantage for the playoffs, so the game was insignificant in the standings. It was of interest solely because Joe Montana would be making his long-awaited comeback after two years on the sidelines with elbow problems.

Young got the starting call against Detroit, leading the 49ers to a 7-6 halftime advantage. Then Montana entered the game in the second half in monsoon-like conditions. In a driving rain storm at Candlestick, he was ineffective on the club's first two possessions. On his third series, he converted a third-down play and finally began to look like the old familiar Montana. After getting a first down, he took a sack, then scrambled for 16 yards, before drilling a nine-yard touchdown pass to Brent Jones.

On the next series, he hit on five straight passes and marched the team 76 yards for another score, capping it with an eight-yard pass to Amp Lee, and giving the 49ers a 24-6 lead.

Montana showed he had not lost his touch, despite being out of action for two seasons. He completed 15 of 21 passes for 126 yards and two scores and ran three times for 28 yards. More importantly, he directed the 49ers to 17 points on three straight drives.

Pierce Holt (78) and Michael Carter (95) gang up to stop Chicago's Brad Muster for a loss.

Montana passed the 35,000-yard mark in career passing in this game, a plateau reached by only four other quarterbacks in NFL history: Fran Tarkenton, Dan Fouts, Johnny Unitas and Dan Marino.

The 24-6 victory enabled San Francisco to complete the season with a 14-2 record. After a week off, the 49ers first playoff opponent was the Washington Redskins. Playing in a quagmire at Candlestick Park, the 49ers handled the Redskins, 20-13, despite suffering four turnovers.

San Francisco scored first when Steve Young connected with John Taylor on a five-yard scoring pass. Washington responded with a Chip Lohmiller field goal. Mike Cofer added a 23-yard field goal, and as time was running out in the half, Young hit Brent Jones on a 16-yard slant-in to give the 49ers a 17-3 halftime lead.

Washington made it interesting in the third quarter when Chip Lohmiller kicked a 32-yard field goal, and Mark Rypien directed a 66-yard scoring drive capped by his own one-yard run. With 14 minutes left to play, San Francisco had a slim 17-13 lead. Cofer added one final 33-yard field goal and the 49ers came away with an uninspired 20-13 win.

Jerry Rice was the leading receiver for San Francisco, catching six passes for 88 yards. Ricky

Watters rushed for 83 yards on 18 carries, and Steve Young completed 20 of 30 for 221 yards.

On the defensive side, San Francisco had five sacks, including three by Pierce Holt.

San Francisco was now one step away from the Super Bowl. The Dallas Cowboys were the only ones standing in the way.

The NFL brought in turf expert George Toma to replace the Candlestick sod that had been decimated by the combination of a month-long downpour and the playoff game between the Redskins and 49ers.

San Francisco got off to a dubious start against Dallas on the third play of the game, when Young caught the Cowboys in a blitz and launched a beautiful 63-yard touchdown pass to Jerry Rice. The play was nullified, however, by a Guy McIntyre holding penalty and the 49ers failed to score on the drive.

Dallas took the early lead on a Sean Elliot field goal, but San Francisco responded with a drive of its own, capped by Young's one-yard run that gave the 49ers a 7-3 lead.

But Dallas took control of the game midway through the second quarter and into the third, scoring on four straight possessions and virtually controlling the ball throughout the third quarter. San Fran-

Brent Jones 1987–

The tight end must maintain a delicate balance between the brutal savagery of offensive-line play and the subtle precision of an NFL passing game. It is a thin line that is difficult to walk, one that requires a unique blend of finesse and strength. It requires a man with uncommon athletic skill and a special mental focus.

The San Francisco 49ers have always recognized the importance of the tight end and have been blessed with a long line of skilled players in this position. From Monty Stickles through Ted Kwalick, to Russ Francis and John Frank, the tight end has always played an important role in the San Francisco offense.

In the 49ers record book, the passing categories are domi- nated by wide receivers, however, with names like Jerry Rice, John Taylor, Gene Washing- ton and Dwight Clark. In 1990, a new name emerged when Brent Jones had 56 receptions, setting a team record for catches by a tight end. Jones has been a force to be reckoned with ever since.

The development of Brent Jones has been of prime importance to the 49ers' offensive scheme. Along with two of the finest wide receivers in pro football, Jerry Rice and John Taylor, Jones is the man who keeps opposing defenses honest. Defenders cannot afford to double- team Rice and Taylor at the expense of Jones. He has become a legitimate deep threat and an important third-down receiver.

In 1992, his sixth season with the 49ers, Jones' contribution to the San Francisco offense was finally noticed around the league and he was selected to his first Pro Bowl. He is just the second 49er tight end, besides Ted Kwalick in 1971 and 1972, to be so honored.

But the best was yet to come for Jones. In 1993, he was selected to another Pro Bowl after catching 68 passes for 735 yards. A year later, he relived his dream by capturing another Super Bowl ring as San Fran- cisco defeated San Diego in Super Bowl XXIX.

Jones had a humble start with the 49ers in 1987 when he joined the club as a free agent. Originally drafted by the Pittsburgh Steelers in the fifth round in 1986, he was waived late in the year after spending most of the season on injured reserve with a neck problem.

The 49ers were a logical stop in Jones' search for an NFL job, having grown up in San Jose and having played college ball at nearby Santa Clara. It also helped that Coach Bill Walsh was familiar with Jones' abilities after watching him perform at the 1985 East-West Shrine game. Walsh was happy to give the tight end a closer look.

But there didn't appear to be much room on the 49er roster for Jones. The club was set at tight end. Starter John Frank, a devastating run blocker, was in his prime and on the verge of becoming a Pro Bowl player, while veteran Russ Francis added valuable experience and leadership. But Brent Jones persevered. He made a place for himself on the squad by showing hustle and grit on special teams.

During those first two years, Jones saw limited action on offense and caught just 10 passes, but two of those receptions were for touchdowns. Most importantly, his determination did not go unnoticed by the 49er coaches.

Then, late in the 1988 season, Jones got the chance he'd been waiting for and used it to display his talent for the end zone. In a dramatic game against the Philadelphia Eagles, the 49ers scored three touchdowns in the final seven minutes to pull out a 38-28 win. Jones scored the game-

winning touchdown on a 25-yard pass over the middle which was left open when Rice and Taylor were double-teamed. It was the start of an important new role for Jones as the man who would take the pressure off San Francisco's dangerous wide receivers.

Prior to the 1989 season, tight end John Frank decided he had played enough football. He retired in order to finish medical school and become a surgeon. Jones won the starting job and soon became an intricate part of the 49er passing game.

In his first year as a starter, Jones caught 40 passes for 500 yards and five touchdowns. He saved his best for clutch moments. Against the New York Giants in an important late season game, he caught five passes and had a 17-yard touchdown reception. Then Jones scored a touchdown in all three of the club's post-season games, as the 49ers made their drive to Super Bowl XXIV. The culminating moment of Jones' season came in the Super Bowl against Denver when he hauled in a seven-yard reception for a touchdown.

"That was like a dream come true," Jones said. "Just being there and winning the game was important to me but scoring in the Super Bowl is something I'll never forget."

In 1990, Jones came into his own as a receiver. Early in the season he had his best game ever, nabbing five passes for 125 yards against Atlanta and

scoring on a 67-yard reception. He ended the year with 56 catches for 747 yards and set club records for a tight end in both categories. He also had five touchdown receptions.

A knee injury hampered Jones during the 1991 season and he spent nearly two months on injured reserve. With Jones gone, the offense struggled. When he returned, the team was rejuvenated and went on to win its final six games of the year. Despite missing seven games, Jones caught 27 passes in 1991 for 417 yards.

Jones is valuable to the club as more than just a pass catcher. His desire to win has been an inspiration to club members. That was never more evident than late in the 1992 season when the 49ers needed a win over rival New Orleans to maintain their lead in the NFC Western Division. In that game, Jones was forced to the sidelines late in the third quarter after taking a vicious hit on a 20-yard catch.

"I couldn't breathe," Jones said. "I tried to get up and the official told me to stay down where I was."

Jones left the game with a rib injury. He slapped a pad on his rib and returned in the fourth quarter to catch two touchdown passes as the 49ers rallied to beat the Saints, 21-20. Jones caught the game winner, an eight-yard scoring pass, with 46 seconds remaining on the clock.

"I saw the coverage on that play and knew I was getting the ball,"

Jones said. "We ran the same play for our earlier touchdown. I was going to run a hook behind the safety. Steve Young read the defense and did the smart thing. He threw it up and out so either I caught the ball or nobody caught it."

One of the biggest thrills of the 1992 season for Jones was the return of Joe Montana on a Monday Night Football game against Detroit on the final day of the season. It was Montana's first appearance in nearly two years.

Jones was Montana's favorite target that night. Montana connected with Jones on a 16-yard pass on third down to keep a 49er drive alive, then hit him with a nine-yard scoring pass. It was Montana's first touchdown pass in two years.

"I wanted to keep that ball," Jones said. "I think I was more excited than Joe was."

Dana Stubblefield (94) was named NFL Defensive Rookie of the Year in 1993 after registering 10.5 sacks that season. He was a first-round selection of the 49ers in 1993. Here Stubblefield pressures Philadelphia Eagles quarterback Bubby Brister (6).

cisco lost the ball on three turnovers and had possession for just nine plays in the period. When the third quarter came to an end, the 49ers were fortunate to be trailing just 17-13.

The Cowboys increased their lead to 24-13 when Emmitt Smith hauled in a 16-yard touchdown pass from Troy Aikman just two minutes into the final quarter.

With time winding down, Steve Young gave the 49ers new life when he led the offense 93 yards in nine plays, cutting the Dallas lead to 24-20 with 4:20 minutes left to play. Then disaster struck. On Dallas' ensuing drive, Aikman hit Alvin Harper with a 15-yard pass over the middle, and the shifty wide receiver raced another 45 yards to the nine-yard line. Three plays later, the Cowboys scored the clinching touchdown.

Dallas quarterback Troy Aikman blistered the 49ers' secondary for 322 passing yards and Emmit Smith ran for 114.

Steve Young connected 25 of 35 for 313 yards but suffered two interceptions. Ricky Watters was the club's leading rusher, gaining 66 yards on 11 carries.

Associated Press honored Steve Young, Jerry Rice and Harris Barton by naming them All-Pro at the end of the season. Steve Young was named the league's Most Valuable Player and was named recipient of the team's Len Eshmont Award.

Jerry Rice continued to catch passes and score touchdowns at an unprecedented pace. He set an NFL record when he caught his 101st touchdown pass midway through the year to break the league's career touchdown reception mark.

1993 Coach George Seifert spent the offseason pondering a route back to the Super Bowl and came to the conclusion defense was the secret to getting there.

In the annual college draft, he chose a pair of defensive linemen in the first round. Dana Stubblefield, a 6 foot 2, 300-pounder from the University of Kansas, was the 26th player selected overall. Then with the 49ers' other first-round choice, the 27th overall, Seifert picked Tennessee's Todd Kelly.

In the later rounds, Seifert continued to search for defensive players. He selected cornerback Adrian Hardy with his second-round choice and Pittsburgh State linebacker Troy Wilson in the seventh round.

Michigan quarterback Elvis Grbac, an eighth-round choice, was brought in as a backup to Steve Young.

San Francisco opened the 1993 regular season in Pittsburgh against the Steelers. It took the 49ers just one series to get the offense in gear.

On their first possession of the year, the 49ers put together a 12-play drive that covered 61 yards as Steve Young mixed short passes with running plays to set up Mike Cofer's 37-yard field goal.

Just over a minute later, 49ers cornerback Mike McGruder intercepted a pass from Steelers quarterback Mike Tomczak, giving the 49ers the ball at the Steelers 34. From there, it took just four plays for the 49ers to record their first touchdown of the season, a

Ken Norton, Jr. 1994–

It's tough to grow up in the shadow of the man who broke Muhammad Ali's jaw and took away his heavyweight title. To establish himself outside of the legacy of his famous father, Ken Norton, Jr., knew he'd have to do something extraordinary.

In 1994 he did. Norton became the first professional football player ever to win three straight Super Bowl rings. He did it with two different clubs.

The 6'2", 243-pound inside linebacker left the Dallas Cowboys to join the 49ers as a free agent prior to the 1994 season after signing a six-year $9.6 million contract. It was a godsend for San Francisco, which was in desperate need of defensive help.

After losing the NFC Championship Game to the Cowboys for the second straight year in 1993, San Francisco sought to retool its linebacking corps. It was the club's most obvious weakness. Team president Carmen Policy went after linebackers with gusto, signing San Diego's Gary Plummer, New Orleans' Rickey Jackson and Norton. But it was Norton's acquisition that was the most satisfying. By bringing Norton aboard, the 49ers not only strengthened their own club, they weakened their conference rivals.

But things were not as rosy as Norton expected in his early days as a 49er. He was acquired as an aggressive run-stopper and earned a reputation as an intense competitor with great speed and quickness. In 1993, he played in his first Pro Bowl after leading the Super Bowl champion Cowboys in tackles, with 159, and in sacks, with 10. But some critics felt those statistics were an illusion. And in the first six games of 1994, the 49ers began to wonder if the critics weren't correct.

The first half of the 1994 season did not go as Norton expected. The 49ers defense was woefully porous. That became most evident against Philadelphia in the fifth game of the season as the Eagles ran over the 49ers like a pack of wild mustangs. They gained 191 yards rushing and handed the 49ers their worst defeat in nearly two decades, 40-8. An unknown rookie named Charlie Garner picked up 111 of those yards.

After being throttled by the Eagles, San Francisco's rushing defense was ranked 12th in the league. At that point, a run at the Super Bowl seemed unlikely, if not downright impossible.

That was also about the time Norton began to hear the murmurs. Local broadcasters and sports reporters claimed he was an overpaid free agent bust. Some felt he was damaged goods. Scouts and coaches said he looked unsure of himself and tentative on plays. And for a linebacker, indecisiveness is the worst possible sin.

"We were all getting used to a new system at the beginning of the season," said Gary Plummer, who joined the 49ers in 1994 after eight seasons with the San Diego Chargers. "There was a little confusion at times, people wondering where to go on different coverages. Eventually we got it together though."

And there was some credence to the rumor that Norton was damaged merchandise, although he claims he was healthy. His physical problem began midway through the 1993 season in a game against the Philadelphia Eagles. Norton remembers grabbing a ball carrier and holding tight, then something in his upper arm giving way. On the Dallas sideline, he told the trainer he had a cramp. The team doctor took a look and explained that the entire right bicep muscle had ripped away from the bone and had bunched up into a knot.

Rather then having surgery done on the bicep, Norton played out the season. Every day for nearly three months Norton felt the cramp-like pain in his upper arm. He had trouble lifting his right arm above his shoulder but still he continued to play.

In February, after leading the Cowboys to the Super Bowl and playing in his first Pro Bowl, Norton had surgery performed. It was over three months after the injury occurred.

After the debacle against Philadelphia everything slowly fell into place for Norton. He began to feel comfortable about the time his ex-teammates, the Dallas Cowboys, came to town. Appropriately enough, Norton had one of his best games of the season against Dallas. The 49ers held All-Pro running back Emmitt Smith to 87 yards rushing. San Francisco defeated Dallas, 21-14.

"Early in the season I was being used a little differently than I was being used in Dallas," Norton said. "With the 49ers, I was supposed to check certain keys and do certain things before going to the ball. With the Cowboys, my job was to fly to the ball, make the play, get a tackle."

Eventually the 49ers began using Norton the way Dallas did, letting him loose to freelance. The results were seen immediately, especially by his former teammates.

"I felt a lot more comfortable once they turned me loose," Norton said. "In the Dallas game, I was ready to do whatever it took to win. I was playing for pride there."

And he did himself proud, combining with Plummer to record 15 tackles. More importantly, they took Emmitt Smith out of the game in the second half.

"That was basic smash-mouth football," Plummer said. "I could see Ken was ready for it. He always does a good job preparing himself physically and mentally for a game. But against Dallas he was like his old self. He was trash-talking and you could tell he was hyped."

Trash talk is something new in the 49er repertoire. Norton brought it to the club and helped instill a new attitude among the defensive crew in 1994. Along with Richard Dent and Deion Sanders, he added a sense of bravado to the 49ers that bordered on cockiness.

Although Norton is now acclaimed as one of the best middle linebackers in the game, it is a relatively new position for him. In fact, Norton didn't even begin to play football until he was a junior in high school. The reason: Ken Norton, Sr., the former heavyweight champion of the world, forbid his son from playing football because he felt the sport was too dangerous.

Norton eventually earned All-America honors as a linebacker at UCLA, then was drafted by the Dallas Cowboys in the second round in 1988, the 41st player selected overall. During his first five seasons at Dallas, he was used primarily as an outside linebacker. In 1993, he moved to inside linebacker and recorded a career-high 159 tackles during the year, earning his first Pro Bowl berth. It was the second straight season that he led the team in tackles.

It was a move the 49ers are glad he made.

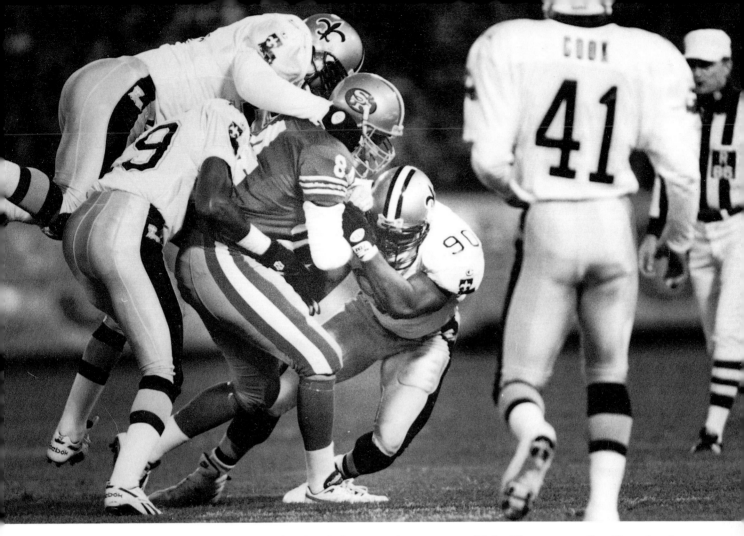

Tight end Brent Jones (84) is dragged down by a band of New Orleans Saints defenders. Jones has emerged as a clutch receiver for San Francisco and has been selected to play in three Pro Bowls.

five-yard pass from Steve Young to Jerry Rice.

Pittsburgh's next series lasted just four plays before 49ers linebacker Keith DeLong recovered a Barry Foster fumble. San Francisco capitalized on the miscue when Young hooked up with Rice for their second touchdown of the game just six seconds into the second quarter.

The Steelers were able to put three points on the board before halftime as Gary Anderson split the uprights with a 29-yard field goal. But as the two clubs left the field for intermission, San Francisco was clearly in control, 17-3.

Pittsburgh clawed back into the game, cutting the 49ers' lead to 17-13 late in the third quarter after a touchdown by Barry Foster and another Anderson field goal. But Steve Young fired his third scoring pass of the day to Brent Jones early in the fourth quarter, putting the game out of reach. In San Francisco's 24-13 win over Pittsburgh, Young completed 24 of 36 passes for 240 yards and three touchdowns. Jerry Rice caught eight passes for 78 yards

and two scores. Ricky Watters was San Francisco's leading rusher with 46 yards on 14 carries.

The Cleveland Browns handed the 49ers their first loss of the season in week two. Four turnovers haunted San Francisco as the Browns capitalized on the miscues to tally 17 points in the second quarter. Young, who completed 19 of 33 passes for 274 yards, suffered three interceptions. The 49ers scored on a pair of field goals by Mike Cofer and Marc Logan's four-yard run late in the second quarter. But Cleveland held San Francisco scoreless in the second half and triumphed, 23-12.

Ricky Watters had his first 100-yard rushing game of the season in week three as the 49ers downed the Atlanta Falcons 37-30 in a shoot-out at Candlestick Park. The lead changed hands five times as quarterbacks Bobby Hebert and Steve Young matched each other with three touchdown passes apiece.

After falling behind 13-9 in the first half, San Francisco responded with four second-half touchdowns. Young sparked the effort, completing 18 of 22 passes for 210 yards, including scoring passes to Nate Singleton, Brent Jones and Jamie Williams. Jerry Rice added a touchdown on a 43-yard run.

In week six, the 49ers took a 3-2 record to Texas

Stadium in a much-anticipated meeting with the defending Super Bowl champion Dallas Cowboys. It was San Francisco's first attempt to avenge its loss to Dallas in the 1992 NFC Championship Game.

San Francisco got on the scoreboard just three minutes into the game when linebacker Johnny Johnson stripped the football from Cowboys running back Emmitt Smith and cornerback Eric Davis picked it up and dashed 47 yards to the end zone.

After Dallas kicker Eddie Murray's 48-yard field goal made the score 7-3, the 49ers struck again. They mounted a 12-play, 73-yard drive late in the first quarter that was capped by Mike Cofer's 25-yard field goal.

In the second quarter, ex-49er Charles Haley came back to haunt his old teammates. He sacked Young and forced a fumble, which was recovered by the Cowboys at the San Francisco 18. Four plays later Emmitt Smith danced into the end zone to give Dallas a 13-10 lead. Just before the half ended, Murray added a 29-yard field goal to give the Cowboys a 16-10 advantage at the intermission.

Late in the third quarter, San Francisco took the lead again at 17-16, when Young hit tight end Brent Jones with a 12-yard touchdown pass. But that would be the end of scoring for San Francisco.

The game slipped away on the 49ers' next possession as Marc Logan fumbled at his own 39 and the Cowboys recovered. They needed just two plays to put the ball in the end zone as Troy Aikman hooked up with Michael Irvin on a 36-yard scoring pass. It was just one of Irvin's 12 receptions for 168 yards. The score gave Dallas a 23-17 lead with an entire quarter left to play. San Francisco had trouble mounting an attack and the Cowboys held on to defeat the 49ers 26-17.

San Francisco won six consecutive games after losing to Dallas. The club's most impressive offensive displays came in beating the Rams 40-17 and the Tampa Bay Bucs 45-21.

Against the Rams, Steve Young passed for 245 yards and one touchdown, and ran for another 57 yards. Fullback Marc Logan scored twice, while Ricky Watters added a touchdown.

Young blistered the Bucs as well, completing 23 of 29 passes for 311 yards and four touchdowns. Jerry Rice was on the receiving end of all four scoring passes. He had eight receptions for 172 yards.

With a 9-3 record and sole possession of first place in the NFC West, the 49ers traveled to Atlanta. Once again quarterbacks Hebert and Young got into a throwing match.

Young struck first by hitting running back Amp Lee with a six-yard touchdown pass in the first quarter. Hebert responded with a five-yard scoring pass to wide receiver Andre Rison.

Rathman gave the 49ers a 14-7 lead when he capped a 14-play, 77-yard drive with a two-yard run. Cofer added a 32-yard field goal to give San Francisco a 17-7 lead at the half. The 49ers upped their advantage to 24-7 early in the third quarter when Steve Young scrambled 10 yards for a touchdown. Then the game slipped away.

Hebert capitalized on several 49er mistakes in the second half to rally the Falcons. He took advantage of Dexter Carter's fumbled punt early in the fourth quarter to throw a touchdown pass to Mike Haynes, cutting San Francisco's lead to 24-14. With six minutes left, Hebert hooked up with Rison again to make the score 24-21. Then with three minutes left he drove Atlanta 38 yards in eight plays to set up Norm Johnson's 47-yard field goal, which tied the game at 24-24.

On the ensuing kickoff, Dexter Carter fumbled again. The Falcons recovered and Johnson kicked a 37-yard field goal with 28 seconds left to win the game.

A week later the 49ers were out for blood and the Detroit Lions happened to be in the way. San Francisco demolished the Lions 55-17 generating a season-high 565 yards in offense as six different players scored touchdowns. The victory gave the 49ers the NFC Western Division crown.

Steve Young and wide receiver John Taylor got the 49ers rolling early against Detroit. They hooked up on the third play from scrimmage for a 68-yard touchdown. Minutes later Young threw his second scoring pass, a 20-yarder to wide receiver Sanjay Beach.

Detroit kicker Jason Hanson answered with a 51-yard field goal, but that was as close as the Lions would get. After the ensuing kickoff Young needed just one play to hit Jerry Rice with an 80-yard touchdown pass.

On the 49ers' next series, Young guided the team on a 14-play, 72-yard drive. Fullback Tom Rathman capped it with a two-yard touchdown plunge. After one half of play, the 49ers led 31-10.

Young finished the game 17 of 23, passing for 354 yards and four touchdowns. Amp Lee was the 49ers leading rusher with 66 yards on 18 carries. He also caught six passes for 50 yards and a touchdown.

Deion Sanders 1994

By just about anyone's standards, Deion Sanders was a bargain. He signed with the 49ers for $1 million in 1994. But there was a catch. He'd also collect a $500,000 bonus if the club won the NFC title and another $250,000 bonus if San Francisco won the Super Bowl.

Of course, Sanders walked away with the $750,000 in bonuses, and probably guaranteed himself 10 times that amount in endorsement fees, after the 49ers whipped the Chargers in Super Bowl XXIX.

Along the way, Sanders was named the 1994 NFL Defensive Player of the Year. He helped loosen up one of the most conservative teams in pro football. And he turned out to be the missing piece to the 49ers' defensive puzzle, solidifying a unit that was considered unfocused early in the season.

Sanders came to San Francisco by way of Atlanta, where he played for five years after being the fifth player chosen in the 1989 NFL draft. Back then, he inked a $4.4 million contract over four years, plus his own licensing deal with NFL properties. In signing with San Francisco, he passed up several more lucrative offers, including a $17-million, four-year deal with the New Orleans Saints.

His logic for doing so was impeccable. He had one goal, to win a Super Bowl and add a large diamond-studded Super Bowl ring to his collection of ostentatious jewelry. The San Francisco 49ers were the best possible vehicle for Sanders to hitch a ride to Miami for Super Bowl XXIX.

"Winning was the most important thing for me," Sanders said upon signing with San Francisco. "I want to play in a Super Bowl. The 49ers have already won four Super Bowls. I'm here to make it five."

"Everyone here knew we were getting probably the best cover man in football," said then 49er defensive coordinator Ray Rhodes. "That's exactly what we wanted.

What we didn't realize was that he has a tremendous work ethic. He did everything we asked him in practice. He studied hard and learned the coverages. And there was none of the showy stuff. That attitude rubbed off on some other guys and everyone worked a little harder."

Tom Holmoe, the 49ers secondary coach, had the task of reviewing coverages with Sanders when the All-Pro defensive back reported to the team. As they went through the 49ers' complicated playbook, Sanders absorbed the various zone coverages and defensive switches before politely asking Holmoe, "But mostly I'll be playing man-to-man, right?"

"Some people were worried that Deion would be too flashy and that he might be a problem," Harris Barton said. "But he was here for about five minutes and everybody realized he was a good guy who was going to fit in."

In his first outing with the 49ers, after just three days of practice, Sanders lined up at right corner against the Los Angeles Rams. He was in mid-season form, blanketing the Rams' receivers as only two passes were thrown in his direction. Both were incomplete.

Sanders has picked up many nicknames during his days as a two-sport professional athlete, budding rap star, amateur dancer and one-man commercial endorsement machine. Among them are "Neon Deion," a moniker he despises, and "Prime Time," a name he seems to enjoy. In his second game with the 49ers, he lived up to his "Prime Time" handle.

Against the New Orleans Saints, San Francisco held a precarious 17-13 lead with less than a minute to play. New Orleans quarterback Jim Everett had directed his club to the San Francisco 30-yard line and was poised to score. He fired a pass in the flat that hung a little too long. Sanders intercepted it and returned it 74 yards for a game-saving touchdown.

"Deion baited Everett on that," said defensive end Richard Dent said. "He kind of lurked back there until Everett released the pass then just exploded to the ball."

Sanders interception return turned a nail-biter into certain victory for San Francisco. But it wasn't the only game he helped save. He changed the course of several contests during the 1994 season with outstanding plays. The 49ers' second matchup with the Los Angeles Rams is another case in point.

San Francisco scored with just under two minutes left in the game to take a 31-27 lead over Los Angeles. After the ensuing kickoff quarterback Chris Miller engineered a drive that took the Rams to the 49ers' 38-yard line with 55 seconds remaining.

Sanders was lined up to defend against Rams wide receiver Flipper Anderson. Anderson beat Sanders deep in the end zone and Miller's pass was on line for what appeared to be a certain touchdown. Just as the ball was to settle into Anderson's hands for the score that would put Los Angeles ahead, Sanders came diving out of nowhere to flick the ball away from Anderson and save the day for San Francisco.

"On the film I saw the kind of play Deion made to get to that ball," said Ray Rhodes. "You can't teach people something like that. For Deion to get to that ball took incredible athletic skill. You just don't see that kind of speed and quickness. I don't think I've ever seen anyone recover to make a play like that, especially at such a critical point in a game."

And, of course, there was the 49ers game with Atlanta, Deion's first trip back to the Georgia Dome. In that one, he displayed his flair for the dramatic by intercepting a Jeff George pass, then high-stepping down the sideline past the Falcons bench on the way to a 93-yard touchdown.

But Sanders was a catalyst for the 49ers in other ways, too. He brought a new attitude to a team viewed as somber, conservative and business-like throughout the league. He instilled fun in the 49er locker room.

"To tell you the truth, I was a little surprised when I first got here and saw the attitude of some of these guys," Sanders said. "For years, I watched Jerry Rice and Steve Young and Ricky Watters kick people's butts. I thought they must have a lot of fun doing it. But I found out they were never quite satisfied. Even when they won, they had the feeling they didn't win big enough. We needed to change that."

By playing in Super Bowl XXIX, Sanders became the first athlete ever to participate in the Super Bowl and the World Series. He also played in the college World Series and was on a Florida State football team that was a couple of votes shy of being a national champion.

Playing for the Atlanta Braves during the 1992 World Series against Cincinnati, he batted .533 with five stolen bases in four games. Although the Braves lost the series, the Reds were impressed enough to make a trade for Sanders a year later.

But for Sanders, professional sports is more than competition. It's entertainment and part of the entertainment business entails fancy threads, gold chains, gaudy rings, expensive cars and sex appeal.

"The field is my stage," he said. "And I love to perform. I play to make people have fun."

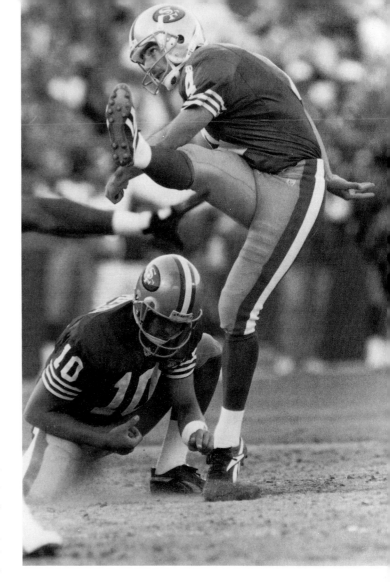

Kicker Doug Brien was a third-round draft pick of the 49ers in 1994. As a rookie, he was 4th in the NFC in scoring with 105 points. Klaus Wilmsmeyer (10) is the holder.

Dexter Carter rushed one time for 50 yards and a touchdown.

The 49ers ended the regular season with a 10-6 record after home losses to Houston and Philadelphia, then met the New York Giants in the NFC divisional playoff. It turned into the Ricky Watters show at Candlestick Park as Watters scored a playoff-record five touchdowns and the 49ers annihilated the Giants 44-3.

The 49ers didn't waste time getting on the scoreboard. They took the opening kickoff and marched 80 yards in eight plays. Watters put the finishing touch on the drive, scoring on a one-yard plunge. It was the first of three touchdowns he scored in the opening half as the 49ers built a 23-3 lead.

Watters added two more touchdowns in the third quarter before he called it a day. He rushed for 118 yards on 24 carries. Marc Logan added 40 yards on nine carries and one touchdown. Steve Young connected on 17 of 22 passes for 226 yards as the 49ers racked up 413 yards of total offense to just 194 yards for New York.

On the defensive side of the ball, safety Tim McDonald led the club with five tackles. His first-quarter interception also led to the 49ers' second score. Defensive back Eric Davis got into the action with an interception while defensive lineman Dana Stubblefield supplied inside pressure and recorded two sacks.

In the NFC Championship Game, the 49ers faced the Dallas Cowboys for the second straight season. The Cowboys looked tough on the opening drive as they marched 75 yards in 11 plays and scored on Emmitt Smith's five-yard run.

Early in the second quarter, the 49ers retaliated. Steve Young directed a nine-play, 80-yard drive and capped it by connecting with fullback Tom Rathman for a seven-yard touchdown.

Unfortunately, that was the highlight of the day for San Francisco. Dallas took control of the contest after that, scoring 21 unanswered points in the second quarter. Fullback Daryl Johnston pounded the first nail in the 49ers' coffin as he scored on a four-yard run. Troy Aikman then threw touchdown passes to Emmitt Smith and Jay Novacek, giving Dallas a 28-7 lead at the half.

Late in the third quarter, the 49ers tried to make another run at the Cowboys. They put together a 43-yard drive and scored on Watters' four-yard rush. As the fourth quarter opened, the 49ers trailed 28-14. That's when the key series of the game transpired.

Cowboys backup quarterback Bernie Kosar took the field after Aikman was knocked silly and left the game with a concussion. Kosar faced a third-and-nine from his own 19. The 49ers came with a heavy rush, but Kosar was able to avoid it and connect with Michael Irvin for 12 yards and a first down. Three plays later, he found wide receiver Alvin Harper on a 42-yard scoring pass to give the Cowboys an insurmountable 35-14 lead.

Steve Young scored one last touchdown for the 49ers late in the fourth quarter, but it was meaningless. The Cowboys held on to win 38-21. Young completed 27 of 45 passes for 287 yards and one touchdown. He was also the 49ers' leading rusher, picking up 38 yards on seven carries and one touchdown.

Although the 49ers did not advance to the Super Bowl, they led the NFL in scoring, with 473 points, and total offense, averaging 402 yards per game.

Steve Young completed 68 percent of his passes

and set a club record by passing for 4,023 yards. The club's leading ground gainer was Ricky Watters, who rushed for 950 yards and 10 touchdowns.

Jerry Rice recorded 98 receptions for 1,503 yards and 15 touchdowns and was named NFL Offensive Player of the Year by Associated Press. He also received the Len Eshmont Award, the team's most prestigious honor.

Dana Stubblefield was named NFL Defensive Rookie of the Year after registering 10.5 sacks.

Steve Young, Jerry Rice, Tim McDonald, Harris Barton, Guy McIntyre, Brent Jones and Jesse Sapolu were all selected to play in the Pro Bowl.

1994

The road to Super Bowl XXIX actually began in an elevator as the 1993 season came to a close. That's when 49ers owner Eddie DeBartolo and team president Carmen Policy were heading to the 49ers locker room in the final moments of the 1993 NFC Championship Game between Dallas and San Francisco.

San Francisco was about to drop its second straight NFC title to the Cowboys and DeBartolo was hot. He let Policy know he didn't want to lose to the Cowboys again. In no uncertain terms, he told Policy to find the players San Francisco needed to stop Dallas' string of wins over the 49ers, no matter what they cost.

The newly implemented NFL salary cap put a lid on how much money Policy could spend, but not on how creatively he could spend it.

During the off-season, Policy signed Chicago Bears All-Pro defensive end Richard Dent, Dallas Cowboys All-Pro linebacker Ken Norton, New Orleans Saints All-Pro linebacker Rickey Jackson, San Diego Chargers linebacker Gary Plummer and, in perhaps the biggest coup of his career, Atlanta Falcons All-Pro defensive back Deion Sanders.

To fit this squadron of NFL heavyweights under the salary cap, Policy restructured the contracts of several 49ers players, including Pro Bowlers Jerry Rice, Ricky Watters and Tim McDonald.

The 49ers also had six draft selections in the first three rounds, including two first-round picks. With its first choice, the seventh overall, San Francisco selected Notre Dame defensive tackle Bryant Young. Florida State fullback William Floyd was also a first-round pick.

In the second round, the 49ers chose Syracuse linebacker Kevin Mitchell and Virginia Tech defen-

sive back Tyronne Drakeford. And in the third round, San Francisco selected Cal kicker Doug Brien. All five men played a role in the 49ers' march to the Super Bowl.

One surprise of the draft was linebacker Lee Woodall, a sixth-round pick out of tiny West Chester, a division II college. Woodall would eventually win a starting job with San Francisco.

The 49ers opened the season at Candlestick Park in a Monday night game against the Los Angeles Raiders. Coach Art Shell's Raiders were being billed as a possible Super Bowl team and boasted three wide receivers fast enough to be on the U.S. Olympic sprint team.

"This game will let us know exactly how good we are," Jerry Rice said before the game. "We've got to learn from this and just get better if we're going to be champions."

Rice caught three touchdown passes in the game, of which the third was the most significant. It was Rice's 127th career touchdown and broke Jim Brown's NFL career touchdown record.

As for the rest of the 49ers, they had no problem with the Raiders. San Francisco thrashed Los Angeles 44-14.

The second week of the season was billed as a matchup between quarterbacks Steve Young and Joe Montana as the 49ers traveled to Kansas City to meet the Chiefs. It was the first meeting between the two clubs since Montana's departure for the Midwest.

San Francisco was playing with a decimated offensive line. Out of action were All-Pro tackle Harris Barton and starting right guard Ralph Tamm. During the game, the 49ers lost guard Jesse Sapolu to a pulled hamstring. Tamm's backup, Derrick Deese, also left the game after suffering a slight concussion.

On the defensive side of the ball Richard Dent hobbled to the sideline with a serious knee injury that kept him out of action for all but three plays the rest of the year.

The Chiefs scored first as Montana directed an 11-play, 67-yard drive and capped it with a one-yard pass to tackle Joe Valerio, who was lined up as an eligible receiver. The Chiefs then capitalized on four 49er turnovers to beat the 49ers 24-17.

Montana was 19 of 31, passing for 203 yards and two touchdowns, but it wasn't so much Montana that beat the 49ers as linebacker Derrick Thomas. Thomas made three sacks and wreaked havoc with the 49er offense all day.

Just four days after losing to the Chiefs, the

Jesse Sapolu 1983–1996

Center Jesse Sapolu thought it was a joke. He was in the end zone at Honolulu's Aloha Stadium in February of 1994 for the Pro Bowl along with his position coach from the 49ers, Bobb McKittrick, and Giants center Bart Oates.

While loosening up to play in the game, the three men were discussing the possibility of Oates, who was about to become a free agent, signing with the 49ers. If Oates did sign, McKittrick joked, Sapolu would be forced to move back to guard, a position he played from 1983 to 1988 for the 49ers.

Sapolu laughed, but deep down he did not think the idea was particularly funny. He

figured he'd found a niche for himself at center over the last five seasons, and was finally being recognized by his fellow players and coaches. He was voted to play in the Pro Bowl for the first time after the 1993 season and was the NFC's starting center.

Sapolu had good reason for resisting the move, if it ever happened. The change would mean going against new players and having to learn their habits and tendencies. It would also mean relearning a position he hadn't played in five years while giving up one he'd nearly mastered.

Then, in the late spring of 1994, the

phone rang at Sapolu's Southern California home. It was 49ers coach George Seifert. He told Sapolu that the team was on the verge of signing Bart Oates as a free agent. Seifert went on to say it would mean Sapolu would have to move back to guard. Then Seifert told Sapolu the clincher. The move could help the team return to the Super Bowl.

Sapolu didn't have to think about it. He'd always been taught that the success of the team was more important than the success of the individual. He agreed without question.

"Here's a guy who made the Pro Bowl as a center and then they ask him to move?" running back Ricky Watters marveled. "I don't know if I could do that."

For most teams the move from center to guard isn't such a difficult chore. But the 49ers' offensive scheme depends on quick, mobile linemen who are constantly in motion. Guards are often required to pull and trap. For Sapolu, the move was a big one. He had to relearn where he was required to go on every play in the 49ers' enormous playbook.

Sapolu once relished playing guard. He loved the athletic nature of the position and, according to McKittrick, was naturally suited to play it. McKittrick thinks Sapolu could have made the Pro Bowl four or five times if he had stayed at guard. But the sudden retirement of Randy Cross following the 1988 season forced Sapolu to move to center.

Once he got used to center, Sapolu grew to love it. The center serves as the quarterback of the linemen. If he sniffs out a blitz, he must call an audible at the line of scrimmage, alerting the other linemen to change blocking schemes, much like a quarterback does for the rest of the offense.

McKittrick said Sapolu was an expert at making line calls and was looked upon as a team leader partially because of it. He became a calming presence in the huddle and locker room where emotional players like Guy McIntyre and Ralph Tamm might lose their composure.

Sapolu's soothing nature even extended to the coaching staff on one occasion. In the final preseason game of 1994, Seattle safety Robert Blackmon rammed 49ers fullback Adam Walker long after the whistle blew. It was an obvious cheap shot and head coach George Seifert raced onto the field to give Blackmon a piece of his mind. Seifert was heatedly jawing with Blackmon when Sapolu intervened to restrain the 49ers' head man before he delivered a blow, Woody Hayes-style.

"I miss the leadership (of center)," Sapolu admitted. "When I felt the atmosphere was getting out of control in the huddle, I was able to pop in there with something to stabilize the situation and take the pressure off."

The move from center to guard was just one of the adjustments Sapolu has had to make on his way to becoming a force in the NFL. He originally joined the 49ers in 1983 as an 11th-round draft pick from the University of Hawaii. A native of Apia, Western Samoa, Sapolu brought a laid-back Pacific Islander's attitude to the mainland. He quickly discovered that the Bill Walsh-led 49ers of the 1980s embraced a corporate image. Sapolu's casual attire of shorts and thongs was soon replaced with leather shoes and button-down shirts. He adopted the club's business-like attitude with relish. Moreover, he went about his job quietly, efficiently and without expressing much emotion.

Of course, all that changed when Deion Sanders, William Floyd and Ken Norton joined the team in 1994. For the first time, the 49ers were effusive in their touchdown celebrations. Like many of the coaches, Sapolu wasn't sure about the change. But slowly he has seen the value of what players like Deion Sanders have brought to the 49ers.

"Deion does everything (opposing) fans hate," Sapolu said. "But he doesn't drink. He doesn't go out much. He needs to concentrate on his job and he does it to the best of his ability. I learned a lot from him. My style is different. I'm reserved and focused on what I need to do. I feel like any outside influences would deter me from that.

"I'm as loose as I've ever been and I'm a product of the 49ers system. I'm a little looser now, but at the same time more focused than ever before. We are just adjusting to the times so to speak."

The 1996 season saw Sapolu move back to center. For the last time. Following the season, he underwent surgery to replace a valve in his heart. The procedure wasn't like recovering from a broken foot or a fractured leg. While Sapolu will be able to live a normal life, his football life has come to an end.

Sapolu will always be remembered as the consummate team player. Over 14 seasons, he earned four Super Bowl rings and appeared in two Pro Bowls. It was a dream-like finish for someone whose career started as an injury-riddled nightmare.

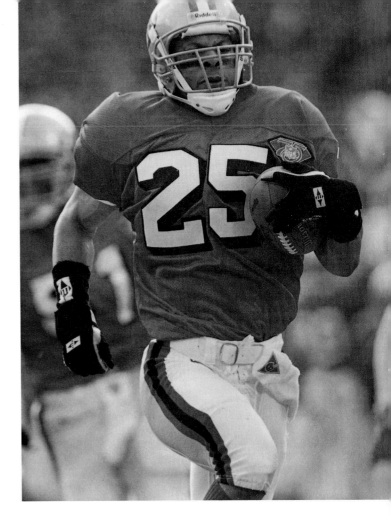

Cornerback Eric Davis dashes for the end zone during the first quarter of the 1994 NFC Championship Game against the Dallas Cowboys. Davis was instrumental in helping the 49ers jump out to a 31-14 halftime lead in that game after intercepting two passes and stripping the ball on another occasion that led to a 49er fumble recovery.

49ers scored a major coup by signing All-Pro cornerback Deion Sanders to a relatively inexpensive one-year deal worth $1 million. The contract also called for Sanders to collect $500,000 if the 49ers won the NFC title and $250,000 for winning the Super Bowl.

"Winning was the big factor," Sanders said after signing the pact. "I want to fulfill my dream and win a Super Bowl here in San Francisco. They've already won four of them. I'm here to help win number five."

San Francisco traveled to Anaheim Stadium in week three, where they traditionally have had their way with the hapless Rams. The 49ers continued to dominate Los Angeles, winning 34-19, but the victory was a little more difficult than usual. This contest didn't swing in the 49ers' direction until the first half was nearly over.

With the game tied at 10, San Francisco had the ball at the Rams one-yard line with enough time for one play. Seifert could call on kicker Doug Brien to put a chip shot through the uprights, or he could go for six points and deflate the upstart Rams.

Seifert opted for the touchdown. When Steve Young slipped between center Bart Oates and guard Derrick Deese to put the 49ers in control 17-10, the Rams were just about cooked.

"I didn't really have any second thoughts about it," Seifert said. "We needed the points and we needed to assert ourselves."

The 49ers set a team record with 177 yards in penalties against Los Angeles, and they lost another offensive lineman. This time Steve Wallace went down with a deep thigh bruise. Ironically, that left center Bart Oates as the senior man on the offensive line. He'd played just three games with the 49ers.

Young completed 79 percent of his passes against Los Angeles, hitting on 31 of 39 for 355 yards and two touchdowns. He also ran for two scores.

The 49ers suffered their worst regular season defeat in nearly 14 years when the Philadelphia Eagles came to town in week five.

It started on the 49ers' first offensive play, an interception off a deflected pass that went through the hands of Jerry Rice. On their second offensive play, the 49ers fumbled. On their third series of the day, Young was sacked for a safety. Philadelphia was ahead 23-0 before San Francisco had registered a first down.

The game was over by halftime as the Eagles posted a 30-8 lead then coasted in the second half to skunk San Francisco 40-8 and run the 49ers' record to 3-2. Philadelphia gained 437 offensive yards to the 49ers' 189.

"We stunk the joint up," safety Tim McDonald said.

The most significant move made by the 49ers all day came late in the third quarter. On third-and-ten at midfield, Seifert sent quarterback Elvis Grbac into the game to replace the beaten and battered Steve Young. But the gesture didn't set well with the normally stoic Young. He stormed off the field, then paced the sideline, cussing and yelling at anyone who would listen.

"I should have changed quarterbacks sooner than that," explained Seifert after the game. "Steve took a shot on the previous play. We have a long season ahead of us and it was obvious to me he could get hurt. We were going to be in passing situations the rest of the game and they were sending everybody."

The monumental loss had an upside to it. The defeat seemed to wake the 49ers from the doldrums.

A week later at Detroit, the 49ers fell behind early 14-0. San Francisco's equipment manager, Bronco Hinek, could have packed the club's bags

Fullback William Floyd (40) runs over Washington Redskins linebacker Kurt Gouveia (54). Floyd joined the 49ers as a first round draft pick in 1994 and established himself as a powerful and explosive runner with excellent pass-catching ability.

right there and settled in to watch another blowout. Instead the 49ers fought back. They stood up and countered the Lions with their own offensive fire-power.

On their third possession of the game, early in the second quarter, the 49ers marched 63 yards in four plays. William Floyd finished the drive by scoring his first pro touchdown on a one-yard plunge.

Just before the half, the 49ers tied the game at 14 by going 42 yards on nine plays. Dexter Carter set up the drive by returning a punt 21 yards. The score came on Ricky Watters' four-yard run behind Floyd's crushing block.

Early in the fourth quarter, Floyd scored the go-ahead touchdown for San Francisco on a one-yard run. He showed his power on the play, using a second effort to burrow through a pile of Lions after initially being stopped short of the goal line. Floyd gained 35 yards rushing and was the 49ers' leading receiver with five receptions.

In the fourth quarter, San Francisco added another touchdown on a five-yard pass from Steve Young to Nate Singleton for a final score of 27-21.

A week later the 49ers traveled to Atlanta for a game the Falcons hyped as a showdown in the NFC West. After 60 minutes of football, it was clear which team was the class of the division. San Francisco steamrolled the Falcons, 42-3.

Steve Young was almost perfect against Atlanta, completing his first 14 passes. He finished with 15 completions in 16 attempts and four touchdowns. But it was Deion Sanders who stole the show.

In his first trip back to Atlanta since joining the 49ers, Sanders got into a slugging match with Falcons All-Pro receiver Andre Rison. Sanders followed that up a few minutes later with a 93-yard interception return, in which he danced joyously past the Falcons bench on his way to the end zone.

The 49ers defense came to life as well. Dana Stubblefield made two sacks, while Todd Kelly and

George Seifert 1989–1996

It's not often that a young man can grow up to fulfill his wildest fantasy. San Francisco 49ers' Coach George Seifert is one of the lucky few.

As a young grid star at San Francisco's Polytechnic High School, located across the street from the 49ers' old Kezar Stadium home, Seifert had dreamed of a life in football. The hard-hitting linebacker and offensive tackle spent his autumn Sundays as an usher at Kezar, one of the perks of being a Poly Parrot football star. There, he was introduced to the innovative coaching style of Frankie Albert, and watched the heroics of the 49ers' Million Dollar Backfield of Y.A. Tittle, Hugh McElhenny, Joe Perry and John Henry Johnson. He personally saw the 49ers grow from a struggling

new NFL franchise into a respected league power.

"It was a great experience for me," Seifert says. "The 49ers were always an exciting team to watch as a kid. I never dreamed that someday I would be back here."

Seifert's dream came true. He graduated from Poly High School and continued his life in football, first as a player at the University of Utah, then as a coach at his alma mater. As it is for all football coaches, Seifert's life became a never-ending odyssey of drifting from one coaching job to the next.

After spending a year at Utah in 1964, Seifert took the head coaching position at tiny Westminster College in Salt Lake City. From there, it was on to Iowa and then Oregon. During all that time, he never forgot

about the 49ers or his old home in San Francisco's Mission District.

Seifert finally got a chance to return to the Bay Area in 1972 when he joined the coaching staff at Stanford University. There he transformed the defensive backfield into the best in the Pacific Eight Conference.

But Seifert was still restless. He had an aching desire to become a head coach. When Cornell University offered Seifert the opportunity to run its football program in 1975, he packed up his family and hit the road again.

Seifert spent two uneventful years in New York trying to turn around the Cornell football program, but to no avail. Then he returned to the Bay Area once more, this time to join the staff of Bill Walsh at Stanford. It was a decision that would profoundly affect the rest of his life.

"I'd say Bill has been one of the most important influences on me as a coach," Seifert says. "He has a great football mind and he's an excellent teacher. His record obviously speaks for itself."

When 49ers' owner Eddie DeBartolo summoned Bill Walsh to team headquarters in 1979 and offered him the job of head coach of the San Francisco 49ers, Walsh accepted and brought Seifert along with him. He eventually made Seifert San Francisco's defensive coordinator.

"George has a unique aptitude for the technical aspects of the game," Walsh said. "He is not a light, quick-witted, amusing type of coach, but a very demanding, no-nonsense, business-oriented man who quickly gets the respect of players because of his expertise and willingness to work long hours."

Veteran NFL observers know that it is the offense that brings fans to the stadium on Sunday, but it is the defense that wins games at the professional level. While the offensive wizardry of Bill Walsh got headlines in the Bay Area, the San Francisco defense under Seifert quietly stifled opponents.

Seifert's silent efficiency did not go unnoticed by other coaches and general managers around the league. It was just a matter of time before he

was approached with head coaching offers. Cleveland and Indianapolis were among the first to come knocking at Seifert's door, but he refused. He was satisfied playing second fiddle to Walsh. He was happy to be back home living out his childhood dream.

"George wasn't overly ambitious in the sense that he was scheming to get the head coaching job," team president Carmen Policy said. "He was patient and content to wait for it."

Finally, in 1989, Seifert's life came full circle. With the retirement of Bill Walsh, he was named the 12th head coach of the San Francisco 49ers. The odyssey had ended. Just 30 years after serving as an usher at Kezar Stadium, Seifert became the first native San Franciscan to lead the San Francisco 49ers.

"George and I had worked together for nine of my ten years with the 49ers and, before that, in my two years at Stanford," Walsh said. "He is a bright, conscientious and hard-working man who was ready to take on the responsibility of being a pro head coach."

But Walsh's hand-picked successor faced a daunting task when he took over the 49ers. Seifert replaced a coaching legend, a man who led the 49ers to three Super Bowls. It was a little like taking the place of Knute Rockne at Notre Dame or John Wooden at UCLA; anything but a championship was unacceptable. It didn't help that Walsh was selected to

Pro Football's Hall of Fame in his first year of eligibility. Seifert's chore was to usher the "Team of the Eighties" into the 1990s.

The transition has been smooth but not always easy. In his rookie season at the helm of the 49ers, Seifert guided the club to the NFL's best record and its fourth Super Bowl victory, a 55-10 thrashing of the Denver Broncos. In 1994, Seifert once again took the 49ers to the Super Bowl, where they pummeled the San Diego Chargers, 49-26.

Through the 1994 season, Seifert posted a 81-24 record and a phenomenal .771 winning percentage. The only active NFL coach who approaches Seifert's penchant for winning games is Miami's Don Shula. In his first six seasons, Seifert won five Western Division titles, two NFC Championships and two Super Bowls.

Seifert's tenure has not been without controversy. Some of his most difficult decisions have involved personnel matters. He was roundly criticized for losing Ronnie Lott and Roger Craig to free agency in 1991. And before the 1992 season, Seifert unloaded All-Pro defensive lineman Charles Haley after a series of off-field problems.

But his most delicate juggling act has been to appease the fragile egos of his superstar players, including Joe Montana, Steve Young, Deion Sanders and Jerry Rice. Seifert also has heard the wrath of the fans over the loss of longtime 49er hero, Joe Montana.

"One of the most difficult jobs of a coach is replacing a veteran who has been loyal and given you years of hard work and dedication," Bill Walsh said. "It is not easy to ask them to step aside. But for the good of the team and the franchise, it is something that has to be done. Some coaches just can't deal with it, and as a result the team will go into a state of decline because they hold onto the veterans a little too long."

Seifert has done an excellent job bringing in new assistant coaches as well. Because of the team's success, the 49ers' staff is constantly raided by other NFL teams. In recent years, the 49ers have lost coaches Mike Shanahan, Mike Holmgren, Dennis Green, Ray Rhodes and Sherm Lewis.

And through it all, Seifert's mentor, Bill Walsh, watches closely.

"The team could be in disarray," Walsh said of the many challenges that have confronted Seifert as coach. "But everything has been handled very well. Seifert got them through Lott and Craig okay, which could have been a real problem. George has been able to maintain leadership. He's done an excellent job."

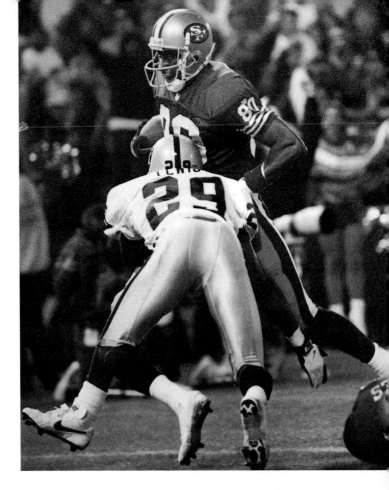

Jerry Rice (80) scores his 126th career touchdown against the Los Angeles Raiders in the opening game of the 1994 season. Rice tied the NFL's all-time touchdown record held by Jim Brown. Later in the game Rice scored again to break Brown's mark.

rookie Bryant Young each had a sack. Troy Wilson got into the act in the fourth quarter, sacking quarterback Perry Klein on two successive plays.

The Tampa Bay Bucs were the 49ers' next victims. San Francisco completely dominated the Bucs, gaining 411 yards to 123 for Tampa Bay, and picking up 24 first downs against the Bucs' eight. The 49ers defense continued to improve, holding the Bucs scoreless until the fourth quarter when the game was already decided.

San Francisco's running attack began to show signs of life as Ricky Watters had his first 100-yard rushing game of the season. He picked up 103 yards on 14 carries and two touchdowns. His first score came midway through the first quarter and gave the 49ers a 7-0 lead.

Steve Young was impeccable once again. He completed 20 of 26 passes for 255 yards and one touchdown to wide receiver Ed McCaffrey.

San Francisco had posted a 6-2 record when they got a week's rest with a bye at the midway point of the season. That's about the time the 49ers began preparing for another showdown with the Dallas Cowboys.

The 49ers-Cowboys matchup was billed around the league as a probable precursor to the NFC Championship Game. If it was it didn't begin as the 49ers had hoped.

Dallas got on the board first as Emmitt Smith scored on a four-yard run. Meanwhile, the 49ers offense had trouble getting started. Young completed only three passes for 16 yards in the opening half. It was enough to keep the 49ers close as the clubs went into the locker room tied 7-7.

In the second half, Young settled down and found his rhythm. He located Jerry Rice in single-coverage late in the third quarter and hit him with a 57-yard touchdown pass. Rice out-leaped Dallas cornerback Larry Brown to make a spectacular catch and put San Francisco ahead for the first time.

Later, Young connected with Brent Jones on a game-clinching 13-yard pass. He ended the game completing 12 of 21 passes for 183 yards and two touchdowns.

But the 49ers defense really made the difference in this game. Emmitt Smith gained 78 yards on 26 carries, but in the crucial second half he was held to just 26 yards rushing.

The secondary also made some big plays, intercepting Troy Aikman three times. Safety Merton

Hanks came up with two clutch interceptions which stopped Dallas drives. Deion Sanders also had an interception. Rickey Jackson, Dana Stubblefield and Bryant Young put on the pressure up front, providing one sack each.

"It was a great victory for the defense," Hanks said. "A lot of the new players were brought here specifically to help us beat Dallas. We did, but we'll probably face them again."

A week later, the 49ers got a scare from the Los Angeles Rams on a Sunday night at Candlestick.

After taking a 21-6 lead into the locker room at halftime, the 49ers allowed the Rams to claw their way back into the game. On their first three possessions of the second half, the Rams drove for three touchdowns. Finally, it took an 18-yard pass from Steve Young to Jerry Rice with 1:56 left to put the 49ers in front, 31-27. It was the third touchdown of the night for Rice, who caught a team-record 16 passes for 165 yards in the game.

After Rice's score, Los Angeles had one more opportunity to win it. Quarterback Chris Miller guided the Rams to the 49ers 38-yard line. With 55 seconds left, wide receiver Flipper Anderson had Deion Sanders beat in the end zone. Sanders recovered in the nick of time to make a spectacular diving play, flicking the ball away from Anderson just before it settled into his waiting hands.

Once again Young was nearly flawless. He com-

Quarterback Steve Young eludes the grasp of San Diego Chargers defensive lineman Leslie O'Neal during Super Bowl XXIX. Young passed for 325 yards and a record six touchdowns in addition to rushing for 49 yards. He was an unanimous choice as the game's MVP.

pleted 30 of 44 passes for 325 yards and four touchdowns, and gained 23 yards rushing.

In late November, the 49ers scoured the country in search of a pass rush specialist for the upcoming playoffs. They found defensive end Tim Harris at Larry's Surf and Turf, his restaurant in Capitola, California, and told him to report to the 49ers practice facility. Harris signed a contract for the NFL minimum, but with one incentive. He was to receive a $5,000 bonus for each sack he recorded, giving new meaning to the term "hit man."

Over the Thanksgiving weekend, San Francisco clinched the NFC West title with a 35-14 win over the New Orleans Saints at the Superdome.

It marked the 12th straight year the 49ers won at least 10 regular season games, an NFL record. It was also the eighth time in nine years they'd captured the NFC West crown.

San Francisco used the final four games of the season to prepare for the playoffs. But they did it in glorious fashion. They trounced the Falcons 50-14 on a day Seifert claimed the 49ers were inconsistent.

They rolled over the San Diego Chargers 38-15, and the Denver Broncos 42-19, putting together a 10-game winning streak and a 13-2 record. It allowed the 49ers to clinch the home-field advantage throughout the playoffs.

San Francisco dropped its final regular season game to Minnesota 21-14, but many of the team's starters were on the sideline by halftime, resting up for the long road ahead.

It was a record-breaking season for the 49ers in many respects. They scored 505 points, an average of 31.6 per game, shattering the franchise mark of 475 point in 1984. They also scored a club-record 66 touchdowns.

Several individuals found their way into the NFL and club record books. Jerry Rice scored 15 touchdowns to bring his NFL-record total to 139. He also joined James Lofton and Steve Largent as the only players to catch passes for 13,000 yards in their careers. Rice's 112 receptions also set a new club mark.

Steve Young threw for 3,969 yards and broke Joe Montana's club record by throwing 35 touchdown passes in a season. His 112.8 quarterback rating was the highest in league history and his 70.3 completion percentage set a team record. He became the first player ever to lead the NFL in passing four years in a row and was named the league's MVP for the second time.

Ricky Watters was the club's leading rusher. He gained 877 yards on 239 carries and six touchdowns. Rookie William Floyd picked up 305 yards and six touchdowns.

Safety Merton Hanks had seven interceptions while Deion Sanders had six. Sanders set a single-season team record with 303 yards in interception returns and three touchdowns.

Rice, Young and Deion Sanders were named All-Pro, and coach George Seifert was named coach of the year in a Sporting News poll of the league's coaches.

After a first-round playoff bye, the 49ers prepared to face the Chicago Bears, who had defeated the Minnesota Vikings in the wild card game to advance to the divisional playoff. Chicago survived with solid defense and a no-frills offense. The club consisted largely of overachieving and unknown players led by quarterback Steve Walsh. Not a single Bear was named to the Pro Bowl. San Francisco was made a 17-point favorite.

On a soggy Saturday at Candlestick Park, San

Steve Young 1987–

Trying to escape from the shadow of Joe Montana is a little like following in the footsteps of God. The shoes are too big for any mere mortal to fill.

Steve Young is accustomed to following in the path of legends. After all he is the great-great-great grandson of religious leader Brigham Young, and when he matriculated to BYU, the university named for his famous ancestor, he replaced record-setting quarterback Jim Mc-Mahon. Young has spent a lifetime stepping forward to meet new challenges.

Young's most difficult task, however, was succeeding Joe Montana as the starting quarterback of the 49ers. To Northern California football fans, Montana is a football deity. And as Young has discovered, replacing a god is next to impossible.

As 49er trades go, Young has turned into one of the team's all-time bargains. The former Tampa Bay Buccaneer quarterback

joined the San Francisco 49ers in 1987 in exchange for a second- and fourth-round draft choice. He moved west with the reputation of being an outstanding athlete who was a little unorthodox, a quarterback who ran first and threw as an afterthought. His previous employers, the Bucs and the Los Angeles Express of the USFL, relied on Young's athleticism and improvisational skills to move the football. Many people wondered if a free-wheeling quarterback like Young would fit into San Francisco's regimented offensive system, one that calls for a disciplined quarterback with the ability to quickly read defenses.

For four seasons, Young had few opportunities to show his ability. He was the highest paid clipboard holder in the NFL, waiting patiently as Montana's backup. Young watched from the sidelines as Montana led the 49ers to Super Bowl wins in 1988 and 1989, and nearly a third straight title in 1990. As

Montana improved with age, Young wondered if he'd ever get a chance to command the 49ers' high-powered attack.

But that quickly changed during the 49ers' training camp in 1991, when elbow problems led to surgery for three-time Super Bowl MVP Joe Montana. Suddenly Young was handed the starting quarterback job and thrust into the spotlight. It was the chance Young had been waiting for.

"This has always been Joe's offense, but I knew if I had a chance to take some snaps, I could make things happen," Young said. "It's frustrating for any professional athlete to wait on the sidelines. I just wanted a chance to show what I could do."

Young got off to a rocky debut in 1991 as Montana's heir. The 49ers started with losses in two of their first three games and naturally, all blame for the club's misfortunes was heaped on the shoulders of Young.

Then, in his fourth

start of the season against the Los Angeles Rams, Young began to perform. With Los Angeles leading 10-3 and time running out in the half, Young guided the 49ers 65 yards in less than two minutes to tie the score. The drive silenced critics who said Young couldn't lead a two-minute offense like Montana.

In the second half of the game, Young fired a 62-yard scoring pass to Jerry Rice and San Francisco went on to beat the Rams, 27-10. Young finished the game with 21 completions in 31 attempts for 288 yards, two touchdowns and no interceptions. It seemed as if he'd turned the corner.

"That was an important game in terms of confidence," Young said. "We needed a win, but it was also important because I felt the offense was beginning to run smoothly."

But midway through the season, Young suffered a knee injury and the 49ers stumbled along to a 4-6 record. They ended the season with six straight wins but finished out of the playoffs for the first time since 1982.

Although Young was criticized for the 49ers poor showing in the standings, he ended the 1991 season with a 101.3 quarterback rating and won the NFL passing title. He became the third 49er quarterback to lead the NFL in passing, joining John Brodie who did it in 1970 and Joe Montana who won it in 1987 and 1989.

Young's career took off in 1992, when he put together his most impressive season and became the first 49er quarterback since Joe Montana in 1983 to start

every league game. For the second straight year he was the NFL's highest-rated passer. His 107 rating made him the first quarterback in history to have a rating of over 100 in consecutive seasons. He finished first in all four quarterback ranking categories, leading the league in completion percentage (66.7), touchdown passes (25), average yards per attempt (8.62), and interception percentage (1.7). He also rushed for 537 yards and led the NFL with a 7.1-yard rushing average. To top it off, he was named the starting quarterback in the Pro Bowl and the league's Most Valuable Player.

More importantly to Young, he proved to teammates and fans he could win under pressure. He pulled out three games in which the 49ers were trailing in the fourth quarter, and two more in which they were tied late in the game. The 49ers finished the 1992 season with a 14-2 record, the best in the NFL.

But for some people that was still not enough. For over a decade, the 49ers have been Joe Montana's team—he was the driver of the 49ers' finely-tuned offensive machine. Bay Area fans have been reluctant to hand over the keys to Young.

For many, that reluctance has been a matter of style. Montana was considered the smooth, stylish quarterback who threw effortless touchdown passes and rallied the team when it needed to score in the final seconds of a big game.

"People are always going to remember Joe," Young said. "He's one of the greatest to ever play

the game. But our styles are very different."

Indeed, Young brings a different element to the 49ers' offense, an ingredient that opposing defenses didn't see from Joe Montana. On a bad day Young can run 40 yards in 4.5 seconds, a speed which gives defensive coordinators nightmares and puts him in the upper echelon of the league's players. That game-breaking speed, and the scrambling ability that goes with it, adds a new dimension to the 49ers with Young at the helm.

As the 1992 season came to a close, many of Young's teammates noticed a more relaxed approach from their quarterback. It appeared the torch had finally been passed. Young had matured as a quarterback.

"He's got a better grasp of the offense under pressure now," Tom Rathman said. "During a two-minute offense or when he has to audible, he is a lot more calm. It used to take him a while to see the defense and audible. Now he's right on top of it."

Former offensive coordinator Mike Shanahan agreed. "I think his timing is better. I think his awareness of where his receivers are and his progression has improved. When he does scramble, he's looking to throw the football instead of just taking off. That just comes with increased playing time."

The increased playing time paid off in 1994. That's when Young took control of the team and came into his own as the best quarterback in pro football. He ended the regular season with his third straight passing title and was named

league MVP. But he saved his best performance for the biggest game of his life.

Young has heard all the whispers about his inability to win the big one, but in Super Bowl XXIX he had the type of game quarterbacks only dream about.

He started the heroics early by throwing a 44-yard touchdown pass to Jerry Rice before two minutes had ticked off the clock. Three minutes later he fired a 51-yard scoring pass to Ricky Watters.

In just seven plays and five minutes, Young directed the 49ers 138 yards for two touchdowns.

But that wasn't enough for the overeager Young. He ended the day by completing 24 of 36 passes for 325 yards and a Super Bowl record six touchdowns. In addition, Young ran five times for 49 yards, an average of 9.8 yards per carry. Young was the unanimous choice as Super Bowl MVP.

"That was probably my best effort," Young said. "I hope there will be more Super Bowls to come. But under the circumstances, with what it meant and everything, that had to be my best game. It was the kind of performance, under the pressure of the Super Bowl, that you have to feel very good about.

"Beating San Diego was the big one. We had to face the Cowboys (in the NFC Championship Game), then win the Super Bowl and we did that. I think our performance in those games kind of set us apart from the rest of the pack."

And Steve Young's performance may have been the best of the bunch.

Francisco ran over the Bears 44-15. After fumbling the ball away on their opening drive, the 49ers scored on six straight possessions. By halftime, the 49ers had racked up a 27-point lead.

William Floyd started the scoring for San Francisco with a two-yard run in the first quarter. Tight end Brent Jones got into the act, capping a 54-yard scoring drive by hauling in an eight-yard touchdown pass from Steve Young. Then Floyd added another touchdown on a four-yard run and Doug Brien added a 36-yard field goal. Finally, Young scored on a six-yard run to end the first half's fireworks. But that was all San Francisco needed as it took a 30-3 score to the locker room.

Floyd added his third touchdown of the game midway through the third quarter, then most of the offensive starters found a cozy spot for themselves on the bench.

"The 49ers played like what they are, the best team in football," Bears coach Dave Wannstedt said after the game.

The 49er offensive line dominated the Bears as San Francisco rushed for 145 yards and five scores. When Young took to the air, he completed 16 of 22 passes for 143 yards.

Defensively, San Francisco allowed just 247 yards. Tim Harris, Rhett Hall and Bryant Young all scored sacks.

The game's most exciting moment came just before halftime when Young scored and took a shot from Chicago defensive back Shaun Gayle in the end zone. Young jumped up and spiked the ball at Gayle's feet. Then Brent Jones, Bart Oates and Jerry Rice quickly came to Young's defense and wrestled Gayle to the turf. William Floyd found himself in the middle of the pack. After a shoving match with 290-pound defensive end Alonzo Spellman, Floyd picked him up and tossed him about 10 feet, knocking him to the ground.

"You can't allow people to take shots at your franchise player," said Oates. "You have to put a stop to it right then and there."

The victory put San Francisco in the NFC Championship Game for the sixth time in seven years. Dallas also advanced to the title contest after beating the Green Bay Packers in the playoffs. It was the third straight championship match between the two teams and their sixth postseason meeting since 1970. Going into the game, the 49ers had won only one of the six postseason matchups with Dallas.

The Cowboys flew into San Francisco at less than full strength. Emmitt Smith was still feeling the effects of a pulled hamstring and Michael Irvin was limping noticeably. Both men were expected to have a rough time on the Candlestick Park turf, which was a mess after two weeks of nearly non-stop rain. As a result, bookmakers installed the 49ers as seven-point favorites over Dallas.

The 49ers started like they were shot from a cannon. After William Floyd and Ricky Watters roughed up a couple of Dallas players in the end zone prior to the game, San Francisco took the field and scored an amazing 21 unanswered points in less than five minutes.

"There was a lot of intensity right from the start," Rice said. "The fireworks began when we went to warm up."

Defensive back Eric Davis got things going on the third play from scrimmage when he intercepted a pass intended for Kevin Williams and returned it 44 yards for a score.

On the Cowboys' next possession, Davis was in the right place again. Three plays after the kickoff, Troy Aikman completed a pass to Michael Irvin, but Davis stripped it and Tim McDonald recovered at the Dallas 39. From there, Steve Young went to the air. He hit Ricky Watters on a swing pass and the Niners' running back turned it into a 29-yard score.

On the ensuing kickoff, Adam Walker stripped the ball from Dallas return man Kevin Williams and 49er kicker Doug Brien recovered. The 49ers were in business again at the Cowboys 35. They took just seven plays to score, with Floyd running it in from the one-yard line.

Dallas battled to stay in the game, but was never closer than 10 points. Every time Dallas climbed out of its hole the 49ers countered with another big play. One of the biggest occurred after the Cowboys cut the lead to 24-14 just before halftime. With eight seconds left, Steve Young hooked up with Jerry Rice on a 28-yard scoring pass.

"That was the play of the game," Young said. But it wasn't enough to bury the Cowboys.

Young guided the 49ers to yet another touchdown late in the third quarter. After a 10-play, 70-yard drive, Young ran the ball in from the three to give San Francisco a 38-21 lead.

In the fourth quarter, Dallas was forced to pass and the 49ers came with an all-out rush as Tim Harris and Rhett Hall picked up two sacks apiece. Still, the Cowboys scored on Aikman's 10-yard pass to Irvin midway through the fourth quarter, cutting San

Francisco's lead to 38-28.

Minutes later the Cowboys were driving again. That's when coach Barry Switzer made the biggest blunder of the game.

With five minutes on the clock, Aikman found Irvin deep in San Francisco territory. Deion Sanders appeared to have Irvin covered and he broke up the pass. But the Cowboys didn't see it that way. They complained long and hard that Sanders had interfered with Irvin.

Switzer was irate. He stormed over to a referee then bumped him with a hip. The referee threw a yellow flag and Switzer was penalized 15 yards for unsportsmanlike conduct. The penalty moved Dallas back to its own 42-yard line where it faced third-and-25. On fourth down, Aikman was sacked, ending the Cowboys' chances.

Defeating Dallas was exhilarating for San Francisco, but the best was yet to come. Super Bowl XXIX and the San Diego Chargers loomed up ahead.

San Diego was led by quarterback Stan Humphries and running back Natrone Means on offense. Its defense boasted the best linebacker in the business, Junior Seau.

Steve Young would admit later that the long wait was worth it. In the biggest game of his career, he threw a Super Bowl-record six touchdown passes and was named MVP as the 49ers stomped San Diego 49-26. San Francisco became the first team in NFL history to win five Super Bowls.

The 49ers struck swiftly and efficiently against the Chargers. On the third play of the game, with just 1:22 gone, Jerry Rice caught a Steve Young pass over the middle and raced 44 yards to the end zone. It was the quickest touchdown in Super Bowl history.

Young never let up. On the 49ers' next possession, he connected with Ricky Watters on a 51-yard touchdown pass as the 49ers went 79 yards in four plays. On San Francisco's first three possessions, Young was eight of nine passing with three touchdowns. By game's end, he had completed 24 of 36 passes for 325 yards and six touchdowns, in addition to rushing for 49 yards.

The game was never in doubt. San Francisco controlled the contest at halftime, 28-10, then added a pair of touchdowns in the third quarter to ice it. Midway through the fourth quarter, coach George Seifert was seen smiling on the sideline, a sure sign the game was progressing smoothly for San Francisco. In the end, even third-string quarterback Bill Musgrave saw action, connecting on a six-yard pass.

"It was amazing," said guard Jesse Sapolu. "We were in sync. It was like a symphony, with Steve Young conducting, and everybody doing their job. Every time we didn't score we were disappointed."

Three of the scores came from running back Ricky Watters, who gained 47 yards rushing. Jerry Rice also scored three touchdowns. He emerged from the game with new Super Bowl career records for points (42), catches (28), yards (512) and touchdowns (7).

On defense, cornerback Eric Davis continued his outstanding play. He intercepted his fourth pass of the postseason after making just one during the regular season.

And there were other firsts. Linebacker Ken Norton became the first player ever to win three straight Super Bowls, doing it in 1992 and 1993 with Dallas before joining the 49ers in 1994. And Deion Sanders became the first man to play in both a Super Bowl and a World Series.

"To win a championship when those are the expectations, that's tough," Seifert said. "Yet that makes it more rewarding. This team had a chance to be a part of history. They became the first to win five Super Bowls and they did it on the 75th anniversary of the league."

In the losers' locker room, coach Bobby Ross had nothing but praise for the 49ers.

"You don't run into teams like that very often," Ross said. "Their execution is unbelievable. They operate on another level."

Two-time Pro Bowl defensive tackle Dana Stubblefield was NFL Defensive Rookie of the Year in 1993.

1995

Two key members of the Super Bowl champion 49ers defected prior to the 1995 season: All Pro running back Ricky Watters and defensive back Deion Sanders, the 1994 Defensive Player of the Year. Watters was replaced by San Francisco native Derek Loville, while Marquez Pope took over for Sanders at cornerback.

San Francisco opened the season against the New Orleans Saints at the Superdome. It needed the late game defensive heroics of Tyronne Drakeford and Eric Davis to escape the Big Easy with a 24-22 victory.

After a scoreless first quarter the 49ers jumped out to a 14-0 lead on a pair of big plays: one by the offense and one on defense.

Naturally, Jerry Rice scored the first 49er touchdown of the season hauling in a 50-yard pass from Steve Young. It was the first of Rice's six receptions for 87 yards.

On New Orleans ensuing possession, safety Tim McDonald intercepted a Jim Everett pass and scooted 52 yards to score and put San Francisco on top 14-0. It looked like the rout was on, but a series of 49er turnovers helped the Saints stay in the game.

Quarterback Steve Young took a beating early and was forced to the sideline with a sprained neck in the second quarter. He was replaced by backup quarterback Elvis Grbac, who had his first pass attempt intercepted by Sean Lumpkin and returned for a New Orleans touchdown.

Young returned to action in the second half and put on quite a show, ending the day with 21 completions in 27 attempts for 260 yards. He also led the 49ers in rushing with 50 yards. Young was aided by fullback William Floyd, who gained 48 yards on 10 carries, and Derek Loville, who added 49 yards on 14 carries.

But it was the defense which rode to San Francisco's rescue in the game's final minutes. Nursing a 24-22 lead, San Francisco needed several big defensive plays to preserve the win.

Cornerback Eric Davis was San Francisco's first savior on New Orleans' final series. He made a diving, left-handed deflection of a long pass intended for Michael Haynes that would have been a touchdown.

Two plays later, with just over a minute to go, cornerback Tyronne Drakeford blitzed off the left corner on fourth-and-10 and hammered Everett as he prepared to release a pass. The ball bounced wildly on the artificial turf before Drakeford scooped it up to preserve the win.

"That was a gutsy call by (defensive coordinator) Pete Carroll," said safety Tim McDonald. "We were playing in a zone and needed a big play."

After defeating the Atlanta Falcons 41-10 in week two, quarterback Drew Bledsoe and the hot New England Patriots invaded 3Com Park, San Francisco's new name for Candlestick Park. The 49ers' defense confused Bledsoe with a wide-array of blitzes to post a 28-3 win. The Patriots' second-year quarterback was sacked four times and completed just 21 of 51 passes. Safety Merton Hanks intercepted two Bledsoe passes and Lee Woodall picked off one.

Jerry Rice was the offensive catalyst for San Francisco hauling in two touchdown passes. He had six receptions for 87 yards. Young completed 29 of 42 passes for 284 yards and three touchdowns. Derek Loville paced the 49ers' ground game with 58 yards on 12 carries.

Sporting a 3-0 record San Francisco traveled to the Silverdome in Pontiac, Mich. They left with their first loss of the season as the Detroit Lions squeaked out a 27-24 win on Monday Night Football. San Francisco had a chance to tie it on the game's final play, but kicker Doug Brien missed a 40-yard field goal.

First round draft pick Bryant Young has been a starter at defensive tackle in his first two seasons.

The New York Giants were next on the 49ers' schedule. The game turned into an old-fashioned display of helmet-banging football as San Francisco topped New York 20-6.

"I would say today was the most physical game I have ever played," said Jerry Rice, who suffered a mild concussion in the second quarter then returned to score a touchdown late in the first half. It was Rice's sixth touchdown reception in five games.

It took nearly an entire half for the 49ers explosive offense to get in gear. Fullback William Floyd scored the 49ers' first touchdown on a one-yard run with 1:57 left in the half. After holding the Giants on four plays San Francisco took over again, and 26 seconds before intermission, Young found Rice on a 16-yard scoring pass. The two late touchdowns broke open a close defensive struggle and gave San Francisco a 20-6 lead heading into the locker room.

On the defensive side of the ball, San Francisco held New York to 237 total yards. Giants running back Rodney Hampton gained just 27 yards rushing. Hampton was forced to leave the field in the second half with a broken hand.

Rookie 49er receiver J.J. Stokes made his first NFL appearance, wearing a padded cast for protection over the hand he broke in training camp. The first reception of his career was on a 14-yard pass from Young.

Rice was not the only man in scarlet and gold to leave the field feeling dizzy or sore. Steve Young suffered a shoulder injury that required an MRI exam. Merton Hanks suffered a severe thigh bruise, Dennis Brown injured his right knee and required arthroscopic surgery, Derek Loville sustained a bruised left thigh, and receiver Nate Singleton broke his collarbone.

"This was a tough, physical ballgame," 49ers coach George Seifert said. "You could tell by looking around the locker room after the game that there was a lot of hitting going on out there today."

San Francisco's season appeared to be in jeopardy after losing to the Indianapolis Colts, 18-17, in week six. Not only did the 49ers look sluggish but they lost starting quarterback Steve Young, who suffered damage to his throwing shoulder and was sidelined for four weeks.

The defeat left the 49ers with a 4-2 record, a game behind the St. Louis Rams in the NFC West.

Young took the field with a sore passing arm and a severe case of the flu, then took a beating from the Colts. Indianapolis used an assortment of blitzes to register six sacks and grind Young into the artificial turf all afternoon.

"They created some havoc for us out there," said tackle Steve Wallace. "Usually we can pick them up and make adjustments, but we didn't do it very well today."

"Steve Young was sick as a dog," Harris Barton said. "He's a brave guy. If Steve's not in the game, we don't win."

San Francisco scored its first touchdown on a five-yard pass from Young to Rice in the second quarter and took a 7-6 lead into the locker room. Derek Loville added a score midway through the third quarter on a four-yard run. Three field goals by Colts kicker Cary Blanchard, who was cut by the 49ers in preseason, helped stake the Colts to a 15-14 lead, but a 51-yard field goal by Doug Brien midway through the final period put San Francisco on top, 17-15.

Blanchard responded with his own 41-yard kick, his fourth field goal of the day, to supply the winning margin for Indianapolis.

San Francisco managed just 269 yards on offense, the club's lowest total in nearly two years. Despite putting in one of their poorest efforts of the season the 49ers still had a chance to win the game. But kicker Doug Brien sent a 46-yard field goal far

Tom Rathman 1986 - 1993

Tom Rathman belonged to an earlier era when football was a battle between unknown warriors in mud and rain and snow. Players wore cageless leather helmets, blocking and tackling was a respected art, and games were decided in the bloody trenches.

With his crewcut hair style, firm jutting jaw, and midwestern sense of hard work and fair play, Rathman personified football's infancy. He had the look of an All-American fullback and exhibited his Nebraska-fed passion for the game every time he handled the pigskin.

Rathman's running style

was unmistakable. For eight seasons he was the San Francisco 49ers beast of burden; a pile-driving ball carrier eager to lower a shoulder and knock people flat. He preferred running over opponents rather than scampering around them. He believed in the motto: "three yards and a cloud of dust."

Rathman joined the 49ers in 1986 when he was selected out of the University of Nebraska in the third round of the NFL college draft. At Nebraska, Rathman was used mainly as a blocking back until his senior year when he was given a featured role in the

offense. He responded to the challenge by gaining 881 yards and was named to the All-Big Eight team.

In San Francisco, Rathman was reunited with ex-Nebraska teammate Roger Craig in the 49er backfield. And once again Rathman was called on to pave the way for his backfield mate. The duo proved to be a lethal combination for opponents. In 1987, Rathman's second year with the club, he combined with Craig to give the 49ers one of the most potent running games in the league. San Francisco gained 2,237 yards on the ground that season to lead the NFC in rushing. Although Rathman started just seven games he contributed 257 yards on 62 carries for a 4.1 yard average. More importantly, he proved to be a devastating lead blocker for Craig, a role he came to relish.

"We asked Tom to do a number of different things for us," Coach George Seifert said. "If we needed blocking, he'd block. When we needed tough yardage, quite often we'd look to Tom. When we needed a receiver out of the backfield, he filled that role too. He was the ultimate team player."

"All I wanted to do was win football games," Rathman said. "Whatever the coaches wanted me to do I'd do, whether it was play on special teams or run with the football."

Indeed, Rathman turned into one of the league's most versatile backs. He worked long and hard to polish his pass catching skills and blossomed into one of the NFL's top receiving backs, a role which would have stunned any observer of Nebraska Cornhusker football. During four seasons of varsity play at Nebraska, Rathman caught just five passes. He never considered himself a pass receiving threat. But the 49ers find a way of using just about everybody in their offensive attack and Rathman proved to be an integral part of the San Francisco passing game.

"We saw that Tom had great hands so it was just natural that he be used as a receiver in our system," said former 49er offensive coordinator Mike Holmgren, who was credited with refining Rathman's role as a receiver. "At Nebraska he was used as a power back. They never asked him to

catch passes. It wasn't as if he couldn't do it. We did the same thing with Roger Craig. He wasn't used as a receiver either until he got to the 49ers."

Suddenly, the six-foot-one, 235-pound Rathman found himself in a new role. He was no longer just a big, bruising runner and blocker. He became part of the 49ers so-called finesse system of football, a cog in one of the most advanced passing games in the NFL.

Rathman made the most of it. In 1988 he caught 42 passes for 382 yards, averaging over nine yards per reception. By 1989 he had nearly as many receptions as rushing attempts. He caught 73 passes that season to lead NFC running backs, while rushing just 79 times. He gained 616 yards receiving in 1989 and averaged over eight yards a catch.

"It was kind of a surprise to me that I would be used as a receiver that much," Rathman said. "It gives me a chance to get out in the open field and run with the ball."

Rathman had his best day as a receiver in a 1989 game against New England when he caught 11 passes for 103 yards. He set personal highs in both categories as San Francisco crushed the Patriots, 37-20.

Although Rathman became a respected receiver he also made a name for himself around the league as a punishing blocker who paved the way for his backfield mates. He got as much satisfaction from knocking down linebackers as he did in scoring touchdowns.

"Part of Roger Craig's effectiveness came from the way he used Rathman as a lead blocker to set up defenders," said Matt

Millen, a former 49er teammate, who also played against Rathman as a member of the Redskins and Raiders. "I'm not taking anything away from Roger but Rathman could really clear people out and open up a hole. You can't say enough about him. You don't see many fullbacks like him anymore."

But like all running backs, Rathman dearly wanted to carry the football and he dreamed about packing the pigskin when the 49ers were near the goal line. Indeed, San Francisco counted on Rathman to get the tough yards, and between 1990 and 1993, no 49er back was more effective than their rugged fullback on carries inside the 10-yard line. Rathman averaged six touchdowns a year on carries from the red zone.

Rathman's ability near the goal line was never more evident than in Super Bowl XXIV. Against the Denver Broncos' top-rated defense Rathman bulled into the end zone on two different occasions. It was the first multiple touchdown rushing game of his career and it couldn't have happened in a more important contest.

"That was a big thrill for me," Rathman said. "I was really looking forward to that game, playing for a Super Bowl title. I wanted to prove myself against the best. Of course the most important thing is to win but it was really satisfying to have a hand in the scoring."

Rathman seemed to save his best for postseason competition. In 14 playoff games, Rathman rushed for nearly 300 yards and averaged 4.5 yards per carry. He also

scored six touchdowns. The only 49ers to gain more yardage in playoff competiton were Roger Craig, Ricky Watters, and Wendell Tyler. And only Craig has more rushing touchdowns.

"I had a great opportunity to work with one of the best offenses in football," Rathman said. "The 49ers gave me an opportunity to show what I could do. I'm grateful for that."

right with 46 seconds to go. It turned out to be Brien's last game as a 49er. He was cut later in the week and the 49ers signed veteran kicker Tony Zendejas.

Young finished the game completing 28 of 40 passes for 229 yards and a touchdown.

Backup quarterback Elvis Grbac got his first start in a 49ers uniform the following week against the St. Louis Rams. He looked like the second coming of Joe Montana as he led the 49ers to a 44-10 shellacking of the Rams.

San Francisco got inspired play from its defense which supplied a pair of touchdowns, both by linebacker Ken Norton Jr. He returned two interceptions for scores.

But it was safety Dedrick Dodge who got the 49ers rolling. He intercepted a Chris Miller pass on the Rams' first possession, setting up the 49ers on the Rams 35-yard line. Grbac then took the field for the first time. Trying to rattle the 49ers new starting quarterback, St. Louis blitzed. Grbac picked it up and rolled right to buy time. He spotted John Taylor running a post pattern and hit him in stride for a touchdown.

On the Rams next possession, Norton made his first interception and returned it 21 yards for a score.

"It's nice to have a 14-point lead spotted to you," Grbac said. "It gives you a little confidence and you can go out and do what you have to do.

Grbac added a four-yard touchdown pass to Jerry Rice just before the half ended to give San Francisco a 24-3 lead. He finished the game 11 of 14 for 119 yards and two touchdowns. Floyd was the 49ers leading rusher with 49 yards on nine carries.

With a 5-2 record the 49ers were riding high after beating the Rams. Next on the schedule were the lowly New Orleans Saints. New Orleans had a 1-6 record and was on the verge of self-destruction as it prepared to travel to 3Com Park. San Francisco was favored by 14 points.

But in a shocking turn of events, New Orleans defeated the 49ers 11-7. Even worse came the news, immediately following the game, that fullback William Floyd and tight end Brent Jones were lost for the season with knee injuries.

Floyd was injured late in the fourth quarter as he tried to tackle Rufus Porter, who recovered a Ted Popson fumble.

San Francisco controlled the ball for all but three plays in the first quarter but was unable to score. The club's one first quarter scoring opportuni-

ty was thwarted when Tony Zendejas' 37-yard field goal attempt was blocked. Early in the second quarter the 49ers scored their only touchdown on a one-yard sneak by quarterback Elvis Grbac.

The 49ers were victimized by turnovers and poor special teams play. Three of the 49ers' drives ended in turnovers: two interceptions thrown by Grbac and a fumble lost by tight end Popson.

Despite the poor showing, San Francisco had a chance to pull out a victory late in the game. Facing a 3rd-and-18 with 2:30 to play Grbac's pass to Rice near the goal line went incomplete off Rice's fingertips

"Our backs are to the wall now," said tackle Steve Wallace. "We've just got to get back on our feet and get ready to play again next week."

The loss dropped the 49ers into a tie for first place in the NFC West with the Falcons and Rams at 5-3.

The loss overshadowed Jerry Rice's eight receptions for 108 yards, giving Rice the NFL record for career pass receiving yardage. He finished the game with 14,040 career yards.

Grbac continued to play well. He completed 29 of 42 passes for 243 yards.

In the locker room after the game, the silence was snapped by head coach George Seifert who said, "Keep your heads up. It can't get any worse than this."

He was wrong. The worst was yet to come. The 49ers hit rock bottom a week later, losing to the expansion Carolina Panthers at home, 13-7.

"If there is a point lower than low, that's where I'm at," safety Tim McDonald said following the debacle. "Maybe I'll wake up and find out I'm dreaming. Or having a nightmare."

If there was a bright spot it was that tight end Brent Jones made a miraculous recovery. After being told he would miss the remainder of the season with a knee injury suffered just a week earlier, he was in uniform against the Panthers.

Carolina managed just 204 yards of total offense but 49er turnovers proved to be the difference. San Francisco lost the ball five times - three of them inside the Panthers' five-yard line - and in the process became the first defending NFL champion to lose to an expansion team.

The disaster began late in the first quarter. San Francisco was driving for what appeared to be a touchdown but former 49er cornerback Tim McKyer

Forty Niners Owner Edward J. DeBartolo Jr. and quarterback Steve Young chat prior to a game during the 1994 Super Bowl season.

Merton Hanks 1991-

Merton Hanks was just another anonymous member of the 49ers defensive unit until San Francisco took on the Dallas Cowboys midway through the 1994 season.

At stake was home field advantage throughout the playoffs and the incalculable psychological advantage that goes to the victor in such a titantic struggle between the NFL's two best teams.

Silhouetted against that backdrop safety Merton Hanks decided to stage his own coming out party. He kicked it off early by diving to stop a crucial third down pass intended for Cowboys receiver Alvin Harper. The pass was ruled incomplete, but replays later showed Hanks actually intercepted it.

In the second quarter with the score tied at 7-7 the Cowboys were driving for the go-ahead touchdown deep in 49ers territory. Once again Hanks was on Harper. Aikman's pass was a little behind Harper and Hanks got a hand on it. Then Harper batted the ball upward. Hanks made the most of the moment. As the ball floated away from Harper, Hanks nabbed it at the one-yard line.

Hanks saved his play of the day for the crucial fourth quarter. With six minutes left in the game, the 49ers had a precarious 14-7 lead. Dallas was driving, however, and advanced to the San Francisco seven-yard line. On second-and-goal Hanks' assignment was to cover Emmitt Smith, a dangerous receiver out of the back-field, who already had five receptions in the game. But on this play Smith's job was to protect the passer.

"I was watching Emmitt closely," Hanks said. "He stayed in to block. I just drifted toward my left and read Troy's eyes."

Aikman's eyes told Hanks the pass would be coming over the middle. Hanks stepped up, intercepted the pass at the goal line, and killed another Cowboys scoring opportunity. This one clinched the contest. San Francisco went on to record a 21-14 win.

Besides the two interceptions, Hanks batted away four passes and made four tackles. It was enough to leave Hanks' defensive backfield mate, Deion Sanders, breathless.

"That was a Pro Bowl performance," Sanders said. "If he isn't selected this year then something is wrong with the system."

Apparently there is nothing wrong with the system because Hanks was named to the Pro Bowl squad for the first time in 1994. Alongside him in Hawaii were two other members of the 49ers secondary: cornerback Deion Sanders and safety Tim McDonald. Coincidentally, the last time that many players from the San Francisco secondary made the Pro Bowl, in 1984, when Ronnie Lott, Eric Wright, Dwight Hicks and Carlton Williamson all made the team, the 49ers won the Super Bowl.

Interestingly enough, Hanks wasn't even the 49ers starting safety at the beginning of the 1994 season. Dana Hall laid claim to the free safety spot while Hanks was playing the corner position later won by Deion Sanders. After the acquisition of Neon Deion, Hanks was moved to free safety and Hall was benched.

Hanks was a largely unheralded defensive back when the 49ers selected him in the fifth round of the 1991 draft. He had been an All America cornerback at the University of Iowa, but at the scouting combine that year Hanks had a bad day. He was clocked in the 40-yard dash at nearly 4.7, considered a good time for a quick outside linebacker, but a snail's pace for a cornerback.

Ray Rhodes, who served as the 49ers' defensive backs coach at the time, decided to give Hanks a second look. In a private workout for Rhodes, Hanks ran a 4.58. Head coach George Seifert was not thoroughly convinced on the Iowa-man's worth, however. After four rounds of the draft passed without Hanks being selected, Rhodes begged Seifert to pick him.

The 49ers took a chance and Hanks insisted they got the steal of the decade. During his first two seasons Hanks was a spot starter at cornerback. Former 49er Pro Bowl cornerback Eric Wright, who had retired to the coaching ranks, was given the chore of making a star out of Hanks. It almost wore him out.

"Mert had a lot to learn," Wright said. "He had a lot of natural ability, a lot of athletic talent. He was actually easy to work with because he listened and was willing to take direction. He really wanted to become a good defensive back."

Early in the 1993 season, Hanks got his shot. He took over at free safety for Hall after Hall suffered a sprained ankle.

It soon became obvious that the 6-foot-2, 185 pound Hanks was a rising star. In mid-November 1993 he was named NFC Defensive Player-of-the-Week after intercepting two passes against New Orleans and returning them 94 yards. One interception was returned 67 yards for a touchdown.

Hanks also had a big week off the field. His wife Marva, a former star basketball player for the Iowa Hawkeye women's basketball team, gave birth to a daughter named Milan. It was the second child for the Hanks'. The oldest daughter is named Maya Angelou Hanks after the acclaimed poet and novelist.

But 1994 was clearly Hanks' breakthrough season. At least one national magazine recognized Hanks' on-field contributions that season. Sports Illustrated named Hanks to its All-Pro team, the only 49er on the defensive side of the ball to be so honored. He had a career-high seven interceptions, tops on the club. Coach George Seifert now says the ability was there all along.

"When Merton first came to camp you could see that he was going to be a player," Seifert said. "He has always had a tremendous nose for the ball, which is essential for a free safety. He's one of those guys that just loves to play, who's always in the middle of the action. The thing that he really has going for him is his great work ethic. He's always trying to improve himself. Because of that he'll just continue to get better."

Seifert's prognosis rang true in 1995 when Hanks was selected to his second straight Pro Bowl. Once again he proved to be among the most opportunistic players in football. Midway through the 1995 campaign, when the 49ers faced the Dallas Cowboys in their biggest game of the year, Hanks scooped up a Michael Irvin fumble early in the game and dashed 38 yards for a touchdown.

"It's really amazing how many big defensive plays he's made over the past two seasons," Seifert said. "That play against Dallas really set the tone for the game. Steve Young was out and the offense had been struggling. We needed the defense to come up big that day and Merton was just one of several players who did."

Since taking the starting job in 1994, Hanks has intercepted 12 passes, third best in the NFL over the 1994 and 1995 seasons behind Arizona's Aeneas Williams and Oakland's Terry McDaniel. Much of that can be attributed to Hanks' ability to lull quarterbacks into throwing dangerous passes.

"He has surprising quickness," said Wright. "He kind of hangs back there and a quarterback thinks he can sneak a pass in. But Mert's got a good burst to the ball and I think a lot of quarterbacks are surprised by that. He covers a lot of ground back there and you really don't notice until you see it on film."

Although quarterbacks around the NFL may be surprised by Hanks' quickness and big play capabilities, the 49er free safety certainly isn't.

"Right now I'd say I'm the best free safety in the league," Hanks said. "There are a few people that make All Pro teams on reputation but I think I've passed those guys now."

Most of the NFL already agrees.

stepped in front of an Elvis Grbac pass and returned it 96 yards for a touchdown.

The 49ers spent the rest of the day playing catch-up as Grbac completed 26 of 37 passes for 327 yards. Rice caught eight passes for 111 yards. Loville had six receptions for 55 yards, Taylor had four receptions for 69 yards, and Jones caught four passes for 64 yards.

But the 49ers receivers suffered through a string of unbelievably rotten luck. Midway through the second quarter, Jerry Rice snagged a Grbac pass at the 12 and was heading for the end zone when Carolina cornerback Tyrone Poole slapped the ball out of Rice's hands at the one. The ball bounded out the back of the end zone for a touchback, giving the Panthers a first down at the 20.

Then on the 49ers first series in the second half, John Taylor took off with a reception, going 40 yards to the Carolina one, where Poole again knocked the ball out of his hands. This time it was recovered by linebacker Sam Mills.

Late in the fourth quarter the 49ers grim prospects turned black as Grbac went down with a sprained ankle. He was replaced by third-string quarterback Cary Conklin, who hadn't thrown a pass that counted since 1993.

"There's something different about this year," tackle Steve Wallace said after the loss. "In four of the last six games it's come down to do or die in the final two minutes and we haven't been able to do it. You can't expect to win consistently in this league by putting that type of pressure on yourself."

With a 5-4 record, San Francisco's season looked bleak. The 49ers were playing without their starting quarterback and fullback, and had just dropped consecutive games to two of the NFL's weakest clubs. Next on their schedule were the mighty Dallas Cowboys.

The 49ers were traveling into the eye of the tornado, Irving, Texas, the home of Deion Sanders, Troy Aikman, Michael Irvin, and Emmitt Smith. Dallas had a 7-1 record. The entire football world was predicting a Dallas blowout. Las Vegas had the Cowboys as 13 point favorites.

San Francisco relished the challenge, its biggest in perhaps a decade. It responded by scoring 17 points in the first five minutes of the game, including 14 in the opening 1:25, and plastered Dallas 38-20.

The onslaught started quickly as Grbac hit Jerry Rice on an 81-yard touchdown pass on the second play from scrimmage. On the Cowboys'

Originally a fifth round selection in 1991, Merton Hanks has developed into one of the NFL's premier defensive backs.

ensuing possession, Marquez Pope popped Irvin after a catch, knocking the ball loose. Merton Hanks recovered and raced 38 yards for a touchdown. On the next possession, linebacker Rickey Jackson intercepted Aikman's pass at the 28-yard line leading to Jeff Wilkins' 26-yard field goal.

Just like that, San Francisco had a 17-0 lead.

Late in the first quarter defensive tackle Dana Stubblefield made his presence known as he smothered quarterback Troy Aikman on a third down play. The sack left Aikman grimacing in pain and forced him to the locker room for the rest of the game with a bruised knee. Aikman was replaced by backup Wade Wilson.

By halftime the 49ers had posted a 31-7 lead.

When it was over, Rice had five catches for 161 yards, his highest yardage total ever against Dallas. Grbac was 20 of 30 for 305 yards and two touchdowns. Loville gained 61 yards on 23 carries and one touchdown.

Dallas was held to a season low 296 yards. Michael Irvin had four receptions for 37 yards, while Smith gained 100 yards rushing on 18 carries.

"There's a lot of big smiles in our locker room," tight end Brent Jones said after the victory. "They're the classic team that's cocky and arrogant. They were talking about how we disrespected them, but how did we disrespect them? We rocked them twice last year. They forgot to respect the world champions."

A win over Dallas was the catalyst San Francisco needed. It responded by thrashing the Miami Dolphins 44-20 and the St. Louis Rams 41-13 in the ensuing two weeks to resume first place in the NFC West.

Against St. Louis, the 49ers' defense took center stage. Four interceptions, two by Tyronne Drakeford and one each by Eric Davis and Tim McDonald, led to 24 San Francisco points. Davis returned his interception 86 yards for a score and the secondary totaled 171 yards in runbacks, a franchise record. Davis' return was the sixth defensive touchdown of the season, tying a team record set in 1983.

"A good pass rush helped us out," safety Tim McDonald said. "With our defensive line, we turn teams into one-dimensional clubs. They've got to throw the ball to move it and that makes it easier for us to get our interceptions."

Steve Young returned to action against St. Louis after a five-game layoff and had his first pass intercepted. He settled down to complete 21 of 32 passes for 226 yards and three touchdowns.

J.J. Stokes had the best game of his rookie season with five catches for 65 yards and two scores. His first touchdown came after taking a short pass from Young and racing parallel to the goal line through several tacklers. The 16-yard touchdown reception actually covered about 65 yards.

"We haven't peaked," said center Bart Oates. "We're getting ready for that December run."

The 49ers continued their playoff surge a week later beating the Buffalo Bills 27-17. Once again the defense came through with the game-turning play.

In the third quarter, with the game tied 10-10, the Bills faced first and goal at the 49ers one-yard line. Buffalo running back Thurman Thomas was on the bench nursing a sore back and leg cramps. On first down rookie fullback Darick Holmes took the handoff and launched himself skyward in the direction of the goal line. Somewhere over the line of scrimmage he was met head-on by linebacker Gary Plummer.

"It was a lead play and I didn't see him," Holmes said. "He hit me and just knocked the ball out. It was a great hit. He hit me high, right on the ball."

"In situations like that I like to hang back so I can kind of launch myself," Plummer said.

The ball squirted loose in the Buffalo backfield where linebacker Lee Woodall picked it up and sprinted 96 yards for a touchdown. It was the seventh touchdown scored by the 49ers' defense setting a franchise record.

"That was a great play," cornerback Eric Davis said. "It totally changed their mindset. To come that close and come up with nothing."

Instead of dropping behind 17-10, the 49ers took a 17-10 lead and quickly added a field goal to build a 20-10 lead early in the fourth quarter

"It was the biggest emotional swing I've ever felt in my career," tight end Brent Jones said. "It was unbelievable."

The defense didn't do all the scoring. Running backs Adam Walker and Derek Loville each added a touchdown. Loville had one of his best games of the season rushing for 88 yards on 24 carries and catching 10 passes for 86 yards. Young completed 28 of 44 passes for 243 yards. He failed to throw a touchdown pass for the first time in 18 straight regular season games.

San Francisco beat the Carolina Panthers, 31-10, in its 14th game of the season to post a 10-4 record and clinch the NFC West title. The 49ers needed victories in their final two games of the season to secure the home field advantage throughout the playoffs. The Minnesota Vikings and Atlanta Falcons were the 49ers' remaining opponents.

San Francisco defeated the Minnesota Vikings 37-30 for its sixth consecutive victory, but the winning streak came to a dramatic close a week later as the Atlanta Falcons stopped the 49ers, 28-27. By defeating San Francisco, Atlanta secured itself a playoff spot and thwarted the 49ers' effort to obtain home-field advantage throughout the playoffs.

The 49ers' loss was troubling for several reasons. After scoring on its first three possessions, on drives of 80, 78 and 65 yards, San Francisco's offense was unable to move the ball consistently in the second half against Atlanta's 29th-ranked defense.

Furthermore, the Falcons gained 363 yards against the 49ers' top-ranked defense, with most of it coming after backup quarterback Bobby Hebert took over in the second half.

Most importantly, the 49ers did not show the killer instinct needed to finish off opponents, especial-

Ricky Watters 1991-1994

A running back in the National Football League survives on bravado. It's not a position for timid men unsure of their talents.

But few athletes can match Ricky Watters for bluster and boastfulness. He reported to the 49ers' rookie camp in 1991 with the swagger of Jim Brown, the moves of O. J. Simpson, and the confidence of Joe Namath.

Drafted out of Notre Dame on the second round in 1991, the San Francisco 49ers expected Watters to be a solid running threat. Coach George Seifert looked to Watters to resurrect San Francisco's once proud ground game, a rushing attack which suddenly turned anemic in 1990. Watters was the man tabbed to succeed the departing Roger Craig and inject life into the San Francisco ground game.

Unfortunately, in his first season, Watters proved to be more style than substance. Instead of being a rookie sensation, Watters became one of the club's walking wounded. During his first week in training camp he suffered a broken foot while trying to make a cut and was placed on injured reserve. The broken bone took nearly two months to heal. Midway through the season he was ready to come back and joined the team as a member of the practice squad. His presence was short-lived though because he broke his hand and was put on injured reserve for the remainder of the season.

With his rookie season a disaster most 49er veterans began to feel Watters was another drafting mistake; one of those college phenoms who didn't have the strength, speed or stamina to play in the NFL. He was like a shiny, new 12-cylinder Jaguar that remained in the garage because it always had engine problems.

"If you would have asked me I would have told you the team made a mistake in drafting him," tackle Harris Barton said. "Most of us thought he was a bust."

With Watters out of the lineup his sideline braggadacio became annoying to some of the team's senior members. The flashy style and colorful apparel, which included diamond ear rings and enough gold jewelry to satisfy the Spanish Conquistadors, was no longer a source of amusement.

Watters' stock sunk with the coaching staff as well. In fact, expectations for Watters dropped so low after that disappointing first season the 49ers used their second-round choice in 1992 to select another running back. This time, Florida State's Amp Lee was expected to answer the club's prayers.

But Watters saw the handwriting on the wall. He was determined to prove himself in the NFL so he prepared himself for the 1992 season like never before. He began a strict martial arts program that required a newfound sense of discipline and inner strength, and he passionately devoted himself to the 49ers' off-season training program. He also got some fatherly advice from veteran tight end Jamie Williams who told Watters he had the physical ability to become a star in the NFL. It was just a matter of maturity and mental preparation. Watters could make it, but only if he wanted it badly enough.

When Watters reported to camp in top-notch shape the team veterans and coaching staff took notice. His stock began to rise steadily when he carried the ball like Walter Payton in the 1992 preseason games. But the shadow of rookie Amp Lee always lurked behind him. When the 49ers opened the season against the New York Giants Watters got the starting nod. He quickly let his teammates know it was the right decision.

On his first carry in the NFL Watters took a handoff from Steve Young and dashed past All-Pro linebacker Lawrence Taylor on his way to a 13-yard gain. He quickly sprinted back to the huddle and said excitedly to anyone who would listen, "They can't stop me. Give me the ball. They can't stop me."

"We all laughed at him," said tackle Steve Wallace. "He was so cocky."

But Watters gained 100 yards on 13 carries and 50 yards on five receptions that afternoon. The linemen

stopped laughing after they saw what Watters could do. The 49ers went on to rout the Giants.

"I always knew I could do it," Watters said. "Some people think I'm too cocky or something but that's just the way I have to be. I have to make myself feel invincible. You can't run onto the field for an NFL football game and not think you're the best because you'll end up getting hurt." Watters' first game as a 49er was a harbinger of things to come. He exceeded all the club's expectations in the early part of the season. Through his first five games Watters gained 397 yards rushing, including 87 against the hated Los Angeles Rams. It was enough to make the veterans forget about Roger Craig and begin to accept Watters, gold chains and all.

"In my 14 years here, Ricky was the most talented running back we had," center Jesse Sapolu said. "When you talk about cutting ability and reading the hole, Ricky was special."

Watters quick feet and intuitive cuts earned him the nickname "jiggle joints" around the 49er compound. And around the league his spin move was hailed as the best in the NFL.

"That was something I did since I was a kid playing in the street," Watters said. "I watched Tony Dorsett of the Cowboys spin that way and I copied it, I guess. It gets me out of traffic. I stopped doing the spins at Notre Dame because they thought I was dancing too much. They wanted me to hit the hole running hard and straight. My dad was the one who said I ought to go back to using the spin move."

Watters unequivocably won the respect of the 49er linemen in a late-season

game against the New Orleans Saints that turned out to be one of the most important of 1992. Watters came through with an impressive performance as he was called on 25 times and gained 115 yards. On one second quarter touchdown drive, Watters carried eight times for 60 yards. It was his third straight 100-yard game. He also caught three passes for 11 yards as San Francisco pulled out a dramatic 21-20 win over New Orleans at Candlestick.

"That's the kind of game I like," Watters said. "We planned to throw against them and then alternate the run and pass but the defense backed off too far; they had only three linemen up front. We decided to run the ball. And we ran it and ran it and ran it."

Watters was not a one-dimensional running back. Like Roger Craig before him, Watters was also a sure-handed receiver out of the backfield. In fact, it was a talent that prompted Notre Dame Coach Lou Holtz to use Watters as a flanker during his sophmore year with the Irish. His pass catching ability was not lost on former 49er offensive coordinator Mike Shanahan, who made Watters an integral part of the 49ers passing game.

But it was Watters running ability that electrified the 49er offense in 1992. With five games left in the season, Watters was making a run at the NFC's rushing title. He also had a chance at breaking the team's single-season rushing record (1,502 yards) set by Roger Craig in 1988. Then he suffered a bruised shoulder against the Philadelphia Eagles and saw limited action through the remainder of the regular season.

Despite the injury,

Watters was determined to pass a major landmark during his first complete season in the NFL. He desperately wanted to gain 1,000 yards rushing in a season. Oddly enough, Watters has the distinction of doing it twice in one year.

Against Tampa Bay, he passed the 1,000 yard mark, then lost three yards on his final carry of the game to finish with 998 yards. He had to wait until the last day of the season to do it again when he carried three times for 15 yards against Detroit. Watters ended the year with 1,013 yards joining Roger Craig, Wendell Tyler, Delvin Williams, J.D. Smith and Joe Perry as the only 49ers ever to rush for 1,000 yards in a season. It was a feat he was never able to duplicate with San Francisco. In 1993 he rushed for 950 yards and in 1994 gained 877 yards on the ground.

"It wasn't that big a deal," Watters insisted. "It was just a matter of time. I knew I would get it."

"Ricky Watters made San Francisco more difficult to defend," former 49er coach Bill Walsh said. "With Watters you couldn't concentrate just on Steve Young and Jerry Rice. He was a dangerous threat as a receiver or running back."

ly in critical games. Twice in the fourth quarter the 49ers had a chance to put the game on ice with a touchdown. Both times they had to settle for a field goal.

San Francisco's last scoring opportunity was especially distressing. The 49ers led 24-22 and seemed to be marching toward paydirt. With a first down at the Atlanta 15, the drive suddenly turned sour. Atlanta's defense stuffed the 49ers on two straight plays and on third down Young was sacked by Atlanta linebacker Jesse Tuggle. The 49ers settled for a field goal that increased their lead to five points, then it was time for the defense to perform. Instead, it fell on its face.

San Francisco stopped Atlanta on its first three plays to set up a fourth-and-five situation. With two minutes to play, the Falcons were forced to go for the first down.

On the fourth down play San Francisco put almost no pressure on Hebert and he found Eric Metcalf for a 23-yard completion to set up a first down near midfield. On the next play Hebert again faced little pressure and hit Terance Mathis with a short pass over the middle. Mathis broke free in the secondary and outraced several 49ers to score the winning touchdown.

Jerry Rice provided several offensive highlights in the game. He caught 12 passes for 153 yards, scored a touchdown, and threw a 41-yard touchdown pass to J.J. Stokes. His 12 catches gave him a team record 122 for the season and a single-season NFL record of 1,848 yards. They also allowed Rice to pass Art Monk as the NFL's all-time reception leader with 942.

Steve Young completed 31 of 44 passes for 316 yards in the game, but didn't throw a scoring pass.

Derek Loville gained 62 yards in 15 carries and had nine receptions for 47 yards. He ended the season with 10 rushing touchdowns to tie a team record. J.J. Stokes had one of the best games of his rookie season, catching five passes for 106 yards, including one touchdown.

The 49ers finished the season as the NFL's highest scoring team for the fourth straight year and were second in total offensive yardage. They also led the NFL in total defense, based on yards allowed, for only the second time in their history.

Although the 49ers lost the home-field advantage throughout the playoffs, they still had a first round bye and the chance to play their first postseason game at

Linebacker Gary Plummer is one of the reasons for the 49ers improved defense in 1994 and 1995.

home. San Francisco met the Green Bay Packers, coached by former 49ers offensive coordinator Mike Holmgren, in the first round. It was a day filled with calamities.

San Francisco's bad luck began on its first play from scrimmage. Steve Young threw a pass to fullback Adam Walker as he swung out of the backfield. Walker, playing with a broken thumb, made the catch and was hit by linebacker Wayne Simmons. The ball popped loose. Cornerback Craig Newsome picked it up and dashed 31 yards for a Green Bay touchdown.

The play proved disastrous for two reasons. Not only did the Packers score the touchdown that gave them a 7-0 lead and the momentum that would propel them to a 27-17 upset of San Francisco, it also ended All-Pro tackle Harris Barton's day. He injured his left ankle and was lost for all but one series in the game.

The play was just a precursor of the misfortune awaiting San Francisco, which looked sluggish and unprepared for the Packers. On its next possession

Green Bay stunned the 49ers defense, needing just four plays to go 62 yards for another touchdown.

Green Bay ultimately built a 21-0 lead largely on the wizardry of quarterback Brett Favre, the NFL's MVP. He completed 15 of his first 16 passes and spread his throws around to a variety of receivers. Favre connected with tight end Keith Jackson on a three-yard scoring pass and receiver Mark Chmura on a 13-yard touchdown pass.

San Francisco was finally able to get on the scoreboard with less than two minutes to play in the half, driving 77 yards on 12 plays. But instead of coming away with seven points, the 49ers had to settle for a 21-yard field goal.

Midway through the third quarter, the 49ers looked like they might make a game of it. They drove 80 yards in 14 plays, capped by Young's one-yard touchdown run, cutting Green Bay's lead to 21-10. But the Packers wouldn't let up. They responded with two Chris Jacke field goals putting the game out of reach, 27-10, late in the fourth quarter.

Without a reliable ground game and battling a huge deficit, Steve Young experienced one of his most frustrating days as a 49er. He threw an NFL playoff-record 65 passes, completing 32 for 328 yards and no touchdowns. He also was intercepted twice, fumbled once, was sacked three times, and had 17 passes knocked away.

Young also supplied the 49ers with their only running threat. He gained 77 yards rushing, mostly because he was being chased out of the pocket all afternoon. The rest of the 49ers' backfield combined to rush for 10 yards on nine carries.

Rice tried to help Young carry the load. He caught 11 passes for 117 yards but gained only 10 yards after his receptions.

"They appeared to be the stronger team today," Seifert said of the Packers. "They executed extremely well offensively and defensively. I can't say our players didn't go into the game emotionally prepared. I thought they did. The other team beat us to the punch and we never recovered."

Among the 49ers who retired after the 1995 season were wide receiver John Taylor, center Bart Oates, and linebacker Rickey Jackson. Taylor finished his 10th NFL season with 29 receptions for 387 yards and two touchdowns. He will be remembered best for catching the game-winning pass against Cincinnati in Super Bowl XXIII with just 34 seconds to play.

Jackson, a 15-year veteran, registered nine sacks in 1995 and finished with 136 for his career to place in the top-five sack specialists in league history.

Oates was named to the Pro Bowl in 1995. It was the fourth time he was selected for the game during his 11-year career.

Just days after the 49ers were eliminated from the playoffs, San Francisco's former head coach, Bill Walsh, was rehired as a consultant. His job was to teach offensive coordinator Marc Trestman the subtle nuances of the West Coast offense devised by Walsh during his tenure with the 49ers in the 1980s.

San Francisco's need for a multi-purpose back was addressed through free agency. The 49ers signed former San Jose State and New York Jets star Johnny Johnson, who sat out the 1995 season, and former Stanford and Cleveland Browns fullback Tommy Vardell.

To bolster the pass rush, San Francisco signed Chris Doleman, who had nine sacks for the Atlanta Falcons in 1995, and Roy Barker. The 49ers also used their first pick in the 1996 draft on a pass rusher. In the second round they selected 6-foot-3, 246 pound USC defensive end Israel Ifeanyi.

1996

Bill Walsh rejoined the San Francisco coaching staff prior to the 1996 season as a consultant, although his role was never fully understood by players, fans or fellow coaches and he proved to be more of a distraction than a help.

The 49ers acquired veteran defensive ends Chris Doleman and Roy Barker, and drafted USC's Israel Ifeanyi in the second round to upgrade the club's weak pass rush. To assist on offense, fullback Tommy Vardell, running back Terry Kirby and guard Ray Brown were signed. The 49ers gambled by signing former Jets star running back Johnny Johnson, who sat out the 1995 season with a bad back. The gamble blew up in the club's face when Johnson lasted through two practices, never suited up for a preseason game and was cut prior to the start of the regular season. The most productive rookie turned out to be a third round draft pick, wide receiver Terrell Owens.

San Francisco got off to a rocky start in 1996. Although it defeated the lowly New Orleans Saints, 27-11, quarterback Steve Young was roughed up and sacked three times. On one sack, he was forced to leave the game to have his chin stitched.

Despite injuries to offensive linemen Steve Wallace and Ray Brown, the 49ers piled up 157 yards on the ground. Derek Loville led the way with 61 yards on 16

Gary Plummer 1994-

The 49ers season hung in the balance late in 1995 as San Francisco faced the Buffalo Bills on Monday Night Football. With the game tied 10-10 in the third quarter Buffalo faced a first-and-goal at the 49ers one-yard line.

While Buffalo running back Thurman Thomas nursed a sore back and leg cramps, rookie fullback Darick Holmes entered the game to replace him. On first down Bills quarterback Jim Kelly called on Holmes. The rookie took Kelly's handoff, saw a slight hole open over right guard and launched himself in the direction of the end zone. He never reached it.

As Holmes was leaping toward paydirt, 49er linebacker Gary Plummer was flinging his body in the opposite direction, right at Holmes. The two flying bodies collided head-on somewhere over the line of scrimmage. The football popped out and danced crazily in the Bills' backfield.

"It was a lead play and I didn't see him," Holmes said. "He hit me and just knocked the ball out. It was a great hit. He hit me high, right on the ball."

"In situations like that I like to hang back so I can kind of launch myself," Plummer said.

San Francisco linebacker Lee Woodall picked up the loose ball and sprinted 96 yards for a touchdown. Instead of dropping behind the Bills 17-10, the 49ers took a 17-10 lead. The 14-point swing provided the 49ers with the momentum they needed in the second half to defeat Buffalo 27-17 and post a 9-4 record.

"That was a great play," cornerback Eric Davis said. "It totally changed their mindset. To come that close and end up with nothing has got to be frustrating and discouraging."

"It was the biggest emotional swing I've ever felt in my career," tight end Brent Jones said. "It was unbelievable."

The game-turning play was one of the most dramatic in Plummer's NFL career. It also exemplified the type of momentum adjustment provided by the 49ers' defense throughout the 1995 season. San Francisco scored eight touchdowns on the defensive side of the ball that season, a team record. Plummer's dynamic play at inside linebacker was one of the reasons.

"I'll tell you one thing, it's hard to find people who are as dedicated and work as hard as Gary Plummer," coach George Seifert said. "He stays in great shape with his offseason workouts. He prepares himself better than just about anyone before each game with film reviews of the opposing team. He's a great asset to this team and a tremendous leader."

Plummer proved his value to the 49ers in 1994, his first season with the club. San Francisco spent nearly $1.2 million to acquire Plummer's services over a two-year period. The free agent inside linebacker was expected to step in and become the club's primary run stopper. He did just that. In 1993, a year before Plummer's arrival San Francisco allowed an average of 112 yards rushing per game. In 1994, with Plummer in the middle, the 49ers relinquished an average of 83 yards rushing per game, nearly 30 yards less.

More importantly, by shoring up the defense, with the addition of Plummer, Ken Norton Jr., Deion Sanders, and Bryant Young, the 49ers reached their ultimate goal; a record-setting fifth Super Bowl title.

"That's why I signed with the 49ers," Plummer said. "The money was good, but it was the lure of playing for a Super Bowl that was the biggest attraction for me. Winning a Super Bowl was the ultimate. Now I guess I'm getting greedy because I want to play in another one."

Plummer's Super Bowl ring took on added significance because he got it at the expense of his former club: the San Diego Chargers.

"I was happy to see the Chargers make it to the Super Bowl," Plummer said. "I still have a lot of friends over there. Some people accused me of talking trash about them but that wasn't true. I don't know where that idea got started. I had a bit of grudge with their owner (Alex Spanos) but none of the players."

Plummer's offseason workout regimen, one of the most vigorous in football, may keep him in shape long enough to reach his goal of playing in another Super Bowl. Indeed, his exercise routine has become legendary in recent years. Plummer maintains a full gym at his home near San Diego's Scripps Ranch that would impress even Arnold Schwarzenegger. He often challenges younger teammates to participate in one of his "typical" workouts.

"There have been a lot of guys who have come over and tried to keep up with me," Plummer said. "They probably think I'm just some old stiff, but I've laid out a few guys."

One player unable to keep up with Plummer's pace was San Diego Chargers running back Eric Bieniemy. Bieniemy, who is 10 years younger than Plummer, tried to stay with Plummer on the treadmill but collapsed in exhaustion.

"Yeah, I basically passed out working out with him," Bieniemy admitted. "I've always tried to keep it quiet, but I guess people know now. Plummer killed

me. I think he set me up though. I'm going to get him back. I'm not sure how yet, but I'll find a way."

Plummer's road to the top of the NFL was not an easy one. He was never highly recruited. After graduating from Mission San Jose High School in Fremont, California he played two seasons of football at Ohlone College. Plummer transferred to the University of California for his junior year and made the team as a walk-on. At Cal he earned a starting berth at nose tackle, despite weighing just 210 pounds, and was named the team's defensive MVP.

After graduating from Cal in 1982 the NFL didn't show much interest in Plummer's services. He was shunned in the annual draft and signed with the USFL's Oakland Invaders, where he was the club's defensive captain. He played three seasons with the Invaders and was the team's all-time leading tackler.

The San Diego Chargers signed Plummer as a free agent in 1986 after the USFL folded. By that time he was no longer a 210-pound lineman. Instead, due to the wonders of weight training, Plummer was a 6-foot-2, 245-pound run thumper. In his third NFL game, Plummer was named a starter at inside linebacker and never relinquished the position. During his NFL rookie season, he led the Chargers in fumble recoveries with three, and had 98 tackles. Between 1986 and 1993, Plummer was the Chargers' leading tackler with 792 stops.

The highlight of Plummer's stint with the Chargers may have been the 1990 season. That's

when he led the team in tackles and also became a scoring threat on offense. In coach Dan Henning's goal line offense Plummer often lined up as a blocking back. He scored two touchdowns in 1990. The first coming on a two-yard scoring pass from Billy Joe Tolliver against Pittsburgh. The second score was against Denver on a one-yard plunge.

But Plummer would gladly give up those touchdowns for another shot at a Super Bowl.

"Playing in a Super Bowl with the 49ers was like a dream for me," Plummer said. "I didn't have the same feeling in my first 11 years of football that I did playing with San Francisco. The enjoyment I got out of football after joining the 49ers was more than anyone could ever believe."

carries. Tommy Vardell added 33 yards on eight carries. Loville and Vardell each scored a touchdown. Steve Young added 52 rushing yards and was 18-of-29 through the air for 199 yards.

The St. Louis Rams provided little competition for the 49ers in week two as San Francisco compiled its first shutout in seven years with a 34-0 win. The defense dominated the game, limiting the Rams to 105 yards in offense, the lowest total allowed by the 49ers since 1977. San Francisco gave up just six first downs, accumulated seven sacks and scored on a pair of safeties. Defensive tackle Bryant Young made two sacks and was credited with the pressure that caused one safety. Chris Doleman and Roy Barker each had a sack that led to a fumble. And it was turnovers that led to the 49ers big day as they started four drives inside the Rams 35-yard line.

Steve Young aggravated a pulled groin muscle in the second quarter while running toward the sideline and throwing an incomplete pass. He was removed from the game early in the third quarter after twice being flushed from the pocket and sliding to avoid being tackled. It was a dead giveaway that the groin was bothering him since Young rarely slides to avoid contact. Young completed 15-of-18 passes for 138 yards before he was replaced by Elvis Grbac. Grbac was 6-of-12 for 86 yards.

San Francisco scored three times on the ground. Derek Loville paced the 49ers with 49 yards on 12 carries and one touchdown. Tommy Vardell gained 44 yards and added a touchdown, and Dexter Carter scored from one yard out late in the game.

Nate Singleton, the 49ers' third wideout, was lost for the season with a broken clavicle.

After a bye week, San Francisco suffered its first loss of the season, 23-7 to the Carolina Panthers. San Francisco gained twice as many yards as its opponent but Carolina, despite playing with a backup quarterback, was better prepared and more physical than its NFC West rival.

Early in the second quarter, reserve quarterback Steve Beuerlein staked the Panthers to a 17-0 lead. Beuerlein's favorite target was former 49er tight end Wesley Walls, who caught two scoring passes.

The 49ers scored their only points of the day midway through the third quarter as Steve Young connected with Derek Loville for a 44-yard score on what appeared to be a broken play. It was Young's first touchdown pass of the season.

Young endured another punishing day. He was sacked four times and was hit at least a dozen other times while unloading the football. He completed 24-of-40 passes for 267 yards. Jerry Rice had 10 receptions for 127 yards and Derek Loville caught six passes for 85 yards. Young originally was diagnosed with a hamstring problem after the game. Later it was discovered he suffered a stress fracture of the pubic bone.

The running game was nonexistent against Carolina. San Francisco gained just 48 yards with Loville picking up 20 on seven carries.

San Francisco rebounded by throttling the futile Atlanta Falcons 39-17. It was a victory supplied by the defense which forced four Atlanta turnovers, including an interception returned 55 yards for a touchdown by Marquez Pope.

Quarterback Steve Young remained on the sideline against Atlanta nursing his injuries while Elvis Grbac got his first start of the season. Grbac put in a workmanlike day completing 22-of-36 passes including a 16-yard scoring pass to Ted Popson. J.J. Stokes caught seven passes for 88 yards but also dropped an easy throw.

The most impressive pass of the day came from running back Terry Kirby, who fired a 24-yard touchdown ball to Jerry Rice. It was Rice's first scoring reception of the season. Kirby also gained 14 yards on four carries. The 49ers finished the day with 150 yards on the ground, but that statistic was misleading because 67 yards were gained on one play by Anthony Lynn late in the game.

Most of the 49ers points were supplied by kicker Jeff Wilkins, who tied Ray Wersching's team record by making six field goals in six attempts, including a 46-yarder that equaled his career-best.

San Francisco improved its record to 4-1 by routing the Rams for the second time in the season, 28-11. The fabled touchdown tandem of Elvis Grbac to Ted Popson was the reason. Grbac, starting his second straight game in place of the injured Steve Young, hooked up with his tight end for a pair of touchdowns. He also found Jerry Rice with a 31-yard scoring pass. Grbac finished with 20 completions in 32 attempts for 222 yards.

The 49er defense did the dirty work. The Rams crossed the 50-yard line just once in their first seven possessions and scored their only touchdown after recovering a blocked punt at the three-yard line with less than two minutes to play in the game. San Francisco registered five sacks including three by the incomparable Bryant Young, and forced four turnovers. Merton Hanks intercepted two passes.

Terry Kirby had the best rushing day by a 49er

back thus far in the season with 73 yards on 13 carries. He added 57 yards on five receptions.

With a 4-1 record, San Francisco was poised for a Monday night showdown with the 5-1 Green Bay Packers, who were led by former 49ers offensive coordinator Mike Holmgren. But the Packers got the best of San Francisco, 23-20, as Chris Jacke split the uprights with a 53 yard field goal after 3:41 of overtime. There were several controversial plays that put the Packers in position to win the game.

San Francisco took a 17-6 halftime lead after Elvis Grbac connected with Jerry Rice on a pair of touchdown strikes. Midway through the third quarter the Packers scored on a 59-yard pass from Brett Favre to Don Beebe. Replays showed that Beebe probably trapped the ball while making a diving catch and was also touched down by defensive back Marquez Pope. Instead the officials ruled it a touchdown after Beebe got up and sprinted 30 yards to the end zone.

San Francisco had a chance to put the game away late in the fourth quarter. With the game tied at 17, Marquez Pope intercepted a pass and returned it to the Packers 12-yard line with 2:13 to go. At that point Coach George Seifert chose to play it safe to set up a field goal. He ordered three runs which forced Green Bay to use its time outs. Jeff Wilkins 28-yard field goal attempt was good and the 49ers had a 20-17 lead with 1:50 to go.

San Francisco appeared to have stopped Green Bay on its possession but a pass interference call against Steve Israel gave Green Bay a first down. The officials added 15 yards and tossed Israel from the game after claiming Israel bumped an official while arguing the call. The penalties gave Green Bay a first down at their own 45 yard line. Seconds later Jacke converted on the field goal that sent the game into overtime.

"We were robbed," Grbac said. "Our defense was playing good. We held them. Then the refs gave them 20 yards in penalties. The game was stolen from us."

San Francisco appeared to be headed to a second straight loss after falling behind the Cincinnati Bengals, 21-0, through nearly two quarters of play. But the unlikliest of heroes, Ted Popson and Terrell Owens, helped get the 49ers back into the game. Popson caught a pair of touchdown passes and Owens grabbed a 45-yard scoring pass with 2:08 left to tie the game at 21. Then Dedrick Dodge intercepted a Jeff Blake pass with 1:48 remaining and the 49ers were back in business at their own 32. Behind a limping Steve Young, who replaced an injured Elvis Grbac, the 49ers drove to the 15. That's when Seifert called the most unexpected of plays, a

naked bootleg with an obviously injured Young, hobbling, limping and skipping into the end zone. It was a play nobody in the stadium expected.

The injuries continued for Young the following week. On the third play of the game against the Houston Oilers at the Astrodome, Young was flushed out of the pocket. He was smacked by a pair of Oiler linebackers and suffered a concussion. With both Young and Grbac injured, the 49ers turned to third-stringer Jeff Brohm. Brohm completed 19-of-30 passes for 176 yards and one touchdown as San Francisco squeaked by the Oilers 10-9. Brohm threw a game-winning 20-yard scoring pass to Terrell Owens midway through the fourth quarter. Brohm was also the 49ers leading rusher with 35 yards on nine carries.

After beating the New Orleans Saints, 24-17, to post a 7-2 record, San Francisco hosted the Super Bowl champion Dallas Cowboys. Early in the game, Coach Seifert appeared to have organized a flawless game plan. The 49ers controlled the ball for nearly 12 minutes in the first quarter and outgained Dallas 139 yards to 0 enroute to a 10-0 lead. But Steve Young took another pounding, absorbing three big hits in the second quarter that knocked him out of action.

Dallas tied the score at 10 early in the fourth quarter. Behind Elvis Grbac, the 49ers rebounded with a nine-play drive that covered 69 yards. Terry Kirby capped the drive with a 27 yard run to put the 49ers in front 17-10.

After stopping a Dallas drive at the nine-yard line the 49ers had the game in their control with six minutes left to play. Then on first down, Grbac tried to force a pass over the middle and it was intercepted by linebacker Fred Strickland. Cowboys quarterback Troy Aikman wasted no time finding Eric Bjornson for the game-tying touchdown. The Cowboys won in overtime, 20-17, on Chris Boniol's 29-yard field goal.

"We made some mistakes and it really cost us," said Jerry Rice. "I felt like we let that one get away."

The 49ers rebounded with three consecutive wins over the Baltimore Ravens, Washington Redskins and Atlanta Falcons. Steve Young returned to action against the Redskins and tied an NFL single-game record by completing 20 straight passes. San Francisco looked poised to make another Super Bowl run. Then the upstart Carolina Panthers came to town.

In a battle for dominance in the NFC West, Carolina outplayed San Francisco for the second time in the season and walked away with a 30-24 victory. In truth, the 49ers self-destructed. They were penalized 15 times, a team record, for 121 yards. And defensive leader Gary Plummer was ejected from the game after a personal foul.

"That was an embarrassing display," Seifert said. "For whatever reason, we became unglued and had too many mistakes, too many penalties."

Despite the mistakes, San Francisco had a chance to win the game. San Francisco overcame a 30-17 third quarter deficit, cutting it to 30-24 on a five-yard pass from Young to Rice with eight minutes to play. On their next possession Young got the 49ers into Carolina territory with a 33 yard run. Two plays later, a high pass from Young bounced off Terrell Owens' hands and was intercepted by Eric Davis, ending the 49ers hopes.

The 49ers reestablished themselves against Pittsburgh a week later, scoring 16 points in the opening six minutes of the game and breezing to a 25-15 victory. Jerry Rice started the scoring by hauling in a four-yard pass from Steve Young. On the Steelers ensuing possession, Bryant Young registered a sack on quarterback Mike Tomczak, giving the 49ers a 9-0 lead.

San Francisco got the ball on the free kick and quickly moved into scoring position again at the four-yard line after a pass interference penalty. This time Young connected with William Floyd for the touchdown that put the game out of reach.

The 49ers ended the regular season with a 24-14 win over the Detroit Lions, giving them a 12-4 record and a tie for first place in the NFC West with the Carolina Panthers. Nevertheless, they were relegated to a wild card spot in the playoffs because of two regular season losses to the Panthers. Their first round opponent would be the Philadelphia Eagles.

On a wet and muddy field at 3Com Park, San Francisco blanked the Eagles 14-0. The 49ers limited the Eagles to just four second half first downs and knocked quarterback Ty Detmer out of action.

The most significant play of the game came early in the second quarter as Steve Young scored the 49ers first touchdown. As he crossed the goal line on a nine-yard quarterback draw Young was crushed by two Eagles and suffered a pair of broken ribs. Although Young continued to play it was obvious he was in pain. He completed 14-of-21 passes for 161 yards and a three-yard touchdown to Rice, and ran for 65 yards on 11 carries.

Young's injury would doom the 49ers playoff hopes as they took on the Green Bay Packers the following week. He lasted just nine plays as Green Bay demolished the 49ers, 35-14.

Desmond Howard ruined the 49ers' chances by returning a punt 71 yards for a touchdown just three minutes into the game, then followed it with a 46 yard punt return to set up another touchdown minutes later.

Elvis Grbac replaced Young in the first quarter and played reasonably well, completing 19-of-36 for 125 yards and an eight-yard touchdown pass to Terry Kirby. But Grbac was not helped by the fumbles and dropped passes.

Green Bay took a 21-7 lead into the locker room, but the 49ers briefly got back into the game after the second half kickoff. Jeff Wilkins' kick skipped past return man Don Beebe and Steve Israel pounced on the ball at the four-yard line. From there Grbac scored on a bootleg run cutting the Packers lead to 21-14. That was as close as the 49ers got. On the Packers' next possession, Brett Favre led a 72 yard drive for the decisive touchdown.

"That was the key drive of the game," Seifert said. "We were hanging in there until that point but we were unable to stop them. That was demoralizing because they were able to run on us at will."

Despite being eliminated from the Super Bowl competition, several 49ers posted impressive individual season statistics. Steve Young won his fifth NFL passing title and Jerry Rice had 108 receptions to lead the NFL. On the defensive side Roy Barker ended the season with 12 1/2 sacks, Chris Doleman had 11 sacks and Bryant Young had 11 1/2 sacks. Young was also named the Len Eshmont Award winner.

Less than two weeks after the playoff loss to Green Bay, George Seifert stepped down as the 49ers head coach and offensive coordinator Marc Trestman was fired. University of California Coach Steve Mariucci was hired to replace Seifert. Seifert left the 49ers with a 108-35 record and .755 percentage, the highest winning percentage in NFL history . He also won two Super Bowls during his eight years at the helm.

"I had a fairy tale job," Seifert said. "I got to coach in my home town for the team I watched as a kid. It's just time for a change. It's the natural process in sports. You don't stay the head coach for infinity."

Records
&
Statistics

The records listed in this section include only those statistics compiled since 1950, when the 49ers joined the National Football League. However, team leaders in categories such as passing, rushing and receiving are provided for the years 1946-1949. Statistics have been compiled through the 1995 season.

49ers All-Time Draft

1950
(Drafted Alternately 9-10)

1. **NOMELLINI, LEO**
   T, 6-3, 260, Minnesota
2. **CAMPORA, DON**
   T, 6-3, 270, Pacific
3. **COLLINS, RAY**
   T, 6-0, 230, LSU
4. **BAILEY, MORRIS**
   E, 6-2, 215, Texas Christian
5. **KANE, HARRY**
   C, 6-1, 215, Pacific
6. **VAN POOL, DON**
   E, 6-3, 225, Oklahoma
7. **BERRY, LINDY**
   B, 6-0, 180, Texas Christian
8. **WILLIAMS, ELLERY**
   E, 6-2, 200, Santa Clara
9. **ZINACH, PETE**
   B, 6-0, 190, West Virginia
10. **CELERI, BOB**
    B, 5-10, 175 California
11. **DOW, HARLEY**
    T, 6-2, 220, San Jose State
12. **BURKE, DON**
    B, 6-0, 235, Southern Cal
13. **CECCONI, LOU**
    B, 5-8, 171, Pittsburgh
14. **PAYNE, TOM**
    E, 6-2, 200, Santa Clara
15. **GRAMPSEY, LEO**
    E, 6-1, 195, St. Bonaventure
16. **SHAW, CHARLEY**
    G, 6-3, 195, Oklahoma A&M
17. **VAN METER, CLIFF**
    B, 6-1, 198, Tulane
18. **GENITO, RALPH**
    B, 5-11, 180, Kentucky
19. **KLEIN, FORREST**
    G, 6-0, 205, California
20. **NIX, JACK**
    E, 6-2, 205, Southern Cal
21. **ALKER, GUERIN**
    C, 6-1, 207, Loyola
*22. **WILSON, BILLY**
    E, 6-3, 198, San Jose State
23. **WILLIAMS, JIM**
    E, 6-2, 185, Rice
24. **WYMAN, BILL**
    T, 6-2, 220, Rice
25. **DUNN, BOB**
    G, 6-2, 200, Dayton
26. **POWERS, JIM**
    B, 6-0, 183, Southern Cal
27. **JOHNSON, KEN**
    G, 6-3, 200, Pacific
28. **HALL, CHARLEY**
    B, 6-1, 190, Arizona
29. **WHELAN, BOB**
    B, 5-11, 175, Boston U.
30. **STILLWELL, BOB**
    E, 6-0, 200, Southern Cal

1951
(Drafted Alternately 2-3)

1. **TITTLE, Y.A.**
   QB, 6-0, 190, LSU
2. **SCHABARUM, PETE**
   HB, 5-11, 185, California
3. **MIXON, BILL**
   HB, 5-11, 197, Georgia
4. **Choice To Cleveland**
5. **STEERE, DICK**
   T, 6-3, 225, Drake
6. **STRICKLAND, BISHOP**
   HB, 5-10, 195, Southern Cal
7. **FORBES, DICK**
   E, 6-2, 215, St. Ambrose
8. **ARENAS, JOE**
   HB, 5-11, 180, Omaha
9. **VAN ALSTYNE, BRUCE**
   E, 6-3, 205, Stanford
10. **FEHER, NICK**
    G, 6-0, 220, Georgia
11. **JESSUP, BILL**
    E, 6-1, 195, Southern Cal
12. **MONACHINO, JIM**
    HB, 5-10, 190, California
13. **MARVIN, DICK**
    E, 6-3, 190, Georgia Tech
14. **BERRY, REX**
    B, 5-11, 180, Brigham Young
15. **SPARKS, DAVE**
    G, 6-1, 228, South Carolina
16. **WHITE, BOB**
    B, 5-11, 174, Stanford
17. **MICHALIK, ART**
    G, 6-2, 225, St. Ambrose
18. **MURPHY, JIM**
    T, 6-3, 240, Xavier
19. **PHILLIPS, JOHN**
    B, 6-0, 178, Mississippi State
20. **TATE, AL**
    T, 5-11, 210, Illinois
21. **BROWN, HARDY**
    B, 6-0, 195, Tulsa
22. **WINSLOW, DWIGHT**
    B, 6-3, 205, Boise J.C.
23. **BRUNSWALD, WALLY**
    HB, 6-0, 170, Gustavus Adolphus
24. **KINSFORD, TOM**
    B, 5-11, 180, Montana
25. **PETERSON, MIKE**
    E, 6-1, 210, Denver
26. **CARPENTER, KEITH**
    T, 6-3, 226, San Jose State
27. **LUNG, RAY**
    G, 5-9, 209, Oregon
28. **ROHAN, JACK**
    HB, 6-0, 185, Loras College
29. **GARNETT, S.P.**
    T, 6-3, 215, Kansas
30. **FASKE, JERRY**
    HB, 5-9, 190, Iowa

1952
(Drafted Alternately, 8-9)

1. **McELHENNY, HUGH**
   HB, 6-1, 198, Washington
2. **TONEFF, BOB**
   T, 6-2, 252, Notre Dame
3. **TIDWELL, BILLY**
   HB, 5-9, 178, Texas A&M
4. **CAMPBELL, MARION**
   T, 6-3, 245, Georgia
5. **O'DONAHUE, PAT**
   E, 6-1, 205, Wisconsin
6. **BEASLEY, JIM**
   C, 6-4, 215, Tulsa
7. **ROBISON, DON**
   B, 6-1, 190, California
8. **SMITH, JERRY**
   T, 6-1, 230, Wisconsin
9. **CHRISTIAN, GLEN**
   HB, 5-10, 180, Idaho
10. **WEST, CARL**
    B, 6-2, 214, Mississippi
11. **KIMMEL, J.D.**
    T, 6-4, 245, Army-Houston
12. **SNYDER, FRED**
    E, 6-1, 180, Loyola
13. **YEAGER, RUDY**
    T, 6-3, 210, LSU
14. **SIMONS, FRANK**
    E, 6-3, 195, Nebraska
15. **NORMAN, HALDO**
    E, 6-3, 200, Gustavus Adolphus
16. **MYERS, BOB**
    B, 6-2, 185, Stanford
17. **BALDOCK, AL**
    E, 6-2, 200, Southern Cal
18. **CAREY, BILL**
    E, 6-4, 219, Michigan State
19. **TALARICO, SAM**
    T, 6-0, 207, Indiana
20. **YATES, JESS**
    E, 6-2, 190, LSU
21. **OFFIELD, GENE**
    E, 5-11, 195, Hardin-Simmons
22. **COZAD, JIM**
    T, 6-2, 215, Santa Clara
23. **GLAZIER, BILL**
    E, 6-1, 189, Arizona
24. **KRUEGER, RALPH**
    T, 6-3, 225, California
25. **LAUGHLIN, HENRY**
    B, 6-1, 200, Kansas
26. **KANE, DICK**
    G, 6-3, 215, Cincinnati
27. **SCHAFF, WALDO**
    T, 6-3, 210, Oklahoma A&M
28. **PALUMBO, JOE**
    G, 5-10 1/2, 205, Virginia
29. **MOSHER, CHUCK**
    E, 6-3, 200, Colorado
30. **PATRICK, DICK**
    C, 6-2, 215, Oregon

1953
(Drafted Alternately 9-8-7)

1. **(A) Bonus Choice:
   BABCOCK, HARRY**
   E, 6-2, 196, Georgia
1. **(B) STOLHANDSKE, TOM**
   E, 6-2, 210, Texas
2. **MORRIS, GEORGE**
   C, 6-3, 235, Georgia Tech
3. **ST. CLAIR, BOB**
   T, 6-7, 250, Tulsa-USF
4. **FULLERTON, ED**
   B, 6-0, 205, Maryland
5. **MILLER, HAL**
   T, 6-4, 249, Georgia Tech
6. **Choice to Chicago Bears**
7. **CARR, PAUL**
   B, 6-0, 205, Houston
8. **HOGLAND, DOUG**
   T, 6-3, 225, Oregon State
9. **LEDYARD, HAL**
   QB, 6-0 1/2, 185, Chattanooga
10. **BROWN, PETE**
    G, 6-2, 217, Georgia Tech
11. **CHARLTON, AL**
    B, 5-11, 185, Washington State
12. **LEACH, CARSON**
    G, 5-10, 218, Duke
13. **EARLEY, BILL**
    B, 6-1, 198, Washington
14. **FLETCHER, TOM**
    B, 6-0, 195, St. Mary's & Arizona State
15. **GENTHNER, CHARLEY**
    T, 6-2, 225, Texas
16. **DURIG, FRED**
    B, 6-1, 200, Bowling Green
17. **LATHAM, HUGH**
    T, 6-3, 225, San Diego State
18. **WACHOLZ, STAN**
    E, 6-3 1/2, 200, San Jose State
19. **DuCLOS, KING**
    E, 6-3, 218, Texas Western
20. **HUIZINGA, RAY**
    T, 6-5, 230, Northwestern
21. **BAHNSEN, KEN**
    B, 5-10, 200, North Texas State
22. **ROBBINS, LAVERNE**
    G, 5-11 1/2, 225, Midwestern
23. **HUNT, TRAVIS**
    T, 6-1, 220, Alabama
24. **MORGAN, ED**
    B, 6-1, 195, Tennessee
25. **STOCKERT, ERNIE**
    E, 6-6, 220, UCLA
26. **COOPER, HARLEY**
    B, 6-1, 195, Arizona State
27. **McCLEOD, RALPH**
    E, 6-4, 205, LSU
28. **NOVIKOFF, TOM**
    B, 6-0, 195, Oregon
29. **STILLWELL, DON**
    E, 6-1, 180, Southern Cal
30. **No pick as result of BONUS CHOICE**

Future Arrival—Redshirt

1954

(Drafted 10th)

1. **FALONEY, BERNIE**
   QB, 6-1, 190, Maryland
2. **RUCKA, LEO**
   G, 6-3, 225, Omaha
3. **KORCHECK, STEVE**
   C, 6-1, 205, George Washington
4. **BOXHOLD, CHARLIE**
   HB, 5-11, 186, Maryland
5. **MINCEVICH, FRANK**
   G, 6-2, 245, South Carolina
6. **SAGELY, FLOYD**
   E, 6-1, 187, Arkansas
7. **YOUNGELMAN, SID**
   T, 6-3, 247, Alabama
8. **Choice to Cleveland**
9. **CONNOLLY, TED**
   G, 6-3, 230, Santa Clara-Tulsa
10. **GOSS, DON**
    T, 6-5, 260, SMU
11. **SKOCKO, JOHN**
    E, 6-3, 220, Southern Cal
12. **EASTERWOOD, HAL**
    C, 6-0, 195, Mississippi State
13. **WILLIAMS, MORGAN**
    G, 6-1 1/2, 195, Texas Christian
14. **WILLIAMS, SAM**
    HB, 6-1, 190, California
15. **PALUMBO, SAM**
    G, 6-2, 220, Notre Dame
16. **FIVEASH, BOBBY**
    HB, 5-11, 185, Florida State
17. **KAUTZ, KARL**
    T, 6-2, 245, Texas Tech
18. **KAY, MORRIS**
    E, 6-2, 204, Kansas
19. **EDMISTON, BOB**
    T, 6-2, 255, Temple-Michigan State
20. **DiPIETRO, FRANK**
    B, 6-1, 197, Georgia
21. **ALSUP, HOWARD**
    T, 6-4, 230, Middle Tennessee State
22. **REYNOLDS, RALPH**
    B, 6-0, 186, North Texas State
23. **FENSTEMAKER, LEROY**
    QB, 6-2, 205, Rice
24. **DANIELS, JERRY**
    T, 6-1, 230, Tennessee Tech
25. **PLATT, JOHN**
    FB, 6-2, 215, Elon-Kentucky
26. **BELLO, PETE**
    C, 6-0, 205, Pasadena City College
27. **BAKER, ED**
    G, 6-1 1/2, 225, Omaha
28. **GARBRECHT, BOB**
    FB, 6-1, 205, Rice
29. **DUNN, TED**
    B, 6-1, 200, Murray State-Washington (Missouri)
30. **FOLKS, DON**
    E, 6-2, 210, Houston

1955

(Drafted Alternately 8-9)

1. **MOEGLE, DICK**
   HB, 6-0, 180, Rice
2. **MORZE, FRANK**
   T, 6-4, 245, Boston College
3. **HARDY, CARROLL**
   HB, 6-0, 185, Colorado
4. **HAZELTINE, MATT**
   C, 6-2, 201, California
5. **KRAEMER, ELDRED**
   T, 6-3, 235, Pittsburgh
6. **LUNA, BOBBY**
   HB, 5-11, 183, Alabama
7. **DEAN, JOHN**
   QB, 6-1, 195, VPI
* 8. **MEYERS, FRED**
   QB, 6-2, 205, Oklahoma
* 9. **PREZIOSIO, FRED**
   QB, 6-2, 245, Purdue
10. **ASHBACHER, RON**
    E, 6-3, 220, Oregon State
11. **RATELLA, RUDY**
    E, 6-3 1/2, 215, Omaha
*12. **PALATELLA, LOU**
    T, 6-2, 230, Pittsburgh
13. **GASKELL, RICHIE**
    E, 6-2, 195, George Washington
14. **McKEITHAN, NICK**
    HB, 6-1, 195, Duke
15. **HESS, BURDETTE**
    G, 6-0, 220, Idaho
16. **HALL, JIM**
    E, 6-2, 195, Auburn
17. **NEWTON, BOB**
    G, 6-2, 220, San Diego State
18. **PHEISTER, RON**
    E, 6-2, 210, Oregon
19. **GARZOLI, JOHN**
    T, 6-7, 265, California
20. **DYER, GLEN**
    QB, 6-5, 200, Texas
21. **MADEROS, GEORGE**
    E, 6-1, 195, Chico State
22. **VANN, PETE**
    QB, 6-1, 189, Army
*23. **GUNNARI, TOM**
    T, 6-2, 220, Washington State
24. **HEASTON, BOB**
    G, 6-2, 222, Cal Poly-SLO
25. **WADE, DEWEY**
    E, 6-1, 225, Kansas State
26. **KERR, JOHNNY**
    E, 6-0, 170, Purdue
*27. **SHOCKEY, DICK**
    QB, 6-3, 210, Marquette
28. **SANDERS, DON**
    HB, 6-0, 185, Stanford
*29. **KNIEDINGER, OTTO**
    T, 6-2, 230, Penn State
*30. **GONGOLA, BOB**
    QB, 6-3, 180, Illinois

1956

(Drafted Alternately 1-2)

1. **MORRALL, EARL**
   QB, 6-1, 190, Michigan State
2. **BOSLEY, BRUCE**
   T, 6-2, 240, West Virginia
3. **HERCHMAN, BILL**
   T, 6-2, 249, Texas Tech
4. **PAJACZKOWSKI, FRANK**
   HB, 6-0, 187, Richmond
5. **Choice to Los Angeles**
6. **SARDISCO, TONY**
   G-LB, 6-2, 210, Tulane
*7. **BARNES, LARRY**
   FB, 6-1, 215, Colorado A&M
8. **SMITH, CHARLES**
   E, 6-2, 200, Abilene Christian
9. **COX, JIM**
   E, 6-3, 190, Cal Poly-SLO
10. **ZALESKI, JERRY**
    HB, 5-10, 195, Colorado A&M

11. **PELL, STEWART**
    T, 6-4, 225, North Carolina
12. **SWEDBERG, ROGER**
    TE, 6-1, 220, Iowa
13. **MOODY, RALPH**
    HB, 6-0, 195, Kansas
*14. **OWENS, R.C.**
    E, 6-3, 205, College of Idaho
15. (A) **HENDERSON, REED**
    G-T, 6-2, 235, Utah State
15. (B) **BOYD, GENE**
    (Choice from Pittsburgh)
    HB, 6-0, 200, Abilene Christian
16. **HERRING, GEORGE**
    QB, 6-3, 200, Mississippi
17. **WEIS, RICHARD**
    T, 6-1, 230, Mississippi
*18. **YELVERTON, BILLY**
    TE, 6-4, 215, Mississippi
19. **ARRIGONI, PETE**
    HB, 6-0, 185, Arizona
20. **SCARBROUGH, BOB**
    C-G, 6-1, 210, Auburn
21. **JOYNER, L.C.**
    HB-E, 6-1, 185, Contra Costa J.C.
22. **WESSMAN, CLARENCE**
    E, 6-3, 235, San Jose State
23. **MONROE, MIKE**
    HB, 6-1, 205, Washington
24. **WALLACE, ED**
    G, 6-3, 260, San Diego J.C.
25. **GOAD, PAUL**
    HB, 6-0, 200, Abilene Christian
26. **LOUDD, ROMMIE**
    E, 6-0, 215, UCLA
27. **GUSTAFSON, JERRY**
    QB, 6-2, 190, Stanford
*28. **DREW, JERRY**
    FB, 5-10, 195, California
29. **BENSON, DEAN**
    E, 6-3, 195, Willamette
*30. **MITCHELL, BOB**
    G-T, 6-0, 204, Puget Sound

1957

(Drafted 2nd)

1. **BRODIE, JOHN**
   QB, 6-1, 195, Stanford
2. **WOODSON, ABE**
   HB, 5-11, 188, Illinois
3. **Choice to Los Angeles**
4. (A) **RIDLON, JIM**
   HB, 6-1, 195, Syracuse
4. (B) **SANDUSKY, MIKE**
   (Choice from Chicago Cardinals)
   G, 5-11, 228, Maryland
5. **RUBKE, KARL**
   C, 6-4, 235, Southern Cal
6. (A) **HUNTER, JIM**
   HB, 6-0, 195, Missouri
6. (B) **RHODES, BILL**
   (Choice from Philadelphia)
   HB, 6-0, 200, Western State
*7. **DUGAN, FRED**
   E, 6-3, 195, Dayton
8. **PITTS, ERNIE**
   E, 6-2, 190, Denver
*9. **BRUECKMAN, CHARLES**
   C-LB, 6-2, 218, Pittsburgh
*10. **HURST, JERRY**
   T, 6-7, 240, Middle Tennessee
*11. **DAVIS, TOM**
   HB, 6-2, 205, LSU
*12. **SINGTON, FRED**
   T-G, 6-1, 225, Alabama

13. **MACKEY, CHARLES**
    E, 6-4, 190, Arizona State
14. **WARZEKA, RON**
    T, 6-3, 235, Montana State
*15. **KAISER, EARL**
    HB, 6-0, 195, Houston
16. **KRISTOPAITIS, VIC**
    FB, 6-2, 205, Dayton
17. **KUHN, DAVE**
    C-LB, 6-1, 220, Kentucky
*18. **GUY, RICHARD**
    G, 6-3, 225, Ohio State
19. **BABB, GENE**
    FB, 6-2, 210, Austin
20. **DeLOACH, SID**
    G, 6-1, 220, Duke
21. **WILCOX, FRED**
    HB, 6-1, 185, Tulane
22. **TRIPP, PAUL**
    T, 6-3, 240, Idaho State
23. **THOMAS, JOHN**
    E, 6-5, 215, Pacific
24. **LADNER, JOHN**
    E, 6-2, 205, Wake Forest
25. **MEYER, RAY**
    FB, 5-11, 210, Lamar Tech
*26. **TOPPING, TOM**
    T-G, 6-2, 215, Duke
27. **VICIC, DON**
    FB, 6-1, 210, Ohio State
28. **CURTIS, BILL**
    HB, 6-3, 180, TCU
29. **HALLBECK, VERN**
    LB, 6-2, 213, TCU
30. **PARKS, GEORGE**
    QB, 6-2, 205, Lamar Tech

1958

(Drafted Alternately 8-9)

1. (A) **PACE, JIM**
   (Choice from Pittsburgh)
   HB, 6-0, 195, Michigan
1. (B) **KRUEGER, CHARLES**
   T, 6-4, 230, Texas A&M
*2. **NEWMAN, BOB**
   QB, 6-2, 190, Washington State
3. **HOPPE, BOB**
   HB, 6-0, 190, Auburn
4. **VARONE, JOHN**
   HB, 5-11, 190, Miami
5. **ATKINS, BILL**
   HB, 6-1, 200, Auburn
6. **SCHMIDT, HENRY**
   T, 6-4, Trinity College
7. **Choice traded to Detroit**
8. (A) **MILLS, RON**
   HB, 6-1, 180, West Texas State
*8. (B) **BURTON, LEON**
   (Choice from Chicago Cardinals)
   HB, 5-9, 170, Arizona State
9. **TROUTMAN, GEORGE**
   C, 6-4, 260, Capitol (Ohio)
*10. **HECKMAN, VEL**
   T, 6-0, 230, Florida
*11. **WHARTON, ROBERT**
   T, 6-2, 238, Houston
12. **WILLIAMS, PETE**
    T, 6-1, 225, Lehigh
13. (A) **DUKES, HAROLD**
    E, 6-2, 225, Michigan State
13. (B) **YORE, JAMES**
    (Choice from Pittsburgh)
    FB, 6-2, 225, Indiana
14. **FIELDS, MAX**
    HB, 5-10, 185, Whittier College

Future Arrival—Redshirt

15. **Choice traded to Detroit**
16. **SHIRKEY, GEORGE**
    T, 6-4, 250, Stephen F. Austin
17. **WHITTENBORN, JOHN**
    T, 6-2, 238, SE Missouri State
18. **MORRIS, DENNIT**
    G-LB, 6-1, 230, Oklahoma
19. **MUSHATT, RANNIE**
    G, 6-4, 244, Grambling
20. **MERTENS, JERRY**
    E, 6-0, 185, Drake
21. **CHRISTIAN, DON**
    HB, 6-0, 190, Arkansas
22. **HARTMAN, BRUCE**
    T, 6-0, 245, Luther College
23. **FIELDS, LARRY**
    HB, 6-0, 200, Utah
*24. **MACKEY, DEE**
    E, 6-5, 227, E. Texas State
25. **KAUZMAREK, BILL**
    C, 6-0, 225, SW Missouri State
*26. **HILL, HILLARD**
    E, 6-1, 188, Southern Cal
27. **WITUCKI, BOB**
    E, 6-3, 225, Notre Dame
28. **WARREN, GARLAND**
    C, 6-1, 225, No. Texas State
29. **HODGES, HERMAN**
    HB, 6-2, 210, Sam Houston
*30. **STAHURA, TED**
    T, 6-0, 250, Pittsburgh State

1959
(Drafted 6th)
1. (A) **BAKER, DAVE**
   HB, 6-0, 190, Oklahoma
1. (B) **JAMES, DAN**
   (Choice from Pittsburgh)
   C, 6-2, 250, Ohio State
2. **HARRISON, BOB**
   LB, 6-2, 227, Oklahoma
3. **DOVE, EDDIE**
   HB, 6-2, 183, Colorado
4. **CLARK, MONTE**
   DT, 6-6, 260, Southern Cal
5. **GEREMIA, FRANK**
   T, 6-3, 245, Notre Dame
6. **BAVARO, WALLY**
   T, 6-4, 245, Holy Cross
*7. (A) **COLCHICO, DAN**
   E, 6-4, 225, San Jose State
7. (B) **ROGERS, DON**
   (Choice from Chicago Cardinals)
   LB, 6-2, 245, South Carolina
8. **AKIN, LEWIS**
   E, 6-4, 210, Vanderbilt
9. **GREEN, ROBERT**
   HB, 5-11, 175, Florida
10. **NAGURSKI, BRONKO**
    T, 6-2, 225, Notre Dame
11. **HAYS, JACK**
    HB, 6-2, 190, Trinity College
12. **KORUTZ, BILL**
    C, 6-2, 250, Dayton
13. **LOPASKY, BILL**
    G, 6-2, 235, West Virginia
14. **DUKES, MICHAEL**
    FB-LB, 6-3, 218, Clemson
15. **BELLAND, JOE**
    HB, 5-10, 182, Arizona State
16. **COOK, BOB**
    HB, 6-3, 185, Idaho State
17. **JURCZAK, JEROME**
    C, 6-2 1/2, 220, St. Benedict's

Future Arrival—Redshirt

18. **COWLEY, JACK**
    T, 6-2, 210, Trinity College
*19. **OSBORNE, TOM**
    HB, 6-3, 195, Hastings
    (Nebraska)
*20. **DEESE, TOBY**
    T, 5-10, 185, Georgia Tech
21. **CARR, LUTHER**
    HB, 5-10, 185, Washington
22. **McQUEEN, BURNIO**
    E, 6-3, 200, North Carolina A&T
23. **DOLLAHAN, BRUCE**
    T, 6-3, 225, Illinois
24. **CHUDY, CRAIG**
    E, 6-3, 200, UCLA
*25. **GEE, ROY**
    G, 6-2, 200, Trinity College
26. **YOUNG, ED**
    E, 6-2, 215, Louisville
27. **SEMENKO, MEL**
    T, 6-2, 200, Colorado
28. **McCLUSKEY, MIKE**
    HB, 6-0, 185, Washington
29. **BOLTON, JACK**
    T, 6-3, 235, Puget Sound
30. **CARTER, LOWELL**
    E-LB, 6-3, 230, Denver

1960
(Drafted Alternately 10-11)
1. **STICKLES, MONTY**
   E, 6-3, 232, Notre Dame
*2. (A) **KAMMERER, CARL**
   LB, 6-3, 237, Pacific
2. (B) **MAGAC, MIKE**
   (Choice from Washington)
   G, 6-2, 225, Missouri
3. **BREEDLOVE, ROD**
   C-LB, 6-2, 215, Maryland
4. **NORTON, RAY**
   HB, 6-2, 184, San Jose State
5. **ROHDE, LEN**
   T, 6-4, 235, Utah State
6. **MURCHISON, OLA**
   E, 6-3, 211, Pacific
7. **WATERS, BOB**
   QB, 6-2, 188, Presbyterian
8. (A) **MATHIS, BILL**
   (Choice from Washington)
   HB, 6-1, 200, Clemson
8. (B) **FUGLER, MAX**
   C-LB, 6-2, 224, LSU
9. **WASDEN, BOB**
   C-LB, 6-2, 220, Auburn
10. **BRANCH, MEL**
    E, 6-2, 220, LSU
11. (A) **PITTS, ED**
    (Choice from Pittsburgh)
    T, 6-2, 230, South Carolina
*11. (B) **HANSEN, ERNEST**
    C, 6-4, 250, Arizona State
12. **WILLIAMS, JIM**
    T, 6-1, 255, North Carolina
    College
*13. **HINSHAW, DEAN**
    T, 6-6, 240, Idaho State
14. **CAMPBELL, GARY**
    QB, 6-0, 199, Whittier
15. **DOWDLE, MIKE**
    FB-LB, 6-4, 225, Texas
16. **HEINEKE, JIM**
    TB, 6-2, 230, Wisconsin
17. **GONSOULIN, AUSTIN**
    HB, 6-3, 205, Baylor
18. **ROBINSON, CARL**
    T, 6-5, 245, South Carolina State

19. **PATE, BOBBY**
    HB, 6-0, 175, Presbyterian
20. **WOODWARD, JIM**
    T, 6-5, 228, Lamar Tech

1961
(Drafted Alternately 9-10)
1. (A) **JOHNSON, JIM**
   (Choice from Pittsburgh)
   HB, 6-2, 184, UCLA
1. (B) **CASEY, BERNIE**
   (Choice from Baltimore)
   FB, 6-4, 215, Bowling Green
1. (C) **KILMER, BILL**
   QB, 6-0, 190, UCLA
2. **LAKES, ROLAND**
   C-T, 6-4, 245, Wichita
3. **COOPER, BILL**
   FB, 6-2, 215, Muskingum
4. (A) **THOMAS, AARON**
   (Choice from Pittsburgh)
   E, 6-3, 208, Oregon
4. (B) **MESSER, DALE**
   HB, 5-10, 175, Fresno
5. (A) **McCREARY, BOB**
   T, 6-5, 250, Wake Forest
*5. (B) **MILLER, CLARK**
   (Choice from Dallas)
   T, 6-5, 245, Utah State
*6. **McCLELLAN, MIKE**
   HB, 6-0, 185, Oklahoma
7. **PURDIN, RAY**
   HB, 6-0, 185, Northwestern
8. **PLUMLEY, NEILL**
   T, 6-6, 240, Oregon State
*9. (A) **DONOHUE, LEON**
   (Choice from Pittsburgh)
   T, 6-4, 245, San Jose State
9. (B) **NINO, EVERISTO**
   T, 6-4, 243, E. Texas State
10. **HYNES, PAUL**
    HB, 6-0, 210, Louisiana Tech
11. **PARRILLI, TONY**
    LB, 6-1, 220, Illinois
*12. **COFFEY, DON**
    E, 6-2, 190, Memphis State
*12. (A) **HACKLER, TOMMY**
    (Choice from Pittsburgh)
    E, 6-4, 217, Tennessee
13. (B) **FINCKE, JULIUS**
    T, 6-3, 260, McNeese State
14. **WORRELL, BILL**
    T, 6-2, 240, Georgia
*15. **SAMS, BOB**
    T, 6-2, 250, Central State
    (Oklahoma)
16. **FULLER, CHARLIE**
    HB, 5-11, 170, San Francisco
    State
17. **JEWELL, TOM**
    G, 6-1, 240, Idaho State
*18. **McFARLAND, KAY**
    E-HB, 6-2, 180, Colorado State
19. **SIMPSON, TOM**
    C-OT, 6-3, 245, Davidson
20. **PEERY, JERRY**
    G-DT, 6-3, 245, Central State
    (Oklahoma)

1962
(Drafted 8th)
1. **ALWORTH, LANCE**
   HB, 6-0, 180, Arkansas
2. **PINE, ED**
   LB, 6-4, 230, Utah

3. **ADAMS, BILLY RAY**
   FB, 6-2, 215, Mississippi
*4. (A) **DEAN, FLOYD**
   LB, 6-4, 245, Florida
*4. (B) **SIEMINSKI, CHARLIE**
   (Choice from Dallas)
   DT, 6-4, 245, Penn State
5. (A) **WOODS, TED**
   (Choice from St. Louis
   Cardinals)
   HB, 6-1, 194, Colorado
*5. (B) **LIND, MIKE**
   FB, 6-2, 215, Notre Dame
6. (A) **LUHNOW, KEITH**
   (Choice from Washington)
   FB, 6-3, 220, Santa Ana J.C.
6. (B) **BROWN, JERRY**
   (Choice from Pittsburgh)
   G, 6-1, 230, Mississippi
6. (C) **WINTER, BILL**
   G, 6-1, 235, West Virginia
7. **BURRELL, JOHN**
   E, 6-3, 190, Rice
8. **VOLLENWEIDER, JAMES**
   HB-FB, 6-1, 210, Miami (FL)
9. **ROBERTS, JIM**
   T, 6-3, 240, Mississippi
10. **COUSTILLAC, REGIS**
    C, 6-2, 224, Pittsburgh
11. **JEPSON, LARRY**
    C, 6-5, 230, Furman
12. **McPIKE, MILTON**
    E, 6-2, 225, Kirksville Teachers
13. **PIEROVICH, GEORGE**
    LB-FB, 6-2, 225, California
14. **EASTERLY, DICK**
    DB, 5-11, 185, Syracuse
15. **OSBORNE, RAY**
    T, 6-6, 235, Mississippi State
16. **FRANK, RON**
    T, 6-6, 232, So. Dakota State
17. **FOLTZ, WALLY**
    E, 6-3, 218, De Pauw
18. **BROWN, GARY**
    T, 6-2, 239, Illinois
19. **BURTON, BOB**
    T, 6-2, 250, Murray State
20. **McFARLAND, RODGER**
    DB, 6-1, 183, Kansas

1963
(Drafted Alternately 8-7)
1. **ALEXANDER, KERMIT**
   HB, 5-11, 186, UCLA
2. **ROCK, WALTER**
   OT-DT, 6-5, 240, Maryland
3. **LISBON, DON**
   HB, 6-0, 190, Bowlng Green
4. **Choice to Chicago**
*4. (A) **ROSDAHL, HARRISON**
   (Choice from Philadelphia)
   G, 6-4, 245, Penn State
4. (B) **CAMPBELL, HUGH**
   (Choice from Washington)
   E, 6-1, 184, Washington State
*5. (A) **BURKE, VERN**
   E, 6-4 1/2, 201, Oregon
*5. (B) **PILOT, JIM**
   (Choice from Pittsburgh)
   FB, 6-1, 205, New Mexico
5. (C) **MOELLER, GARY**
   (Choice from Chicago)
   LB, 6-1, 224, Ohio State
6. **EMERICK, PAT**
   LG, 6-2, 238, Western
   Michigan

DeCOURLEY, ERNEST
DT, 6-6, 250, Moorehead State
. LOCKE, ROGER
E, 6-2, 185, Arizona State
. MACZUZAK, JOHN
T, 6-5, 245, Pittsburgh
0. LOPOUR, DICK
HB, 6-2, 214, Huron
1. SHAFER, STEVE
QB, 6-0, 185, Utah State
2. DENTON, ROBERT
T, 6-2, 240, Mississippi State
3. SHULTZ, DICK
T, 6-3, 240, Ohio University
4. TOBIN, BILL
HB, 5-11, 210, Missouri
15. ROSS, OLLIE
FB, 6-0, 215, West Texas State
6. BOGDALEK, JIM
DT, 6-4, 245, Toledo
7. REED, KEN
G, 6-0, 230, Tulsa
18. SELLERS, JOHN
T, 6-2, 220, Bakersfield J.C.
9. PRICE, BOB
G, 6-1, 230, North Texas State
0. DAVIS, DON
B, 5-11, 220, McMurry

1964
(Drafted 1st)
. PARKS, DAVE
E, 6-2, 195, Texas Tech
. MIRA, GEORGE
QB, 5-11, 183, Miami (FL)
. WILCOX, DAVE
LB, 6-3, 230, Oregon
4. WILSON, JAMES
G, 6-3, 244, George
. JOHNSON, RUDY
FB, 5-11, 200, Nebraska
6. LEWIS, GARY
FB, 6-2 1/2, 227, Arizona State
7. CLARKE, HAGWOOD
DB, 6-0, 196, Florida
8. (A) DAUGHERTY, BOB
HB, 6-2, 185, Tulsa
. (B) POOLE, BOB
(Choice from Washington)
TE, 6-4, 216, Clemson
9. MUDD, HOWARD
G, 6-3, 237, Hillsdale
*10. POLSER, FRED
T, 6-5, 235, East Texas State
11. ALMQUIST, DENNIS
G, 6-1, 218, Idaho
*12. LONG, JIM
FB, 6-1, 202, Fresno State
13. BROWN, ROBERT
DT, 6-5, 263, Arkansas A&M
14. BEARD, ED
T, 6-2, 235, Tennessee
15. GRIFFIN, JAMES
E, 6-3 1/2, 230, Grambling
16. GORDON, CORNELL
DB, 5-11, 180, North Carolina A&T
*17. BRUSVAN, KEN
T, 6-4, 223, Oregon State
*18. COLE, JERRY
E, 6-4, 215, Southwest Texas State
19. RAWSON, LARRY
B, 5-11, 209, Auburn
20. BAKER, GENE
G, 6-1, 235, Whitworth

1965
(Drafted 2nd)
1. (A) WILLARD, KEN
FB, 6-2, 230, North Carolina
1. (B) DONNELLY, GEORGE
(Choice from Cleveland)
DB, 6-3, 202, Illinois
2. CERNE, JOE
C, 6-2, 237, Northwestern
3. (A) SCHWEICKERT, BOB
(Choice from N.Y. Giants)
HB, 6-1, 191, Virginia Poly
3. (B) NORTON, JIM
T, 6-4, 247, Washington
3. (C) CHAPPLE, JACK
(Choice from Baltimore)
LB, 6-2, 225, Stanford
*4. TODD, LARRY
FL, 6-1, 190, Arizona State
*5. McCORMICK, DAVE
T, 6-6, 250, LSU
6. Choice to Cleveland
7. Choice to Green Bay
8. Choice to Minnesota
9. SWINFORD, WAYNE
DB, 6-0 1/2, 185, Georgia
*10. CAPPADONA, ROBERT
HB, 6-2, 225, Northeastern
*11. MASS, STEVE
T, 6-2, 270, Detroit
*12. PLUMP, DAVE
HB, 6-0, 190, Fresno State
13. SCHUMACHER, GREG
LB, 6-3, 230, Illinois
14. ANDRUSKI, FRANK
DB, 6-0, 185, Utah
15. PABIAN, JOE
T, 6-3, 270, West Virginia
*16. HETTEMA, DAVE
T, 6-3 1/2, 230, New Mexico
17. FRKETICH, LEN
E, 6-3, 220, Oregon State
*18. STANDRIDGE, LEON
E, 6-3, 220, San Diego State
19. FORD, DALE
QB-DB, 6-1, 200, Washington State
*20. DUNCAN, DENNIS
HB, 6-1, 200, Louisiana College

1966
(Drafted Alternately 10-11)
1. HINDMAN, STAN
DE-G, 6-3, 235, Mississippi
*2. WINDSOR, BOB
E, 6-4, 224, Kentucky
3. (A) RANDOLPH, ALVIN
(Choice from Dallas)
DB, 6-2, 193, Iowa
3. (B) BLAND, DAN
DB, 5-11, 190, Mississippi State
*4. PARKER, DON
G, 6-3, 240, Virginia
5. (A) PHILLIPS, MEL
(Choice from Dallas)
DB, 6-0, 190, North Carolina A&T
5. (B) SMITH, STEVE
TE, 6-5, 240, Michigan
6. JOHNSON, CHARLES
DT, 6-2, 266, Louisville
7. Choice to Baltimore
8. WITCHER, DICK
E, 6-3, 210, UCLA

9. KRAMER, KENT
TE, 6-5, 235, Minnesota
10. SBRANTI, RON
LB, 6-2, 228, Utah
11. RIDLEHUBER, PRESTON
DB, 6-2, 195, Georgia
12. LOEBACH, LYALL
T, 6-5, 248, Simpson
*13. JACKSON, JIM
DB, 5-11, 185, Western Illinois
*14. COLLETT, ELMER
G, 6-4, 225, San Francisco State
*15. SAFFOLD, S.T.
E, 6-3, 205, San Jose State
16. LeCLAIR, JIM
QB, 6-1, 195, C.W. Post
17. BRELAND, JIM
G, 6-2, 230, Georgia Tech
*18. PARSON, RON
E, 6-5, 240, Austin Peay
*19. FITZGERALD, DICK
T, 6-1, 250, Nebraska
20. WALKER, WILLIE
LB, 6-3, 220, Baylor

1967
(Drafted Alternately 11-13)
1. (A) SPURRIER, STEVE
(Choice from Atlanta)
QB, 6-2, 203, Florida
1. (B) BANASZEK, CAS
LB, 6-3, 245, Northwestern
2. HOLZER, TOM
T, 6-4, 248, Louisville
3. (A) NUNLEY, FRANK
(Choice from Pittsburgh)
LB, 6-2, 230, Michigan
3. (B) TUCKER, BILL
HB, 6-2, 232, Tennessee A&I
4. TRIMBLE, WAYNE
DB, 6-3, 205, Alabama
5. Choice to Atlanta
6. CUNNINGHAM, DOUG
HB, 5-11, 185, Mississippi
7. JACKSON, MILT
DB, 6-3, 185, Tulsa
8. JOHNSON, WALTER
LB, 6-4, 235, Tuskegee
9. BRIGGS, BOB
T, 6-3, 248, Heidelberg
10. MYERS, PHIL (Chip)
FL, 6-4, 185, NW Oklahoma
11. CARMANN, KEN
DT, 6-4, 265, Kearney (Nebraska)
12. HALL, JAMES
LB, 6-3, 230, Tuskegee
13. GIBBS, RICH
DB, 6-1, 187, Iowa
14. LeBLANC, DALTON
FL, 5-11, 175, NE Louisiana
15. SPENCER, CLARENCE
FL, 6-4, 200, Louisville
16. TEMPLEMAN, BART
C, 6-3, 248, Eastern Montana
17. TALBOTT, DAN
QB, 6-0, 180, North Carolina

1968
(Drafted Alternately 14-15)
1. BLUE, FORREST
C, 6-5, 248, Auburn
2. Choice traded to St. Louis
3. (A) OLSSEN, LANCE
(Choice from Detroit)
T, 6-5, 267, Purdue

3. (B) VANDERBUNDT, SKIP
LB, 6-3, 234, Oregon
4. FULLER, JOHN
E, 6-0, 175, Lamar Tech
5. LEE, DWIGHT
RB, 6-2, 190, Michigan State
6. (A) JOHNSON, LEO
(Choice from New Orleans)
FL, 6-2, 185, Tennessee State
6. (B) BELK, BILL
DE, 6-3, 240, Maryland State
7. RICHARDSON, JERRY
LB, 6-2, 218, Mississippi
8. (A) BROWN, CHARLES
(Choice from N.Y. Giants)
T, 6-5, 246, Augustana
8. (B) GRAY, TOM
FL, 5-9, 174, Morehead State
9. BOYETT, CASEY
E, 6-1, 188, Brigham Young
10. HART, TOMMY
LB, 6-3, 215, Morris Brown
11. FITZGIBBONS, DENNIS
G, 6-1, 260, Syracuse
12. JOHNSON, HENRY
QB, 6-0, 180, Fisk
13. MITRAKOS, TOM
C, 6-4, 220, Pittsburgh
14. MOORE, ALEX
RB, 6-1, 200, Norfolk State
15. SPENCER, CLARENCE
FL, 6-2, 188, Louisville
16. ROSENOW, TOM
DT, 6-3, 250, Northern Illinois
17. PATERA, DENNIS
K, 6-0 214, Brigham Young

1969
(Drafted 16th)
1. (A) KWALICK, TED
(Choice from New Orleans)
TE, 6-4, 230, Penn State
1. (B) WASHINGTON, GENE
FL, 6-1, 186, Stanford
2. Choice to Pittsburgh via Cleveland
3. Choice to Dallas
4. (A) SNIADECKI, JIM
(Choice from Detroit)
LB, 6-2, 220, Indiana
4. (B) MOORE, GENE
RB, 6-1, 200, Occidental
5. EDWARDS, EARL
DT, 6-6, 276, Wichita State
6. THOMAS, JIM
RB, 6-1, 216, Texas-Arlington
7. VAN SINDEREN, STEVE
F, 6-4, 255, Washington State
8. LOPER, MIKE
T, 6-4, 230, Brigham Young
9. CRAWFORD, HILTON
DB, 6-1, 195, Grambling
10. CHAPPLE, DAVE
K, 6-1, 180, Santa Barbara
11. PEAKE, WILLIE
T, 6-3, 260, Alcorn A&M
12. O'MALLEY, JACK
T, 6-4, 250, Southern Cal
13. CHAMPLIN, PAUL
DB, 6-0, 194, Eastern Montana
14. BLACK, TOM
FL, 6-1, 192, East Texas State
15. GOLDEN, GARY
DB, 6-0, 179, Texas Tech

* Future Arrival—Redshirt

16. **HOSKINS, BOB**
LB, 6-2, 235, Wichita State
17. **RUSHING, JOE**
LB, 6-2, 216, Memphis State

1970
(Drafted 9th)
1. **HARDMAN, CEDRICK**
DE, 6-3, 250, North Texas State
1. **(B) TAYLOR, BRUCE**
(Choice from Washington)
DB, 6-0, 180, Boston U.
2. **Choice to Los Angeles**
3. **ISENBARGER, JOHN**
(Choice from Philadelphia via
Los Angeles)
RB, 6-3, 205, Indiana
4. **WASHINGTON, VIC**
WR, 5-11, 180, Wyoming
5. **McARTHUR, GARY**
T, 6-5, 247, Southern Cal
6. **CLARK, RUSTY**
QB, 6-2, 212, Houston
7. **STRONG, JIM**
RB, 6-2, 204, Houston
8. **CAMPBELL, CARTER**
LB, 6-3, 214, Weber State
9. **RILEY, PRESTON**
WR, 6-1, 180, Memphis State
10. **SCHREIBER, LARRY**
RB, 6-0, 193, Tennessee Tech
11. **CROCKETT, DANNY**
WR, 6-1, 170, Toledo
12. **TANT, BILL**
T, 6-4, 245, Dayton
13. **VANDERSLICE, JIM**
LB, 6-3, 220, Texas Christian
14. **KING, JACK**
G, 6-2, 245, Clemson
15. **DELSIGNORE, DAVE**
WR, 6-0, 175, Youngstown State
16. **PERKINS, PRODUS**
WR, 6-0, 178, Livingstone
College
17. **CULTON, MIKE**
P, 5-11, 195, LaVerne College

1971
(Drafted Alternately 18-19)
1. **ANDERSON, TIM**
CB, 5-11, 201, Ohio State
2. **(A) JANET, ERNIE**
(Choice from Green Bay)
G, 6-4, 243, Washington
2. **(B) ORDUNA, JOE**
RB, 6-0, 194, Nebraska
3. **(A) DICKERSON, SAM**
(Choice from Philadelphia)
WR, 6-2, 196, Southern Cal
3. **(B) PARKER, WILLIE**
C, 6-3, 238, North Texas State
4. **HARRIS, TONY**
RB, 6-3, 191, Toledo
5. **(A) SHATERNICK, DEAN**
(Choice from Chicago)
T, 6-5, 244, Kansas State
5. **(B) WELLS, GEORGE**
(Choice from N.Y. Giants)
LB, 6-1, 240, New Mexico
State
5. **(C) HUFF, MARTY**
LB, 6-2, 239, Michigan
6. **BRESLER, AL**
WR, 6-1, 185, Auburn
7. **WATSON, JOHN**
T, 6-4, 251, Oklahoma

8. **McCANN, JOHN**
P, 6-2, 170, Arizona State
9. **COUCH, THERMAN**
LB, 6-2, 218, Iowa State
10. **(A) CARDO, RON**
(Choice from New Orleans)
RB, 6-3, 254, Wisconsin State
10. **(B) JENNINGS, ERNIE**
WR, 6-0, 170, Air Force
11. **REED, JOE**
QB, 6-1, 196, Mississippi State
12. **BUNCH, JIM**
DT, 6-3, 254, Wisconsin State
13. **BULLOCK, JOHN**
RB, 5-11, 216, Purdue
14. **DUNSTAN, BILL**
LB, 6-4, 217, Utah State
15. **LENNON, JOHN**
DE, 6-3, 221, Colgate
16. **PURCELL, DAVE**
DT, 6-4, 260, Kentucky
17. **CHARLTON, LEROY**
CB, 6-2, 180, Florida A&M

1972
(Drafted Alternately 19-18)
1. **BEASLEY, TERRY**
WR, 5-11, 186, Auburn
2. **(A) McGILL, RALPH**
(Choice from N.Y. Giants)
CB, 6-0, 181, Tulsa
2. **(B) BARRETT, JEAN**
T, 6-6, 253, Tulsa
3. **DUNBAR, ALLEN**
WR, 6-0, 196, Southern
4. **HALL, WINDLAN**
CB, 5-11, 170, Arizona State
5. **GREENE, MIKE**
LB, 6-4, 233, Georgia
6. **WALKER, JACKIE**
SS, 6-0, 186, Tennessee
7. **HARDY, EDGAR**
G, 6-4, 233, Jackson State
8. **WITTUM, TOM**
P, 6-1, 185, Northern Illinois
9. **BROWN, JERRY**
CB, 5-10, 170, Northwestern
10. **WILLIAMS, STEVE**
DT, 6-4, 251, Western Carolina
11. **LAPUTKA, TOM**
DE, 6-4, 235, Southern Illinois
12. **SETZLER, STEVE**
DE, 6-3, 232, St. Johns
13. **PETTIGREW, LEON**
T, 6-5, 228, San Fernando
Valley State
14. **GUTHRIE, ERIC**
QB, 6-0, 200, Boise State
15. **MADDOX, BOB**
DE, 6-6, 235, Frostburg State
16. **DAVIS, RON**
G, 6-2, 235, Virginia State
17. **ALEXANDER, TED**
RB, 6-0, 192, Langston

1973
(Drafted Alternately 18-19)
1. **HOLMES, MIKE**
CB, 6-1, 180, Texas Southern
2. **HARPER, WILLIE**
(Choice from N.Y. Giants)
LB, 6-2, 205, Nebraska
2. **Choice to St. Louis**
3. **Choice to Denver via
Washington**

4. **Choice to San Diego**
via Washington
5. **(A) FULK, MIKE**
(Choice from Chicago)
LB, 6-3, 229, Indiana
5. **(B) BEVERLY, ED**
WR, 5-11, 172, Arizona State
6. **MOORE, ARTHUR**
DT, 6-5, 253, Tulsa
7. **MITCHELL, JOHN**
LB, 6-3, 229, Alabama
8. **ATKINS, DAVID**
RB, 6-1, 202, Texas-El Paso
9. **PRAETORIUS, ROGER**
RB, 6-3, 228, Syracuse
11. **HUNT, CHARLIE**
LB, 6-3, 218, Florida State
11. **DAHLBERG, TOM**
RB, 6-2, 209, Gustavus
Adolphus
12. **PETTUS, LARRY**
T, 6-4, 228, Tennessee State
13. **KELSO, ALAN**
C, 6-6, 244, Washington
14. **MORRISON, DENNIS**
QB, 6-3, 207, Kansas State
15. **BETTIGA, MIKE**
WT, 6-3, 181, Humbolt State
16. **OVEN, MIKE**
TE, 6-4, 205, Georgia Tech
17. **ERICKSON, BOB**
G, 6-3, 240, North Dakota
State

1974
(Drafted 10th)
1. **(A) JACKSON, WILBUR**
RB, 6-1, 205, Alabama
1. **(B) SANDIFER, BILL**
(Choice from New England)
DT, 6-6, 278, UCLA
2. **(A) FAHNHORST, KEITH**
OT, 6-6, 248, Minnesota
2. **(B) WILLIAMS, DELVIN**
(Choice from Washington)
RB, 6-1, 197, Kansas
3. **Choice to St.   Louis**
4. **(A) HASLERIG, CLINT**
(Choice from N.Y. Jets via
New Orleans)
WR, 6-0, 189, Michigan
4. **Choice to New Orleans**
4. **(B) JOHNSON, SAMMY**
(Choice from Green Bay)
RB, 6-1, 217, North Carolina
5. **Choice to New Orleans**
6. **RAINES, MIKE**
DT, 6-6, 255, Alabama
7. **JOHNSON, KERMIT**
RB, 5-11, 189, UCLA
8. **SCHNEITZ, JIM**
T, 6-3, 253, Missouri
9. **MOORE, MANFRED**
RB, 6-1, 190, Southern Cal
10. **GASPARD, GLEN**
LB, 6-1, 210, Texas
11. **BATTLE, GREG**
S, 5-11, 188, Colorado State
12. **HULL, TOM**
LB, 6-3, 229, Penn State
13. **OWEN, TOM**
QB, 6-1, 195, Wichita State
14. **WILLIAMSON, WALT**
DE, 6-4, 225, Michigan

15. **GRAY, LEONARD**
TE, 6-8, 240, Long Beach
State
16. **CONNORS, JACK**
DB, 5-11, 185, Oregon
17. **STANLEY, LEVI**
G, 6-2, 250, Hawaii

1975
(Drafted Alternately 10-9)
1. **WEBB, JIMMY**
DT, 6-5, 248, Mississippi State
2. **COLLINS, GREG**
LB, 6-3, 228, Notre Dame
3. **Choice to N.Y. Giants**
3. **(A) HART, JEFF**
(Choice from Buffalo)
T, 6-5, 266, Oregon State
3. **(B) MIKE-MAYER, STEVE**
(Choice from Washington)
K, 6-0, 180, Maryland
3. **(C) BAKER, WAYNE**
(Choice from St. Louis)
DT, 6-6, 260, Brigham Young
4. **(A) ELAM, CLEVELAND**
(Choice from New Orleans)
DE, 6-3, 240, Tennessee State
4. **(B) OLIVER, FRANK**
DB, 6-1, 189, Kentucky State
5. **BULLOCK, WAYNE**
RB, 6-0, 232, Notre Dame
6. **Choice to Kansas City**
7. **Choice to Buffalo**
8. **KENDRICK, PRESTON**
LB, 6-1, 217, Florida
9. **(A) JOHNSON, JAMES**
DB, 6-2, 195, Tennessee State
9. **(B) NATALE, DAN**
(Choice from Philadelphia)
TE, 6-3, 223, Penn State
9. **(C) DOUGLAS, CEASER**
(Choice from St. Louis)
T, 6-5, 272, Illinois Wesleyan
10. **LAYTON, DONNIE**
RB, 6-0, 190, South Carolina
State
11. **HERNANDEZ, GENE**
DB, 6-2, 173, Texas Christian
12. **WORLEY, RICK**
QB, 6-1, 195, Howard Payne
13. **MITCHELL, DALE**
LB, 6-3, 211, Southern Cal
14. **HENSON, DAVID**
WR, 6-3, 173, Abilene
Christian
15. **LAVIN, RICH**
TE, 6-5, 223, Western Illinois
16. **& 17. Choices to Baltimore**
for Colts' 15th & 16th in 1976

1976
(Drafted Alternately 4 & 3)
1. **Choice to New England**
1. **(Choice from Houston to
New England)**
2. **(A) CROSS, RANDY**
C, 6-3, 245, UCLA
2. **(B) LEWIS, EDDIE**
(Choice from Tampa Bay)
CB, 6-0, 172, Kansas
3. **(Choice from New Orleans
to Kansas City)**
3. **Choice to Dallas**
4. **RIVERA, STEVE**
(Choice from Philadelphia)
WR, 5-11, 190, California

4. Choice to N.Y. Giants
5. Choice to Cincinnati
5. LEONARD, ANTHONY
(Choice from Detroit)
CB, 5-11, 170, Virginia Union
6. (A) PENNYWELL, ROBERT
LB, 6-1, 222, Grambling
6. (B) BULL, SCOTT
(Choice from St. Louis)
QB, 6-5, 209, Arkansas
7. CHESLEY, JAY
DB, 6-1, 184, Vanderbilt
8. AYERS, JOHN
T, 6-5, 238, West Texas State
9. HARRISON, KENNY
WR, 6-0, 179, Southern
Methodist
10. ROSS, ROBIN
T, 6-4, 248, Washington State
11. HOFER, PAUL
RB, 6-0, 186, Mississippi
12. LOPER, GERALD
G, 6-2, 245, Florida
13. BRUMFIELD, LARRY
CB, 6-0, 171, Indiana State
14. MILLER, JOHNNY
G, 6-1, 241, Livingstone
15. STIDHAM, HOWARD
LB, 6-2, 214, Tennessee Tech
16. LEWIS, REGGIE
DE, 6-1, 215, San Diego State
17. JENKINS, DARRYL
RB, 6-2, 235, San Jose State

1977
(Drafted 16th)
1. Choice to New England
2. Choice to New England
3. BOYD, ELMO
(Choice from Houston)
WR, 5-11, 185, Eastern
Kentucky
3. Choice to N.Y. Jets
4. BLACK, STAN
S, 6-0, 204, Mississippi State
5. Choice to Buffalo
6. (A) BURNS, MIKE
(Choice from Buffalo)
CB, 6-0, 184, Southern Cal
6. (B) HARLAN, JIM
C, 6-5, 241, Howard Payne
7. VAN WAGNER, JIM
RB, 6-0, 202, Michigan Tech
8. Choice to N.Y. Giants
9. POSEY, DAVID
K, 5-11, 167, Florida
10. Choice to Tampa Bay
11. BILLICK, BRIAN
TE, 6-5, 232, Brigham Young
12. MARTIN, SCOTT
T, 6-4, 257, North Dakota

1978
(Drafted 7th)
1. (A) MacAFEE, KEN
TE, 6-4, 250, Notre Dame
1. (B) BUNZ, DAN
(Choice from Miami)
LB, 6-4, 230, Long Beach
State
2. Choice to Buffalo
2. DOWNING, WALT
(Choice from Chicago)
G, 6-3, 254, Michigan

3. Choice to Buffalo
3. HUGHES, ERNIE
(Choice from Baltimore)
G, 6-3, 253, Notre Dame
4. LeCOUNT, TERRY
WR, 5-10, 172, Florida
5. Choice to Baltimore
5. (A) REESE, ARCHIE
(Choice from Houston via
Kansas City and Chicago)
DT, 6-3, 263, Clemson
5. (B) THREADGILL, BRUCE
(Choice from Miami)
DB, 6-0, 190, Mississippi State
6. Choice from Minnesota to
Washington
6. WALKER, ELLIOTT
RB, 5-11, 193, Pittsburgh
7. QUILLAN, FRED
C, 6-5, 240, Oregon
8. Choice to Washington
9. (A) REDDEN, HERMAN
DB, 6-2, 190, Howard
9. (B) MOORE, DEAN
(Choice from Detroit)
LB, 6-2, 210, Iowa
9. (C) McDANIELS, STEVE
(Choice from Denver)
T, 6-6, 276, Notre Dame
10. CONNELL, MIKE
P, 6-1, 200, Cincinnati
11. McCRAY, WILLIE
DE, 6-5, 234, Troy State
12. (A) IRONS, DAN
T, 6-7, 260, Texas Tech
12. (B) CONNORS, ROD
(Supplemental Draft)
RB, 6-2, 190, Southern Cal

1979
(Drafted 1st)
1. Choice to Buffalo
2. OWENS, JAMES
RB, 5-11, 188, UCLA
3. Choice to Seattle
3. MONTANA, JOE
(Choice from Dallas via
Seattle)
QB, 6-2, 200, Notre Dame
4. Choice to Buffalo
5. (A) SEABRON, TOM
LB, 6-3, 209, Michigan
5. (B) ALDRIDGE, JERRY
(Choice from Detroit)
RB, 6-2, 220, Angelo State
6. VAUGHN, RUBEN
DT, 6-2, 264, Colorado
7. FRANCIS, PHIL
FB, 6-1, 205, Stanford
8. Choice to Green Bay
9. HAMILTON, STEVE
DE, 6-3, 240, Missouri
10. (A) CLARK, DWIGHT
WR, 6-3, 204, Clemson
10. (B) BALLAGE, HOWARD
(Choice from Tampa Bay)
CB, 6-1, 182, Colorado
11. McBRIDE, BILLY
DB, 6-1, 187, Tennessee
State
12. Forfeited choice via supplemental draft of 1978.

1980
(Drafted Alternately 2 & 1)
1. Choice to N.Y. Jets
1. (A) COOPER, EARL
(Choice from N.Y. Jets)
RB, 6-2, 227, Rice
1. (B) STUCKEY, JIM
(Choice from Denver via N.Y.
Jets)
DE, 6-4, 245, Clemson
2. Choice to Buffalo
2. Choice from Detroit to
Minnesota
2. TURNER, KEENA
(Choice from Minnesota)
LB, 6-2, 219, Purdue
3. Choice to Los Angeles
3. (A) MILLER, JIM
(Choice from Minnesota)
P, 5-11, 183, Mississippi
3. (B) PUKI, CRAIG
(Choice from Washington
via Los Angeles)
LB, 6-1, 231, Tennessee
4. (A) CHURCHMAN, RICKY
SS, 6-1, 193, Texas
4. (B) HODGE, DAVID
(Choice from New England
via Los Angeles)
LB, 6-2, 221, Houston
5. TIMES, KEN
DT, 6-2, 246, Southern
6. WILLIAMS, HERB
CB, 6-0, 198, Southern
7. Choice to Cincinnati
8. Choice to Oakland
8. LEOPOLD, BOBBY
(Choice from Oakland)
LB, 6-1, 215, Notre Dame
9. Choice to Detroit via Kansas
City
9. HARTWIG, DAN
(Choice from Oakland)
QB, 6-3, 212, Cal Lutheran
10. Choice to Pittsburgh
11. Choice to Miami
12. Choice to Pittsburgh

1981
(Drafted Alternately 8-10)
1. LOTT, RONNIE
DB, 6-0, 199, Southern Cal
2. (A) HARTY, JOHN
(Choice from Washington)
DT, 6-4, 253, Iowa
2. Choice to Chicago
2. (B) WRIGHT, ERIC
(Choice from Chicago)
DB, 6-1, 180, Missouri
3. WILLIAMSON, CARLTON
DB, 6-0, 204, Pittsburgh
4. Choice to Dallas
5. (A) THOMAS, LYNN
DB, 5-11, 181, Pittsburgh
5. (B) JONES, ARRINGTON
(Choice from Chicago)
FB, 6-0, 230, Winston-Salem
6. KUGLER, PETE
DT, 6-4, 255, Penn State
7. Choice to Philadelphia
8. WHITE, GARRY
RB, 5-11, 201, Minnesota
9. Choice to Cincinnati
10. Choice to Baltimore
11. DeBOSE, RON
TE, 6-5, 229, UCLA

12. (A) OGILVIE, MAJOR
RB, 6-0, 202, Alabama
12. (B) ADAMS, JOE
(Choice from Pittsburgh)
QB, 6-3, 185, Tennessee State

1982
(Drafted 27th)
1. Choice to New England
2. PARIS, WILLIAM "BUBBA"
(Choice from New England)
T, 6-6, 293, Michigan
2. Choice from Washington
to New England
2. Choice to New England
3. Choice to San Diego
4. Choice to New England
5. WILLIAMS, NEWTON
RB, 5-10, 204, Arizona State
6. WILLIAMS, VINCE
(Choice from Oakland)
FB, 6-0, 231, Oregon
6. Choice to New Orleans
7. FERRARI, RON
LB, 6-0, 212, Illinois
8. Choice to New Orleans
9. CLARK, BRYAN
QB, 6-2, 196, Michigan State
10. (A) McLEMORE, DANA
(Choice from Tampa Bay)
DB, 5-10, 183, Hawaii
10. (B) BARBIAN, TIM
DT, 6-3, 230, Western Illinois
11. GIBSON, GARY
LB, 6-1, 215, Arizona
12. WASHINGTON, TIMOTHY
CB, 5-9, 184, Fresno State

1983
(Drafted Alternately 5-8)
1. Choice to San Diego
2. Choice to L.A. Rams
2. CRAIG, ROGER
(Choice from San Diego)
RB, 6-0, 222, Nebraska
3. MONTGOMERY, BLANCHARD
(Choice from L.A. Rams)
LB, 6-2, 236, UCLA
3. Choice to L.A. Rams
4. (Choice from Denver to L.A.
Rams)
4. HOLMOE, TOM
DB, 6-2, 180, Brigham Young
5. ELLISON, RIKI
LB, 6-2, 220, Southern Cal
6. Choice to Tampa Bay
7. MOTEN, GARY
LB, 6-1, 210, Southern
Methodist
8. Choice to San Diego
9. MULARKEY, MIKE
TE, 6-4, 245, Florida
9. Choice from Cleveland to
Chicago
10. MERRELL, JEFF
NT, 6-4, 264, Nebraska
11. SAPOLU, JESSE
G-C, 6-4, 260, Hawaii
12. Choice to Chicago

1984
(Drafted Alternately 23-24)
1. SHELL, TODD
LB, 6-4, 225, Brigham Young
2. Choice to L.A. Raiders

2. **FRANK, JOHN**
(Choice from L.A. Raiders)
TE, 6-3, 225, Ohio State
3. **McINTYRE, GUY**
(Choice from St. Louis)
G, 6-3, 271, Georgia
3. **Choice to St. Louis**
4. **Choice from Tampa Bay to Seattle**
4. **Choice to San Diego**
5. **(A) CARTER, MICHAEL**
(Choice from Atlanta)
DT, 6-2, 281, Southern Methodist
5. **Choice from Denver to Atlanta**
5. **Choice to St. Louis**
5. **(B) FULLER, JEFF**
(Choice from Washington, via L.A. Raiders)
LB-S, 6-2, 216, Texas A&M
6. **Choice to Atlanta**
7. **Choice to New England**
8. **Choice to San Diego**
9. **(A) MILLER, LEE**
(Choice from Chicago)
DB, 6-1, 186, Cal State-Fullerton
9. **(B) HARMON, DERRICK**
RB 5-10, 202, Cornell
10. **MORITZ, DAVE**
WR, 6-0, 181, Iowa
11. **PENDELTON, KIRK**
WR, 6-3, 191, Brigham Young
12. **Choice from Chicago to Miami**
13. **Choice to San Diego**

1985

(Drafted 16th in 1st; 28th 2-12)
1. **RICE, JERRY**
WR, 6-2, 220, Mississippi Valley State
1. **Choice to New England**
2. **Choice to New England**
3. **MOORE, RICKY**
(Choice from New England)
RB, 6-11, 236, Alabama
3. **Choice to New England**
4. **Choice to Buffalo**
5. **COLLIE, BRUCE**
OT, 6-6, 275, Texas-Arlington
6. **BARRY, SCOTT**
QB, 6-2, 190, UC-Davis
7. **Choice to San Diego**
8. **Choice to New England**
9. **Choice to San Diego**
10. **Choice to Seattle**
11. **WOOD, DAVID**
DE, 6-4, 250, Arizona
12. **CHUMLEY, DONALD**
DT, 6-4, 259, Georgia

1986

(Drafted 18th)
1. **Choice to Dallas**
1. **Choice from Dallas to Buffalo**
2. **Choice from Buffalo to Detroit**
2. **ROBERTS, LARRY**
(Choice from Detroit)
DE, 6-3, 264, Alabama
2. **Choice to Washington**

3. **(A) RATHMAN, TOM**
(Choice from Buffalo)
FB, 6-1, 232, Nebraska
3. **(B) McKYER, TIM**
(Choice from Philadelphia)
CB, 6-0, 174, Texas-Arlington
3. **Choice from Detroit to L.A. Rams**
3. **(C) TAYLOR, JOHN**
WR, 6-1, 185, Delaware State
4. **(A) HALEY, CHARLES**
(Choice from Cleveland via L.A. Rams)
LB, 6-5, 230, James Madison
4. **(B) WALLACE, STEVE**
(Choice from Washington via L.A. Rams)
T, 6-5, 276, Auburn
4. **(C) FAGAN, KEVIN**
DT, 6-3, 260, Miami (Fla.)
5. **Choice to San Diego**
5. **MILLER, PAT**
(Choice from Dallas)
LB, 6-1, 220, Florida
6. **Choice to Washington**
6. **GRIFFIN, DON**
(Choice from N.Y. Jets)
FS, 6-0, 176, Middle Tennessee State
7. **Choice to New England**
8. **(A) POPP, JIM**
(Choice from Philadelphia)
TE, 6-5, 239, Vanderbilt
8. **(B) SNIPES, ROOSEVELT**
('85 Supplemental Draft)
RB, 5-9, 175, Florida State
9. **CHERRY, TONY**
RB, 5-7, 187, Oregon
10. **(A) STINSON, ELLISTON**
WR, 5-10, 175, Rice
10. **(B) HALLMAN, HAROLD**
(Choice from Washington)
NG, 5-11, 234, Auburn
11. **Choice to San Diego**
12. **Choice to Tampa Bay**

1987

(Drafted 22nd)
1. **(A) BARTON, HARRIS**
T, 6-3, 260, North Carolina
1. **(B) FLAGLER, TERRENCE**
(Choice from Washington)
RB, 6-0, 200, Clemson
2. **BREGEL, JEFF**
(Choice from Philadelphia)
G, 6-4, 280, Southern California
2. **Choice to Tampa Bay**
3. **Choice to Buffalo**
4. **Choice to Tampa Bay**
5. **JOKISCH, PAUL**
WR, 6-7, 230, Michigan
6. **WHITE, BOB**
LB, 6-2, 246, Penn State
7. **DeLINE, STEVE**
K, 5-11, 180, Colorado State
8. **GRAYSON, DAVID**
LB, 6-2, 220, Fresno State
9. **SHELLEY, JO NATHAN**
CB, 6-0, 176, Mississippi
10. **PAYE, JOHN**
(Choice from New England via L.A. Raiders)
QB, 6-3, 205, Stanford
11. **Choice to L.A. Raiders from Philadelphia via 49ers**

11. **NICHOLAS, CALVIN**
WR, 6-4, 208, Grambling
12. **Choice to L.A. Raiders**

1988

(Drafted 25th)
1. **Choice to L.A. Raiders**
2. **(A) STUBBS, DANNY**
(Choice from L.A. Raiders)
DE, 6-4, 260, Miami (Fla.)
2. **(B) HOLT, PIERCE**
(Choice from Philadelphia via Tampa Bay)
DE/DT, 6-4, 280, Angelo State
2. **Choice to Tampa Bay**
3. **ROMANOWSKI, BILL**
LB, 6-4, 231, Boston College
4. **HELTON, BARRY**
(Choice from Chicago via L.A. Raiders)
P, 6-3, 205, Colorado
4. **Choice to Tampa Bay**
5. **Choice to N.Y. Jets**
5. **Choice to Buffalo**
6. **Choice to Tampa Bay**
7. **BRYANT, KEVIN**
LB, 6-2, 223, Delaware State
8. **CLARKSON, LARRY**
T, 6-7, 303, Montana
9. **BONNER, BRIAN**
LB, 6-1, 220, Minnesota
10. **FOLEY, TIM**
K, 5-10, 210, Georgia Southern
11. **BROOKS, CHET**
CB, 5-11, 191, Texas A&M
12. **MIRA, JR., GEORGE**
LB, 6-0, 230, Miami (FL)

1989

(Drafted 28th)
1. **DeLONG, KEITH**
LB, 6-2, 235, Tennessee
2. **WALLS, WESLEY**
TE, 6-5, 246, Mississippi
3. **HENDERSON, KEITH**
FB, 6-1, 220, Georgia
4. **BARBER, MIKE**
WR, 5-10, 172, Marshall
5. **(A) JACKSON, JOHNNY**
(Choice from the L.A. Raiders)
CB/S, 6-1, 204, Houston
5. **(B) Choice to L.A. Raiders, plus 49ers' No. 8 (224th overall)**
6. **HENDRICKSON, STEVE**
LB, 6-0, 245, California
7. **Choice to San Diego**
Wes Chandler trade, 1988
8. **Choice to L.A. Raiders for Raiders' No. 5 (122nd overall)**
9. **HARMON, RUDY**
LB, 6-1, 230, LSU
10. **SINCLAIR, ANDY**
C, 6-3, 285, Stanford
11. **(A) BELL, JIM**
(Choice from L.A. Raiders)
RB, 6-0, 205, Boston College
11. **(B) McGEE, NORM**
WR, 6-0, 180, North Dakota
12. **(A) GOSS, ANTONIO**
(Choice from L.A. Raiders, Milt McColl trade, 1988)
LB, 6-4, 228, North Carolina

12. **(B) Choice to L.A. Raiders, plus 49ers' No. 12 in 1990, for Raiders' No. 11 (290th overall) in 1989**

1990

(Drafted 28th)
1. **CARTER, DEXTER**
RB, 5-9, 170, Florida State
2. **(A) BROWN, DENNIS**
(Choice from Minnesota through Dallas, 1990 trade with Cowboys that sent RB Terrence Flagler, DE Daniel Stubbs, 49ers' No. 3 (81st) and No. 11 (304th) picks in 1990 to Dallas for Cowboys' No. 2 (47th) and No. 3 (68th) picks in 1990.)
2. **(B) DAVIS, ERIC**
CB, 5-11, 178, Jacksonville State
3. **(A) LEWIS, RONALD**
(Choice from Kansas City through Dallas via above Dallas trade)
WR, 5-11, 173, Florida State
3. **(B) Choice to Dallas via above Dallas trade**
4. ***(A) CALIGUIRE, DEAN**
(Choice from L.A. Raiders, 1990 trade with Raiders that sent 49ers' No. 4 (109th) and No. 5 (137th) picks in 1990 for Raiders' No. 4 (89th) pick in 1990.)
G/C, 6-2, 282, Pittsburgh
4. **(B) Choice to L.A. Raiders via above L.A. trade**
5. **Choice to L.A. Raiders via above L.A. trade**
6. **POLLACK, FRANK**
T/G, 6-4, 277, Northern Arizona
7. **Choice to San Diego, 1988 trade with Chargers for Wes Chandler**
8. **PICKENS, DWIGHT**
WR, 5-10, 170, Fresno State
9. **HAGGINS, ODELL**
NT, 6-2, 271, Florida State
10. **HARRISON, MARTIN**
DE, 6-5, 240, Washington
11. **(A) SHELTON, ANTHONY**
(Choice from Miami, 1990 draft day trade with Dolphins that sent CB Tim McKyer to Miami for Dolphins' No. 11 (289th) pick in 1990 and No. 2 pick in 1991.)
S, 6-1, 195, Tennessee State
11. **(B) Choice to Dallas via above Dallas trade**
12. **Choice to L.A. Raiders, 1989 draft day trade with Raiders that sent 49ers' No. 12B in 1989 for Raiders' No. 11 in 1989. The 49ers selected RB Jim Bell of Boston College.**

Three teams selected ahead of the 49ers, who passed on the original choice of 8th in the round and 89th overall.

1991
(Drafted 26th)
1. WASHINGTON, TED
NT/DE, 6-4, 299, Louisville
2. (A) WATTERS, RICKY
(Choice from Cincinnati)
RB, 6-1, 212, Notre Dame
2. Choice to Cincinnati
2. (B) JOHNSON, JOHN
LB, 6-3, 230, Clemson
3. Choice to Green Bay
4. DONAHUE, MITCH
(Choice from Green Bay)
LB, 6-2, 254, Wyoming
4. Choice to Cincinnati
5. (A) HANKS, MERTON
(Choice from Green Bay)
CB, 6-2, 185, Iowa
5. (B) BOATSWAIN, HARRY
T, 6-4, 295, New Haven
6. BOWLES, SCOTT
T, 6-5, 280, North Texas State
7. CANLEY, SHELDON
RB, 5-9, 195, San Jose State
8. HARGAIN, TONY
WR, 6-0, 188, Oregon
9. RIDDICK, LOUIS
S, 6-2, 217, Pittsburgh
10. HOLDBROOKS, BYRON
NT/DE, 6-5, 280, Alabama
11. SLAUGHTER, BOBBY
WR, 5-11,171, Louisiana Tech
12. CONFER, CLIFF
DE, 6-0, 270, Michigan State

1992
(Drafted 18th)
1. HALL, DANA
S, 6-2, 206, Washington
2. LEE, AMP
RB, 5-11, 200, Florida State
3. BOLLINGER, BRIAN
G, 6-5, 285, North Carolina
4. THOMAS, MARK
DE, 6-5, 259, North Carolina
State
4. Choice to Green Bay
5. Choice to Green Bay

6. Choice to Green Bay
6. RUSSELL, DAMIEN
(Choice from Pittsburgh)
S, 6-1, 204, Virginia Tech
7. Choice to Pittsburgh
8. Choice to Pittsburgh from
Green Bay
8. Choice to Pittsburgh
9. HAGAN, DARIAN
Return Specialist, 5-9, 191,
Colorado
10. MAYFIELD, COREY
NT, 6-2, 280, Oklahoma
11. COVINGTON, TOM
TE, 6-3, 241, Georgia Tech
12. LeBOUNTY, MATT
DE, 6-4, 254, Oregon

1993
(Drafted 26th)
1. Choice to Phoenix from
Kansas City
1. Choice to New Orleans from
Phoenix
1. (A) STUBBLEFIELD, DANA
(Choice from New Orleans)
DE, 6-2, 302, Kansas
1. (B) KELLY, TODD
DE, 6-2, 259, Tennessee
2. Choice to San Diego from L.A.
Raiders
2. HARDY, ADRIAN
(Choice from San Diego)
CB, 5-11, 194, Northwestern
State
2. Choice to Green Bay
2. Choice to L.A. Raiders from
Dallas
3. Choice to L.A. Raiders from
New Orleans
3. Choice to San Diego
4. Choice to San Diego
5. SMITH, ARTIE
(Choice from Phoenix)
DE, 6-4, 303, Louisiana Tech
5. Choice to San Diego
6. DALMAN, CHRIS
G-C, 6-3, 285, Stanford
7. WILSON, TROY

DE, 6-4, 235, Pittsburg State
8. GRBAC, ELVIS
(Choice from Minnesota)
QB, 6-5, 232, Michigan
8. Choice to San Diego

1994
(Drafted 23rd)
1. (A) YOUNG, BRYANT
(Choice from LA Rams)
DT, 6-2, 276, Notre Dame
1. Choice to L.A. Rams from San
Diego
1. Choice to Dallas
1. (B) FLOYD, WILLIAM
(Choice from Dallas)
FB, 6-1, 242, Florida State
2. (A) MITCHELL, KEVIN
(Choice from Green Bay)
LB, 6-1, 260, Syracuse
2. Choice to L.A. Rams
2. (B) DRAKEFORD, TYRONNE
(Choice from Dallas)
CB, 5-9, 185, Virginia Tech
3. Compensatory Choice to
Green Bay
3. (A) BRIEN, DOUG
(Compensatory Choice)
K, 5-11, 177, California
3. (B) FLEMMING, CORY
(Choice from Denver)
WR, 6-1, 207, Tennessee
3. Choice to Kansas City
3. Choice to Denver from Dallas
3. Choice to LA Rams from
Philadelphia
4. Choice to LA Raiders
5. Choice to Green Bay from
Denver
5. PETERSON, TONY
LB, 6-0, 223, Notre Dame
6. Choice to Green Bay from San
Diego
6. WOODALL, LEE
LB, 6-0, 220, West Chester
6. Choice to Green Bay from
Philadelphia
7. Choice to Dallas

1995
(Drafted 30th)
1A. STOKES, J.J.
(Choice from Cleveland)
WR, 6-4, 217, UCLA
1B. Choice to Cleveland
2. Choice to L.A. Rams
3. Choice to Cleveland
4A. Choice to Cleveland from
Kansas City
4B. HANSHAW, TIM
T/G, 6-5, 300, Brigham Young
5. Choice to Detroit
6. ARMSTRONG, ANTONIO
LB, 6-1, 234, Texas A&M
7. COLEMAN, HERB
DE, 6-4, 285, Trinity
International

1996
(Drafted 23rd)
1. Choice to Baltimore
2. (A) IFEANYI, ISRAEL
(Choice from Oakland)
LB/DE, 6-3, 246, USC
3. OWENS, TERRELL
WR, 6-2, 213, Tenn-Chattanooga
4. (A) Choice to Oakland
4. (B) PRICE, DARYL
(Compensatory selection)
DE, 6-3, 274, Colorado
5. UWAEZUOKE, IHEANYI
WR, 6-2, 195, California
6. PITTS, STEPHEN
RB, 5-10, 192, Penn. State
7. (A) MANUEL, SEAN
TE, 6-2, 245, New Mexico St.
7. (B) MANUEL, SAM
(Compensatory selection)
LB, 6-2, 235, New Mexico St.

1997
(Drafted 26th)
1. DRUCKENMILLER, JIM
QB, 6-4, 230, Virginia Tech
2. EDWARDS, MARC
(Choice from Philadelphia)
RB, 5-11, 236, Notre Dame
3. CLARK, GREG
(Choice from Indianapolis)
TE, 6-2, 262, Stanford

49ers All-Time Roster—1946-1996

-A-
Abramowicz, Danny, WR, Xavier
(OH), 1973-74
Albert, Frank, QB, Stanford,
1946-52
Adridge, Ben, HB, Oklahoma State,
1952
Aldridge, Jerry, RB, Angelo State,
1980
Alexander, Kermit, HB, UCLA,
1963-69
Alexander, Mike, WR, Penn State,
1993
Allen, Nate, CB, Texas Southern,
1975
Anderson, Terry, WR, Bethune-
Cookman, 1980
Anderson, Tim, S, Ohio State, 1975
Arenas, Joe, HB, Omaha, 1951-57
Asmus, Jim, P, Hawaii, 1987
Atkins, Bill, HB, Auburn, 1958-59
Atkins, Dave, RB, Texas-El Paso,
1973
Audick, Dan, T-G, Hawaii, 1981-82

Ayers, John, G, West Texas State,
1976-86

-B-
Babb, Gene, FB, Austin, 1957-58
Babcock, Harry, E, Georgia, 1953-
55
Bahnsen, Ken, FB, North Texas
State, 1953
Bahr, Matt, K, Penn State, 1981
Baker, Dave, HB, Oklahoma, 1959-
61
Baker, Wayne, DT, BYU, 1975
Balatti, Ed, E, Oakland High (CA),
1946-48
Baldassin, Mike, LB, Washington,
1977-78
Baldwin, John, C, Centenary, 1947
Banaszek, Cas, T, Northwestern,
1967-77
Banducci, Bruno, G, Stanford,
1946-54
Barber, Mike, WR, Marshall, 1989
Barker, Roy, DT, North Carolina,
1996-current

Barnes, Larry, FB, Colorado, 1957
Barnett, Oliver, DL, Kentucky, 1995
Barnes, Tomur, CB, North Texas,
1993
Barrett, Jean, T, Tulsa, 1973-80
Bartolo, Steve, RB, Colorado State,
1988
Barton, Harris, T, North Carolina,
1987-current
Bassi, Dick, G, Santa Clara,
1946-47
Beach, Sanjay, WR, Colorado State,
1991, 93
Beals, Alyn, E, Santa Clara,
1946-51
Beard, Ed, LB, Tennessee,
1965-72
Beasley, Terry, WR, Auburn, 1972-
75
Beatty, Ed, C, Mississippi, 1955-56
Beeson, Terry, LB, Kansas, 1982
Beisler, Randy, T, Indiana,
1969-74
Belser, Ceaser, LB, Arkansas
AM&N, 1974

Belk, Bill, DE, Maryland State, 1968-
74
Benefield, David, LB, CSU
Northridge, 1996-current
Benjamin, Guy, QB, Stanford, 1981-
83
Bentz, Roman, T, Tulane, 1948
Berry, Rex, HB, BYU, 1951-56
Bettiga, Mike, WR, Humbolt State,
1973
Beverly, Ed, WR, Arizona State,
1973
Black, Stan, DB, Mississippi State,
1977
Blackmore, Richard, CB, Mississippi
State, 1983
Blount, Ed, QB, Washington State,
1987
Blue, Forrest, C, Auburn, 1968-74
Board, Dwaine, DE, North Carolina
A&T, 1979-87
Boatswain, Harry, T, New Haven,
1991-93
Bollinger, Brian, G, North Carolina,
1992-94

Bono, Steve, QB, UCLA, 1989-93
Boone, J.R., HB, Tulsa, 1952
Bosley, Bruce, C-G, West Virginia, 1956-68
Bouza, Matt, WR, California, 1981
Boyd, Elmo, WR, Eastern Kentucky, 1978
Boykin, Greg, FB, Northwestern, 1978
Bradley, Ed, LB, Wake Forest, 1977-78
Braggonier, Dennis, DB, Stanford, 1974
Brandes, John, TE, Cameron, 1993
Brandon, Michael, DE, Florida, 1995-current
Bregel, Jeff, G, USC, 1987-89
Bridewell, Jeff, QB, UC-Davis, 1993
Bristor, John, S. Waynesburg, 1979
Britt, Charlie, HB, Georgia, 1964
Brock, Clyde, T, Utah State, 1963
Brockhaus, Jeff, K, Missouri, 1987
Brodie, John, QB, Stanford, 1957-73
Brohm, Jeff, QB, Louisville, 1996-current
Brooks, Chet, S, Texas A&M, 1988-89
Brown, Dennis, DE, Washington, 1990-current
Brown, Hardy, LB, Tulsa, 1951-56
Brown, Hurlie, S, Miami (FL), 1993
Brown, Pete, C, Georgia Tech, 1953-54
Brown, Ray, G, Arkansas State, 1996-current
Brown, Ray, RB, South Carolina, 1987
Browner, Keith, LB, USC, 1987
Bruce, Gail, E, Washington, 1948-52
Bruer, Bob, TE, Mankato State, 1979-80
Brumfield, Jackson, E, Southern Mississippi, 1954
Bruney, Fred, HB, Ohio State, 1953, 1956
Bryant, Bob, T, Texas Tech, 1946-49
Bryant, Junior, DE, Notre Dame, 1993-current
Buckley, Curtis, S. E. Texas State, 1996-current
Bull, Scott, QB, Arkansas, 1976-78
Bungarda, Ken, T, Missouri, 1980
Bunz, Dan, LB, Long Beach State, 1978-84
Burch, Swift, DE, Temple, 1993
Burke, Don, LB, USC, 1950-54
Burke, Vern, E, Oregon State, 1965
Burns, Mike, DB, USC, 1977
Burt, Jim, NT, Miami (FL), 1989
Butler, John, S, Principia, 1987

-C-

Caldwell, Mike, WR, California, 1995-current
Calhoun, Mike, DT, Notre Dame, 1980
Caliguire, Dean, C, Pittsburgh, 1991
Calvelli, Tony, C, Stanford, 1949
Campbell, Carter, LB, Weber State, 1970
Campbell, Marion, T, Georgia, 1954-55
Campora, Don, T, Pacific, 1950, 1952
Carapella, Al, T, Miami (FL), 1951-55

Carolan, Brett, TE, Washington State, 1994-95
Carpenter, John, T, Michigan, 1949
Carr, Earl, RB, Florida, 1978
Carr, Eddie, HB, Olney High (PA), 1947-49
Carr, Paul, LB, Houston, 1955-58
Carter, Dexter, RB, Florida State, 1990-96
Carter, Michael, NT, SMU, 1984-92
Casanega, Ken, HB, Santa Clara, 1946, 1948
Casey, Bernie, E, Bowling Green, 1961-66
Cason, Jim, HB, LSU, 1948-52, 1954
Cassara, Frank, FB, St. Mary's, 1954
Cathcart, Royal, HB, Santa Barbara State, 1950
Cathcart, Sam, HB, Santa Barbara State, 1949-50, 1952
Cavanaugh, Matt, QB, Pittsburgh, 1983-85
Caveli, Tony, C, Stanford, 1949
Ceresino, Gordy, LB, Stanford, 1979
Cerne, Joe, C, Northwestern, 1965-67
Chandler, Wes, WR, Florida, 1988
Chapple, Jack, LB, Stanford, 1965
Cherry, Tony, RB, Oregon, 1986-87
Childs, Jason, T, North Dakota, 1993
Choma, John, G-C, Virginia, 1981-83
Churchman, Ricky, S, Texas, 1980-81
Clark, Bryan, QB, Michigan State, 1982-83
Clark, Don, G, USC, 1948-49
Clark, Dwight, WR, Clemson, 1979-87
Clark, Mario, CB, Oregon, 1984
Clark, Mike, DE, Florida, 1982
Clark, Monte, T, USC, 1959-61
Cline, Tony, DE, Miami (FL), 1976
Cochran, Mark, T, Baylor, 1987
Cofer, Mike, K, North Carolina State, 1988-93
Colchico, Dan, E, San Jose State, 1960-64, 67
Collett, Elmer, G, San Francisco State, 1967-72
Collie, Bruce, T-G, Texas Arlington, 1985-89, 1992
Collier, Floyd, T, San Jose State, 1948
Collier, Tim, CB, East Texas State, 1982-83
Collins, Glen, DE, Mississippi State, 1987
Collins, Greg, LB, Notre Dame, 1975
Collins, Ray, T, LSU, 1950-52
Comeaux, Darren, LB, Arizona State, 1987
Conklin, Cary, QB, Washington, 1995
Conlee, Gerry, C, St. Mary's, 1946-47
Connell, Mike, P, Cincinnati, 1978
Conner, Clyde, E, Pacific, 1956-63
Connolly, Ted, G, Santa Clara Tulsa, 1954, 1956-62
Cook, Toi, DB, Stanford, 1994
Cooke, Bill, DE, Massachusetts-Amherst, 1976

Cooper, Adrian, TE, Oklahoma, 1996-current
Cooper, Bill, FB, Muskingum, 1961-64
Cooper, Earl, FB-TE, Rice, 1980-85
Cooper, George, LB, Michigan State, 1987
Cordileone, Lou, G-LB, Clemson, 1961
Cornelius, Charles, DB, Bethune-Cookman, 1979-80
Courtney, Matt, S, Idaho State, 1987
Cousineau, Tom, LB, Ohio State, 1986-87
Covington, Tom, TE, Georgia Tech, 1992-93
Cowlings, Al, DE, USC, 1979
Cox, Greg, S, San Jose State, 1988, 1990-91
Cox, James, G, Stanford, 1948
Craig, Roger, FB, Nebraska, 1983-90
Crawford, Derrick, WR, Memphis State, 1986
Cribbs, Joe, RB, Auburn, 1986-87
Crist, Chuck, DB, Penn State, 1978
Cross, Bob, T, Kilgore J.C., 1956-57
Cross, Randy, G-C, UCLA, 1976-88
Crow, John David, HB, Texas A&M, 1965-68
Crowe, Paul, HB, St. Mary's, 1948
Crowell, Otis, T, Hardin-Simmons, 1947
Cullity, Dave, T, Utah, 1989
Cunningham, Doug, RB, Mississippi, 1967-73

-D-

Dahms, Tom, T, San Diego State, 1957
Dalman, Chris, G-C, Stanford, 1993-current
Daniels, Clem, RB, Prarie View, 1968
Daughtery, Bob, HB, Tulsa, 1966-67
Davis, Eric, CB, Jacksonville State, 1990-95
Davis, Kyle, C, Oklahoma, 1978
Davis, Johnny, FB, Alabama, 1981
Davis, Tommy, K, LSU, 1959-69
Dean, Floyd, LB, Florida, 1963-64
Dean, Fred, DE, Louisiana Tech, 1981-85
Dean, Kevin, LB, Texas Christian, 1987
DeBerg, Steve, QB, San Jose State, 1977-80
Deese, Derrick, G, Southern Cal, 1992-current
DeLong, Keith, LB, Tennessee, 1989-93
Dent, Richard, DE, Tennessee State, 1994
Diaz-Infante, David, G, San Jose State, 1993
Dixon, Al, TE, Iowa State, 1984
Dodge, Dedrick, S, Florida State, 1994-current
Doleman, Chris, DE, Pittsburgh, 1996-current
Domres, Marty, QB, Columbia, 1976
Donnelly, George, DB, Illinois, 1965-67
Donohue, Leon, T, San Jose State, 1962-64
Donohue, Mitch, LB, Wyoming, 1991-93

Dove, Eddie, HB, Colorado, 1959-62
Dow, Harley, G, San Jose State, 1950
Dowdle, Mike, LB, Texas, 1963-65
Downing, Tim, DE, Washington State, 1993
Downing, Walt, C-G, Michigan, 1978-83
Downs, Bob, HB, Northwestern, 1962-66
Drake, Joe, NT, Arizona, 1987
Drakeford, Tyronne, DB, Virginia Tech, 1994-current
Dressel, Chris, TE, Stanford, 1987
Dressel, Robert, C, Purdue, 1993
DuBose, Doug, RB, Nebraska, 1987-88
Dugan, Fred, E, Dayton, 1958-59
Duncan, Maury, QB, San Francisco State, 1954-55
Dungy, Tony, DB, Minnesota, 1979
Durdan, Don, HB, Oregon State, 1946-47
Durham, Darius, WR, San Diego State, 1983
Durrette, Michael, G, West Virginia, 1986-87

-E-

Easley, Walt, FB, West Virginia, 1981-82
Edwards, Earl, DT, Wichita, 1969-72
Elam, Cleveland, DE, Tennessee State, 1976-78
Elia, Bruce, LB, Ohio State, 1976-78
Elliott, Charles, T, Oregon, 1948
Elliott, Lenvil, RB, NE Missouri State, 1979-81
Ellison, Riki, LB, USC, 1983-89
Elston, Art, C, South Carolina, 1946-48
Enderle, Dick, G, Minnesota, 1976
Endriss, Al, E, San Francisco State, 1952
Ervins, Rickey, RB, Southern California, 1995
Eshmont, Len, HB, Fordham, 1946-49
Etcheverry, Sam, QB, Denver, 1963
Etienne, LeRoy, LB, Nebraska, 1990
Evans, Kevin, WR, San Jose State, 1993
Evans, Ray, G, Texas Western, 1949-50
Evansen, Paul, G, Oregon State, 1948

-F-

Fagan, Kevin, DE, Miami (FL), 1987-93
Fahnhorst, Jim, LB, Minnesota, 1984-90
Fahnhorst, Keith, T, Minnesota, 1974-87
Faison, Derrick, WR, Howard, 1993
Faryniarz, Brett, LB, San Diego State, 1993
Faylor, John, S, Santa Clara, 1987
Feher, Nick, G, Georgia, 1951-54
Fernandez, Mervyn, WR, San Jose State, 1993
Ferrari, Ron, LB, Illinois, 1982-86
Ferrell, Bob, RB, UCLA, 1976-80
Fisk, Bill, E, USC, 1946-47
Flagler, Terrence, RB, Clemson, 1987-89

Flores, Mike, DE, Louisville, 1995
Floyd, William, FB, Florida State, 1994-current
Forrest, Ed, C, Santa Clara, 1946-47
Foster, Roy, G, Southern Cal, 1991-93
Fountaine, Jamal, DE, Washington, 1995
Francis, Phil, RB, Stanford, 1979-80
Francis, Russ, TE, Oregon, 1982-87
Franceschi, Pete, HB, San Francisco, 1946
Frank, John, TE, Ohio State, 1984-88
Franz, Tracy, G, San Jose State, 1987
Freitas, Jesse, QB, Santa Clara, 1946
Fuller, Jeff, S-LB, Texas A&M, 1984-89
Fuller, John, DB, Lamar Tech, 1968-72

-G-

Gagliano, Bob, QB, Utah State, 1986-87
Gaiters, Bob, HB, New Mexico State, 1962-63
Galiffa, Arnie, QB, West Point, 1954
Galigher, Ed, DT, UCLA, 1977-79
Garlin, Don, HB, USC, 1949-50
Garnett, Scott, NT, Washington, 1985
Garrett, Len, TE, New Mexico Highlands, 1975
Gash, Thane, S, East Tennessee State, 1992
Gavric, Momcilo, K, Belgrade, 1969
Gehrke, Fred, HB, Utah, 1950
Gervais, Rick, S, Stanford, 1981-83
Gilbert, Lewis, TE, Florida, 1980
Gladney, Tony, WR, Nevada-Las Vegas, 1987
Glover, Clyde, DE, Fresno State, 1987
Goad, Paul, FB, Abilene Christian, 1956
Gonsoulin, Austin, DB, Baylor, 1967
Gonzaga, John, T, Mt. Diablo High (CA), 1956-59
Goss, Antonio, LB, North Carolina, 1989, 1991-current
Gossett, Bruce, K, Richmond, 1970-74
Grant, Alan, CB, Stanford, 1992
Gray, Tim, DB, Texas A&M, 1979
Grbac, Elvis, QB, Michigan, 1993-96
Green, Jacob, DE, Texas A&M, 1992
Greenlee, Fritz, LB, Arizona, 1969
Greer, Terry, WR, Alabama State, 1987-89
Gregory, Garlin, G, Louisiana Tech, 1946-47
Grgich, Visco, G, Santa Clara, 1946-52
Griffin, Don, CB, Middle Tennessee State, 1986-93

-H-

Hadley, Ron, LB, Washington, 1987-88
Haley, Charles, LB, James Madison, 1986-91
Hall, Dana, S, Washington, 1992-94
Hall, Darryl, S, Washington, 1995

Hall, Forrest, HB, San Francisco, 1948
Hall, Parker, HB, Mississippi, 1946
Hall, Rhett, DT, University of California, 1994
Hall, Windian, S, Arizona State, 1972-75
Hanks, Merton, CB, Iowa, 1991-current
Hanley, Dick, C, Fresno State, 1947
Hanshaw, Tim, G, Brigham Young, 1995-current
Hantla, Bob, G, Kansas, 1954-55
Hardman, Cedrick, DE, North Texas State, 1970-79
Hardy, Adrian, CB, Northwestern State, 1993-94
Hardy, Andre, FB, St. Mary's, 1987
Hardy, Carroll, HB, Colorado, 1955
Hardy, Edgar, G, Jackson State, 1973
Hardy, Kevin, DT, Notre Dame, 1968
Harkey, Lem, HB, Emporia State, 1955
Harmon, Derrick, RB-KR, Cornell, 1984-86
Harper, Willie, LB, Nebraska, 1973-83
Harris, Joe, LB, Georgia Tech, 1978
Harris, Tony, WR, Toledo, 1971
Harris, Tim, LB-DE, Memphis State, 1991, 92 1994-95
Harrison, Bob, LB, Oklahoma, 1959-61, 1965-67
Harrison, Dennis, DE, Vanderbilt, 1986
Harrison, Kenny, WR, SMU, 1976-78
Harrison, Martin, LB, Washington, 1990-93
Hart, Tom, DE, Morris Brown, 1968-76
Hart, Jeff, T, Oregon State, 1975
Harty, John, DT, Iowa, 1981-83, 86
Hayes, Bob, WR, Florida A&M, 1975
Hays, Harold, LB, Southern Mississippi, 1968-69
Hazeltine, Matt, LB, California, 1955-68
Heller, Ron, TE, Oregon State, 1987-88
Helton, Barry, P, Colorado, 1988-90
Henderson, Keith, FB, Georgia, 1989-92
Henderson, Thomas, LB, Langston, 1980
Hendrickson, Steve, LB, California, 1989
Henke, Ed, E, USC, 1951-52, 1955-60
Henley, Thomas, WR, Stanford, 1987
Herchman, Bill, T, Texas Tech, 1956-59
Hettema, Dave, T, New Mexico, 1967
Hicks, Dwight, S, Michigan, 1979-85
Hill, John, C, Lehigh, 1985
Hillman, Jay, FB, Boston, 1993
Hilton, Scott, LB, Salem College, 1979-80
Hindman, Stan, DE, Mississippi, 1966-71, 1973-74
Hoage, Terry, S, Georgia, 1993
Hobbs, Homer, G, Georgia, 1949-50
Hofer, Paul, RB, Mississippi, 1976-81

Hoffman, Gary, T, Santa Clara, 1987
Hogan, Mike, FB, Tennessee-Chattanooga, 1979
Hogland, Doug, G, Oregon State, 1953-55
Holladay, Bob, HB, Tulsa, 1956-57
Holland, John Robert, CB, Sacramento State, 1993
Hollas, Hugo, DB, Rice, 1974
Holmes, Mike, DB, Texas Southern, 1974-75
Holmoe, Tom, S, BYU, 1983-89
Holt, Pierce, DE, Angelo State, 1988-92
Holzer, Tom, DE, Louisville, 1967
Horn, Bob, LB, Oregon State, 1982-83
Horne, Dick, E, Oregon, 1947
Hoskins, Bob, DT, Wichita State, 1970-75
Howell, Clarence, E, Texas A&M, 1948
Hoyle, Wilson, K, Wake Forest, 1993
Huff, Gary, QB, Florida State, 1980
Huff, Marty, LB, Michigan, 1972
Hughes, Ernie, G, Notre Dame, 1978-80
Hull, Tom, LB, Penn State, 1974
Hunt, Charlie, LB, Florida State, 1973

-I-

Ifeanyi, Israel, DE, Southern California, 1996-current
Isenberger, John, RB, Indiana, 1970-73
Israel, Steve, CB, Pittsburgh, 1995-96

-J-

Jackson, Jim, HB, Western Illinois, 1966-67
Jackson, Johnnie, S, Houston, 1989-92
Jackson, Randy, RB, Wichita, 1973
Jackson, Ricky, LB, LSU, 1994-95
Jackson, Wilbur, RB, Alabama, 1974-79
Jarmolowich, Mike, LB, Maryland, 1993
Jennings, Rick, WR, Maryland, 1977
Jessup, Bill, E, USC, 1951-52, 1954-58
Joelson, Greg, DE, Arizona State, 1991
Johnson, Bill, C, Tyler J.C., 1948-56
Johnson, Charlie, DT, Louisville, 1966-67
Johnson, Charles, DB, Grambling, 1979-80
Johnson, Eric, S, Washington State, 1979
Johnson, Gary, DT, Grambling, 1984-85
Johnson, James, LB, San Diego State, 1987
Johnson, Jim, HB, UCLA, 1961-76
Johnson, John, LB, Clemson, 1991-93
Johnson, John Henry, HB, St. Mary's/Arizona State, 1954-56
Johnson, Kermit, RB, UCLA, 1975-76
Johnson, Leo, WR, Tennessee State, 1969-70
Johnson, Rudy, HB, Nebraska, 1964-65

Johnson, Sammy, RB, North Carolina, 1974-76
Jones, Arrington, FB, Winston Salem, 1981
Jones, Brent, TE, Santa Clara, 1987-current
Jones, Larry, WR, NE Missouri State, 1978
Jordan, Darin, LB, Northeastern, 1991-94
Judie, Ed, LB, Northern Arizona, 1982-83
Jury, Bob, S, Pittsburgh, 1978

-K-

Kammerer, Carl, LB, Pacific, 1961-62
Keeble, Jerry, LB, M innesota, 1987
Keever, Carl, LB, Boise State, 1987
Kelcher, Louie, NT, SMU, 1984
Kelly, Gordon, LB, Georgia, 1960-61
Kelly, Todd, DE, Tennessee, 1993-94
Kelm, Larry, LB, Texas A&M, 1993
Kemp, Jeff, QB, Dartmouth, 1986
Kennedy, Allan, T, Washington State, 1981-84
Kennedy, Sam, LB, San Jose State, 1988
Kenny, Charles, G, San Francisco, 1947
Kilgore, Jon, P, Auburn, 1969
Kilmer, Bill, QB, UCLA, 1961-66
Kimbrough, Elbert, HB, Northwestern, 1962-66
Kirby, Terry, RB, Virginia, 1996-current
Kirk, Randy, LB, San Diego State, 1996-current
Knafelc, Gary, E, Colorado, 1963
Knutson, Steve, G-T, USC, 1978
Kopay, Dave, HB, Washington, 1964-67
Korff, Mark, LB, Florida, 1987
Kovach, Jim, LB, Kentucky, 1985
Kraemer, Eldred, G, Pittsburgh, 1955
Krahl, Jim, DT, Texas Tech, 1980
Kramer, Kent, TE, Minnesota, 1966
Krueger, Charles, DT, Texas A&M, 1959-73
Krueger, Rolf, DE, Texas A&M, 1972-74
Kugler, Pete, DT, Penn State, 1981-83, 1986-90
Kuykendall, Fulton, LB, UCLA, 1985
Kuzman, John, T, Fordham, 1946
Kwalick, Ted, TE, Penn State, 1969-74
Kyles, Troy, WR, Howard, 1992

-L-

LaBounty, Matt, DE, Oregon, 1992-93
Lakes, Roland, DT, Wichita State, 1961-70
Land, Fred, T, LSU, 1948
Land, Mel, DE, Michigan State, 1980
Larson, Bill, TE, Colorado State, 1975
LaRose, Dan, DE, Missouri, 1965
Lash, Jim, WR, Northwestern, 1976
Latimer, Al, CB, Clemson, 1980
Laughlin, Bud, FB, Kansas, 1955
Lawrence, Amos, RB, North Carolina, 1981-82
Lawson, Steve, G, Kansas, 1976
LeBounty, Matt, DE, Oregon, 1992-93
LeCount, Terry, WR, Florida, 1978

Ledyard, Hal, QB, UT Chattanooga, 1953
Lee, Amp, RB, Florida State, 1992-93
Lee, Dwight, RB, Michigan State, 1968
Lee, Mark, CB, Washington, 1991
Leonard, Jim, C, Santa Clara, 1985
Leonard, Tony, CB, Virginia Union, 1976
Leopold, Bobby, LB, Notre Dame, 1980-83
Lewis, Eddie, DB, Kansas, 1976-79
Lewis, Gary, FB, Arizona State, 1964-69
Lewis, Kevin, CB, Northwestern State, 1991-92
Lewis, Ron, WR, Florida State, 1990-92
Lilly, Kevin, NT, Tulsa, 1988-89
Lillywhite, Verl, HB, USC, 1948-51
Lind, Mike, FB, Notre Dame, 1963-64
Lindstrom, Chris, DT, Boston College, 1983
Lisbon, Don, HB, Bowling Green, 1963-64
Liter, Greg, DE, Iowa State, 1987
Livingston, Howie, HB, Fullerton J.C., 1950
Lockett, J.W., RB, Central (Oklahoma) State, 1961
Logan, Marc, RB, Kentucky, 1992-94
Long, Tim, C, Memphis State, 1987
Looney, Jim, LB, Purdue, 1981
Lopasky, Bill, G, West Virginia, 1961
Lott, Ronnie, CB, USC, 1981-90
Loville, Derek, RB, Oregon, 1994-96
Loyd, Alex, E, Oklahoma State, 1950
Luna, Bob, HB, Alabama, 1955
Lyles, Lenny, HB, Louisville, 1959-60
Lynn, Anthony, RB, Texas Tech, 1996-current

-M-

MacAfee, Ken, TE, Notre Dame, 1978-79
Macauley, John, OL, Stanford, 1984
Mackey, Dee, TE, East Texas State, 1960
Maderos, George, HB, Chico State, 1955-56
Magac, Mike, G, Missouri, 1960-64
Maloney, Norm, E, Purdue, 1948-49
Manley, Joe, LB, Mississippi State, 1953
Mann, Charles, DE, Nevada, 1994
Manuel, Sean, TE, New Mexico State, 1996-current
Margerum, Ken, WR, Stanford, 1986-87
Martin, Bob, LB, Nebraska, 1979
Martin, Derrick, LB, San Jose State, 1987
Martin, Saladin, DB, San Diego State, 1981
Masini, Leonard, FB, Fresno State, 1947-48
Mason, Lindsey, T, Kansas, 1982
Matheson, Riley, G-LB, Texas Western, 1948
Mathews, Ned, HB, UCLA, 1946-47
Matthews, Clay, E, Georgia Tech, 1950, 1953-55

Matuszak, Marv, LB, Tulsa, 1957-58
Maurer, Andy, G, Oregon, 1976
McAlister, Ken, LB-S, San Francisco, 1983
McCaffrey, Ed, WR, Stanford, 1994
McCann, Jim, P, Arizona State, 1971-72
McColl, Milt, LB, Stanford, 1981-87
McCormick, Dave, T, LSU, 1966
McCormick, Tom, HB, Pacific, 1956
McCormick, Walt, C, USC, 1948
McCray, Willie, DE, Troy State, 1978
McDonald, Quintus, LB, Penn State, 1993
McDonald, Tim, S, Southern Cal, 1993-current
McElhenny, Hugh, HB, Washington, 1952-60
McFarland, Kay, HB, Colorado State, 1962-68
McGee, Willie, WR, Alcorn A&M, 1976
McGill, Ralph, CB, Tulsa, 1972-76
McGruder, Michael, CB, Kent State, 1992-93
McGuire, Steve, RB, Miami (FL), 1993
McHan, Lamar, QB, Arkansas, 1963
McIlhenny, Don, HB, SMU, 1961
McIntyre, Guy, G, Georgia, 1984-93
McIntyre, Jeff, LB, Arizona State, 1979
McKenzie, Reggie, LB, Tennessee, 1992
McKoy, Billy, LB, Purdue, 1974
McKyer, Tim, CB, Texas-Arlington, 1986-89
McLemore, Dana, KR-CB, Hawaii, 1982-87
McNeil, Clifton, E, Grambling, 1968-69
Mellekas, John, C, Arizona, 1962
Mellus, John, T, Villanova, 1946
Melville, Dan, P, California, 1979
Mertens, Jerry, HB, Drake, 1958-65
Messer, Dale, HB, Fresno State, 1961-65
Meyers, Bob, FB, Stanford, 1952
Michalik, Art, G, St. Ambrose, 1953-54
Mike, Bob, T, UCLA, 1948-49
Mike-Mayer, Steve, K, Maryland, 1975-76
Mikolas, Doug, NT, Portland State, 1987
Miles, Searcy, QB, San Jose State, 1954-56
Millen, Matt, LB, Penn State, 1990
Miller, Clark, E, Utah State, 1962-68
Miller, Hal, T, Georgia Tech, 1953
Miller, Jim, P, Mississippi, 1980-82
Miller, Johnny, G, Livingston, 1977-78
Milstead, Rod, G, Delaware State, 1994-current
Mira, George, QB, Miami (FL), 1964-68
Mitchell, Dale, LB, USC, 1976
Mitchell, Kevin, LB, Syracuse, 1994-current
Mitchell, Tom, TE, Bucknell, 1974-77
Mixon, Bill, HB, Georgia, 1953-54
Moegle, Dick, HB, Rice, 1955-59
Mojsiejenko, Ralf, P, Michigan State, 1991

Momsen, Bob, G, Ohio State, 1952
Monachino, Jim, HB, California, 1951
Monds, Wonder, DB, Nebraska, 1978
Monroe, Carl, RB-KR, Utah, 1983-87
Montana, Joe, QB, Notre Dame, 1979-92
Montgomery, Blanchard, LB, UCLA, 1983-84
Moore, Dean, LB, Iowa, 1978
Moore, Eugene, RB, Occidental, 1969
Moore, Jeff, RB, Jackson State, 1982-83
Moore, Manfred, RB, USC, 1974-75
Morgan, Joe, T, Southern Mississippi, 1949
Morgan, Melvin, DB, Mississippi Valley, 1979-80
Moroski, Mike, QB, UC Davis, 1986
Morrall, Earl, QB, Michigan State, 1956
Morris, Dennit, LB, Oklahoma, 1958
Morris, George, C, Georgia Tech, 1956
Morrison, Dennis, QB, Kansas State, 1974
Morton, Dave, LB, UCLA, 1979
Morton, John, LB, Texas Christian, 1953
Morze, Frank, C, Boston College, 1957-61
Moss, Anthony, LB, Florida State, 1993
Moten, Gary, LB, SMU, 1983
Mott, Joe, LB, Iowa, 1993
Mudd, Howard, G, Hillsdale, 1964-69
Musgrave, Bill, QB, Oregon, 1991-94
Myers, Chip, E, NW Oklahoma, 1967

-N-

Nehemiah, Renaldo, WR, Maryland, 1982-84
Neville, Tom, Fresno State, 1991
Nicholas, Calvin, WR, Grambling, 1988
Nichols, Mark, LB, Colorado State, 1978
Nicholson, Jim, T, Michigan State, 1981
Nix, Jack, E, USC, 1950
Nixon, Tory, San Diego State, 1985-88
Nomellini, Leo, T, Minnesota, 1950-63
Norberg, Hank, E, Stanford, 1946-47
Nordquist, Mark, G, Pacific, 1976
Norton, Jim, T, Washington, 1965-66
Norton, Ken Jr., LB, UCLA, 1994-current
Norton, Ray, HB, San Jose State, 1960-61
Nunley, Frank, LB, Michigan, 1967-76

-O-

Oates, Bart, C, Brigham Young, 1994-95
Obradovich, Jim, TE, USC, 1976
Odom, Rick, DB, USC, 1978
O'Donahue, Pat, E, Wisconsin, 1952
Olerich, Dave, E, San Francisco, 1967-68, 1972-73

Olssen, Lance, T, Purdue, 1968-69
Orosz, Tom, P, Ohio State, 1983
Osborne, Clancy, LB, Arizona State, 1959-60
Owen, Tom, QB, Wichita State, 1974-75
Owens, James, WR, UCLA, 1979-80
Owens, R.C., HB, College of Idaho, 1957-61
Owens, Terrell, WR, Tenn-Chattanooga, 1996-current

-P-

Pace, Jim, HB, Michigan, 1958
Palatella, Lou, G, Pittsburgh, 1955-58
Paris, Bubba, T, Michigan, 1982-89
Parker, Don, G, Virginia, 1967
Parks, Dave, E, Texas Tech, 1964-67
Parks, Limbo, G, Arkansas, 1987
Parrish, James, T, Temple, 1993
Parsons, Earle, HB, USC, 1946-47
Patera, Dennis, K, BYU, 1968
Patterson, Reno, DE, Bethune-Cookman, 1987
Patton, Ricky, RB, Jackson State, 1980-82
Pavlich, Chuck, G, Muskegon High (MI), 1946
Peery, Ryan, DE, California, 1993
Peets, Brian, TE, Pacific, 1981
Penchion, Bob, T, Alcorn A&M, 1974-75
Peoples, Woody, G, Grambling, 1968-77
Perry, Joe, FB, Compton J.C., 1948-60, 1963
Perry, Scott, S, Williams, 1980
Peterson, Anthony, LB, Notre Dame, 1994-current
Phillips, Mel, DB, North Carolina A&T, 1966-76
Pillers, Lawrence, DE, Alcorn A&M, 1980-84
Pine, Ed, LB, Utah, 1962-64
Plummer, Gary, LB, California, 1994-current
Plunkett, Jim, QB, Stanford, 1976-77
Pollack, Frank, T-G, Northern Arizona, 1990-91, 1994-current
Pollard, Darryl, CB, Weber State, 1987-91
Poole, Bob, E, Clemson, 1964-65
Pope, Marquez, CB, Fresno State, 1995-current
Popson, Ted, TE, Portland State, 1994-96
Powell, Charles, E, San Diego High (CA), 1952-53, 1955-57
Powers, Jim, HB, USC, 1950-53
Price, Daryl, DE, Colorado, 1996-current
Prokop, Joe, P, Cal Poly Pomona, 1991
Puddy, Harold, T, Oregon, 1948
Puki, Craig, LB, Tennessee, 1980-81
Putzier, Rollin, LB, Iowa State, 1989

-Q-

Quillan, Fred, C, Oregon, 1978-87
Quilter, Chuck, T, Tyler J.C., 1949

-R-

Raines, Mike, DT, Alabama, 1974
Ramson, Eason, TE, Washington State, 1979-83

7. **DeCOURLEY, ERNEST**
DT, 6-6, 250, Moorehead State
*8. **LOCKE, ROGER**
E, 6-2, 185, Arizona State
*9. **MACZUZAK, JOHN**
T, 6-5, 245, Pittsburgh
10. **LOPOUR, DICK**
HB, 6-2, 214, Huron
11. **SHAFER, STEVE**
QB, 6-0, 185, Utah State
12. **DENTON, ROBERT**
T, 6-2, 240, Mississippi State
13. **SHULTZ, DICK**
T, 6-3, 240, Ohio University
14. **TOBIN, BILL**
HB, 5-11, 210, Missouri
*15. **ROSS, OLLIE**
FB, 6-0, 215, West Texas State
16. **BOGDALEK, JIM**
DT, 6-4, 245, Toledo
17. **REED, KEN**
G, 6-0, 230, Tulsa
*18. **SELLERS, JOHN**
T, 6-2, 220, Bakersfield J.C.
19. **PRICE, BOB**
G, 6-1, 230, North Texas State
20. **DAVIS, DON**
B, 5-11, 220, McMurry

1964
(Drafted 1st)
1. **PARKS, DAVE**
E, 6-2, 195, Texas Tech
2. **MIRA, GEORGE**
QB, 5-11, 183, Miami (FL)
3. **WILCOX, DAVE**
LB, 6-3, 230, Oregon
*4. **WILSON, JAMES**
G, 6-3, 244, George
5. **JOHNSON, RUDY**
FB, 5-11, 200, Nebraska
*6. **LEWIS, GARY**
FB, 6-2 1/2, 227, Arizona State
7. **CLARKE, HAGWOOD**
DB, 6-0, 196, Florida
*8. (A) **DAUGHERTY, BOB**
HB, 6-2, 185, Tulsa
8. (B) **POOLE, BOB**
(Choice from Washington)
TE, 6-4, 216, Clemson
9. **MUDD, HOWARD**
G, 6-3, 237, Hillsdale
*10. **POLSER, FRED**
T, 6-5, 235, East Texas State
11. **ALMQUIST, DENNIS**
G, 6-1, 218, Idaho
*12. **LONG, JIM**
FB, 6-1, 202, Fresno State
13. **BROWN, ROBERT**
DT, 6-5, 263, Arkansas A&M
14. **BEARD, ED**
T, 6-2, 235, Tennessee
15. **GRIFFIN, JAMES**
E, 6-3 1/2, 230, Grambling
16. **GORDON, CORNELL**
DB, 5-11, 180, North Carolina A&T
*17. **BRUSVAN, KEN**
T, 6-4, 223, Oregon State
*18. **COLE, JERRY**
E, 6-4, 215, Southwest Texas State
19. **RAWSON, LARRY**
B, 5-11, 209, Auburn
20. **BAKER, GENE**
G, 6-1, 235, Whitworth

1965
(Drafted 2nd)
1. (A) **WILLARD, KEN**
FB, 6-2, 230, North Carolina
1. (B) **DONNELLY, GEORGE**
(Choice from Cleveland)
DB, 6-3, 202, Illinois
2. **CERNE, JOE**
C, 6-2, 237, Northwestern
3. (A) **SCHWEICKERT, BOB**
(Choice from N.Y. Giants)
HB, 6-1, 191, Virginia Poly
3. (B) **NORTON, JIM**
T, 6-4, 247, Washington
3. (C) **CHAPPLE, JACK**
(Choice from Baltimore)
LB, 6-2, 225, Stanford
*4. **TODD, LARRY**
FL, 6-1, 190, Arizona State
*5. **McCORMICK, DAVE**
T, 6-6, 250, LSU
6. Choice to Cleveland
7. Choice to Green Bay
8. Choice to Minnesota
9. **SWINFORD, WAYNE**
DB, 6-0 1/2, 185, Georgia
*10. **CAPPADONA, ROBERT**
HB, 6-2, 225, Northeastern
*11. **MASS, STEVE**
T, 6-2, 270, Detroit
*12. **PLUMP, DAVE**
HB, 6-0, 190, Fresno State
13. **SCHUMACHER, GREG**
LB, 6-3, 230, Illinois
14. **ANDRUSKI, FRANK**
DB, 6-0, 185, Utah
15. **PABIAN, JOE**
T, 6-3, 270, West Virginia
*16. **HETTEMA, DAVE**
T, 6-3 1/2, 230, New Mexico
17. **FRKETICH, LEN**
E, 6-3, 220, Oregon State
*18. **STANDRIDGE, LEON**
E, 6-3, 220, San Diego State
19. **FORD, DALE**
QB-DB, 6-1, 200, Washington State
*20. **DUNCAN, DENNIS**
HB, 6-1, 200, Louisiana College

1966
(Drafted Alternately 10-11)
1. **HINDMAN, STAN**
DE-G, 6-3, 235, Mississippi
*2. **WINDSOR, BOB**
E, 6-4, 224, Kentucky
3. (A) **RANDOLPH, ALVIN**
(Choice from Dallas)
DB, 6-2, 193, Iowa
3. (B) **BLAND, DAN**
DB, 5-11, 190, Mississippi State
*4. **PARKER, DON**
G, 6-3, 240, Virginia
5. (A) **PHILLIPS, MEL**
(Choice from Dallas)
DB, 6-0, 190, North Carolina A&T
5. (B) **SMITH, STEVE**
TE, 6-5, 240, Michigan
6. **JOHNSON, CHARLES**
DT, 6-2, 266, Louisville
7. Choice to Baltimore
8. **WITCHER, DICK**
E, 6-3, 210, UCLA

9. **KRAMER, KENT**
TE, 6-5, 235, Minnesota
10. **SBRANTI, RON**
LB, 6-2, 228, Utah
11. **RIDLEHUBER, PRESTON**
DB, 6-2, 195, Georgia
12. **LOEBACH, LYALL**
T, 6-5, 248, Simpson
*13. **JACKSON, JIM**
DB, 5-11, 185, Western Illinois
*14. **COLLETT, ELMER**
G, 6-4, 225, San Francisco State
*15. **SAFFOLD, S.T.**
E, 6-3, 205, San Jose State
16. **LeCLAIR, JIM**
QB, 6-1, 195, C.W. Post
17. **BRELAND, JIM**
G, 6-2, 230, Georgia Tech
*18. **PARSON, RON**
E, 6-5, 240, Austin Peay
*19. **FITZGERALD, DICK**
T, 6-1, 250, Nebraska
20. **WALKER, WILLIE**
LB, 6-3, 220, Baylor

1967
(Drafted Alternately 11-13)
1. (A) **SPURRIER, STEVE**
(Choice from Atlanta)
QB, 6-2, 203, Florida
1. (B) **BANASZEK, CAS**
LB, 6-3, 245, Northwestern
2. **HOLZER, TOM**
T, 6-4, 248, Louisville
3. (A) **NUNLEY, FRANK**
(Choice from Pittsburgh)
LB, 6-2, 230, Michigan
3. (B) **TUCKER, BILL**
HB, 6-2, 232, Tennessee A&I
4. **TRIMBLE, WAYNE**
DB, 6-3, 205, Alabama
5. Choice to Atlanta
6. **CUNNINGHAM, DOUG**
HB, 5-11, 185, Mississippi
7. **JACKSON, MILT**
DB, 6-3, 185, Tulsa
8. **JOHNSON, WALTER**
LB, 6-4, 235, Tuskegee
9. **BRIGGS, BOB**
T, 6-3, 248, Heidelberg
10. **MYERS, PHIL (Chip)**
FL, 6-4, 185, NW Oklahoma
11. **CARMANN, KEN**
DT, 6-4, 265, Kearney (Nebraska)
12. **HALL, JAMES**
LB, 6-3, 230, Tuskegee
13. **GIBBS, RICH**
DB, 6-1, 187, Iowa
14. **LeBLANC, DALTON**
FL, 5-11, 175, NE Louisiana
15. **SPENCER, CLARENCE**
FL, 6-4, 200, Louisville
16. **TEMPLEMAN, BART**
C, 6-3, 248, Eastern Montana
17. **TALBOTT, DAN**
QB, 6-0, 180, North Carolina

1968
(Drafted Alternately 14-15)
1. **BLUE, FORREST**
C, 6-5, 248, Auburn
2. Choice traded to St. Louis
3. (A) **OLSSEN, LANCE**
(Choice from Detroit)
T, 6-5, 267, Purdue

3. (B) **VANDERBUNDT, SKIP**
LB, 6-3, 234, Oregon
4. **FULLER, JOHN**
E, 6-0, 175, Lamar Tech
5. **LEE, DWIGHT**
RB, 6-2, 190, Michigan State
6. (A) **JOHNSON, LEO**
(Choice from New Orleans)
FL, 6-2, 185, Tennessee State
6. (B) **BELK, BILL**
DE, 6-3, 240, Maryland State
7. **RICHARDSON, JERRY**
LB, 6-2, 218, Mississippi
8. (A) **BROWN, CHARLES**
(Choice from N.Y. Giants)
T, 6-5, 246, Augustana
8. (B) **GRAY, TOM**
FL, 5-9, 174, Morehead State
9. **BOYETT, CASEY**
E, 6-1, 188, Brigham Young
10. **HART, TOMMY**
LB, 6-3, 215, Morris Brown
11. **FITZGIBBONS, DENNIS**
G, 6-1, 260, Syracuse
12. **JOHNSON, HENRY**
QB, 6-0, 180, Fisk
13. **MITRAKOS, TOM**
C, 6-4, 220, Pittsburgh
14. **MOORE, ALEX**
RB, 6-1, 200, Norfolk State
15. **SPENCER, CLARENCE**
FL, 6-2, 188, Louisville
16. **ROSENOW, TOM**
DT, 6-3, 250, Northern Illinois
17. **PATERA, DENNIS**
K, 6-0 214, Brigham Young

1969
(Drafted 16th)
1. (A) **KWALICK, TED**
(Choice from New Orleans)
TE, 6-4, 230, Penn State
1. (B) **WASHINGTON, GENE**
FL, 6-1, 186, Stanford
2. Choice to Pittsburgh via Cleveland
3. Choice to Dallas
4. (A) **SNIADECKI, JIM**
(Choice from Detroit)
LB, 6-2, 220, Indiana
4. (B) **MOORE, GENE**
RB, 6-1, 200, Occidental
5. **EDWARDS, EARL**
DT, 6-6, 276, Wichita State
6. **THOMAS, JIM**
RB, 6-1, 216, Texas-Arlington
7. **VAN SINDEREN, STEVE**
F, 6-4, 255, Washington State
8. **LOPER, MIKE**
T, 6-4, 230, Brigham Young
9. **CRAWFORD, HILTON**
DB, 6-1, 195, Grambling
10. **CHAPPLE, DAVE**
K, 6-1, 180, Santa Barbara
11. **PEAKE, WILLIE**
T, 6-3, 260, Alcorn A&M
12. **O'MALLEY, JACK**
T, 6-4, 250, Southern Cal
13. **CHAMPLIN, PAUL**
DB, 6-0, 194, Eastern Montana
14. **BLACK, TOM**
FL, 6-1, 192, East Texas State
15. **GOLDEN, GARY**
DB, 6-0, 179, Texas Tech

Future Arrival—Redshirt

16. **HOSKINS, BOB**
LB, 6-2, 235, Wichita State
17. **RUSHING, JOE**
LB, 6-2, 216, Memphis State

1970
(Drafted 9th)
1. **HARDMAN, CEDRICK**
DE, 6-3, 250, North Texas State
1. **(B) TAYLOR, BRUCE**
(Choice from Washington)
DB, 6-0, 180, Boston U.
2. **Choice to Los Angeles**
3. **ISENBARGER, JOHN**
(Choice from Philadelphia via Los Angeles)
RB, 6-3, 205, Indiana
4. **WASHINGTON, VIC**
WR, 5-11, 180, Wyoming
5. **McARTHUR, GARY**
T, 6-5, 247, Southern Cal
6. **CLARK, RUSTY**
QB, 6-2, 212, Houston
7. **STRONG, JIM**
RB, 6-2, 204, Houston
8. **CAMPBELL, CARTER**
LB, 6-3, 214, Weber State
9. **RILEY, PRESTON**
WR, 6-1, 180, Memphis State
10. **SCHREIBER, LARRY**
RB, 6-0, 193, Tennessee Tech
11. **CROCKETT, DANNY**
WR, 6-1, 170, Toledo
12. **TANT, BILL**
T, 6-4, 245, Dayton
13. **VANDERSLICE, JIM**
LB, 6-3, 220, Texas Christian
14. **KING, JACK**
G, 6-2, 245, Clemson
15. **DELSIGNORE, DAVE**
WR, 6-0, 175, Youngstown State
16. **PERKINS, PRODUS**
WR, 6-0, 178, Livingstone College
17. **CULTON, MIKE**
P, 5-11, 195, LaVerne College

1971
(Drafted Alternately 18-19)
1. **ANDERSON, TIM**
CB, 5-11, 201, Ohio State
2. **(A) JANET, ERNIE**
(Choice from Green Bay)
G, 6-4, 243, Washington
2. **(B) ORDUNA, JOE**
RB, 6-0, 194, Nebraska
3. **(A) DICKERSON, SAM**
(Choice from Philadelphia)
WR, 6-2, 196, Southern Cal
3. **(B) PARKER, WILLIE**
C, 6-3, 238, North Texas State
4. **HARRIS, TONY**
RB, 6-3, 191, Toledo
5. **(A) SHATERNICK, DEAN**
(Choice from Chicago)
T, 6-5, 244, Kansas State
5. **(B) WELLS, GEORGE**
(Choice from N.Y. Giants)
LB, 6-1, 240, New Mexico State
5. **(C) HUFF, MARTY**
LB, 6-2, 239, Michigan
6. **BRESLER, AL**
WR, 6-1, 185, Auburn
7. **WATSON, JOHN**
T, 6-4, 251, Oklahoma

8. **McCANN, JOHN**
P, 6-2, 170, Arizona State
9. **COUCH, THERMAN**
LB, 6-2, 218, Iowa State
10. **(A) CARDO, RON**
(Choice from New Orleans)
RB, 6-3, 254, Wisconsin State
10. **(B) JENNINGS, ERNIE**
WR, 6-0, 170, Air Force
11. **REED, JOE**
QB, 6-1, 196, Mississippi State
12. **BUNCH, JIM**
DT, 6-3, 254, Wisconsin State
13. **BULLOCK, JOHN**
RB, 5-11, 216, Purdue
14. **DUNSTAN, BILL**
LB, 6-4, 217, Utah State
15. **LENNON, JOHN**
DE, 6-3, 221, Colgate
16. **PURCELL, DAVE**
DT, 6-4, 260, Kentucky
17. **CHARLTON, LEROY**
CB, 6-2, 180, Florida A&M

1972
(Drafted Alternately 19-18)
1. **BEASLEY, TERRY**
WR, 5-11, 186, Auburn
2. **(A) McGILL, RALPH**
(Choice from N.Y. Giants)
CB, 6-0, 181, Tulsa
2. **(B) BARRETT, JEAN**
T, 6-6, 253, Tulsa
3. **DUNBAR, ALLEN**
WR, 6-0, 196, Southern
4. **HALL, WINDLAN**
CB, 5-11, 170, Arizona State
5. **GREENE, MIKE**
LB, 6-4, 233, Georgia
6. **WALKER, JACKIE**
SS, 6-0, 186, Tennessee
7. **HARDY, EDGAR**
G, 6-4, 233, Jackson State
8. **WITTUM, TOM**
P, 6-1, 185, Northern Illinois
9. **BROWN, JERRY**
CB, 5-10, 170, Northwestern
10. **WILLIAMS, STEVE**
DT, 6-4, 251, Western Carolina
11. **LAPUTKA, TOM**
DE, 6-4, 235, Southern Illinois
12. **SETZLER, STEVE**
DE, 6-3, 232, St. Johns
13. **PETTIGREW, LEON**
T, 6-5, 228, San Fernando Valley State
14. **GUTHRIE, ERIC**
QB, 6-0, 200, Boise State
15. **MADDOX, BOB**
DE, 6-6, 235, Frostburg State
16. **DAVIS, RON**
G, 6-2, 235, Virginia State
17. **ALEXANDER, TED**
RB, 6-0, 192, Langston

1973
(Drafted Alternately 18-19)
1. **HOLMES, MIKE**
CB, 6-1, 180, Texas Southern
2. **HARPER, WILLIE**
(Choice from N.Y. Giants)
LB, 6-2, 205, Nebraska
2. **Choice to St. Louis**
3. **Choice to Denver via Washington**

4. **Choice to San Diego**
via Washington
5. **(A) FULK, MIKE**
(Choice from Chicago)
LB, 6-3, 229, Indiana
5. **(B) BEVERLY, ED**
WR, 5-11, 172, Arizona State
6. **MOORE, ARTHUR**
DT, 6-5, 253, Tulsa
7. **MITCHELL, JOHN**
LB, 6-3, 229, Alabama
8. **ATKINS, DAVID**
RB, 6-1, 202, Texas-El Paso
9. **PRAETORIUS, ROGER**
RB, 6-3, 228, Syracuse
11. **HUNT, CHARLIE**
LB, 6-3, 218, Florida State
11. **DAHLBERG, TOM**
RB, 6-2, 209, Gustavus Adolphus
12. **PETTUS, LARRY**
T, 6-4, 228, Tennessee State
13. **KELSO, ALAN**
C, 6-6, 244, Washington
14. **MORRISON, DENNIS**
QB, 6-3, 207, Kansas State
15. **BETTIGA, MIKE**
WT, 6-3, 181, Humbolt State
16. **OVEN, MIKE**
TE, 6-4, 205, Georgia Tech
17. **ERICKSON, BOB**
G, 6-3, 240, North Dakota State

1974
(Drafted 10th)
1. **(A) JACKSON, WILBUR**
RB, 6-1, 205, Alabama
1. **(B) SANDIFER, BILL**
(Choice from New England)
DT, 6-6, 278, UCLA
2. **(A) FAHNHORST, KEITH**
OT, 6-6, 248, Minnesota
2. **(B) WILLIAMS, DELVIN**
(Choice from Washington)
RB, 6-1, 197, Kansas
3. **Choice to St. Louis**
4. **(A) HASLERIG, CLINT**
(Choice from N.Y. Jets via New Orleans)
WR, 6-0, 189, Michigan
4. **Choice to New Orleans**
4. **(B) JOHNSON, SAMMY**
(Choice from Green Bay)
RB, 6-1, 217, North Carolina
5. **Choice to New Orleans**
6. **RAINES, MIKE**
DT, 6-6, 255, Alabama
7. **JOHNSON, KERMIT**
RB, 5-11, 189, UCLA
8. **SCHNEITZ, JIM**
T, 6-3, 253, Missouri
9. **MOORE, MANFRED**
RB, 6-1, 190, Southern Cal
10. **GASPARD, GLEN**
LB, 6-1, 210, Texas
11. **BATTLE, GREG**
S, 5-11, 188, Colorado State
12. **HULL, TOM**
LB, 6-3, 229, Penn State
13. **OWEN, TOM**
QB, 6-1, 195, Wichita State
14. **WILLIAMSON, WALT**
DE, 6-4, 225, Michigan

15. **GRAY, LEONARD**
TE, 6-8, 240, Long Beach State
16. **CONNORS, JACK**
DB, 5-11, 185, Oregon
17. **STANLEY, LEVI**
G, 6-2, 250, Hawaii

1975
(Drafted Alternately 10-9)
1. **WEBB, JIMMY**
DT, 6-5, 248, Mississippi State
2. **COLLINS, GREG**
LB, 6-3, 228, Notre Dame
3. **Choice to N.Y. Giants**
3. **(A) HART, JEFF**
(Choice from Buffalo)
T, 6-5, 266, Oregon State
3. **(B) MIKE-MAYER, STEVE**
(Choice from Washington)
K, 6-0, 180, Maryland
3. **(C) BAKER, WAYNE**
(Choice from St. Louis)
DT, 6-6, 260, Brigham Young
4. **(A) ELAM, CLEVELAND**
(Choice from New Orleans)
DE, 6-3, 240, Tennessee State
4. **(B) OLIVER, FRANK**
DB, 6-1, 189, Kentucky State
5. **BULLOCK, WAYNE**
RB, 6-0, 232, Notre Dame
6. **Choice to Kansas City**
7. **Choice to Buffalo**
8. **KENDRICK, PRESTON**
LB, 6-1, 217, Florida
9. **(A) JOHNSON, JAMES**
DB, 6-2, 195, Tennessee State
9. **(B) NATALE, DAN**
(Choice from Philadelphia)
TE, 6-3, 223, Penn State
9. **(C) DOUGLAS, CEASER**
(Choice from St. Louis)
T, 6-5, 272, Illinois Wesleyan
10. **LAYTON, DONNIE**
RB, 6-0, 190, South Carolina State
11. **HERNANDEZ, GENE**
DB, 6-2, 173, Texas Christian
12. **WORLEY, RICK**
QB, 6-1, 195, Howard Payne
13. **MITCHELL, DALE**
LB, 6-3, 211, Southern Cal
14. **HENSON, DAVID**
WR, 6-3, 173, Abilene Christian
15. **LAVIN, RICH**
TE, 6-5, 223, Western Illinois
16. & 17. **Choices to Baltimore**
for Colts' 15th & 16th in 1976

1976
(Drafted Alternately 4 & 3)
1. **Choice to New England**
1. **(Choice from Houston to New England)**
2. **(A) CROSS, RANDY**
C, 6-3, 245, UCLA
2. **(B) LEWIS, EDDIE**
(Choice from Tampa Bay)
CB, 6-0, 172, Kansas
3. **(Choice from New Orleans to Kansas City)**
3. **Choice to Dallas**
4. **RIVERA, STEVE**
(Choice from Philadelphia)
WR, 5-11, 190, California

4. **Choice to N.Y. Giants**
5. **Choice to Cincinnati**
5. **LEONARD, ANTHONY**
   (Choice from Detroit)
   CB, 5-11, 170, Virginia Union
6. **(A) PENNYWELL, ROBERT**
   LB, 6-1, 222, Grambling
6. **(B) BULL, SCOTT**
   (Choice from St. Louis)
   QB, 6-5, 209, Arkansas
7. **CHESLEY, JAY**
   DB, 6-1, 184, Vanderbilt
8. **AYERS, JOHN**
   T, 6-5, 238, West Texas State
9. **HARRISON, KENNY**
   WR, 6-0, 179, Southern
   Methodist
10. **ROSS, ROBIN**
    T, 6-4, 248, Washington State
11. **HOFER, PAUL**
    RB, 6-0, 186, Mississippi
12. **LOPER, GERALD**
    G, 6-2, 245, Florida
13. **BRUMFIELD, LARRY**
    CB, 6-0, 171, Indiana State
14. **MILLER, JOHNNY**
    G, 6-1, 241, Livingstone
15. **STIDHAM, HOWARD**
    LB, 6-2, 214, Tennessee Tech
16. **LEWIS, REGGIE**
    DE, 6-1, 215, San Diego State
17. **JENKINS, DARRYL**
    RB, 6-2, 235, San Jose State

1977
(Drafted 16th)
1. **Choice to New England**
2. **Choice to New England**
3. **BOYD, ELMO**
   (Choice from Houston)
   WR, 5-11, 185, Eastern
   Kentucky
3. **Choice to N.Y. Jets**
4. **BLACK, STAN**
   S, 6-0, 204, Mississippi State
5. **Choice to Buffalo**
6. **(A) BURNS, MIKE**
   (Choice from Buffalo)
   CB, 6-0, 184, Southern Cal
6. **(B) HARLAN, JIM**
   C, 6-5, 241, Howard Payne
7. **VAN WAGNER, JIM**
   RB, 6-0, 202, Michigan Tech
8. **Choice to N.Y. Giants**
9. **POSEY, DAVID**
   K, 5-11, 167, Florida
10. **Choice to Tampa Bay**
11. **BILLICK, BRIAN**
    TE, 6-5, 232, Brigham Young
12. **MARTIN, SCOTT**
    T, 6-4, 257, North Dakota

1978
(Drafted 7th)
1. **(A) MacAFEE, KEN**
   TE, 6-4, 250, Notre Dame
1. **(B) BUNZ, DAN**
   (Choice from Miami)
   LB, 6-4, 230, Long Beach
   State
2. **Choice to Buffalo**
2. **DOWNING, WALT**
   (Choice from Chicago)
   G, 6-3, 254, Michigan

3. **Choice to Buffalo**
3. **HUGHES, ERNIE**
   (Choice from Baltimore)
   G, 6-3, 253, Notre Dame
4. **LeCOUNT, TERRY**
   WR, 5-10, 172, Florida
5. **Choice to Baltimore**
5. **(A) REESE, ARCHIE**
   (Choice from Houston via
   Kansas City and Chicago)
   DT, 6-3, 263, Clemson
5. **(B) THREADGILL, BRUCE**
   (Choice from Miami)
   DB, 6-0, 190, Mississippi State
6. **Choice from Minnesota to
   Washington**
6. **WALKER, ELLIOTT**
   RB, 5-11, 193, Pittsburgh
7. **QUILLAN, FRED**
   C, 6-5, 240, Oregon
8. **Choice to Washington**
9. **(A) REDDEN, HERMAN**
   DB, 6-2, 190, Howard
9. **(B) MOORE, DEAN**
   (Choice from Detroit)
   LB, 6-2, 210, Iowa
9. **(C) McDANIELS, STEVE**
   (Choice from Denver)
   T, 6-6, 276, Notre Dame
10. **CONNELL, MIKE**
    P, 6-1, 200, Cincinnati
11. **McCRAY, WILLIE**
    DE, 6-5, 234, Troy State
12. **(A) IRONS, DAN**
    T, 6-7, 260, Texas Tech
12. **(B) CONNORS, ROD**
    (Supplemental Draft)
    RB, 6-2, 190, Southern Cal

1979
(Drafted 1st)
1. **Choice to Buffalo**
2. **OWENS, JAMES**
   RB, 5-11, 188, UCLA
3. **Choice to Seattle**
3. **MONTANA, JOE**
   (Choice from Dallas via
   Seattle)
   QB, 6-2, 200, Notre Dame
4. **Choice to Buffalo**
5. **(A) SEABRON, TOM**
   LB, 6-3, 209, Michigan
5. **(B) ALDRIDGE, JERRY**
   (Choice from Detroit)
   RB, 6-2, 220, Angelo State
6. **VAUGHN, RUBEN**
   DT, 6-2, 264, Colorado
7. **FRANCIS, PHIL**
   FB, 6-1, 205, Stanford
8. **Choice to Green Bay**
9. **HAMILTON, STEVE**
   DE, 6-3, 240, Missouri
10. **(A) CLARK, DWIGHT**
    WR, 6-3, 204, Clemson
10. **(B) BALLAGE, HOWARD**
    (Choice from Tampa Bay)
    CB, 6-1, 182, Colorado
11. **McBRIDE, BILLY**
    DB, 6-1, 187, Tennessee
    State
12. **Forfeited choice via supple-
    mental draft of 1978.**

1980
(Drafted Alternately 2 & 1)
1. **Choice to N.Y. Jets**
1. **(A) COOPER, EARL**
   (Choice from N.Y. Jets)
   RB, 6-2, 227, Rice
1. **(B) STUCKEY, JIM**
   (Choice from Denver via N.Y.
   Jets)
   DE, 6-4, 245, Clemson
2. **Choice to Buffalo**
2. **Choice from Detroit to
   Minnesota**
2. **TURNER, KEENA**
   (Choice from Minnesota)
   LB, 6-2, 219, Purdue
3. **Choice to Los Angeles**
3. **(A) MILLER, JIM**
   (Choice from Minnesota)
   P, 5-11, 183, Mississippi
3. **(B) PUKI, CRAIG**
   (Choice from Washington
   via Los Angeles)
   LB, 6-1, 231, Tennessee
4. **(A) CHURCHMAN, RICKY**
   SS, 6-1, 193, Texas
4. **(B) HODGE, DAVID**
   (Choice from New England
   via Los Angeles)
   LB, 6-2, 221, Houston
5. **TIMES, KEN**
   DT, 6-2, 246, Southern
6. **WILLIAMS, HERB**
   CB, 6-0, 198, Southern
7. **Choice to Cincinnati**
8. **Choice to Oakland**
8. **LEOPOLD, BOBBY**
   (Choice from Oakland)
   LB, 6-1, 215, Notre Dame
9. **Choice to Detroit via Kansas
   City**
9. **HARTWIG, DAN**
   (Choice from Oakland)
   QB, 6-3, 212, Cal Lutheran
10. **Choice to Pittsburgh**
11. **Choice to Miami**
12. **Choice to Pittsburgh**

1981
(Drafted Alternately 8-10)
1. **LOTT, RONNIE**
   DB, 6-0, 199, Southern Cal
2. **(A) HARTY, JOHN**
   (Choice from Washington)
   DT, 6-4, 253, Iowa
2. **Choice to Chicago**
2. **(B) WRIGHT, ERIC**
   (Choice from Chicago)
   DB, 6-1, 180, Missouri
3. **WILLIAMSON, CARLTON**
   DB, 6-0, 204, Pittsburgh
4. **Choice to Dallas**
5. **(A) THOMAS, LYNN**
   DB, 5-11, 181, Pittsburgh
5. **(B) JONES, ARRINGTON**
   (Choice from Chicago)
   FB, 6-0, 230, Winston-Salem
6. **KUGLER, PETE**
   DT, 6-4, 255, Penn State
7. **Choice to Philadelphia**
8. **WHITE, GARRY**
   RB, 5-11, 201, Minnesota
9. **Choice to Cincinnati**
10. **Choice to Baltimore**
11. **DeBOSE, RON**
    TE, 6-5, 229, UCLA

12. **(A) OGILVIE, MAJOR**
    RB, 5-11, 202, Alabama
12. **(B) ADAMS, JOE**
    (Choice from Pittsburgh)
    QB, 6-3, 185, Tennessee State

1982
(Drafted 27th)
1. **Choice to New England**
2. **PARIS, WILLIAM "BUBBA"**
   (Choice from New England)
   T, 6-6, 293, Michigan
2. **Choice from Washington
   to New England**
2. **Choice to New England**
3. **Choice to San Diego**
4. **Choice to New England**
5. **WILLIAMS, NEWTON**
   RB, 5-10, 204, Arizona State
6. **WILLIAMS, VINCE**
   (Choice from Oakland)
   FB, 6-0, 231, Oregon
6. **Choice to New Orleans**
7. **FERRARI, RON**
   LB, 6-0, 212, Illinois
8. **Choice to New Orleans**
9. **CLARK, BRYAN**
   QB, 6-2, 196, Michigan State
10. **(A) McLEMORE, DANA**
    (Choice from Tampa Bay)
    DB, 5-10, 183, Hawaii
10. **(B) BARBIAN, TIM**
    DT, 6-3, 230, Western Illinois
11. **GIBSON, GARY**
    LB, 6-1, 215, Arizona
12. **WASHINGTON, TIMOTHY**
    CB, 5-9, 184, Fresno State

1983
(Drafted Alternately 5-8)
1. **Choice to San Diego**
2. **Choice to L.A. Rams**
2. **CRAIG, ROGER**
   (Choice from San Diego)
   RB, 6-0, 222, Nebraska
3. **MONTGOMERY, BLANCHARD**
   (Choice from L.A. Rams)
   LB, 6-2, 236, UCLA
3. **Choice to L.A. Rams**
4. **(Choice from Denver to L.A.
   Rams)**
4. **HOLMOE, TOM**
   DB, 6-2, 180, Brigham Young
5. **ELLISON, RIKI**
   LB, 6-2, 220, Southern Cal
6. **Choice to Tampa Bay**
7. **MOTEN, GARY**
   LB, 6-1, 210, Southern
   Methodist
8. **Choice to San Diego**
9. **MULARKEY, MIKE**
   TE, 6-4, 245, Florida
9. **Choice from Cleveland to
   Chicago**
10. **MERRELL, JEFF**
    NT, 6-4, 264, Nebraska
11. **SAPOLU, JESSE**
    G-C, 6-4, 260, Hawaii
12. **Choice to Chicago**

1984
(Drafted Alternately 23-24)
1. **SHELL, TODD**
   LB, 6-4, 225, Brigham Young
2. **Choice to L.A. Raiders**

2. **FRANK, JOHN**
(Choice from L.A. Raiders)
TE, 6-3, 225, Ohio State
3. **McINTYRE, GUY**
(Choice from St. Louis)
G, 6-3, 271, Georgia
3. **Choice to St. Louis**
4. **Choice from Tampa Bay to Seattle**
4. **Choice to San Diego**
5. **(A) CARTER, MICHAEL**
(Choice from Atlanta)
DT, 6-2, 281, Southern Methodist
5. **Choice from Denver to Atlanta**
5. **Choice to St. Louis**
5. **(B) FULLER, JEFF**
(Choice from Washington, via L.A. Raiders)
LB-S, 6-2, 216, Texas A&M
6. **Choice to Atlanta**
7. **Choice to New England**
8. **Choice to San Diego**
9. **(A) MILLER, LEE**
(Choice from Chicago)
DB, 6-1, 186, Cal State-Fullerton
9. **(B) HARMON, DERRICK**
RB 5-10, 202, Cornell
10. **MORITZ, DAVE**
WR, 6-0, 181, Iowa
11. **PENDLETON, KIRK**
WR, 6-3, 191, Brigham Young
12. **Choice from Chicago to Miami**
13. **Choice to San Diego**

1985
(Drafted 16th in 1st; 28th 2-12)
1. **RICE, JERRY**
WR, 6-2, 220, Mississippi Valley State
1. **Choice to New England**
2. **Choice to New England**
3. **MOORE, RICKY**
(Choice from New England)
RB, 6-11, 236, Alabama
3. **Choice to New England**
4. **Choice to Buffalo**
5. **COLLIE, BRUCE**
OT, 6-6, 275, Texas-Arlington
6. **BARRY, SCOTT**
QB, 6-2, 190, UC-Davis
7. **Choice to San Diego**
8. **Choice to New England**
9. **Choice to San Diego**
10. **Choice to Seattle**
11. **WOOD, DAVID**
DE, 6-4, 250, Arizona
12. **CHUMLEY, DONALD**
DT, 6-4, 259, Georgia

1986
(Drafted 18th)
1. **Choice to Dallas**
1. **Choice from Dallas to Buffalo**
2. **Choice from Buffalo to Detroit**
2. **ROBERTS, LARRY**
(Choice from Detroit)
DE, 6-3, 264, Alabama
2. **Choice to Washington**

3. **(A) RATHMAN, TOM**
(Choice from Buffalo)
FB, 6-1, 232, Nebraska
3. **(B) McKYER, TIM**
(Choice from Philadelphia)
CB, 6-0, 174, Texas-Arlington
3. **Choice from Detroit to L.A. Rams**
3. **(C) TAYLOR, JOHN**
WR, 6-1, 185, Delaware State
4. **(A) HALEY, CHARLES**
(Choice from Cleveland via L.A. Rams)
LB, 6-5, 230, James Madison
4. **(B) WALLACE, STEVE**
(Choice from Washington via L.A. Rams)
T, 6-5, 276, Auburn
4. **(C) FAGAN, KEVIN**
DT, 6-3, 260, Miami (Fla.)
4. **Choice to San Diego**
5. **MILLER, PAT**
(Choice from Dallas)
LB, 6-1, 220, Florida
6. **Choice to Washington**
6. **GRIFFIN, DON**
(Choice from N.Y. Jets)
FS, 6-0, 176, Middle Tennessee State
7. **Choice to New England**
8. **(A) POPP, JIM**
(Choice from Philadelphia)
TE, 6-5, 239, Vanderbilt
8. **(B) SNIPES, ROOSEVELT**
('85 Supplemental Draft)
RB, 5-9, 175, Florida State
9. **CHERRY, TONY**
RB, 5-7, 187, Oregon
10. **(A) STINSON, ELLISTON**
WR, 5-10, 175, Rice
10. **(B) HALLMAN, HAROLD**
(Choice from Washington)
NG, 5-11, 234, Auburn
11. **Choice to San Diego**
12. **Choice to Tampa Bay**

1987
(Drafted 22nd)
1. **(A) BARTON, HARRIS**
T, 6-3, 260, North Carolina
1. **(B) FLAGLER, TERRENCE**
(Choice from Washington)
RB, 6-0, 200, Clemson
2. **BREGEL, JEFF**
(Choice from Philadelphia)
G, 6-4, 280, Southern California
2. **Choice to Tampa Bay**
3. **Choice to Buffalo**
4. **Choice to Tampa Bay**
5. **JOKISCH, PAUL**
WR, 6-7, 230, Michigan
6. **WHITE, BOB**
LB, 6-2, 246, Penn State
7. **DeLINE, STEVE**
K, 5-11, 180, Colorado State
8. **GRAYSON, DAVID**
LB, 6-2, 220, Fresno State
9. **SHELLEY, JO NATHAN**
CB, 6-0, 176, Mississippi
10. **PAYE, JOHN**
(Choice from New England via L.A. Raiders)
QB, 6-3, 205, Stanford
11. **Choice to L.A. Raiders from Philadelphia via 49ers**

11. **NICHOLAS, CALVIN**
WR, 6-4, 208, Grambling
12. **Choice to L.A. Raiders**

1988
(Drafted 25th)
1. **Choice to L.A. Raiders**
2. **(A) STUBBS, DANNY**
(Choice from L.A. Raiders)
DE, 6-4, 260, Miami (Fla.)
2. **(B) HOLT, PIERCE**
(Choice from Philadelphia via Tampa Bay)
DE/DT, 6-4, 280, Angelo State
2. **Choice to Tampa Bay**
3. **ROMANOWSKI, BILL**
LB, 6-4, 231, Boston College
4. **HELTON, BARRY**
(Choice from Chicago via L.A. Raiders)
P, 6-3, 205, Colorado
4. **Choice to Tampa Bay**
5. **Choice to N.Y. Jets**
5. **Choice to Buffalo**
6. **Choice to Tampa Bay**
7. **BRYANT, KEVIN**
LB, 6-2, 223, Delaware State
8. **CLARKSON, LARRY**
T, 6-7, 303, Montana
9. **BONNER, BRIAN**
LB, 6-1, 220, Minnesota
10. **FOLEY, TIM**
K, 5-10, 210, Georgia Southern
11. **BROOKS, CHET**
CB, 5-11, 191, Texas A&M
12. **MIRA, JR., GEORGE**
LB, 6-0, 230, Miami (FL)

1989
(Drafted 28th)
1. **DeLONG, KEITH**
LB, 6-2, 235, Tennessee
2. **WALLS, WESLEY**
TE, 6-5, 246, Mississippi
3. **HENDERSON, KEITH**
FB, 6-1, 220, Georgia
4. **BARBER, MIKE**
WR, 5-10, 172, Marshall
5. **(A) JACKSON, JOHNNY**
(Choice from the L.A. Raiders)
CB/S, 6-1, 204, Houston
5. **(B) Choice to L.A. Raiders, plus 49ers' No. 8 (224th overall)**
6. **HENDRICKSON, STEVE**
LB, 6-0, 245, California
7. **Choice to San Diego**
Wes Chandler trade, 1988
8. **Choice to L.A. Raiders for Raiders' No. 5 (122nd overall)**
9. **HARMON, RUDY**
LB, 6-1, 230, LSU
10. **SINCLAIR, ANDY**
C, 6-3, 285, Stanford
11. **(A) BELL, JIM**
(Choice from L.A. Raiders)
RB, 6-0, 205, Boston College
11. **(B) McGEE, NORM**
WR, 6-0, 180, North Dakota
12. **(A) GOSS, ANTONIO**
(Choice from L.A. Raiders, Milt McColl trade, 1988)
LB, 6-4, 228, North Carolina

12. **(B) Choice to L.A. Raiders, plus 49ers' No. 12 in 1990, for Raiders' No.11 (290th overall) in 1989**

1990
(Drafted 28th)
1. **CARTER, DEXTER**
RB, 5-9, 170, Florida State
2. **(A) BROWN, DENNIS**
(Choice from Minnesota through Dallas, 1990 trade with Cowboys that sent RB Terrence Flagler, DE Daniel Stubbs, 49ers' No. 3 (81st) and No. 11 (304th) picks in 1990 to Dallas for Cowboys' No. 2 (47th) and No. 3 (68th) picks in 1990.)
2. **(B) DAVIS, ERIC**
CB, 5-11, 178, Jacksonville State
3. **(A) LEWIS, RONALD**
(Choice from Kansas City through Dallas via above Dallas trade)
WR, 5-11, 173, Florida State
3. **(B) Choice to Dallas via above Dallas trade**
4. ***(A) CALIGUIRE, DEAN**
(Choice from L.A. Raiders, 1990 trade with Raiders that sent 49ers' No. 4 (109th) and No. 5 (137th) picks in 1990 for Raiders' No. 4 (89th) pick in 1990.)
G/C, 6-2, 282, Pittsburgh
4. **(B) Choice to L.A. Raiders via above L.A. trade**
5. **Choice to L.A. Raiders via above L.A. trade**
6. **POLLACK, FRANK**
T/G, 6-4, 277, Northern Arizona
7. **Choice to San Diego, 1988 trade with Chargers for Wes Chandler**
8. **PICKENS, DWIGHT**
WR, 5-10, 170, Fresno State
9. **HAGGINS, ODELL**
NT, 6-2, 271, Florida State
10. **HARRISON, MARTIN**
DE, 6-5, 240, Washington
11. **(A) SHELTON, ANTHONY**
(Choice from Miami, 1990 draft day trade with Dolphins that sent CB Tim McKyer to Miami for Dolphins' No. 11 (289th) pick in 1990 and No. 2 pick in 1991.)
S, 6-1, 195, Tennessee State
11. **(B) Choice to Dallas via above Dallas trade**
12. **Choice to L.A. Raiders, 1989 draft day trade with Raiders that sent 49ers' No. 12B in 1989 for Raiders' No. 11 in 1989. The 49ers selected RB Jim Bell of Boston College.**

Three teams selected ahead of the 49ers, who passed on the original choice of 8th in the round and 89th overall.

1991
(Drafted 26th)
1. **WASHINGTON, TED**
   NT/DE, 6-4, 299, Louisville
2. **(A) WATTERS, RICKY**
   (Choice from Cincinnati)
   RB, 6-1, 212, Notre Dame
2. **Choice to Cincinnati**
2. **(B) JOHNSON, JOHN**
   LB, 6-3, 230, Clemson
3. **Choice to Green Bay**
4. **DONAHUE, MITCH**
   (Choice from Green Bay)
   LB, 6-2, 254, Wyoming
4. **Choice to Cincinnati**
5. **(A) HANKS, MERTON**
   (Choice from Green Bay)
   CB, 6-2, 185, Iowa
5. **(B) BOATSWAIN, HARRY**
   T, 6-4, 295, New Haven
6. **BOWLES, SCOTT**
   T, 6-5, 280, North Texas State
7. **CANLEY, SHELDON**
   RB, 5-9, 195, San Jose State
8. **HARGAIN, TONY**
   WR, 6-0, 188, Oregon
9. **RIDDICK, LOUIS**
   S, 6-2, 217, Pittsburgh
10. **HOLDBROOKS, BYRON**
    NT/DE, 6-5, 280, Alabama
11. **SLAUGHTER, BOBBY**
    WR, 5-11,171, Louisiana Tech
12. **CONFER, CLIFF**
    DE, 6-0, 270, Michigan State

1992
(Drafted 18th)
1. **HALL, DANA**
   S, 6-2, 206, Washington
2. **LEE, AMP**
   RB, 5-11, 200, Florida State
3. **BOLLINGER, BRIAN**
   G, 6-5, 285, North Carolina
4. **THOMAS, MARK**
   DE, 6-5, 259, North Carolina
   State
4. **Choice to Green Bay**
5. **Choice to Green Bay**

6. **Choice to Green Bay**
6. **RUSSELL, DAMIEN**
   (Choice from Pittsburgh)
   S, 6-1, 204, Virginia Tech
7. **Choice to Pittsburgh**
8. **Choice to Pittsburgh from**
   Green Bay
8. **Choice to Pittsburgh**
9. **HAGAN, DARIAN**
   Return Specialist, 5-9, 191,
   Colorado
10. **MAYFIELD, COREY**
    NT, 6-2, 280, Oklahoma
11. **COVINGTON, TOM**
    TE, 6-3, 241, Georgia Tech
12. **LeBOUNTY, MATT**
    DE, 6-4, 254, Oregon

1993
(Drafted 26th)
1. **Choice to Phoenix from**
   Kansas City
1. **Choice to New Orleans from**
   Phoenix
1. **(A) STUBBLEFIELD, DANA**
   (Choice from New Orleans)
   DE, 6-2, 302, Kansas
1. **(B) KELLY, TODD**
   DE, 6-2, 259, Tennessee
2. **Choice to San Diego from L.A.**
   Raiders
2. **HARDY, ADRIAN**
   (Choice from San Diego)
   CB, 5-11, 194, Northwestern
   State
2. **Choice to Green Bay**
2. **Choice to L.A. Raiders from**
   Dallas
3. **Choice to L.A. Raiders from**
   New Orleans
3. **Choice to San Diego**
4. **Choice to San Diego**
5. **SMITH, ARTIE**
   (Choice from Phoenix)
   DE, 6-4, 303, Louisiana Tech
5. **Choice to San Diego**
6. **DALMAN, CHRIS**
   G-C, 6-3, 285, Stanford
7. **WILSON, TROY**

DE, 6-4, 235, Pittsburg State
8. **GRBAC, ELVIS**
   (Choice from Minnesota)
   QB, 6-5, 232, Michigan
8. **Choice to San Diego**

1994
(Drafted 23rd)
1. **(A) YOUNG, BRYANT**
   (Choice from LA Rams)
   DT, 6-2, 276, Notre Dame
1. **Choice to L.A. Rams from San**
   Diego
1. **Choice to Dallas**
1. **(B) FLOYD, WILLIAM**
   (Choice from Dallas)
   FB, 6-1, 242, Florida State
2. **(A) MITCHELL, KEVIN**
   (Choice from Green Bay)
   LB, 6-1, 260, Syracuse
2. **Choice to L.A. Rams**
2. **(B) DRAKEFORD, TYRONNE**
   (Choice from Dallas)
   CB, 5-9, 185, Virginia Tech
3. **Compensatory Choice to**
   Green Bay
3. **(A) BRIEN, DOUG**
   (Compensatory Choice)
   K, 5-11, 177, California
3. **(B) FLEMMING, CORY**
   (Choice from Denver)
   WR, 6-1, 207, Tennessee
3. **Choice to Kansas City**
3. **Choice to Denver from Dallas**
3. **Choice to LA Rams from**
   Philadelphia
4. **Choice to LA Raiders**
5. **Choice to Green Bay from**
   Denver
5. **PETERSON, TONY**
   LB, 6-0, 223, Notre Dame
6. **Choice to Green Bay from San**
   Diego
6. **WOODALL, LEE**
   LB, 6-0, 220, West Chester
6. **Choice to Green Bay from**
   Philadelphia
7. **Choice to Dallas**

1995
(Drafted 30th)
1A. **STOKES, J.J.**
   (Choice from Cleveland)
   WR, 6-4, 217, UCLA
1B. **Choice to Cleveland**
2. **Choice to L.A. Rams**
3. **Choice to Cleveland**
4A. **Choice to Cleveland from**
   Kansas City
4B. **HANSHAW, TIM**
   T/G, 6-5, 300, Brigham Young
5. **Choice to Detroit**
6. **ARMSTRONG, ANTONIO**
   LB, 6-1, 234, Texas A&M
7. **COLEMAN, HERB**
   DE, 6-4, 285, Trinity
   International

1996
(Drafted 23rd)
1. **Choice to Baltimore**
2. **(A) IFEANYI, ISRAEL**
   (Choice from Oakland)
   LB/DE, 6-3, 246, USC
3. **OWENS, TERRELL**
   WR, 6-2, 213, Tenn-Chattanooga
4. **(A) Choice to Oakland**
4. **(B) PRICE, DARYL**
   (Compensatory selection)
   DE, 6-3, 274, Colorado
5. **UWAEZUOKE, IHEANYI**
   WR, 6-2, 195, California
6. **PITTS, STEPHEN**
   RB, 5-10, 192, Penn. State
7. **(A) MANUEL, SEAN**
   TE, 6-2, 245, New Mexico St.
7. **(B) MANUEL, SAM**
   (Compensatory selection)
   LB, 6-2, 235, New Mexico St.

1997
(Drafted 26th)
1. **DRUCKENMILLER, JIM**
   QB, 6-4, 230, Virginia Tech
2. **EDWARDS, MARC**
   (Choice from Philadelphia)
   RB, 5-11, 236, Notre Dame
3. **CLARK, GREG**
   (Choice from Indianapolis)
   TE, 6-2, 262, Stanford

49ers All-Time Roster—1946-1996

-A-
Abramowicz, Danny, WR, Xavier (OH), 1973-74
Albert, Frank, QB, Stanford, 1946-52
Adridge, Ben, HB, Oklahoma State, 1952
Aldridge, Jerry, RB, Angelo State, 1980
Alexander, Kermit, HB, UCLA, 1963-69
Alexander, Mike, WR, Penn State, 1993
Allen, Nate, CB, Texas Southern, 1975
Anderson, Terry, WR, Bethune-Cookman, 1980
Anderson, Tim, S, Ohio State, 1975
Arenas, Joe, HB, Omaha, 1951-57
Asmus, Jim, P, Hawaii, 1987
Atkins, Bill, HB, Auburn, 1958-59
Atkins, Dave, RB, Texas-El Paso, 1973
Audick, Dan, T-G, Hawaii, 1981-82

Ayers, John, G, West Texas State, 1976-86

-B-
Babb, Gene, FB, Austin, 1957-58
Babcock, Harry, E, Georgia, 1953-55
Bahnsen, Ken, FB, North Texas State, 1953
Bahr, Matt, K, Penn State, 1981
Baker, Dave, HB, Oklahoma, 1959-61
Baker, Wayne, DT, BYU, 1975
Balatti, Ed, E, Oakland High (CA), 1946-48
Baldassin, Mike, LB, Washington, 1977-78
Baldwin, John, C, Centenary, 1947
Banaszek, Cas, T, Northwestern, 1967-77
Banducci, Bruno, G, Stanford, 1946-54
Barber, Mike, WR, Marshall, 1989
Barker, Roy, DT, North Carolina, 1996-current

Barnes, Larry, FB, Colorado, 1957
Barnett, Oliver, DL, Kentucky, 1995
Barnes, Tomur, CB, North Texas, 1993
Barrett, Jean, T, Tulsa, 1973-80
Bartolo, Steve, RB, Colorado State, 1988
Barton, Harris, T, North Carolina, 1987-current
Bassi, Dick, G, Santa Clara, 1946-47
Beach, Sanjay, WR, Colorado State, 1991, 93
Beals, Alyn, E, Santa Clara, 1946-51
Beard, Ed, LB, Tennessee, 1965-72
Beasley, Terry, WR, Auburn, 1972-75
Beatty, Ed, C, Mississippi, 1955-56
Beeson, Terry, LB, Kansas, 1982
Beisler, Randy, T, Indiana, 1969-74
Belser, Ceaser, LB, Arkansas AM&N, 1974

Belk, Bill, DE, Maryland State, 1968-74
Benefield, David, LB, CSU Northridge, 1996-current
Benjamin, Guy, QB, Stanford, 1981-83
Bentz, Roman, T, Tulane, 1948
Berry, Rex, HB, BYU, 1951-56
Bettiga, Mike, WR, Humbolt State, 1973
Beverly, Ed, WR, Arizona State, 1973
Black, Stan, DB, Mississippi State, 1977
Blackmore, Richard, CB, Mississippi State, 1983
Blount, Ed, QB, Washington State, 1987
Blue, Forrest, C, Auburn, 1968-74
Board, Dwaine, DE, North Carolina A&T, 1979-87
Boatswain, Harry, T, New Haven, 1991-93
Bollinger, Brian, G, North Carolina, 1992-94

Bono, **Steve,** QB, UCLA, 1989-93
Boone, J.R., HB, Tulsa, 1952
Bosley, Bruce, C-G, West Virginia, 1956-68
Bouza, Matt, WR, California, 1981
Boyd, Elmo, WR, Eastern Kentucky, 1978
Boykin, Greg, FB, Northwestern, 1978
Bradley, Ed, LB, Wake Forest, 1977-78
Braggonier, Dennis, DB, Stanford, 1974
Brandes, John, TE, Cameron, 1993
Brandon, Michael, DE, Florida, 1995-current
Bregel, Jeff, G, USC, 1987-89
Bridewell, Jeff, QB, UC-Davis, 1993
Bristor, John, S. Waynesburg, 1979
Britt, Charlie, HB, Georgia, 1964
Brock, Clyde, T, Utah State, 1963
Brockhaus, Jeff, K, Missouri, 1987
Brodie, John, QB, Stanford, 1957-73
Brohm, Jeff, QB, Louisville, 1996-current
Brooks, Chet, S, Texas A&M, 1988-89
Brown, Dennis, DE, Washington, 1990-current
Brown, Hardy, LB, Tulsa, 1951-56
Brown, Hurlie, S, Miami (FL), 1993
Brown, Pete, C, Georgia Tech, 1953-54
Brown, Ray, G, Arkansas State, 1996-current
Brown, Ray, RB, South Carolina, 1987
Browner, Keith, LB, USC, 1987
Bruce, Gail, E, Washington, 1948-52
Bruer, Bob, TE, Mankato State, 1979-80
Brumfield, Jackson, E, Southern Mississippi, 1954
Bruney, Fred, HB, Ohio State, 1953, 1956
Bryant, Bob, T, Texas Tech, 1946-49
Bryant, Junior, DE, Notre Dame, 1993-current
Buckley, Curtis, S. E. Texas State, 1996-current
Bull, Scott, QB, Arkansas, 1976-78
Bungarda, Ken, T, Missouri, 1980
Bunz, Dan, LB, Long Beach State, 1978-84
Burch, Swift, DE, Temple, 1993
Burke, Don, LB, USC, 1950-54
Burke, Vern, E, Oregon State, 1965
Burns, Mike, DB, USC, 1977
Burt, Jim, NT, Miami (FL), 1989
Butler, John, S, Principia, 1987

-C-

Caldwell, Mike, WR, California, 1995-current
Calhoun, Mike, DT, Notre Dame, 1980
Caliguire, Dean, C, Pittsburgh, 1991
Calvelli, Tony, C, Stanford, 1949
Campbell, Carter, LB, Weber State, 1970
Campbell, Marion, T, Georgia, 1954-55
Campora, Don, T, Pacific, 1950, 1952
Carapella, Al, T, Miami (FL), 1951-55

Carolan, Brett, TE, Washington State, 1994-95
Carpenter, John, T, Michigan, 1949
Carr, Earl, RB, Florida, 1978
Carr, Eddie, HB, Olney High (PA), 1947-49
Carr, Paul, LB, Houston, 1955-58
Carter, Dexter, RB, Florida State, 1990-96
Carter, Michael, NT, SMU, 1984-92
Casanega, Ken, HB, Santa Clara, 1946, 1948
Casey, Bernie, E, Bowling Green, 1961-66
Cason, Jim, HB, LSU, 1948-52, 1954
Cassara, Frank, FB, St. Mary's, 1954
Cathcart, Royal, HB, Santa Barbara State, 1950
Cathcart, Sam, HB, Santa Barbara State, 1949-50, 1952
Cavanaugh, Matt, QB, Pittsburgh, 1983-85
Caveli, Tony, C, Stanford, 1949
Ceresino, Gordy, LB, Stanford, 1979
Cerne, Joe, C, Northwestern, 1965-67
Chandler, Wes, WR, Florida, 1988
Chapple, Jack, LB, Stanford, 1965
Cherry, Tony, RB, Oregon, 1986-87
Childs, Jason, T, North Dakota, 1993
Choma, John, G-C, Virginia, 1981-83
Churchman, Ricky, S, Texas, 1980-81
Clark, Bryan, QB, Michigan State, 1982-83
Clark, Don, G, USC, 1948-49
Clark, Dwight, WR, Clemson, 1979-87
Clark, Mario, CB, Oregon, 1984
Clark, Mike, DE, Florida, 1982
Clark, Monte, T, USC, 1959-61
Cline, Tony, DE, Miami (FL), 1976
Cochran, Mark, T, Baylor, 1987
Cofer, Mike, K, North Carolina State, 1988-93
Colchico, Dan, E, San Jose State, 1960-64, 67
Collett, Elmer, G, San Francisco State, 1967-72
Collie, Bruce, T-G, Texas Arlington, 1985-89, 1992
Collier, Floyd, T, San Jose State, 1948
Collier, Tim, CB, East Texas State, 1982-83
Collins, Glen, DE, Mississippi State, 1987
Collins, Greg, LB, Notre Dame, 1975
Collins, Ray, T, LSU, 1950-52
Comeaux, Darren, LB, Arizona State, 1987
Conklin, Cary, QB, Washington, 1995
Conlee, Gerry, C, St. Mary's, 1946-47
Connell, Mike, P, Cincinnati, 1978
Conner, Clyde, E, Pacific, 1956-63
Connolly, Ted, G, Santa Clara Tulsa, 1954, 1956-62
Cook, Toi, DB, Stanford, 1994
Cooke, Bill, DE, Massachusetts-Amherst, 1976

Cooper, Adrian, TE, Oklahoma, 1996-current
Cooper, Bill, FB, Muskingum, 1961-64
Cooper, Earl, FB-TE, Rice, 1980-85
Cooper, George, LB, Michigan State, 1987
Cordileone, Lou, G-LB, Clemson, 1961
Cornelius, Charles, DB, Bethune-Cookman, 1979-80
Courtney, Matt, S, Idaho State, 1987
Cousineau, Tom, LB, Ohio State, 1986-87
Covington, Tom, TE, Georgia Tech, 1992-93
Cowlings, Al, DE, USC, 1979
Cox, Greg, S, San Jose State, 1988, 1990-91
Cox, James, G, Stanford, 1948
Craig, Roger, FB, Nebraska, 1983-90
Crawford, Derrick, WR, Memphis State, 1986
Cribbs, Joe, RB, Auburn, 1986-87
Crist, Chuck, DB, Penn State, 1978
Cross, Bob, T, Kilgore J.C., 1956-57
Cross, Randy, G-C, UCLA, 1976-88
Crow, John David, HB, Texas A&M, 1965-68
Crowe, Paul, HB, St. Mary's, 1948
Crowell, Otis, T, Hardin-Simmons, 1947
Cullity, Dave, T, Utah, 1989
Cunningham, Doug, RB, Mississippi, 1967-73

-D-

Dahms, Tom, T, San Diego State, 1957
Dalman, Chris, G-C, Stanford, 1993-current
Daniels, Clem, RB, Prarie View, 1968
Daughtery, Bob, HB, Tulsa, 1966-67
Davis, Eric, CB, Jacksonville State, 1990-95
Davis, Kyle, C, Oklahoma, 1978
Davis, Johnny, FB, Alabama, 1981
Davis, Tommy, K, LSU, 1959-69
Dean, Floyd, LB, Florida, 1963-64
Dean, Fred, DE, Louisiana Tech, 1981-85
Dean, Kevin, LB, Texas Christian, 1987
DeBerg, Steve, QB, San Jose State, 1977-80
Deese, Derrick, G, Southern Cal, 1992-current
DeLong, Keith, LB, Tennessee, 1989-93
Dent, Richard, DE, Tennessee State, 1994
Diaz-Infante, David, G, San Jose State, 1993
Dixon, Al, TE, Iowa State, 1984
Dodge, Dedrick, S, Florida State, 1994-current
Doleman, Chris, DE, Pittsburgh, 1996-current
Domres, Marty, QB, Columbia, 1976
Donnelly, George, DB, Illinois, 1965-67
Donohue, Leon, T, San Jose State, 1962-64
Donohue, Mitch, LB, Wyoming, 1991-93

Dove, Eddie, HB, Colorado, 1959-62
Dow, Harley, G, San Jose State, 1950
Dowdle, Mike, LB, Texas, 1963-65
Downing, Tim, DE, Washington State, 1993
Downing, Walt, C-G, Michigan, 1978-83
Downs, Bob, HB, Northwestern, 1962-66
Drake, Joe, NT, Arizona, 1987
Drakeford, Tyronne, DB, Virginia Tech, 1994-current
Dressel, Chris, TE, Stanford, 1987
Dressel, Robert, C, Purdue, 1993
DuBose, Doug, RB, Nebraska, 1987-88
Dugan, Fred, E, Dayton, 1958-59
Duncan, Maury, QB, San Francisco State, 1954-55
Dungy, Tony, DB, Minnesota, 1979
Durdan, Don, HB, Oregon State, 1946-47
Durham, Darius, WR, San Diego State, 1983
Durrette, Michael, G, West Virginia, 1986-87

-E-

Easley, Walt, FB, West Virginia, 1981-82
Edwards, Earl, DT, Wichita, 1969-72
Elam, Cleveland, DE, Tennessee State, 1976-78
Elia, Bruce, LB, Ohio State, 1976-78
Elliott, Charles, T, Oregon, 1948
Elliott, Lenvil, RB, NE Missouri State, 1979-81
Ellison, Riki, LB, USC, 1983-89
Elston, Art, C, South Carolina, 1946-48
Enderle, Dick, G, Minnesota, 1976
Endriss, Al, E, San Francisco State, 1952
Ervins, Rickey, RB, Southern California, 1995
Eshmont, Len, HB, Fordham, 1946-49
Etcheverry, Sam, QB, Denver, 1963
Etienne, LeRoy, LB, Nebraska, 1990
Evans, Kevin, WR, San Jose State, 1993
Evans, Ray, G, Texas Western, 1949-50
Evansen, Paul, G, Oregon State, 1948

-F-

Fagan, Kevin, DE, Miami (FL), 1987-93
Fahnhorst, Jim, LB, Minnesota, 1984-90
Fahnhorst, Keith, T, Minnesota, 1974-87
Faison, Derrick, WR, Howard, 1993
Faryniarz, Brett, LB, San Diego State, 1993
Faylor, John, S, Santa Clara, 1987
Feher, Nick, G, Georgia, 1951-54
Fernandez, Mervyn, WR, San Jose State, 1993
Ferrari, Ron, LB, Illinois, 1982-86
Ferrell, Bob, RB, UCLA, 1976-80
Fisk, Bill, E, USC, 1946-47
Flagler, Terrence, RB, Clemson, 1987-89

Flores, Mike, DE, Louisville, 1995
Floyd, William, FB, Florida State, 1994-current
Forrest, Ed, C, Santa Clara, 1946-47
Foster, Roy, G, Southern Cal, 1991-93
Fountaine, Jamal, DE, Washington, 1995
Francis, Phil, RB, Stanford, 1979-80
Francis, Russ, TE, Oregon, 1982-87
Franceschi, Pete, HB, San Francisco, 1946
Frank, John, TE, Ohio State, 1984-88
Franz, Tracy, G, San Jose State, 1987
Freitas, Jesse, QB, Santa Clara, 1946
Fuller, Jeff, S-LB, Texas A&M, 1984-89
Fuller, John, DB, Lamar Tech, 1968-72

-G-
Gagliano, Bob, QB, Utah State, 1986-87
Gaiters, Bob, HB, New Mexico State, 1962-63
Galiffa, Arnie, QB, West Point, 1954
Galigher, Ed, DT, UCLA, 1977-79
Garlin, Don, HB, USC, 1949-50
Garnett, Scott, NT, Washington, 1985
Garrett, Len, TE, New Mexico Highlands, 1975
Gash, Thane, S, East Tennessee State, 1992
Gavric, Momcilo, K, Belgrade, 1969
Gehrke, Fred, HB, Utah, 1950
Gervais, Rick, S, Stanford, 1981-83
Gilbert, Lewis, TE, Florida, 1980
Gladney, Tony, WR, Nevada-Las Vegas, 1987
Glover, Clyde, DE, Fresno State, 1987
Goad, Paul, FB, Abilene Christian, 1956
Gonsoulin, Austin, DB, Baylor, 1967
Gonzaga, John, T, Mt. Diablo High (CA), 1956-59
Goss, Antonio, LB, North Carolina, 1989, 1991-current
Gossett, Bruce, K, Richmond, 1970-74
Grant, Alan, CB, Stanford, 1992
Gray, Tim, DB, Texas A&M, 1979
Grbac, Elvis, QB, Michigan, 1993-96
Green, Jacob, DE, Texas A&M, 1992
Greenlee, Fritz, LB, Arizona, 1969
Greer, Terry, WR, Alabama State, 1987-89
Gregory, Garlin, G, Louisiana Tech, 1946-47
Grgich, Visco, G, Santa Clara, 1946-52
Griffin, Don, CB, Middle Tennessee State, 1986-93

-H-
Hadley, Ron, LB, Washington, 1987-88
Haley, Charles, LB, James Madison, 1986-91
Hall, Dana, S, Washington, 1992-94
Hall, Darryl, S, Washington, 1995

Hall, Forrest, HB, San Francisco, 1948
Hall, Parker, HB, Mississippi, 1946
Hall, Rhett, DT, University of California, 1994
Hall, Windian, S, Arizona State, 1972-75
Hanks, Merton, CB, Iowa, 1991-current
Hanley, Dick, C, Fresno State, 1947
Hanshaw, Tim, G, Brigham Young, 1995-current
Hantla, Bob, G, Kansas, 1954-55
Hardman, Cedrick, DE, North Texas State, 1970-79
Hardy, Adrian, CB, Northwestern State, 1993-94
Hardy, Andre, FB, St. Mary's, 1987
Hardy, Carroll, HB, Colorado, 1955
Hardy, Edgar, G, Jackson State, 1973
Hardy, Kevin, DT, Notre Dame, 1968
Harkey, Lem, HB, Emporia State, 1955
Harmon, Derrick, RB-KR, Cornell, 1984-86
Harper, Willie, LB, Nebraska, 1973-83
Harris, Joe, LB, Georgia Tech, 1978
Harris, Tony, WR, Toledo, 1971
Harris, Tim, LB-DE, Memphis State, 1991, 92 1994-95
Harrison, Bob, LB, Oklahoma, 1959-61, 1965-67
Harrison, Dennis, DE, Vanderbilt, 1986
Harrison, Kenny, WR, SMU, 1976-78
Harrison, Martin, LB, Washington, 1990-93
Hart, Tom, DE, Morris Brown, 1968-76
Hart, Jeff, T, Oregon State, 1975
Harty, John, DT, Iowa, 1981-83, 86
Hayes, Bob, WR, Florida A&M, 1975
Hays, Harold, LB, Southern Mississippi, 1968-69
Hazeltine, Matt, LB, California, 1955-68
Heller, Ron, TE, Oregon State, 1987-88
Helton, Barry, P, Colorado, 1988-90
Henderson, Keith, FB, Georgia, 1989-92
Henderson, Thomas, LB, Langston, 1980
Hendrickson, Steve, LB, California, 1989
Henke, Ed, E, USC, 1951-52, 1955-60
Henley, Thomas, WR, Stanford, 1987
Herchman, Bill, T, Texas Tech, 1956-59
Hettema, Dave, T, New Mexico, 1967
Hicks, Dwight, S, Michigan, 1979-85
Hill, John, C, Lehigh, 1985
Hillman, Jay, FB, Boston, 1993
Hilton, Scott, LB, Salem College, 1979-80
Hindman, Stan, DE, Mississippi, 1966-71, 1973-74
Hoage, Terry, S, Georgia, 1993
Hobbs, Homer, G, Georgia, 1949-50
Hofer, Paul, RB, Mississippi, 1976-81

Hoffman, Gary, T, Santa Clara, 1987
Hogan, Mike, FB, Tennessee-Chattanooga, 1979
Hogland, Doug, G, Oregon State, 1953-55
Holladay, Bob, HB, Tulsa, 1956-57
Holland, John Robert, CB, Sacramento State, 1993
Hollas, Hugo, DB, Rice, 1974
Holmes, Mike, DB, Texas Southern, 1974-75
Holmoe, Tom, S, BYU, 1983-89
Holt, Pierce, DE, Angelo State, 1988-92
Holzer, Tom, DE, Louisville, 1967
Horn, Bob, LB, Oregon State, 1982-83
Horne, Dick, E, Oregon, 1947
Hoskins, Bob, DT, Wichita State, 1970-75
Howell, Clarence, E, Texas A&M, 1948
Hoyle, Wilson, K, Wake Forest, 1993
Huff, Gary, QB, Florida State, 1980
Huff, Marty, LB, Michigan, 1972
Hughes, Ernie, G, Notre Dame, 1978-80
Hull, Tom, LB, Penn State, 1974
Hunt, Charlie, LB, Florida State, 1973

-I-
Ifeanyi, Israel, DE, Southern California, 1996-current
Isenberger, John, RB, Indiana, 1970-73
Israel, Steve, CB, Pittsburgh, 1995-96

-J-
Jackson, Jim, HB, Western Illinois, 1966-67
Jackson, Johnnie, S, Houston, 1989-92
Jackson, Randy, RB, Wichita, 1973
Jackson, Ricky, LB, LSU, 1994-95
Jackson, Wilbur, RB, Alabama, 1974-79
Jarmolowich, Mike, LB, Maryland, 1993
Jennings, Rick, WR, Maryland, 1977
Jessup, Bill, E, USC, 1951-52, 1954-58
Joelson, Greg, DE, Arizona State, 1991
Johnson, Bill, C, Tyler J.C., 1948-56
Johnson, Charlie, DT, Louisville, 1966-67
Johnson, Charles, DB, Grambling, 1979-80
Johnson, Eric, S, Washington State, 1979
Johnson, Gary, DT, Grambling, 1984-85
Johnson, James, LB, San Diego State, 1987
Johnson, Jim, HB, UCLA, 1961-76
Johnson, John, LB, Clemson, 1991-93
Johnson, John Henry, HB, St. Mary's/Arizona State, 1954-56
Johnson, Kermit, RB, UCLA, 1975-76
Johnson, Leo, WR, Tennessee State, 1969-70
Johnson, Rudy, HB, Nebraska, 1964-65

Johnson, Sammy, RB, North Carolina, 1974-76
Jones, Arrington, FB, Winston Salem, 1981
Jones, Brent, TE, Santa Clara, 1987-current
Jones, Larry, WR, NE Missouri State, 1978
Jordan, Darin, LB, Northeastern, 1991-94
Judie, Ed, LB, Northern Arizona, 1982-83
Jury, Bob, S, Pittsburgh, 1978

-K-
Kammerer, Carl, LB, Pacific, 1961-62
Keeble, Jerry, LB, M innesota, 1987
Keever, Carl, LB, Boise State, 1987
Kelcher, Louie, NT, SMU, 1984
Kelly, Gordon, LB, Georgia, 1960-61
Kelly, Todd, DE, Tennessee, 1993-94
Kelm, Larry, LB, Texas A&M, 1993
Kemp, Jeff, QB, Dartmouth, 1986
Kennedy, Allan, T, Washington State, 1981-84
Kennedy, Sam, LB, San Jose State, 1988
Kenny, Charles, G, San Francisco, 1947
Kilgore, Jon, P, Auburn, 1969
Kilmer, Bill, QB, UCLA, 1961-66
Kimbrough, Elbert, HB, Northwestern, 1962-66
Kirby, Terry, RB, Virginia, 1996-current
Kirk, Randy, LB, San Diego State, 1996-current
Knafelc, Gary, E, Colorado, 1963
Knutson, Steve, G-T, USC, 1978
Kopay, Dave, HB, Washington, 1964-67
Korff, Mark, LB, Florida, 1987
Kovach, Jim, LB, Kentucky, 1985
Kraemer, Eldred, G, Pittsburgh, 1955
Krahl, Jim, DT, Texas Tech, 1980
Kramer, Kent, TE, Minnesota, 1966
Krueger, Charles, DT, Texas A&M, 1959-73
Krueger, Rolf, DE, Texas A&M, 1972-74
Kugler, Pete, DT, Penn State, 1981-83, 1986-90
Kuykendall, Fulton, LB, UCLA, 1985
Kuzman, John, T, Fordham, 1946
Kwalick, Ted, TE, Penn State, 1969-74
Kyles, Troy, WR, Howard, 1992

-L-
LaBounty, Matt, DE, Oregon, 1992-93
Lakes, Roland, DT, Wichita State, 1961-70
Land, Fred, T, LSU, 1948
Land, Mel, DE, Michigan State, 1980
Larson, Bill, TE, Colorado State, 1975
LaRose, Dan, DE, Missouri, 1965
Lash, Jim, WR, Northwestern, 1976
Latimer, Al, CB, Clemson, 1980
Laughlin, Bud, FB, Kansas, 1955
Lawrence, Amos, RB, North Carolina, 1981-82
Lawson, Steve, G, Kansas, 1976
LeBounty, Matt, DE, Oregon, 1992-93
LeCount, Terry, WR, Florida, 1978

Ledyard, Hal, QB, UT Chattanooga, 1953

Lee, Amp, RB, Florida State, 1992-93

Lee, Dwight, RB, Michigan State, 1968

Lee, Mark, CB, Washington, 1991

Leonard, Jim, C, Santa Clara, 1985

Leonard, Tony, CB, Virginia Union, 1976

Leopold, Bobby, LB, Notre Dame, 1980-83

Lewis, Eddie, DB, Kansas, 1976-79

Lewis, Gary, FB, Arizona State, 1964-69

Lewis, Kevin, CB, Northwestern State, 1991-92

Lewis, Ron, WR, Florida State, 1990-92

Lilly, Kevin, NT, Tulsa, 1988-89

Lillywhite, Verl, HB, USC, 1948-51

Lind, Mike, FB, Notre Dame, 1963-64

Lindstrom, Chris, DT, Boston College, 1983

Lisbon, Don, HB, Bowling Green, 1963-64

Liter, Greg, DE, Iowa State, 1987

Livingston, Howie, HB, Fullerton J.C., 1950

Lockett, J.W., RB, Central (Oklahoma) State, 1961

Logan, Marc, RB, Kentucky, 1992-94

Long, Tim, C, Memphis State, 1987

Looney, Jim, LB, Purdue, 1981

Lopasky, Bill, G, West Virginia, 1961

Lott, Ronnie, CB, USC, 1981-90

Loville, Derek, RB, Oregon, 1994-96

Loyd, Alex, E, Oklahoma State, 1950

Luna, Bob, HB, Alabama, 1955

Lyles, Lenny, HB, Louisville, 1959-60

Lynn, Anthony, RB, Texas Tech, 1996-current

-M-

MacAfee, Ken, TE, Notre Dame, 1978-79

Macauley, John, OL, Stanford, 1984

Mackey, Dee, TE, East Texas State, 1960

Maderos, George, HB, Chico State, 1955-56

Magac, Mike, G, Missouri, 1960-64

Maloney, Norm, E, Purdue, 1948-49

Manley, Joe, LB, Mississippi State, 1953

Mann, Charles, DE, Nevada, 1994

Manuel, Sean, TE, New Mexico State, 1996-current

Margerum, Ken, WR, Stanford, 1986-87

Martin, Bob, LB, Nebraska, 1979

Martin, Derrick, LB, San Jose State, 1987

Martin, Saladin, DB, San Diego State, 1981

Masini, Leonard, FB, Fresno State, 1947-48

Mason, Lindsey, T, Kansas, 1982

Matheson, Riley, G-LB, Texas Western, 1948

Mathews, Ned, HB, UCLA, 1946-47

Matthews, Clay, E, Georgia Tech, 1950, 1953-55

Matuszak, Marv, LB, Tulsa, 1957-58

Maurer, Andy, G, Oregon, 1976

McAlister, Ken, LB-S, San Francisco, 1983

McCaffrey, Ed, WR, Stanford, 1994

McCann, Jim, P, Arizona State, 1971-72

McColl, Milt, LB, Stanford, 1981-87

McCormick, Dave, T, LSU, 1966

McCormick, Tom, HB, Pacific, 1956

McCormick, Walt, C, USC, 1948

McCray, Willie, DE, Troy State, 1978

McDonald, Quintus, LB, Penn State, 1993

McDonald, Tim, S, Southern Cal, 1993-current

McElhenny, Hugh, HB, Washington, 1952-60

McFarland, Kay, HB, Colorado State, 1962-68

McGee, Willie, WR, Alcorn A&M, 1976

McGill, Ralph, CB, Tulsa, 1972-76

McGruder, Michael, CB, Kent State, 1992-93

McGuire, Steve, RB, Miami (FL), 1993

McHan, Lamar, QB, Arkansas, 1963

McIlhenny, Don, HB, SMU, 1961

McIntyre, Guy, G, Georgia, 1984-93

McIntyre, Jeff, LB, Arizona State, 1979

McKenzie, Reggie, LB, Tennessee, 1992

McKoy, Billy, LB, Purdue, 1974

McKyer, Tim, CB, Texas-Arlington, 1986-89

McLemore, Dana, KR-CB, Hawaii, 1982-87

McNeil, Clifton, E, Grambling, 1968-69

Mellekas, John, C, Arizona, 1962

Mellus, John, T, Villanova, 1946

Melville, Dan, P, California, 1979

Mertens, Jerry, HB, Drake, 1958-65

Messer, Dale, HB, Fresno State, 1961-65

Meyers, Bob, FB, Stanford, 1952

Michalik, Art, G, St. Ambrose, 1953-54

Mike, Bob, T, UCLA, 1948-49

Mike-Mayer, Steve, K, Maryland, 1975-76

Mikolas, Doug, NT, Portland State, 1987

Miles, Searcy, QB, San Jose State, 1954-56

Millen, Matt, LB, Penn State, 1990

Miller, Clark, E, Utah State, 1962-68

Miller, Hal, T, Georgia Tech, 1953

Miller, Jim, P, Mississippi, 1980-82

Miller, Johnny, G, Livingston, 1977-78

Milstead, Rod, G, Delaware State, 1994-current

Mira, George, QB, Miami (FL), 1964-68

Mitchell, Dale, LB, USC, 1976

Mitchell, Kevin, LB, Syracuse, 1994-current

Mitchell, Tom, TE, Bucknell, 1974-77

Mixon, Bill, HB, Georgia, 1953-54

Moegle, Dick, HB, Rice, 1955-59

Mojsiejenko, Ralf, P, Michigan State, 1991

Momsen, Bob, G, Ohio State, 1952

Monachino, Jim, HB, California, 1951

Monds, Wonder, DB, Nebraska, 1978

Monroe, Carl, RB-KR, Utah, 1983-87

Montana, Joe, QB, Notre Dame, 1979-92

Montgomery, Blanchard, LB, UCLA, 1983-84

Moore, Dean, LB, Iowa, 1978

Moore, Eugene, RB, Occidental, 1969

Moore, Jeff, RB, Jackson State, 1982-83

Moore, Manfred, RB, USC, 1974-75

Morgan, Joe, T, Southern Mississippi, 1949

Morgan, Melvin, DB, Mississippi Valley, 1979-80

Moroski, Mike, QB, UC Davis, 1986

Morrall, Earl, QB, Michigan State, 1956

Morris, Dennit, LB, Oklahoma, 1958

Morris, George, C, Georgia Tech, 1956

Morrison, Dennis, QB, Kansas State, 1974

Morton, Dave, LB, UCLA, 1979

Morton, John, LB, Texas Christian, 1953

Morze, Frank, C, Boston College, 1957-61

Moss, Anthony, LB, Florida State, 1993

Moten, Gary, LB, SMU, 1983

Mott, Joe, LB, Iowa, 1993

Mudd, Howard, G, Hillsdale, 1964-69

Musgrave, Bill, QB, Oregon, 1991-94

Myers, Chip, E, NW Oklahoma, 1967

-N-

Nehemiah, Renaldo, WR, Maryland, 1982-84

Neville, Tom, Fresno State, 1991

Nicholas, Calvin, WR, Grambling, 1988

Nichols, Mark, LB, Colorado State, 1978

Nicholson, Jim, T, Michigan State, 1981

Nix, Jack, E, USC, 1950

Nixon, Tory, San Diego State, 1985-88

Nomellini, Leo, T, Minnesota, 1950-63

Norberg, Hank, E, Stanford, 1946-47

Nordquist, Mark, G, Pacific, 1976

Norton, Jim, T, Washington, 1965-66

Norton, Ken Jr., LB, UCLA, 1994-current

Norton, Ray, HB, San Jose State, 1960-61

Nunley, Frank, LB, Michigan, 1967-76

-O-

Oates, Bart, C, Brigham Young, 1994-95

Obradovich, Jim, TE, USC, 1976

Odom, Rick, DB, USC, 1978

O'Donahue, Pat, E, Wisconsin, 1952

Olerich, Dave, E, San Francisco, 1967-68, 1972-73

Olssen, Lance, T, Purdue, 1968-69

Orosz, Tom, P, Ohio State, 1983

Osborne, Clancy, LB, Arizona State, 1959-60

Owen, Tom, QB, Wichita State, 1974-75

Owens, James, WR, UCLA, 1979-80

Owens, R.C., HB, College of Idaho, 1957-61

Owens, Terrell, WR, Tenn-Chattanooga, 1996-current

-P-

Pace, Jim, HB, Michigan, 1958

Palatella, Lou, G, Pittsburgh, 1955-58

Paris, Bubba, T, Michigan, 1982-89

Parker, Don, G, Virginia, 1967

Parks, Dave, E, Texas Tech, 1964-67

Parks, Limbo, G, Arkansas, 1987

Parrish, James, T, Temple, 1993

Parsons, Earle, HB, USC, 1946-47

Patera, Dennis, K, BYU, 1968

Patterson, Reno, DE, Bethune-Cookman, 1987

Patton, Ricky, RB, Jackson State, 1980-82

Pavlich, Chuck, G, Muskegon High (MI), 1946

Peery, Ryan, DE, California, 1993

Peets, Brian, TE, Pacific, 1981

Penchion, Bob, T, Alcorn A&M, 1974-75

Peoples, Woody, G, Grambling, 1968-77

Perry, Joe, FB, Compton J.C., 1948-60, 1963

Perry, Scott, S, Williams, 1980

Peterson, Anthony, LB, Notre Dame, 1994-current

Phillips, Mel, DB, North Carolina A&T, 1966-76

Pillers, Lawrence, DE, Alcorn A&M, 1980-84

Pine, Ed, LB, Utah, 1962-64

Plummer, Gary, LB, California, 1994-current

Plunkett, Jim, QB, Stanford, 1976-77

Pollack, Frank, T-G, Northern Arizona, 1990-91, 1994-current

Pollard, Darryl, CB, Weber State, 1987-91

Poole, Bob, E, Clemson, 1964-65

Pope, Marquez, CB, Fresno State, 1995-current

Popson, Ted, TE, Portland State, 1994-96

Powell, Charles, E, San Diego High (CA), 1952-53, 1955-57

Powers, Jim, HB, USC, 1950-53

Price, Daryl, DE, Colorado, 1996-current

Prokop, Joe, P, Cal Poly Pomona, 1991

Puddy, Harold, T, Oregon, 1948

Puki, Craig, LB, Tennessee, 1980-81

Putzier, Rollin, LB, Iowa State, 1989

-Q-

Quillan, Fred, C, Oregon, 1978-87

Quilter, Chuck, T, Tyler J.C., 1949

-R-

Raines, Mike, DT, Alabama, 1974

Ramson, Eason, TE, Washington State, 1979-83

Randle, Sonny, E, Virginia, 1967
Randolph, Alvin, DB, Iowa, 1966-70, 1974
Rasley, Rocky, G, Oregon State, 1976
Rathman, Tom, FB, Nebraska, 1986-93
Reach, Kevin, G, Utah, 1987
Reed, Joe, QB, Mississippi State, 1972-74
Reese, Archie, DE, Grambling, 1978-81
Reid, Bill, C, Stanford, 1975
Remington, Bill, C, Washington State, 1946
Renfro, Dick, FB, Washington State, 1946
Reynolds, Jack, LB, Tennessee, 1981-84
Rhodes, Bruce, DB, San Francisco State, 1976
Rhodes, Ray, CB, Tulsa, 1980
Rice, Jerry, WR, Mississippi Valley State, 1985-current
Richardson, Mike, CB, Arizona State, 1989
Ridge, Elston, DE, Nevada-Reno, 1987
Ridlon, Jim, HB, Syracuse, 1957-62
Riley, Preston, WR, Memphis State, 1970-72
Ring, Bill, RB, BYU, 1981-86
Rivera, Steve, WR, California, 1976
Roberson, Vern, DB, Grambling, 1978
Roberts, C.R., FB, USC, 1959-62
Roberts, Larry, DE, Alabama, 1986-93
Robinson, Jimmy, WR, Georgia Tech, 1980
Robnett, Ed, HB, Texas Tech, 1947
Rock, Walter, T, Maryland, 1963-67
Rodgers, Del, RB, Utah, 1987-88
Rogers, Doug, DE, Stanford, 1986
Rohde, Len, T, Utah State, 1960-74
Romanowski, Bill, LB, Boston College, 1988-93
Roskie, Ken, FB, South Carolina, 1946
Rubke, Karl, C, USC, 1957-60, 1962-63, 1965
Rucka, Leo, C, Rice, 1956
Runager, Max, P, South Carolina, 1984-87
Russell, Damien, S, Virginia Tech, 1993

-S-
Sabuco, Tino, C, San Francisco, 1949
Sagely, Floyd, E, Arkansas, 1954-56
Salata, Paul, E, USC, 1949-50
Sanders, Deion, CB, Florida State, 1994
Sandifer, Bill, DT, UCLA, 1974-76
Sandifer, Dan, HB, LSU, 1950
Sapolu, Jesse, G, Hawaii, 1983-96
Sardisco, Tony, G, Tulane, 1956
Satterfield, Alf, T, Vanderbilt, 1947
Saunders, John, DB, Toledo, 1974-75
Schabarum, Pete, HB, California, 1951, 1953-54
Schiechl, John, C, Santa Clara, 1947
Schmidt, Henry, T, USC/Trinity (TX), 1959-60

Scrafford, Kirk, T, Montana, 1995-current
Schreiber, Larry, RB, Tennessee Tech, 1971-75
Scoggins, Eric, LB, USC, 1982
Scotti, Ben, HB, Maryland, 1984
Scrafford, Kurt, T, Montana, 1995
Seabron, Thomas, LB, Michigan, 1979-80
Seal, Paul, TE, Michigan, 1977-79
Seay, Mark, WR, Cal State-Long Beach, 1992-93
Sharkey, Ed, G, Duke/Nevada-Reno, 1955-56
Shaw, Charles, G, Oklahoma State, 1950
Shell, Todd, LB, BYU, 1984-87
Shelley, Jo Nathan, CB, Mississippi, 1987
Sheriff, Stan, LB, Cal Poly-SLO, 1956-57
Sherrard, Mike, WR, UCLA, 1989-92
Shields, Billy, T, Georgia Tech, 1984
Shoener, Hal, E, Iowa, 1948-50
Shumann, Mike, R, Florida State, 1978-79, 1981
Shumon, Ron, LB, Wichita State, 1979
Sieminski, Charlie, T, Penn State, 1963-65
Siglar, Ricky, G-T, San Jose State, 1990
Silas, Sam, DE, Southern Illinois, 1969-70
Simpson, Mike, DB, Houston, 1970-72
Simpson, O.J., RB, USC, 1978-79
Singleton, Nate, WR, Grambling, 1993-current
Singleton, Ron, T, Grambling, 1977-80
Sitko, Emil, HB, Notre Dame, 1950
Skaugstad, Daryle, DT, California, 1983
Smith, Artie, DE, Louisiana Tech, 1993-94
Smith, Charles, E, Abilene Christian, 1956
Smith, Ernie, HB, Compton J.C., 1955-56
Smith, Frankie, CB, Baylor, 1996-current
Smith, George, C, California, 1947
Smith, J.D., HB, North Carolina A&T, 1956-64
Smith, Jerry, G, Wisconsin, 1952-53
Smith, Noland, RB, Tennessee State, 1969
Smith, Steve, E, Michigan, 1966-67
Snead, Norman, QB, Wake Forest, 1974-75
Sniadecki, Jim, LB, Indiana, 1969-73
Solomon, Freddie, WR, Tampa, 1978-85
Soltau, Gordy, E, Minnesota, 1950-58
Sparks, Dave, G, South Carolina, 1951
Spence, Julian, HB, Sam Houston, 1947
Spurrier, Steve, QB, Florida, 1967-75
Standlee, Norm, FB, Stanford, 1946-52
St. Clair, Bob, T, San Francisco-Tulsa, 1953-64
Steptoe, Jack, WR, Utah, 1978

Stevens, Mark, QB, Utah, 1987
Stewart, Andrew, DE, Cincinnati, 1993
Stickles, Monty, E, Notre Dame, 1960-67
Stidham, Howard, LB, Tennessee Tech, 1977
Stits, Bill, HB, UCLA, 1957-58
Stokes, J.J., WR, UCLA, 1995-current
Stolhandske, Tom, LB, Texas, 1955
Stover, Jeff, DE, Oregon, 1982-88
Strickland, Bishop, FB, South Carolina, 1951
Strong, Jim, RB, Houston, 1970
Strzykalski, John, HB, Marquette, 1946-52
Stubblefield, Dana, DE, Kansas, 1993-current
Stubbs, Daniel, DE, Miami (FL), 1988-89
Stuckey, Jim, DE, Clemson, 1980-85
Sullivan, Bob, HB, Holy Cross, 1948
Sullivan, John, S, California, 1987
Sullivan, Kent, P, Cal-Lutheran
Susoeff, Nick, E, Washington State, 1946-49
Sutro, John, T, San Jose State, 1962
Swinford, Wayne, DB, Georgia, 1965-67
Sydney, Harry, FB, Kansas, 1987-91

-T-
Tamm, Ralph, G-C, West Chester, 1992-94
Tanner, Hamp, T, Georgia, 1951
Tausch, Terry, G, Texas, 1989
Tautolo, Terry, LB, UCLA, 1980-81
Taylor, Brian, S, Oregon State, 1993
Taylor, Bruce, CB, Boston U., 1970-77
Taylor, John, WR, Delaware State, 1987-95
Taylor, Roosevelt, S, Grambling, 1969-71
Teresa, Tony, HB, San Jose State, 1958
Thomas, Aaron, E, Oregon State, 1961
Thomas, Chris, WR, Cal Poly-SLO, 1995
Thomas, Chuck, C, Oklahoma, 1987-92
Thomas, Jimmy, RB, Texas-Arlington, 1969-73
Thomas, John, T, Pacific, 1958-67
Thomas, Lynn, DB, Pittsburgh, 1981-82
Thomas, Mark, DE, North Carolina State, 1992-94
Thompson, Tommy, P, Oregon, 1995-current
Thornton, Rupe, G, Santa Clara, 1946-47
Threadgill, Bruce, S, Mississippi State, 1978
Tidwell, Billy, HB, Texas A&M, 1954
Tillman, Spencer, RB, Oklahoma, 1989-91
Times, Ken, DT, Southern (LA), 1980
Titchenal, Bob, E, San Jose State, 1946
Tittle, Y.A., QB, LSU, 1951-60
Toneff, Bob, T, Notre Dame, 1952, 1954-59
Trimble, Wayne, DB, Alabama, 1967

Tubbs, Jerry, LB, Oklahoma, 1958-59
Tucker, Bill, RB, Tennessee A&I, 1967-70
Tuiasosopo, Manu, DT, UCLA, 1984-86
Turner, Keena, LB, Purdue, 1980-90
Turner, Odessa, WR, Northwestern State, 1992-93
Tyler, Wendell, RB, UCLA, 1983-86

-U-
Uwaezuoke, Iheanyi, WR, California, 1996-current

-V-
Van Doren, Bob, E, USC, 1953
Vanderbundt, Skip, LB, Oregon, State, 1969-77
Varajon, Mike, FB, Toledo, 1987
Vardell, Tommy, RB, Stanford, 1996
Vaughan, Ruben, DT, Colorado, 1979
Vaught, Ted, E, Texas Christian, 1953
Veris, Garin, DE, Stanford, 1992
Vetrano, Joe, HB, Southern Mississippi, 1946-49
Vincent, Ted, DT, Wichita State, 1979-80
Visger, George, DT, Colorado, 1980
Vollenweider, Jim, FB, Miami (FL), 1962-63

-W-
Wagner, Lowell, HB, USC, 1949-53, 1955
Walker, Adam, RB, Pittsburgh, 1992-95
Walker, Elliott, RB, Pittsburgh, 1978
Walker, Val Joe, HB, SMU, 1957
Wallace, Bev, QB, Compton J.C., 1947-49
Wallace, Steve, T, Auburn, 1986-96
Walls, Wesley, TE, Mississippi, 1989-93
Walter, Michael, LB, Oregon, 1984-93
Washington, Chris, LB, Iowa State, 1989
Washington, Dave, LB, Alcorn A&M, 1975-76
Washington, Gene, WR, Stanford, 1969-76
Washington, Ted, NT-DE, Louisville, 1991-93
Washington, Tim, CB, Fresno State, 1982
Washington, Vic, RB, Wyoming, 1971-73
Waters, Bob, QB, Presbyterian, 1960-64
Watson, John, T, Oklahoma, 1971-76
Watters, Ricky, RB, Notre Dame, 1991-94
Waymer, Dave, DB, Notre Dame, 1990-91
Webb, Jimmy, DT, Mississippi State, 1975-80
Wells, Mike, TE, San Diego State, 1987
Wersching, Ray, K, California, 1977-87
West, Robert, WR, San Diego State, 1974

White, Bob, HB, Stanford, 1951-52
Whitmore, David, S, Stephen F. Austin, 1991-92
Wilcox, Dave, LB, Oregon, 1964-74
Wilkerson, Jerry, DE, Oregon State, 1980
Wilkins, David, LB, Eastern Kentucky, 1992-93
Wilkins, Jeff, K, Youngstown State, 1995-96
Willard, Ken, FB, North Carolina, 1965-73
Wilks, Greg, LB, Montana State, 1987
Williams, Alfred, DE, Colorado, 1995
Williams, Dave, RB, Colorado, 1977
Williams, Delvin, RB, Kansas, 1974-77
Williams, Gerard, DB, Langston, 1979-80
Williams, Herb, CB, Southern (LA), 1980

Williams, Howie, HB, Howard, 1963
Williams, James, CB, Fresno State, 1996
Williams, Jamie, TE, Nebraska, 1989-93
Williams, Joel, C, Texas, 1948
Williams, John, HB, USC, 1954
Williams, Newton, RB, Arizona State, 1982
Williams, Roy, T, Pacific, 1958-64
Williams, Vince, FB, Oregon, 1982-83
Williamson, Carlton, S, Pittsburgh, 1981-87
Willis, Jamal, RB, Brigham Young, 1995-current
Wilmsmeyer, Klaus, P, Louisville, 1992-94
Wilson, Billy, E, San Jose State, 1951-60
Wilson, Jerry, LB, Auburn, 1960
Wilson, Jim, G, Georgia, 1965-66
Wilson, Karl, DL, LSU, 1993

Wilson, Mike, WR, Washington State, 1981-89
Wilson, Troy, DE, Pittsburg State
Wondolowski, Bill, WR, Eastern Montana, 1969
Woodall, Lee, LB, West Chester, 1994-current
Woods, Don, RB, New Mexico, 1980
Woodson, Abe, HB, Illinois, 1958-64
Woudenberg, John, T, Denver, 1946-49
Wright, Eric, CB, Missouri, 1981-90

-Y-
Yonamine, Wally, HB, Farrington High (HI), 1947
Young, Bryant, DT, Notre Dame, 1994-current
Young, Charle, TE, USC, 1980-82
Young, Steve, QB, BYU, 1987-current

Youngelman, Sid, T, Alabama, 1955
Yowarsky, Walt, C, Kentucky, 1958

-Z-
Zamlynsky, Zigmond, HB, Villanova, 1946
Zendejas, Tony, K, Nevada, 1995

49ers All-Time Coaches

Frank C. (Frankie) Albert (Stanford) Head Coach—1956-58 Assistant—1955
Ed Alsman (Washington) Assistant—1976-77
Bill Atkins (Auburn) Assistant—1976-77
Jerry Attaway (Cal State-Sacramento) Assistant—1983-current
Cas Banaszek (Northwestern) Assistant—1981
Michael Barnes (New York-Cortland) Assistant—1994-current
Ed Beard (Tennessee) Assistant—1974-78
Phil Bengston (Minnesota) Assistant—1951-58
Dwaine Board (North Carolina A&T) Assistant—1990-current
Rick Brooks (Oregon State) Assistant—1975
Jimmy Carr (Morris Harvey) Assistant—1978
Pete Carroll (University of the Pacific) Assistant—1995-96
Matt Cavanaugh (Pittsburgh) Assistant—1996
Jack Christiansen (Colorado State) Head Coach—1963-67 Assistant—1959-63
Monte Clark (Southern Cal) Head Coach—1976
Dan Colchico (San Jose State) Assistant—1967
Bruce Coslet (Pacific) Assistant—1980
Neal Dahlen (San Jose State) Assistant—1979-95
Jim David (Colorado State) Assistant—1964-66
Mark Duncan (Denver) Assistant—1955-62
Dick Enright (Southern Cal) Assistant—1976-77
Lew Erber (Montana State) Assistant—1975
Eddie Erdelatz (St. Mary's) Assistant—1948-49
Jeff Fisher (Southern California) Assistant—1992-93
Chet Franklin (Utah) Assistant—1971-74
Frank Gansz (Navy) Assistant—1978

Doug Gerhart (Occidental) Assistant—1976-77
Mike Giddings (California) Assistant—1968-73
Dennis Green (Iowa) Assistant—1979 & 1986-88
Paul Hackett (UC Davis) Assistant—1983-85
Tommy Hart (Morris Brown) Assistant—1983-91
Norb Hecker (Baldwin-Wallace) Assistant—1979-86
Don Heinrich (Washington) Assistant—1971-75
Howard W. (Red) Hickey (Arkansas) Head Coach—1959-63 Assistant—1955-58
Bob Hollway (Michigan) Assistant—1975
Mike Holmgren (Southern Cal) Assistant—1986-91
Tom Holmoe (Brigham Young) Assistant—1994-95
Mike Holovak (Boston College) Assistant—1969
Ed Hughes (Tulsa) Assistant—1968-70
Carl Jackson (Prairie View A&M) Assistant—1992-96
Milt Jackson (Tulsa) Assistant—1980-82
Bill Johnson (Tyler J.C.) Assistant—1955-67
Larry Kirksey (Eastern Kentucky) Assistant—1994-current
Gregg Knapp (Sacramento State) Assistant—1995-current
Gary Kubiak (Texas A&M) Assistant—1994
Al Lavan (Colorado State) Assistant—1989-90
Jim Lawson (Stanford) Assistant—1946-54
Earl Leggett (LSU) Assistant—1978
Sherman Lewis (Michigan State) Assistant—1983-91
Steve Little (Iowa State) Assistant—1993
Alan Lowry (Texas) Assistant—1992
Lynn, Johnny (UCLA) Assistant—1996
John Marshall (Washington State) Assistant—1989-current

Billie Matthews (Southern) Assistant—1979-82
Pete McCulley (Louisiana Tech) Head Coach—1978
Bobb McKittrick (Oregon State) Assistant—1979-current
Bill McPherson (Santa Clara) Assistant—1979-current
Ken Meyer (Denison) Head Coach—1977 Assistant—1968
Burnie Miller (Wofford) Assistant—1970
Howard Mudd (Hillsdale) Assistant—1977
Jack Myers (UCLA) Assistant—1963
Dick Nolan (Maryland) Head Coach—1968-75
Fred O'Connor (East Stroudsburg State) Head Coach—1978 Assistant—1978
Brian Pariani (UCLA) Assistant—1992-94
Bo Pelini (Ohio State) Assistant—1994-96
Joe Perry (Compton J.C.) Assistant—1968-69
Floyd Peters (San Francisco State) Assistant—1976-77
Dan Radakovich (Penn State) Assistant—1978
Jimmy Raye (Michigan State) Assistant—1977
Ray Rhodes (Tulsa) Assistant—1981-91, 1994
Al Ruffo (Santa Clara) Assistant—1946-47
Doug Scovil (Pacific) Assistant—1970-75
George Seifert (Utah) Head Coach—1989-96 Assistant—1980-88
Mike Shanahan (Eastern Illinois) Assistant—1992-94
Bob Shaw (Ohio State) Assistant—1959
Lawrence T. (Buck) Shaw (Notre Dame) Head Coach—1946-54
Ray Sherman (Fresno State) Assistant—1991-93
Jim Shofner (TCU) Assistant—1967-73 &1977

Mike Solari (San Diego State) Assistant—1992-96
Jim Spavital (Oklahoma State) Assistant—1976-77
Dick Stanfel (San Francisco) Assistant—1971-75
Les Steckel (Kansas) Assistant—1978
George Stewart (Arkansas) Assistant—1996-current
Lynn Stiles (Utah) Assistant—1987-91
Norman P. (Red) Strader (St. Mary's) Head Coach—1955 Assistant—1952
Chuck Studley (Illinois) Assistant—1979-82
Chuck Taylor (Stanford) Assistant—1950
Y.A. Tittle (LSU) Assistant—1965-69
Marc Trestman (Minnesota) Assistant—1995-96
Al Vermeil (Utah State) Assistant—1979-82
Joe Vetrano (Southern Mississippi) Assistant—1953-56
Fred von Appen (Linfield) Assistant—1983-88
Dick Voris (San Jose State) Assistant—1963-67
Bill Walsh (San Jose State) Head Coach—1979-88 Assistant—1996
Mike White (California) Assistant—1978-79
Billy Wilson (San Jose State) Assistant—1961-62,1964-67, 1980
Paul Wiggin (Stanford) Assistant—1968-74
Eric Wright (Missouri) Assistant—1991-93
Sam Wyche (Furman) Assistant—1979-82
Bob Zeman (Wisconsin) Assistant—1989-93
Ernie Zwahlen (Oregon State) Assistant—1968-70

49ers Year-By-Year Scores— All-America Football Conference

1946 (9-5)

Lawrence T. Shaw, Coach

L	7	New York Yankees/S-8	21
W	21	Miami Seahawks/S-15	14
W	32	Brooklyn Dodgers/S-22	13
L	7	At Chicago Rockets/S-29	21
W	34	At Miami Seahawks/O-7	7
W	23	At Los Angeles Dons/O-12	14
L	14	At Buffalo Bills/O-18	17
W	34	At Cleveland Browns/O-27	20
W	27	Buffalo Bills/N-2	14
L	7	Cleveland Browns/N-10	14
L	9	At New York Yankees/N-17	10
W	30	At Brooklyn Dodgers/N-24	14
W	14	Chicago Rockets/N-30	0
W	48	Los Angeles Dons/D-8	7
	307		189

1947 (8-4-2)

Lawrence T. Shaw, Coach

W	23	Brooklyn Dodgers/A-31	7
W	17	Los Angeles Dons/S-7	14
W	14	Baltimore Colts/S-14	7
L	16	New York Yankees/S-21	21
W	41	At Buffalo Bills/S-28	24
T	28	At Baltimore Colts/O-5	28
W	42	Chicago Rockets/O-12	28
L	7	Cleveland Browns/O-26	14
W	26	At Los Angeles Dons/N-2	16
L	16	At New York Yankees/N-9	24
L	14	At Cleveland Browns/N-16	37
W	41	At Chicago Rockets/N-21	16
W	21	At Brooklyn Dodgers/N-27	7
T	21	Buffalo Bills/D-7	21
	327		264

1948 (12-2)

Lawrence T. Shaw, Coach

W	35	Buffalo Bills/A-29	14
W	36	Brooklyn Dodgers/S-5	20
W	41	New York Yankees/S-12	0
W	36	Los Angeles Dons/S-19	14
W	38	At Buffalo Bills/S-26	28
W	31	At Chicago Rockets/O-1	14
W	56	At Baltimore Colts/O-10	14
W	21	At New York Yankees/O-17	7
W	21	Baltimore Colts/O-24	10
W	44	Chicago Rockets/N-7	21
L	7	At Cleveland Browns/N-14	14
W	63	At Brooklyn Dodgers/N-21	40
L	28	Cleveland Browns/N-28	31
W	38	At Los Angeles Dons/D-5	21
	495		248

1949 (9-3/10-4)

Lawrence T. Shaw, Coach

W	31	Baltimore Colts/A-28	17
W	42	Chicago Hornets/S-4	7
W	42	Los Angeles Dons/S-18	14
L	17	At Buffalo Bills/S-25	28
W	42	At Chicago Hornets/S-30	24
W	56	Cleveland Browns/O-9	28
W	51	Buffalo Bills/O-16	7
L	3	At New York Yankees/O-23	24
L	28	At Cleveland Browns/O-30	30
W	28	At Baltimore Colts/N-6	10
W	41	At Los Angeles Dons/N-13	24
W	35	New York Yankees/N-27	14
	416		227

Playoff Game—Dec. 4

(At San Francisco—Kezar)

W	17	New York Yankees	7

Championship Game—Dec. 11

(At San Francisco—Kezar)

L	7	Cleveland Browns	21

49ers Year-By-Year Scores, Dates, Attendance— National Football League

1950 (3-9)

Lawrence T. Shaw, Coach

L	17	New York Yankees (29,600)/S-17	21
L	20	Chicago Bears (35,558)/S-24	32
L	14	Los Angeles Rams (27,262)/O-1	35
L	7	At Detroit (17,337)/O-8	24
L	24	At New York Yankees (5,740)/O-12	29
W	28	Detroit (27,350)/O-22	27
W	17	Baltimore (14,800)/O-29	14
L	21	At Los Angeles Rams (15,952)/N-5	28
L	14	At Cleveland (28,786)/N-12	34
L	0	At Chicago Bears (35,105)/N-19	17
L	21	At Green Bay (13,186)/N-26	25
W	30	Green Bay (19,204)/D-10	14
	213		300

1951 (7-4-1)

Lawrence T. Shaw, Coach

W	24	Cleveland (48,263)/S-30	10
L	14	At Philadelphia (23,827)/O-6	21
W	28	At Pittsburgh (27,124)/O-14	24
L	7	At Chicago Bears (42,296)/O-21	13
W	44	Los Angeles Rams (49,538)/O-28	17
L	16	At Los Angeles Rams (54,346)/N-4	23
W	19	New York Yankees (25,538)/N-11	14
L	21	Chicago Cards (19,658)/N-18	27
T	10	At New York Yankees(10,184)/N-24	10
W	20	At Detroit (46,467)/D-2	10
W	31	Green Bay (15,121)/D-9	19
W	21	Detroit (27,276)/D-16	17
	255		205

1952 (7-5)

Lawrence T. Shaw, Coach

W	17	Detroit (52,750)/S-28	3
W	37	At Dallas Texans (12,566)/O-5	14
W	28	At Detroit (48,842)/O-12	0
W	40	At Chicago Bears (46,338)/O-19	16
W	48	Dallas Texans (26,887)/O-26	21
L	17	Chicago Bears (58,255)/N-2	20
L	14	At New York Giants (54,230)/N-9	23
W	23	At Washington (30,863)/N-16	17
L	9	At Los Angeles Rams (64,450)/N-23	35
L	21	Los Angeles Rams (49,420)/N-30	34
L	7	Pittsburgh (13,886)/D-7	24
W	24	Green Bay (17,579)/D-14	14
	285		221

1953 (9-3)

Lawrence T. Shaw, Coach

W	31	Philadelphia (25,000)/S-27	21
W	31	Los Angeles Rams (41,446)/O-4	30
L	21	At Detroit (56,080)/O-11	24
W	35	At Chicago Bears (36,909)/O-18	28
L	10	Detroit (52,300)/O-25	14
W	24	Chicago Bears (26,308)/N-1	14
W	31	At Los Angeles Rams (85,856)/N-8	27
L	21	At Cleveland (80,698)/N-15	23
W	37	At G.B. in Milwaukee (16,378)/N-22	7
W	38	At Baltimore (26,005)/N-29	21
W	48	Green Bay (31,337)/D-6	14
W	45	Baltimore (23,932)/D-13	14
	372		237

1954 (7-4-1)

Lawrence T. Shaw, Coach

W	41	Washington (32,085)/S-26	7
T	24	At Los Angeles Rams (79,208)/O-3	24
W	23	At G.B. in Milwaukee (15,571)/O-10	17
W	27	At Chicago Bears (42,935)/O-17	24
W	37	Detroit (58,891)/O-24	31
L	27	Chicago Bears (49,833)/O-31	31
L	34	Los Angeles Rams (58,758)/N-7	42
L	7	At Detroit (58,431)/N-14	48
W	31	At Pittsburgh (37,001)/N-20	3
L	13	At Baltimore (23,875)/N-28	17
W	35	Green Bay (32,012)/D-5	0
W	10	Baltimore (25,456)/D-1	7
	313		251

1955 (4-8)

Norman P. Strader, Coach

L	14	Los Angeles Rams (58,772)/S-25	23
L	3	Cleveland (43,595)/O-2	38
W	20	At Chicago Bears (41,651)/O-9	19
W	27	At Detroit (50,179)/O-16	24
L	23	Chicago Bears (56,350)/O-23	34
W	38	Detroit (44,831)/O-30	21
L	14	At Los Angeles Rams (71,832)/N-6	27
L	0	At Washington (25,112)/N-13	7
L	21	At G.B. in Milwaukee (19,099)/N-20	27
L	14	At Baltimore (33,485)/N-27	26
L	7	Green Bay (32,897)/D-4	28
W	35	Baltimore (33,471)/D-11	24
	216		308

1956 (5-6-1)

Frank C. Albert, Coach

L	21	New York Giants (41,751)/S-30	38
W	33	Los Angeles Rams (56,489)/O-7	30
L	7	At Chicago Bears (47,526)/O-14	31
L	17	At Detroit (55,662)/O-21	20
L	21	Chicago Bears (52,612)/O-28	38
L	13	Detroit (46,708)/N-4	17
L	6	At Los Angeles Rams (69,828)/N-11	30
W	17	At Green Bay (17,986)/N-18	16
T	10	At Philadelphia (19,326)/N-25	10
W	20	At Baltimore (37,227)/D-2	17
W	38	Green Bay (32,433)/D-8	20
W	30	Baltimore (43,791)/D-16	17
	233		284

1957 (8-4/8-5)

Frank C. Albert, Coach

L	10	Chicago Cards (35,743)/S-29	20
W	23	Los Angeles Rams (59,637)/O-6	20
W	21	At Chicago Bears (45,310)/O-13	17
W	24	At G.B. in Milwaukee (18,919)/O-20	14
W	21	Chicago Bears (56,693)/O-27	17
W	35	Detroit (59,702)/N-3	31
L	24	At Los Angeles Rams (102,368)/N-10	37
L	10	At Detroit (56,915)/N-17	31
L	21	At Baltimore (50,073)/N-24	27
W	27	At New York Giants (54,121)/D-1	17
W	17	Baltimore (59,950)/D-8	13
W	27	Green Bay (59,100)/D-15	20
	287		295

Playoff Game—Dec. 22

(At San Francisco-Kezar)

L	27	Detroit (60,118)	31

1958 (6-6)

Frank C. Albert, Coach

W	23	Pittsburgh (51,856)/S-28	20
L	3	Los Angeles Rams (59,826)/O-5	33
L	6	At Chicago Bears (45,310)/O-12	28
W	30	At Philadelphia (33,110)/O-19	24
L	14	Chicago Bears (59,441)/O-26	27
W	24	Detroit (59,350)/N-2	21
L	7	At Los Angeles Rams (95,082)/N-9	56
L	21	At Detroit (54,523)/N-16	35
W	33	At G.B. in Milwaukee (43,819)/N-23	12
L	27	At Baltimore (57,557)/N-30	35
W	48	Green Bay (50,793)/D-7	21
W	21	Baltimore (58,334)/D-14	12
	257		324

1959 (7-5)

Howard W. Hickey, Coach

W	24	Philadelphia (41,697)/S-27	14
W	34	Los Angeles Rams (56,028)/O-4	0
L	20	At Green Bay (32,150)/O-11	21
W	34	At Detroit (52,585)/O-18	13
W	20	Chicago Bears (59,045)/O-25	17
W	33	Detroit (59,064)/N-1	7
W	24	At Los Angeles Rams (94,276)/N-8	16
L	3	At Chicago Bears (42,157)/N-15	14
L	14	At Baltimore (56,007)/N-22	45
W	21	At Cleveland (53,763)/N-29	20
L	14	Baltimore (59,075)/D-5	34
L	14	Green Bay (55,997)/D-13	36
	255		237

1960 (7-5)

Howard W. Hickey, Coach

L	19	New York Giants (44,598)/S-25	21
W	13	Los Angeles Rams (53,633)/O-2	9
W	14	At Detroit (49,825)/O-9	10
L	10	At Chicago Bears (48,226)/O-16	27
L	14	At G.B. in Milwaukee (39,914)/O-23	41
W	25	Chicago Bears (55,071)/O-30	7
L	0	Detroit (48,447)/N-6	24
W	26	At Dallas (10,000)/N-20	14
W	30	At Baltimore (57,808)/N-27	22
W	23	At Los Angeles Rams (77,254)/D-4	7
L	0	Green Bay (53,612)/D-10	13
W	34	Baltimore (57,269)/D-18	10
	208		205

1961 (7-6-1)

Howard W. Hickey, Coach

W	35	Washington (43,412)/S-17	3
L	10	At Green Bay (38,624)/S-24	30
W	49	At Detroit (53,155)/O-1	0
W	35	Los Angeles Rams (59,004)/O-8	0
W	38	At Minnesota (34,415)/O-15	24
L	0	At Chicago Bears (49,070)/O-22	31
L	10	At Pittsburgh (19,686)/O-29	20
T	20	Detroit (56,878)/N-5	20
L	7	At Los Angeles Rams (63,766)/N-12	17
W	41	Chicago Bears (52,972)/N-19	31
W	38	Minnesota (43,905)/N-26	28
L	17	At Baltimore (57,641)/D-8	20
W	22	Green Bay (55,722)/D-10	21
L	24	Baltimore (45,517)/D-16	27
	346		143

1962 (6-8)

Howard W. Hickey, Coach

L	14	Chicago (46,052)/S-16	30
L	24	At Detroit (51,032)/S-23	45
W	21	Minnesota (38,407)/S-30	7
W	21	At Baltimore (54,148)/O-7	13
W	34	At Chicago (48,902)/O-14	27
L	13	At G.B. in Milwaukee (46,012)/O-21	31
L	14	Los Angeles Rams (51,033)/O-28	28
L	3	Baltimore (44,875)/N-4	22
L	24	Detroit (43,449)/N-11	38
W	24	At Los Angeles Rams (42,554)/N-18	17
W	24	At St. Louis (17,532)/N-25	17
W	35	At Minnesota (33,076)/D-2	12
L	21	Green Bay (53,769)/D-9	31
L	10	Cleveland (35,274)/D-15	13
	282		331

1963 (2-12)

Coach*

L	20	Minnesota (30,781)/S-15	24
L	14	Baltimore (31,006)/S-22	20
L	14	At Minnesota (28,567)/S-29	45
L	3	At Detroit (44,088)/O-6	26
L	3	At Baltimore (56,962)/O-13	20
W	20	Chicago (35,837)/O-20	14
L	21	At Los Angeles Rams (45,532)/O-27	28
L	7	Detroit (33,511)/N-3	45
W	31	Dallas (29,563)/N-10	24
L	14	At New York Giants (62,982)/N-17	48
L	10	At G.B. in Milwaukee (45,905)/N-24	28
L	17	Los Angeles Rams (33,321)/D-1	21
L	7	At Chicago (46,994)/D-8	27
L	17	Green Bay (31,031)/D-14	21
	198		391

*Coach Red Hickey resigned after third league game and Jack Christiansen was appointed his successor.

1964 (4-10)

Jack Christiansen, Coach

L	17	Detroit (33,204)/S-13	26
W	28	At Philadelphia (57,352)/S-20	24
L	13	St. Louis (30,969)/S-27	23
W	31	Chicago (33,132)/O-4	21
L	14	At G.B. in Milwaukee (47,380)/O-11	24
L	14	At Los Angeles Rams (54,355)/O-18	42
L	22	Minnesota (31,845)/O-25	27
L	7	At Baltimore (60,213)/N-1	37
L	7	At Minnesota (40,408)/N-8	24
W	24	Green Bay (38,483)/N-15	14
L	21	At Chicago (46,772)/N-22	23
L	3	Baltimore (33,642)/N-29	14
W	28	Los Angeles Rams (31,791)/D-6	7
L	7	At Detroit (41,854)/D-13	24
	236		330

1965 (7-6-1)

Jack Christiansen, Coach

W	52	Chicago (31,211)/S-19	24
W	27	Pittsburgh (28,161)/S-26	17
L	24	At Baltimore (57,342)/O-3	27
L	10	At Green Bay (50,858)/O-10	27
W	45	At Los Angeles Rams (34,703)/O-17	21
L	41	Minnesota (40,673)/O-24	42
L	28	Baltimore (43,575)/O-31	34
L	31	At Dallas (30,531)/N-7	39
W	27	At Detroit (52,570)/N-14	21
W	30	Los Angeles Rams (39,253)/N-21	27
W	45	Minnesota (36,748)/N-28	24
W	17	Detroit (38,483)/D-5	14
L	20	At Chicago (43,400)/D-12	61
T	24	Green Bay (45,710)/D-19	24
	421		402

1966 (6-6-2)

Jack Christiansen, Coach

T	20	Minnesota (29,312)/S-11	20
L	14	At Baltimore (56,715)/S-25	36
L	3	At Los Angeles Rams (45,642)/S-30	34
W	21	Green Bay (39,290)/O-9	20
W	44	At Atlanta (54,788)/O-16	7
W	27	Detroit (36,745)/O-23	24
L	3	At Minnesota (45,007)/O-30	28
W	21	Los Angeles Rams (35,372)/N-6	13
T	30	At Chicago (47,079)/N-13	30
L	34	Philadelphia (31,993)/N-20	35
W	41	At Detroit (53,189)/N-24	14
L	7	At G.B. in Milwaukee (48,725)/D-4	20
W	41	Chicago (37,170)/D-11	14
L	14	Baltimore (40,005)/D-18	30
	320		325

1967 (7-7)

Jack Christiansen, Coach

W	27	At Minnesota (39,638)/S-17	21
W	38	Atlanta (30,207)/S-24	7
L	7	At Baltimore (60,238)/O-1	41
W	27	At Los Angeles Rams (60,424)/O-8	24
W	28	At Philadelphia (60,825)/O-15	27
W	27	New Orleans (34,285)/O-22	13
L	3	Detroit (37,990)/O-29	45
L	7	Los Angeles Rams (53,194)/N-5	17
L	28	At Washington (50,326)/N-12	31
L	0	At Green Bay (50,861)/N-19	13
L	9	Baltimore (44,815)/N-26	26
L	14	Chicago (25,613)/D-3	28
W	34	At Atlanta (51,798)/D-10	28
W	24	At Dallas (27,182)/D-16	16
	273		337

1968 (7-6-1)

Dick Nolan, Coach

L	10	At Baltimore (56,864)/S-15	27
W	35	St. Louis (27,557)/S-22	17
W	28	Atlanta (27,477)/S-29	13
L	10	At Los Angeles Rams (69,520)/O-6	24
L	14	Baltimore (32,822)/O-13	42
W	26	At New York Giants (62,958)/O-20	10
W	14	At Detroit (53,555)/O-27	7
L	21	Cleveland (31,359)/N-3	33
L	19	At Chicago (46,978)/N-10	27
T	20	Los Angeles Rams (41,815)/N-17	20
W	45	At Pittsburgh (21,408)/N-24	28
W	27	Green Bay (47,218)/D-1	20
L	20	Minnesota (29,049)/D-8	30
W	14	At Atlanta (44,977)/D-15	12
	303		310

1969 (4-8-2)

Dick Nolan, Coach

L	12	At Atlanta (45,940)/S-21	24
L	7	At G.B. in Milwaukee (48,184)/S-28	14
T	17	Washington (35,184)/O-5	17
L	21	Los Angeles Rams (45,995)/O-12	27
L	7	Atlanta (28,684)/O-19	21
W	24	At Baltimore (60,238)/O-26	21
L	14	Detroit (35,100)/N-2	26
L	30	At Los Angeles Rams (73,975)/N-9	41
W	20	Baltimore (38,472)/N-16	17
L	38	At New Orleans (71,448)/N-23	43
T	24	At Dallas (62,348)/N-27	24
W	42	Chicago (32,826)/D-6	21
L	7	At Minnesota (43,028)/D-14	10
W	14	Philadelphia (25,391)/D-21	13
	277		319

1970 (10-3-1/11-4-1)

Dick Nolan, Coach

W	26	Washington (34,984)/S-20	17
W	34	Cleveland (37,502)/S-27	31
L	20	At Atlanta (58,850)/O-4	21
W	20	At Los Angeles Rams (77,272)/O-11	6
T	20	New Orleans (39,446)/O-18	20
W	19	Denver (39,515)/O-25	14
W	26	Green Bay (59,335)/N-1	10
W	37	At Chicago (45,607)/N-8	16
W	30	At Houston (43,040)/N-15	20
L	7	At Detroit (56,232)/N-22	28
L	13	Los Angeles Rams (59,602)/N-29	30
W	24	Atlanta (41,387)/D-6	20
W	38	At New Orleans (61,940)/D-13	27
W	38	At Oakland Raiders (54,535)/D-20	7
	352		267

NFC Playoff—Dec. 27

(At Bloomington—Metropolitan)

W	17	Minnesota (45,103)	14

NFC Championship—Jan. 3

(At San Francisco-Kezar)

L	10	Dallas (59,364)	17

1971 (9-6/10-7)

Dick Nolan, Coach

L	17	At Atlanta (56,990)/S-19	20
W	38	At New Orleans (81,595)/S-26	20
W	31	At Philadelphia (65,358)/O-3	3
L	13	Los Angeles Rams (44,000)/O-10	20
W	13	Chicago (44,133)/O-17	0
W	26	At St. Louis (50,419)/O-24	14
W	27	New England (45,092)/O-31	10
W	13	At Minnesota (49,784)/N-7	9
L	20	New Orleans (45,138)/N-14	26
L	6	At Los Angeles Rams (80,050)/N-21	17
W	24	At New York Jets (62,936)/N-28	21
L	17	Kansas City (45,306)-MN/D-6	26
W	24	Atlanta (44,584)/D-12	3
W	31	Detroit (45,580)/D-19	27
	300		216

NFC Playoff—Dec. 26

(At San Francisco-Candlestick)

W	24	Washington (45,327)	20

NFC Championship—Jan. 2

(At Irving-Texas)

L	3	Dallas (63,409)	14

1972 (8-5-1/8-6-1)

Dick Nolan, Coach

W	34	San Diego (56,906)*/S-17	3
L	20	At Buffalo (45,825)/S-24	27
W	37	At New Orleans (69,840)/O-1	2
L	7	At Los Angeles Rams (77,382)/O-8	31
L	17	New York Giants (53,284)/O-15	23
T	20	New Orleans (53,571)/O-22	20
W	49	At Atlanta (58,850)/O-29	14
L	24	At G.B. in Milwaukee (47,897)/N-5	34
W	24	Baltimore (57,225)/N-12	21
W	34	At Chicago (65,201)/N-19	21
W	31	At Dallas (65,214)/N-23	10
L	16	Los Angeles Rams (60,175)-MN/D-4	26
W	20	Atlanta (57,523)/D-10	0
W	20	Minnesota (58,502)/D-16	17
	353		249

NFC Playoff—Dec. 23

(At San Francisco-Candlestick)

L	28	Dallas (59,746)	30

*Attendance from 1972 on is actual, does not include "no shows."

1973 (5-9)

Dick Nolan, Coach

L	13	At Miami (68,275)/S-16	21
W	36	At Denver (50,966)/S-23	34
L	20	Los Angeles Rams (57,487)/S-30	40
W	13	At Atlanta (58,850)/O-7	9
L	13	Minnesota (56,438)/O-14	17
W	40	New Orleans (52,881)/O-21	0
L	3	Atlanta (56,825)/O-28	17
L	20	At Detroit (49,531)/N-4	30
L	9	At Washington (54,381)/N-11	33
L	13	At Los Angeles Rams (78,358)/N-18	31
W	20	Green Bay (49,244)-MN/N-26	6
W	38	Philadelphia (51,155)/D-2	28
L	10	At New Orleans (62,490)/D-9	16
L	14	Pittsburgh (52,752)/D-15	37
	262		319

1974 (6-8)

Dick Nolan, Coach

W	17	At New Orleans (65,071)/S-15	13
W	17	At Atlanta (47,686)/S-22	10
L	3	Cincinnati (49,895)/S-29	21
L	9	St. Louis (47,675)/O-6	34
L	13	At Detroit (45,199)-MN/O-14	17
L	14	At Los Angeles Rams (74,070)/O-20	37
L	24	Oakland Raiders (58,524)/O-27	35
L	13	Los Angeles Rams (57,526)-MN/N-4	15
L	14	At Dallas (50,018)/N-10	20
W	34	At Chicago (42,731)/N-17	0
W	27	Atlanta (45,435)/N-24	0
L	0	At Cleveland (24,559)/D-1	7
W	7	Green Bay (45,475)/D-8	6
W	35	New Orleans (40,418)/D-15	21
	226		236

1975 (5-9)

Dick Nolan, Coach

L	17	At Minnesota (48,418)/S-21	27
L	14	Los Angeles Rams (55,072)/S-28	23
W	20	At Kansas City (54,490)/O-5	3
L	3	Atlanta (43,719)/O-12	17
W	35	New Orleans (39,654)/O-19	21
L	16	At New England (60,358)/O-26	24
L	17	Detroit (42,683)/N-2	28
W	24	At Los Angeles Rams (78,995)/N-9	23
W	31	Chicago (41,319)/N-16	3
W	16	At New Orleans (40,328)/N-23	6
L	17	At Philadelphia (56,694)/N-30	27

L	13	Houston (43,767)/D-7	27
L	9	Atlanta (38,501)/D-14	31
L	23	New York Giants (33,939)/D-21	26
	255		286

1976 (8-6)

Monte Clark, Coach

W	26	At Green Bay (54,628)/S-12	14
L	12	Chicago (44,158)/S-19	19
W	37	At Seattle (59,108)/S-26	21
W	17	New York Jets (42,961)/O-3	6
W	16	At Los Angeles Rams (84,483)-MN/O-11	0
W	33	New Orleans (43,160)/O-17	3
W	15	Atlanta (50,240)-SN/O-23	0
L	20	At St. Louis (50,365)/O-31 (OT)-23	
L	21	Washington (56,134)/N-7	24
L	16	At Atlanta (20,058)/N-14	21
L	3	Los Angeles Rams (57,909)/N-21	23
W	20	Minnesota (56,775)-MN/N-29	16
L	7	At San Diego (33,539)/D-5 (OT)-13	
W	27	At New Orleans (42,536)/D-12	7
	270		190

1977 (5-9)

Ken Meyer, Coach

L	0	At Pittsburgh (48,046)-MN/S-19	27
L	15	Miami (40,503)/S-25	19
L	14	At Los Angeles Rams (55,466)/O-2	34
L	0	Atlanta (38,009)/O-9	7
L	17	At New York Giants (70,366)/O-16	20
W	28	Detroit (39,392)/O-23	7
W	20	Tampa Bay (34,750)/O-30	10
W	10	At Atlanta (46,577)/N-6	3
W	10	At New Orleans (41,564)/N-13 (OT)-7	
L	10	Los Angeles Rams (56,779)/N-20	23
W	20	New Orleans (33,702)/N-27	17
L	27	At Minnesota (40,745)/D-4	28
L	35	Dallas (55,848)-MN/D-12	42
L	14	At G.B. in Milwaukee (44,902)/D-18	16
	220		260

1978 (2-14)

Coach*

L	7	At Cleveland (68,973)/S-3	24
L	14	Chicago (49,502)/S-10	16
L	19	At Houston (46,161)/S-17	20
L	10	At New York Giants (71,536)/S-24	27
W	28	Cincinnati (41,107)/O-1	12
L	10	At Los Angeles Rams (59,337)/O-8	27
L	7	New Orleans (37,671)/O-15	14
L	17	Atlanta (34,133)/O-22	20
L	20	At Washington (53,706)/O-29	38
L	10	At Atlanta (55,468)/N-5	21
L	10	St. Louis (33,155)/N-12	16
L	28	Los Angeles Rams (45,022)/N-19	31
L	7	Pittsburgh (51,657)-MN/N-27	24
L	13	At New Orleans (50,068)/D-3	24
W	6	Tampa Bay (30,931)/D-10	3
L	14	At Detroit (56,674)/D-17	33
	219		350

*Pete McCulley was fired after nine games and Fred O'Connor was appointed his successor.

1979 (2-14)

Bill Walsh, Coach

L	22	At Minnesota (46,539)/S-2	28
L	13	Dallas (56,728)/S-9	21
L	24	At Los Angeles Rams (44,303)/S-16	27
L	21	New Orleans (39,727)/S-23	30
L	9	At San Diego (50,893)/S-30	31
L	24	Seattle (44,592)/O-7	35
L	16	At New York Giants (70,352)/O-14	32
W	20	Atlanta (33,952)/O-21	15
L	27	Chicago (42,773)/O-28	28
L	10	At Oakland Raiders (52,764)/N-4	23

L	20	At New Orleans (65,551)/N-11	31
L	28	Denver (42,910)/N-18	38
L	20	Los Angeles Rams (49,282)/N-25	26
L	10	At St. Louis (41,593)/D-2	13
W	23	Tampa Bay (44,506)/D-9	7
L	21	At Atlanta (37,211)/D-16	31
	308		416

1980 (6-10)

Bill Walsh, Coach

W	26	At New Orleans (58,621)/S-7	21
W	24	St. Louis (49,999)/S-14 (OT)-21	
W	37	At New York Jets (50,608)/S-21	27
L	17	Atlanta (56,518)/S-28	20
L	26	At Los Angeles Rams (62,188)/O-5	48
L	14	At Dallas (63,399)/O-12	59
L	17	Los Angeles Rams (55,360)/O-19	31
L	23	Tampa Bay (51,925)/O-26	24
L	13	At Detroit (78,845)/N-2	17
L	16	At G.B. in Milwaukee (54,475)/N-9	23
L	13	At Miami (45,135)/N-16	17
W	12	New York Giants (38,754)/N-23	0
W	21	New England (45,254)/N-30	17
W	38	New Orleans (37,949)/D-7 (OT)-35	
L	10	At Atlanta (55,767)/D-14	35
L	13	Buffalo (37,476)/D-21	18
	320		415

1981 (13-3/16-3)

Bill Walsh, Coach

L	17	At Detroit (62,123)/S-6	24
W	28	Chicago (49,520)/S-13	17
L	17	At Atlanta (56,653)/S-20	34
W	21	New Orleans (44,433)/S-27	14
W	30	At Washington (51,843)/O-4	17
W	45	Dallas (57,574)/O-11	14
W	13	At G.B. in Milwaukee (50,171)/O-18	3
W	20	Los Angeles Rams (59,190)/O-25	17
W	17	At Pittsburgh (52,878)/N-1	14
W	17	Atlanta (59,127)/N-8	14
L	12	Cleveland (52,445)/N-15	15
W	33	At Los Angeles Rams (63,456)/N-22	31
W	17	New York Giants (57,186)/N-29	10
W	21	At Cincinnati (56,796)/D-6	3
W	28	Houston (55,707)/D-13	6
W	21	At New Orleans (43,639)/D-20	17
	357		250

NFC Playoff—Jan. 3

(At San Francisco-Candlestick)

W	38	New York Giants (58,360)	24

NFC Championship—Jan. 10

(At San Francisco-Candlestick)

W	28	Dallas (60,525)	27

Super Bowl XVI—Jan. 24

(At Pontiac, Michigan-Silverdome)

W	26	Cincinnati (81,270)	21

1982 (3-6)*

Bill Walsh, Coach

L	17	Los Angeles Raiders (59,748)/S-12	23
L	21	At Denver (73,899)/S-19	24
W	31	At St. Louis (38,064)/N-21	20
L	20	New Orleans (51,611)/N-28	23
W	30	Los Angeles Rams (58,574)-THN/D-2	24
L	37	San Diego (51,988)-SA/D-11	41
L	7	Atlanta (53,234)-SUN/D-19	17
W	26	At Kansas City (24,319)/D-26	13
L	20	Los Angeles Rams (54,256)/J-2	21
	209		206

*Short season because 1982 was a strike year

1983 (10-6/11-7)

Bill Walsh, Coach

L	17	Philadelphia (55,775)-SA/S-3	22
W	48	At Minnesota (58,167)-THN/S-8	17
W	42	At St. Louis (38,130)/S-18	27
W	24	Atlanta (57,814)/S-25	20
W	33	At New England (54,293)/O-2	13
L	7	Los Angeles Rams (59,119)/O-9	10
W	32	At New Orleans (68,134)/O-16	13
W	45	At Los Angeles Rams (66,070)/O-23	35
L	13	New York Jets (54,796)/O-30	27
L	17	Miami (57,832)/N-6	20
W	27	New Orleans (40,022)/N-13	0
L	24	At Atlanta (32,782)/N-20	28
L	3	At Chicago (40,483)/N-27	13
W	35	Tampa Bay (49,773)/D-4	21
W	23	At Buffalo (38,039)/D-11	10
W	42	Dallas (59,957)-MN/D-19	17
	432		293

NFC Playoff—Dec. 31

(At San Francisco-Candlestick)

W	24	Detroit (58,386)-SA	23

NFC Championship—Jan. 8

(At Washington, DC-RFK)

L	21	Washington (55,363)	24

1984 (15-1/18-1)

Bill Walsh, Coach

W	30	At Detroit (56,782)/S-2	27
W	37	Washington (59,707)-MN/S-10	31
W	30	New Orleans (57,611)/S-16	20
W	21	At Philadelphia (62,771)/S-23	9
W	14	Atlanta (57,990)/S-30	5
W	31	At New York Giants (76,112)-MN/O-8	10
L	17	Pittsburgh (59,110)/O-14	20
W	34	At Houston (39,900)/O-21	21
W	33	At Los Angeles Rams (65,481)/O-28	0
W	23	Cincinnati (58,234)/N-4	17
W	41	At Cleveland (60,092)/N-11	7
W	24	Tampa Bay (57,704)/N-18	17
W	35	At New Orleans (65,177)/N-25	3
W	35	At Atlanta (29,664)/D-2	17
W	51	Minnesota (56,670)-SA/D-8	7
W	19	Los Angeles Rams (59,743)-FN/D-14	16
	475		227

NFC Playoff—Dec. 29

(At San Francisco-Candlestick)

W	21	New York Giants (60,303)-SA	10

NFC Championship—Jan. 6

(At San Francisco-Candlestick)

W	23	Chicago (61,040)	0

Super Bowl XIX—Jan. 26

(At Palo Alto, California-Stanford Stadium)

W	38	Miami (84,059)	16

1985 (10-6/10-7)

Bill Walsh, Coach

L	21	At Minnesota (57,375)/S-8	28
W	35	Atlanta (58,923)/S-15	16
W	34	At Los Angeles Raiders (87,006)/S-22	10
L	17	New Orleans (58,053)/S-29	20
W	38	At Atlanta (44,740)/O-6	17
L	10	Chicago (60,523)/O-13	26
L	21	At Detroit (67,715)/O-20	23
W	28	At Los Angeles Rams (65,939)/O-27	14
W	24	Philadelphia (58,383)/N-3	13

L	16	At Denver (73,173)-MN/N-11	17
W	31	Kansas City (56,447)/N-17	3
W	19	Seattle (57,482)-MN/N-25	6
W	35	At Washington (51,321)/D-1	8
L	20	Los Angeles Rams (60,581)-MN/D-9	27
W	31	At New Orleans (46,065)/D-15	19
W	31	Dallas (60, 114)/D-22	16
	411		263

NFC Wildcard—Dec. 29

(At Meadowlands, N.J.-Giants Stadium)

L	3	New York Giants (75,842)	17

1986 (10-5-1/10-6-1)

Bill Walsh, Coach

W	31	At Tampa Bay (50,780)/S-7	7
L	13	At Los Angeles Rams (65,195)/S-14	16
W	26	New Orleans (58,297)/S-21	17
W	31	At Miami (70,264)/S-28	17
W	35	Indianapolis (57,252)/O-5	14
L	24	Minnesota (58,637)/O-12 (OT)-27
T	10	At Atlanta (55,306)/O-19 (OT)-10
W	31	At G.B. in Milwaukee (50,557)/O-26	27
L	10	At New Orleans (52,234)/N-2	23
W	43	St. Louis (59,172)/N-9	17
L	6	At Washington (54,774)-MN/N-17	14
W	20	Atlanta (58,747)/N-23	0
L	17	New York Giants (59,777)-MN/D-1	21
W	24	New York Jets (58,091)/D-7	10
W	29	At New England (60,787)/D-14	24
W	24	Los Angeles Rams (60,266)-FN/D-19	14
	374		258

NFC Playoff—Jan. 4

(At Meadowlands, N.J.-Giants Stadium)

L	3	New York Giants (76,034)	49

1987 (13-2/13-3)

Bill Walsh, Coach

L	17	At Pittsburgh (55,735)/S-13	30
W	27	At Cincinnati (53,498)/S-20	26
W	41	At New York Giants (16,471)-MN/O-5	21
W	25	At Atlanta (8,684)/O-11	17
W	34	St. Louis (38,094)/O-18	28
W	24	At New Orleans (60,497)/O-25	22
W	31	At Los Angeles Rams (55,328)/N-1	10
W	27	Houston (59,740)/N-8	20
L	24	New Orleans (60,436)/N-15	26
W	24	At Tampa Bay (63,211)/N-22	10
W	38	Cleveland (60,243)-SUN/N-29	24
W	23	At Green Bay (51,118)/D-6	12
W	41	Chicago (63,509)-MN/D-14	0
W	35	Atlanta (54,698)/D-20	7
W	48	Los Angeles Rams (57,953)-SUN/D-27	0
	459		253

NFC Playoff—Jan. 9

(At San Francisco-Candlestick)

L	24	Minnesota (62,547)	36

1988 (10-6/13-6)

Bill Walsh, Coach

W	34	At New Orleans (66,357)/S-4	33
W	20	At New York Giants (75,948)/S-11	17
L	17	Atlanta (60,168)/S-18	34
W	38	At Seattle (62,383)/S-25	7
W	20	Detroit (58,285)/O-2	13
L	13	Denver (61,711)/O-9 (OT)	16
W	24	At Los Angeles Rams (65,450)/O-16	21
L	9	At Chicago (65,293)-MN/O-24	10
W	24	Minnesota (60,738)/O-30	21

L	23	At Phoenix (64,544)/N-6	24
L	3	Los Angeles Raiders (54,448)/N-13	9
W	37	Washington (59,268)-MN/N-21	21
W	48	At San Diego (51,484)/N-27	10
W	13	At Atlanta (44,048)/D-4	3
W	30	New Orleans (62,977)/D-11	17
L	16	Los Angeles Rams (62,444)-MN/D-18	38
	369		294

NFC Playoff—Jan.1
(At San Francisco-Candlestick)

W	34	Minnesota (61,848)	9

NFC Championship—Jan. 8
(At Chicago-Soldier Field)

W	28	At Chicago (66,946)	3

Super Bowl XXIII—Jan. 22
(At Miami-Joe Robbie Stadium)

W	20	Cincinnati (75,129)	16

1989 (14-2/17-2)
George Seifert, Coach

W	30	At Indianapolis (60,111)/S-10	24
W	20	At Tampa Bay (64,087)/S-17	16
W	38	At Philadelphia (66,042)/S-24	28
L	12	Los Angeles Rams (64,250)/O-1	13
W	24	At New Orleans (60,488)/O-8	20
W	31	At Dallas (61,077)/O-15	14
W	37	New England (51,781)/O-22	20
W	23	At New York Jets (62,805)/O-29	10
W	31	New Orleans (60,667)-MN/N-6	13
W	45	Atlanta (59,914)/N-12	3
L	17	Green Bay (62,219)/N-19	21
W	34	New York Giants (63,461)-MN/N-27	24
W	23	At Atlanta (43,128)/D-3	10
W	30	At Los Angeles Rams (67,959)-MN/D-11	27
W	21	Buffalo (60,927)/D-17	10
W	26	Chicago (60,207)/D-24	0
	442		253

NFC Playoff—Jan. 6
(At San Francisco-Candlestick)

W	41	Minnesota (64,585)	13

NFC Championship—Jan. 14
(At San Francisco-Candlestick)

W	30	Los Angeles Rams (64,769)	3

Super Bowl XXIV—Jan. 28
(At New Orleans-Superdome)

W	55	Denver (72,919)	10

1990 (14-2/15-3)
George Seifert, Coach

W	13	At New Orleans (68,629)-MN/S-10	12
W	26	Washington (64,287)/S-16	13
W	19	Atlanta (62,358)/S-23	13
—	—	BYE/S-30	—
W	24	At Houston (59,331)/O-7	21
W	45	At Atlanta (57,921)/O-14	35
W	27	Pittsburgh (64,301)/O-21	7
W	20	Cleveland (63,672)/O-28	17
W	24	At Green Bay (58,835)/N-4	20
W	24	At Dallas (62,966)/N-11	6
W	31	Tampa Bay (62,221)/N-18	7
L	17	Los Angeles Rams (62,533)/N-25	28
W	7	New York Giants (66,092)-MN/D-3	3
W	20	At Cincinnati (60,084)/D-9 (OT)	17
W	26	At Los Angeles Rams (66,619)-MN/D-17	10

L	10	New Orleans (60,112)/D-23	13
W	20	At Minnesota (51,590)/D-30	17
	353		239

NFC Playoff—Jan. 12
(At San Francisco-Candlestick)

W	28	Washington (65,292)	10

NFC Championship—Jan. 20
(At San Francisco-Candlestick)

L	13	New York Giants (66,334)	16

1991 (10-6)
George Seifert, Coach

L	14	At New York Giants (76,319)-MN/S-2	16
W	34	San Diego (60, 753)/S-8	14
L	14	At Minnesota (59,148)/S-15	17
W	27	Los Angeles Rams (63,871)/S-22	10
L	6	At Los Angeles Raiders (91,494)/S-29	12
—	—	BYE/O-6	—
L	34	Atlanta (57,343)/O-13	39
W	35	Detroit (61,240)/O-20	3
W	23	At Philadelphia (65,796)/O-27	7
L	14	At Atlanta (51,259)/N-3	17
L	3	At New Orleans (68,591)/N-10	10
W	14	Phoenix (50,180)/N-17	10
W	33	At Los Angeles Rams (61,881)-MN/N-25	10
W	38	New Orleans (62,092)/D-1	24
W	24	At Seattle (56,711)/D-8	22
W	28	Kansas City (62,672)-SA/D-14	14
W	52	Chicago (60,419)-MN/D-22	14
	393		239

1992 (14-2/15-3)
George Seifert, Coach

W	31	At New York Giants (74,519)/S-6	14
L	31	Buffalo (64,053)/S-13	34
W	31	At New York Jets (71,020)/S-20	14
W	16	At New Orleans (68,591)-SN/S-27	10
W	27	Los Angeles Rams (63,071)/O-4	24
W	24	At New England (54,126)/O-11	12
W	56	Atlanta (63,302)/O-18	17
—	—	BYE/O-25	—
L	14	At Phoenix (47,642)/N-1	24
W	41	At Atlanta (67,404)-MN/N-9	3
W	21	New Orleans (54,895)/N-15	20
W	27	At Los Angeles Rams (65,858)/N-22	10
W	20	Philadelphia (63,374)/N-29	14
W	27	Miami (58,474)/D-6	3
W	20	At Minnesota (60,685)/D-13	17
W	21	Tampa Bay (60,519)/D-20	14
W	24	Detroit (55,907)-MN/D-28	6
	431		236

NFC Playoff—Jan. 9
(At San Francisco-Candlestick)

W	20	Washington (64,991)	13

NFC Championship—Jan. 17

L	20	Dallas (64,920)	30

1993 (10-6/11-7)
George Seifert, Coach

W	24	At Pittsburgh (57,502)/S-5	13
L	13	At Cleveland (78,218)-MN/S-13	23
W	37	Atlanta (63,032)/S-19	30
L	13	At New Orleans (69,041)/S-26	16
W	38	Minnesota (63,071)/O-3	19
—	—	BYE/O-10	—
L	17	At Dallas (65,099)/O-17	26

W	28	Phoenix (62,020)/O-24	14
W	40	Los Angeles Rams (63,417)/O-31	17
—	—	BYE/N-7	—
W	45	At Tampa Bay (43,835)/N-14	21
W	42	New Orleans (66,500)-MN/N22	7
W	35	At Los Angeles Rams (62,143)/N-28	10
W	21	Cincinnati (60,039)-SUN/D-5	8
L	24	At Atlanta (64,688)-SA/D-11	27
W	55	At Detroit (77,052)/D-19	17
L	7	Houston (61,744)-SA/D-25	10
L	34	Philadelphia (61,653)-MN/J-3 (OT)	37
	473		295

NFC Playoff—Jan. 15
(At San Francisco-Candlestick Park)

W	44	New York Giants (67,143)	3

NFC Championship—Jan. 27
(At Irving-Texas Stadium)

L	21	At Dallas (64,902)	38

1994 (13-3/16-3)
George Seifert, Coach

W	44	Los Angeles Raiders (68,032)/S-5	14
L	17	At Kansas City (79,907)/S-11	24
W	34	At Los Angeles Rams (56,479)/S-18	19
W	24	New Orleans (63,971)/S-25	13
L	8	Philadelphia (64,843)/O-2	40
W	27	At Detroit (77,340)/O-9	21
W	42	At Atlanta (67,298)/O-16	3
W	41	Tampa Bay (62,741)/O-23	16
W	37	At Washington (54,335)/N-6	22
W	21	Dallas (69,014)/N-13	14
W	31	Los Angeles Rams (62,774)/N-20	27
W	35	At New Orleans (61,304)/N-28	14
W	50	Atlanta (60,549)/D-4	14
W	38	at San Diego (62,105)/D-11	16
W	42	Denver (64,884)/D-17	19
L	14	at Minnesota (63,326)/D-26	21
	505		296

Records for 49ers Coaches

Coach	Yrs.	Dates	Games	W	L	T	%
Lawrence T. (Buck) Shaw	9	1946-54	116#	72	40	4	.638
Norman P. (Red) Strader	1	1955	12	4	8	0	.333
Frank C. (Frankie) Albert	3	1956-58	37#	19	17	1	.527
Howard W. (Red) Hickey	5*	1959-63	55	27	27	1	.500
Jack Christiansen	5*	1963-67	67	26	38	3	.411
Dick Nolan	8	1968-75	117#	56	56	5	.500
Monte Clark	1	1976	14	8	6	0	.571
Ken Meyer	1	1977	14	5	9	0	.357
Pete McCulley	1+	1978	9	1	8	0	.111
Fred O'Connor	1+	1978	7	1	6	0	.143
Bill Walsh	10	1979-88	166#	102	63	1	.618
George Seifert	8	1989-96	143#	108	35	0	.755
TOTAL	**51**	**1946-present**	**757**	**431**	**313**	**15**	**.569**

*Hickey coached the first three games of 1963; Christiansen the final 11.
+McCulley coached the first nine games of 1978; O'Connor the final seven.
#Includes post-season record.

NFC Playoff—Jan. 7
(At San Francisco-Candlestick Park)

W	44	Chicago Bears (64,644)	15

NFC Championship—Jan. 15
(At San Francisco-Candlestick Park)

W	38	Dallas Cowboys (69,125)	28

Super Bowl XXIX—Jan. 29
(At Miami-Joe Robbie Stadium)

W	49	San Diego Chargers (74,107)	26

1995 (11-5/11-6)
George Seifert, Coach

W	24	At New Orleans (66,627)/S-3	22
W	41	Atlanta (63,627)/S-10	10
W	28	New England (66,179)/S-17	3
L	24	At Detroit (76,236)/S-25-MN	27
W	20	New York Giants (65,536)/O-1	6
L	17	At Indianapolis (60,273)/O-15	18
W	44	At St. Louis Rams (59,915)/O-22	10
L	7	New Orleans (65,272)/O-29	11
L	7	Carolina (61,722)/N-5	13
W	38	At Dallas (65,180)/N-12	20
W	44	At Miami (73,080)/N-20-MN	20
W	41	St. Louis Rams (66,049)/N-26	13
W	27	Buffalo (65,568)/D-3	17
W	31	At Carolina (76,136)/D-10	10
W	37	Minnesota (64,975)/D18-MN	30
L	27	At Atlanta (51,785)/D-24	28
	457		258

NFC Playoff—Jan. 6
(At San Francisco-3Com Park)

L	17	Green Bay (69,311)	27

1996 (12-4/13-5)
George Seifert, Coach

W	27	At New Orleans (63,970)/S-1	11
W	34	St. Louis (63,624)/S-8	0
L	7	At Carolina (72,224)/S-22	23
W	39	Atlanta (62,995)/S-29	17
W	28	At St. Louis (61,260)/O-6	11
L	20	At Green Bay (60,716)/O-14 MN	23
W	28	Cincinnati (63,218)/O-20	21
W	10	At Houston (53,664)/O-27	9
W	24	At New Orleans (53,297)/N-3 SUN	17
L	17	Dallas (68,919)/N-10	20
W	38	Baltimore (51,596)/N-17	20
W	19	At Washington (54,235)/N-24	16
W	34	At Atlanta (46,318)/D-2 MN	10
L	24	Carolina (66,291)/D-8	30
W	25	At Pittsburgh (59,823)/D15	15
W	24	Detroit (61,785)/D-23 MN	14
	398		257

NFC Wildcard—Dec. 29
(At San Francisco-3Com Park)

W	14	Philadelphia (56,460)	0

NFC Playoff—Jan. 4
(At Green Bay-Lambeau Field)

L	14	Green Bay (60,787)	35

49ers Club Leaders By Year

Rushing

Year	Player	Att.	Yds.	Avg.	Long	TD	Rank*
1946	Standlee, Norm	134	683	5.1	—	2	—
1947	Strzykalski, John	143	906	6.3	50	5	—
1948	Strzykalski, John	141	915	6.5	—	4	—
1949	Perry, Joe	115	783	6.8	59	8	—
1950	Perry, Joe	124	647	5.2	78t	5	5
1951	Perry, Joe	136	677	5.0	58t	3	5
1952	Perry, Joe	158	725	4.6	78t	8	3
1953	Perry, Joe	192	1,018	5.3	51t	10	1
1954	Perry, Joe	173	1,049	6.1	58	8	1
1955	Perry, Joe	156	701	4.5	42	2	5
1956	McElhenny, Hugh	185	916	5.0	86t	8	3
1957	McElhenny, Hugh	102	478	4.7	61	1	15
1958	Perry, Joe	125	758	6.1	73t	4	3
1959	Smith, J.D.	207	1,036	5.0	73t	10	2
1960	Smith, J.D.	174	780	4.5	41	5	5
1961	Smith, J.D.	167	823	4.9	33	8	5
1962	Smith, J.D.	258	907	3.5	28	6	6
1963	Smith, J.D.	162	560	3.5	52t	5	13
1964	Kopay, Dave	75	271	3.6	18	0	32
1965	Willard, Ken	189	778	4.1	32	5	4
1966	Willard, Ken	191	763	4.0	49	5	5
1967	Willard, Ken	169	510	3.0	20	5	17
1968	Willard, Ken	227	967	4.3	69t	7	2
1969	Willard, Ken	171	557	3.3	18	7	13
1970	Willard, Ken	236	789	3.3	20	7	9/6
1971	Willard, Ken	216	885	4.0	49	4	15/9
1972	Washington, Vic	141	468	3.3	33	3	42/20
1973	Washington, Vic	151	534	3.5	25	8	32/15
1974	Jackson, Wilbur	174	705	4.1	64	0	17/8
1975	Williams, Delvin	117	631	5.4	52	3	21/13
1976	Williams, Delvin	248	1,203	4.9	80t	7	3/2
1977	Williams, Delvin	268	931	3.5	40	7	10/5
1978	Simpson, O.J.	161	593	3.7	34	1	39/19
1979	Hofer, Paul	123	615	5.0	47	7	33/17
1980	Cooper, Earl	171	720	4.2	47	5	23/12
1981	Patton, Ricky	152	543	3.6	28	4	35/16
1982	Moore, Jeff	85	281	3.3	19	4	37/16
1983	Tyler, Wendell	176	856	4.9	39	4	19/10
1984	Tyler, Wendell	246	1,262	5.1	40	7	5/5
1985	Craig, Roger	214	1,050	4.9	62t	9	13/8
1986	Craig, Roger	204	830	4.1	25	7	13/8
1987	Craig, Roger	215	815	3.8	25	3	8/5
1988	Craig, Roger	310	1,502	4.8	46t	9	3/2
1989	Craig, Roger	271	1,054	3.9	27	6	10/5
1990	Carter, Dexter	114	460	4.0	74t	1	39/19
1991	Henderson, Keith	137	561	4.1	25	2	30/11
1992	Watters, Ricky	206	1,013	4.9	43	9	13/8
1993	Watters, Ricky	208	950	4.6	39	10	12/8
1994	Watters, Ricky	239	877	3.7	23	6	15/8
1995	Loville, Derek	218	723	3.3	27	10	24/13
1996	Kirby, Terry	134	559	4.2	31	3	33/15

t=touchdown

RECEIVING (Based on Number of Catches)

Year	Player	No.	Yds.	Avg.	Long	TD	Rank*
1946	Beals, Alyn	40	586	14.7	—	10	—
1947	Beals, Alyn	47	655	13.9	54	10	—
1948	Beals, Alyn	46	591	12.8	—	14	—
1949	Beals, Alyn	44	678	15.4	—	12	—
1950	Loyd, Alex	32	402	12.6	38	0	18
1951	Soltau, Gordy	59	826	14.0	48t	7	2
1952	Soltau, Gordy	55	774	14.1	49t	7	4
1953	Wilson, Billy	51	840	16.5	61t	10	6
1954	Wilson, Billy	60	830	13.8	43	5	1
1955	Wilson, Billy	53	831	15.7	72t	7	2
1956	Wilson, Billy	60	889	14.8	77t	5	1
1957	Wilson, Billy	52	757	14.6	40	6	1
1958	Conner, Clyde	49	512	10.4	26	5	5
1959	Wilson, Billy	44	540	12.3	57t	4	6
1960	Conner, Clyde	38	531	14.0	65t	2	1

*NFL/NFC Rank

Year	Player	No.	Yds.	Avg.	Long	TD	Rank*
1961	Owens, R.C.	55	1,032	18.8	54	5	7
1962	Casey, Bernie	53	819	15.5	48t	6	11
1963	Casey, Bernie	47	762	16.2	68t	7	14
1964	Casey, Bernie	58	808	13.9	63t	4	6
1965	Parks, Dave	80	1,344	16.8	53t	12	1
1966	Parks, Dave	66	974	14.8	65t	5	3
1967	Witcher, Dick	46	705	15.3	63t	3	17
1968	McNeil, Clifton	71	994	14.0	65t	7	1
1969	Washington, Gene	51	711	13.9	52	3	10
	Cunningham, Doug	51	484	9.5	58	0	11
1970	Washington, Gene	53	1,100	20.8	79t	12	4/3
1971	Kwalick, Ted	52	664	12.8	42t	5	4/2
1972	Washington, Gene	46	918	20.0	62t	12	13/7
1973	Kwalick, Ted	47	729	15.5	48	5	10/6
1974	Schreiber, Larry, RB	30	217	7.2	16	1	60/36
1975	Washington, Gene	44	735	16.7	68t	9	31/10
1976	Washington, Gene	33	457	13.8	55t	6	52/25
	Jackson, Wilbur, RB	33	324	9.8	32	1	53/27
1977	Washington, Gene	32	638	19.9	47t	5	52/22
1978	Solomon, Freddie	31	458	14.8	58	2	83/42
1979	Hofer, Paul, RB	58	662	11.4	44	2	17/7
1980	Cooper, Earl, RB	83	567	6.8	66t	4	2/1
1981	Clark, Dwight	85	1,105	13.0	78t	4	2/1
1982	Clark, Dwight	60	913	15.2	51	5	1/1
1983	Clark, Dwight	70	840	12.0	46t	8	11/5
1984	Craig, Roger, RB	71	675	9.5	64t	3	11/6
1985	Craig, Roger, RB	92	1,016	11.0	73	6	1/1
1986	Rice, Jerry	86	1,570	18.3	66t	15	2/1
1987	Craig, Roger, RB	66	492	7.5	35t	1	3/2
1988	Craig, Roger, RB	76	534	7.0	22	1	7/5
1989	Rice, Jerry	82	1,483	18.1	68t	17	5/4
1990	Rice, Jerry	100	1,502	15.0	64t	13	1/1
1991	Rice, Jerry	80	1,206	15.1	73t	14	5/3
1992	Rice, Jerry	84	1,201	14.3	80t	10	5/3
1993	Rice, Jerry	98	1,503	15.3	80t	15	2/2
1994	Rice, Jerry	112	1,499	13.4	69t	13	2/2
1995	Rice, Jerry	122	1,848	15.1	81t	15	2/2
1996	Rice, Jerry	108	1,254	11.6	39	8	1/1

t=touchdown

PUNTING (Based on Average)

Year	Player	No.	Avg.	Long	Blocked	Rank*
1946	Albert, Frank	54	41.0	73	—	—
1947	Albert, Frank	40	44.0	69	1	—
1948	Albert, Frank	35	44.8	82	—	—
1949	Albert, Frank	31	48.2	72	—	—
1950	Lillywhite, Verl	26	39.1	57	1	11
1951	Albert, Frank	34	44.3	66	0	2
1952	Albert, Frank	68	42.6	70	0	5
1953	Powers, Jim	42	40.6	55	1	8
1954	Brown, Harvey	10	38.4	58	0	11
1955	Luna, Bob	63	40.6	63	3	8
1956	Jessup, Bill	14	40.2	63	0	16
1957	Barnes, Larry	19	47.1	86	0	13
1958	Atkins, Bill	25	39.3	51	0	11
1959	Davis, Tommy	59	45.7	71	0	3
1960	Davis, Tommy	62	44.1	74	0	3
1961	Davis, Tommy	50	44.4	67	0	3
1962	Davis, Tommy	48	45.6	82	0	1
1963	Davis, Tommy	73	45.4	64	2	4
1964	Davis, Tommy	79	45.6	68	0	4
1965	Davis, Tommy	54	45.8	65	0	2
1966	Davis, Tommy	63	41.4	60	0	6
1967	Spurrier, Steve	73	37.6	61	1	12
1968	Spurrier, Steve	68	39.0	54	0	12
1969	Davis, Tommy	23	41.5	55	0	17
1970	Spurrier, Steve	75	38.4	58	0	14/11
1971	McCann, Jim	49	38.7	54	1	25/12
1972	McCann, Jim	64	39.7	63	1	21/10
1973	Wittum, Tom	79	43.7	62	0	4/1
1974	Wittum, Tom	68	41.2	67	1	4/2
1975	Wittum, Tom	67	41.9	64	3	3/2
1976	Wittum, Tom	89	40.8	64	3	3/2
1977	Wittum, Tom	77	36.4	54	3	26/13
1978	Connell, Mike	96	37.3	59	1	21/10

1979	Melville, Dan	71	37.0	53	1	25/14
1980	Miller, Jim	77	40.9	65	0	10/5
1981	Miller, Jim	93	41.5	65	0	15/6
1982	Miller, Jim	44	38.1	80	1‡	25/13
1983	Orosz, Tom	65	39.3	61	1‡	25/11
1984	Runager, Max	56	41.8	59	1	17/17
1985	Runager, Max	86	39.8	57	1‡	26/13
1986	Runager, Max	83	41.6	62	2	10/6
1987	Runager, Max	55	39.2	56	1	22/11
1988	Helton, Barry	78	39.3	53	1	21/11
1989	Helton, Barry	55	40.5	56	1	12/8
1990	Helton, Barry	69	36.8	56	1	28/1
1991	Prokop, Joe	40	38.5	58	0	27/13
1992	Wilmsmeyer, Klaus	49	39.1	58	0	26/14
1993	Wilmsmeyer, Klaus	42	40.9	61	0	23/11
1994	Wilmsmeyer, Klaus	54	41.4	60	0	14/7
1995	Thompson, Tommy	57	40.6	65	0	25/13t
1996	Thompson, Tommy	73	44.1	65	2	10t/4

‡*Recorded to the team*

SCORING

Year	Player	TD	PAT	FG	Points	Rank*
1946	Beals, Alyn	10	1	—	61	—
1947	Beals, Alyn	10	—	—	60	—
1948	Beals, Alyn	14	—	—	84	—
1949	Beals, Alyn	12	1	—	73	—
1950	Soltau, Gordy	1	26	4	44	22
1951	Soltau, Gordy	7	30	6	90	5
1952	Soltau, Gordy	7	34	6	94	—
1953	Soltau, Gordy	6	48	40	114	1
1954	Soltau, Gordy	2	31	11	76	4
1955	Soltau, Gordy	1	27	3	42	24
	Wilson, Billy	7	0	0	42	25
1956	Soltau, Gordy	1	26	13	71	6
1957	Soltau, Gordy	0	33	9	60	9
1958	Soltau, Gordy	0	29	8	53	20
1959	Davis, Tommy	0	31	12	67	9
1960	Davis, Tommy	0	21	12	67	9
1961	Davis, Tommy	0	44	12	80	8
1962	Davis, Tommy	0	36	10	66	16
1963	Davis, Tommy	0	24	10	54	21
1964	Davis, Tommy	0	30	8	54	24
1965	Davis, Tommy	0	52	17	103	4
1966	Davis, Tommy	0	38	16	86	12
1967	Davis, Tommy	0	33	14	75	10
1968	Davis, Tommy	0	26	9	53	19
1969	Willard, Ken	10	0	0	60	21
1970	Gossett, Bruce	0	39	21	102	6/4
1971	Gossett, Bruce	0	32	23	101	5/3
1972	Gossett, Bruce	0	41	18	95	13/7
1973	Gossett, Bruce	0	26	26	104	7/4
1974	Gossett, Bruce	0	25	11	58	25/8
1975	Mike-Mayer, Steve	0	27	14	69	22/9
1976	Mike-Mayer, Steve	0	26	16	74	25/9
1977	Williams, Delvin	9	0	0	54	14/10
1978	Wersching, Ray	0	24	15	69	22/9
1979	Wersching, Ray	0	32	20	92	12/5
1980	Wersching, Ray	0	33	15	78	18/10
1981	Wersching, Ray	0	30	17	81	22/13
1982	Wersching, Ray	0	23	12	59	9/4
1983	Wersching, Ray	0	51	25	126	3/3
1984	Wersching, Ray	0	56	25	131	1/1
1985	Wersching, Ray	0	52	13	91	21/11
1986	Wersching, Ray	0	41	25	116	3/3
1987	Rice, Jerry	23	0	0	128	1/1
1988	Cofer, Mike	0	40	27	121	2/1
1989	Cofer, Mike	0	49	29	136	1/1
1990	Cofer, Mike	0	39	24	111	4/3
1991	Cofer, Mike	0	49	14	91	17/8
1992	Cofer, Mike	0	53	18	107	8/4
1993	Cofer, Mike	0	59	16	107	11t/6
1994	Brien, Doug	0	62	15	105	11t/4
1995	Rice, Jerry	17	1-2pt.	0	104	19/10
1996	Wilkins, Jeff	0	40	30	130	4/2

KICKOFF RETURNS

Year	Player	No.	Yds.	Avg.	Long	TD	Rank*
1946	Eshmont, Len*	10	264	26.4	—	0	
1947	Eshmont, Len*	9	177	19.7	—	0	—
1948	Hall, Forrest	13	369	28.4	—	0	3
1949	Perry, Joe	14	337	24.1	—	0	5
1950	Cathcart, Sam	14	329	23.9	62	0	20
1951	Arenas, Joe	21	542	25.8	49	0	8
1952	McElhenny, Hugh	18	396	22.0	40	0	16
1953	Arenas, Joe	16	551	34.4	82	0	1
1954	Arenas, Joe	16	362	22.6	41	0	11
1955	Arenas, Joe	24	594	24.8	42	0	7
1956	Arenas, Joe	27	801	29.7	96t	1	2
1957	Arenas, Joe	24	657	27.4	64	0	2
1958	Smith, J.D.	15	356	23.7	39	0	8
1959	Lyles, Lenny	25	565	22.6	46	0	10
1960	Lyles, Lenny	17	526	30.9	97t	1	2
1961	Woodson, Abe	27	782	29.0	98t	1	3
1962	Woodson, Abe	37	1,157	31.3	79	0	1
1963	Woodson, Abe	29	935	32.2	103t	3	1
1964	Woodson, Abe	32	880	27.5	70	0	4
1965	Alexander, Kermit	32	741	23.2	46	0	20
1966	Alexander, Kermit	37	984	26.6	56	0	7
1967	Cunningham, Doug	31	826	26.6	94	0	5
1968	Alexander, Kermit	20	360	18.0	35	0	24
1969	Smith, Noland	14	310	22.1	60	0	—
1970	Smith, Noland	14	315	22.5	60	0	16
1971	Washington, Vic	33	858	26.0	74	0	12/8
1972	Washington, Vic	27	771	28.6	98t	1	4/3
1973	Washington, Vic	24	549	22.9	38	0	26/10
1974	Holmes, Mike	25	612	24.5	57	0	15/6
1975	Moore, Manfred	26	650	25.0	52	0	10/5
1976	Leonard, Anthony	26	553	21.3	39	0	29/13
1977	Hofer, Paul	36	871	24.2	48	0	12/7
1978	Williams, Dave	34	745	21.9	89t	1	23/8
1979	Owens, James	41	1,002	24.4	85t	1	5/3
1980	Owens, James	31	726	23.4	101t	1	4/3
1981	Lawrence, Amos	17	437	25.7	92t	1	3/2
1982	McLemore, Dana	16	353	22.1	45	0	18/9
1983	McLemore, Dana	30	576	19.2	39	0	30/14
1984	Monroe, Carl	27	561	20.8	44	0	19/9
1985	Monroe, Carl	28	717	25.6	95t	1	4/3
1986	Crawford, Derrick*	15	280	18.7	34	0	—
1987	Rodgers, Del*	17	358	21.1	50	0	—
1988	DuBose, Doug	32	608	19.0	44	0	27/11
1989	Flagler, Terrence	32	643	20.1	41	0	18/11
1990	Carter, Dexter	41	783	19.1	35	0	21/11
1991	Carter, Dexter	37	839	22.7	98t	1	5/3
1992	Logan, Marc	22	478	21.7	82	0	9/6
1993	Carter, Dexter	25	494	19.8	60	0	18/11
1994	Carter, Dexter	48	1,105	23.0	96t	1	14/11
1995	Carter, Dexter	*23	522	22.7	46	0	—
1996	Carter, Dexter	41	909	22.2	71	0	21/10

t=touchdown

Insufficient returns to qualify for NFL rankings.

FIELD GOALS (Based on Number Made)

Year	Player	Att.	Made	Pct.	Long	Rank*
1946	Vetrano, Joe	7	4	.571	—	—
1947	Vetrano, Joe	8	4	.500	30	—
1948	Vetrano, Joe	8	5	.625	47	—
1949	Vetrano, Joe	4	3	.750	—	—
1950	Soltau, Gordy	7	4	.571	26	9
1951	Soltau, Gordy	18	6	.333	42	10
1952	Soltau, Gordy	12	6	.500	31	6
1953	Soltau, Gordy	15	10	.667	39	4
1954	Soltau, Gordy	18	11	.611	37	4
1955	Soltau, Gordy	12	3	.250	28	10
1956	Soltau, Gordy	20	13	.650	40	2
1957	Soltau, Gordy	15	9	.600	37	7
1958	Soltau, Gordy	21	8	.381	39	8
1959	Davis, Tommy	26	12	.462	43	2
1960	Davis, Tommy	32	19	.594	40	1
1961	Davis, Tommy	22	12	.545	46	9
1962	Davis, Tommy	23	10	.435	42	10
1963	Davis, Tommy	31	10	.645	46	10
1964	Davis, Tommy	25	8	.320	53*	4
1965	Davis, Tommy	27	17	.630	53*	4
1966	Davis, Tommy	31	16	.516	46	12
1967	Davis, Tommy	33	14	.424	50	13

NFL/NFC Rank

Year	Player					
1968	Davis, Tommy	16	9	.563	38	10
1969	Davis, Tommy	10	3	.600	48	24/15
	Gavric, Momcilo	11	3	.273	32	26/17
1970	Gossett, Bruce	31	21	.611	48	6/3
1971	Gossett, Bruce	36	23	.639	48	10/5
1972	Gossett, Bruce	29	18	.621	50	15/5
1973	Gossett, Bruce	33	20	.788	54	1/1
1974	Gossett, Bruce	24	11	.458	46	26/14
1975	Mike-Mayer, Steve	28	14	.500	54	24/13
1976	Mike-Mayer, Steve	28	16	.571	45	15/9
1977	Wersching, Ray	17	10	.588	50	17/5
1978	Wersching, Ray	23	15	.652	45	11/5
1979	Wersching, Ray	24	20	.833	45	3/1
1980	Wersching, Ray	19	15	.789	47	2/1
1981	Wersching, Ray	23	17	.739	45	5/4
1982	Wersching, Ray	17	12	.706	45	17/9
1983	Wersching, Ray	30	25	.833	52	5/3
1984	Wersching, Ray	35	25	.714	53	2/2
1985	Wersching, Ray	21	13	.619	45	25/12
1986	Wersching, Ray	35	25	.714	50	2/3
1987	Wersching, Ray	17	13	.764	45	21/10
1988	Cofer, Mike	38	27	.711	52	3/1
1989	Cofer, Mike	36	29	.806	47	4/2
1990	Cofer, Mike	36	24	.666	56	5/3
1991	Cofer, Mike	28	14	.500	50	26/14
1992	Cofer, Mike	27	18	.666	46	17/8
1993	Cofer, Mike	26	16	.615	46	22t/10t
1994	Brien, Doug	20	15	.750	48	20/7
1995	Wilkins, Jeff	13	12	.923	40	—
1996	Wilkins, Jeff	34	30	.882	49	6t/3

Longest field goal in NFL that year.

PUNT RETURNS (Based on Yards)

Year	Player	No.	Yds.	Avg.	Long	TD	Rank*
1946	Casanega, Ken	18	248	13.8	—	—	—
1947	Vetrano, Joe	12	137	11.4	—	—	—
1948	Cason, Jim	22	309	14.0	—	—	—
1949	Cason, Jim	21	351	16.7	—	—	—
1950	Cathcart, Sam	16	185	11.6	29	0	10
1951	Arenas, Joe	21	272	13.0	51	0	6
1952	McElhenny, Hugh	20	284	14.2	94t	1	5
1953	McElhenny, Hugh	15	104	6.9	25	0	7
1954	Arenas, Joe	23	117	5.1	23	0	6
1955	Arenas, Joe	21	55	2.6	7	0	17
1956	Arenas, Joe	19	117	6.2	67t	1	8
1957	Arenas, Joe	25	80	3.2	26	0	13
1958	McElhenny, Hugh	24	93	3.9	18	0	16
1959	Woodson, Abe	15	143	9.5	65	0	6
1960	Woodson, Abe	13	174	13.4	48	0	1
1961	Woodson, Abe	16	172	10.8	80t	1	4
1962	Woodson, Abe	19	179	9.4	85t	1	4
1963	Woodson, Abe	13	95	7.3	13	0	13
1964	Alexander, Kermit	21	189	9.0	70t	1	8
1965	Alexander, Kermit	35	262	7.5	40	0	7
1966	Alexander, Kermit	30	198	6.6	44t	4	6
1967	Cunningham, Doug	27	249	9.2	57	0	3
1968	Alexander, Kermit	24	87	3.6	26	0	16
1969	Smith, Noland	10	46	4.6	18	0	19
1970	Taylor, Bruce	43	516	12.0	76	0	2/1
1971	Taylor, Bruce	34	235	6.9	38	0	15/6
1972	McGill, Ralph	22	219	10.0	33	0	4/3
1973	Taylor, Bruce	15	207	13.8	61	0	1/1
1974	McGill, Ralph	20	161	8.3	47	0	20/13
1975	McGill, Ralph	31	290	9.4	34	0	18/9
1976	Leonard, Anthony	35	293	8.4	60t	1	20/9
1977	Leonard, Anthony	22	154	7.0	19	0	30/13
1978	Steptoe, Jack	11**	129	11.7	28	0	—
1979	Solomon, Freddie	23	142	6.2	14	0	23/9
1980	Solomon, Freddie	27	298	11.0	57t	2	3/2
1981	Solomon, Freddie	29	173	6.0	19	0	25/13
1982	McLemore, Dana	7**	156	22.3	93t	1	—
1983	McLemore, Dana	31	331	10.7	56t	1	6/2
1984	McLemore, Dana	45	521	11.6	79t	1	4/2
1985	McLemore, Dana	38	258	6.8	22	0	21/9
1986	Griffin, Don	38	377	9.9	76t	1	5/2
1987	McLemore, Dana	21	265	12.6	83t	1	2/2
1988	Taylor, John	44	556	12.6	95t	2	1/1

NFL/NFC Rank

Year	Player						
1989	Taylor, John	36	417	11.6	37	0	5/4
1990	Taylor, John	26	212	8.2	30	0	13/8
1991	Taylor, John	31	267	8.6	24	0	9/5
1992	Grant, Alan	29	249	8.6	46	0	12/6
1993	Carter, Dexter	34	411	12.1	72t	1	5/2
1994	Carter, Dexter	38	321	8.4	26	0	14/11
1995	Carter, Dexter	9**	164	18.2	78t	1	—
1996	Carter, Dexter	36	317	8.8	52	0	18/9

t=touchdown

**Insufficient returns to qualify for NFL rankings.*

INTERCEPTIONS

Year	Player	No.	Yds.	Avg.	Long	TD	Rank*
1946	Casanega, Ken	8	146	18.3	68	—	—
1947	Eshmont, Len	6	72	12.0	—	—	—
1948	Carr, Eddie	7	144	20.6	56	1	—
1949	Cason, Jim	9	152	19.9	—	—	—
1950	Powers, Jim	5	42	8.4	26	0	27
1951	Wagner, Lowell	9	115	12.8	40	0	8
1952	Wagner, Lowell	6	69	11.5	30	0	12
1953	Berry, Rex	7	142	20.3	29	1	8
1954	Berry, Rex	3	69	23.0	34t	1	32
1955	Moegle, Dick	6	50	8.3	37	0	14
1956	Moegle, Dick	6	75	12.5	31t	1	12
1957	Moegle, Dick	8	107	13.4	40	0	6
1958	Ridlon, Jim	4	10	2.5	3	0	23
1959	Baker, Dave	5	75	15.0	29	0	10
1960	Baker, Dave	10	96	9.6	28	0	1
1961	Baker, Dave	6	123	20.5	10	0	11
1962	Woodson, Abe	2	31	15.5	31	0	58
1963	Alexander, Kermit	5	72	17.4	38	0	18
1964	Alexander, Kermit	5	65	13.0	24	0	9
1965	Johnson, Jimmy	6	47	7.8	26	0	10
1966	Alexander, Kermit	4	73	18.3	55	0	25
1967	Alexander, Kermit	5	72	14.4	48	0	17
1968	Alexander, Kermit	9	155	17.2	66t	1	2
1969	Alexander, Kermit	5	39	7.8	22	0	14
1970	Taylor, Bruce	2	70	23.3	70	0	48/24
1971	Taylor, Bruce	3	68	22.7	49	0	65/33
1972	Johnson, Jimmy	4	18	4.5	15	0	43/17
1973	Taylor, Bruce	6	30	5.0	22	0	10/5
1974	McGill, Ralph	5	71	14.2	45	0	19/9
1975	Taylor, Bruce	3	29	9.7	15	0	75/36
1976	Rhodes, Bruce	3	42	14.0	30	0	—
1977	Washington, Dave	2	68	34.0	50	0	93/37
1978	Crist, Chuck	6	59	26.5	32	0	11/10
1979	Hicks, Dwight	5	57	11.4	29	0	28/12
1980	Hicks, Dwight	4	73	18.3	44	0	41/19
	Churchman, Ricky	4	7	1.8	7	0	41/19
1981	Hicks, Dwight	9	239	26.6	72	1	3/2
1982	Hicks, Dwight	3	5	1.7	3	0	22/8
1983	Wright, Eric	7	164	23.4	60t	2	6/4
1984	Turner, Keena	4	51	12.8	21	0	40/17
	Lott, Ronnie	4	26	6.5	15	0	48/21
1985	Lott, Ronnie	6	68	11.3	25	0	16/7
1986	Lott, Ronnie	10	134	13.4	57t	1	1/1
1987	Lott, Ronnie	5	62	12.4	34	0	11/7
	Griffin, Don	5	1	0.2	1	0	14/9
1988	McKyer, Tim	7	11	1.6	7	0	5/6
1989	Lott, Ronnie	5	34	6.8	28	0	16/9
1990	Waymer, Dave	7	64	9.1	24	0	4/4
1991	Waymer, Dave	4	77	19.3	42	0	23/13
1992	Griffin, Don	5	4	0.8	2	0	15/5
1993	McGruder, Michael	5	89	17.8	37	1	14t/6t
1994	Hanks, Merton	7	93	13.3	38	0	4t/4t
1995	Drakeford, Tyronne	5	54	10.8	37	0	16t/10t
	Hanks, Merton	5	31	6.2	23	0	16t/10t
1996	Pope, Marquez	6	98	16.3	55t	1	4t/2t

PASSING

Year	Player	Att.	Comp.	Pct.	Yds.	TD	Int.	Rtg.	Rank*
1946	Albert, Frank	197	104	52.9	1,404	14	14	—	—
1947	Albert, Frank	242	128	52.9	1,692	18	15	—	—
1948	Albert, Frank	264	154	58.3	1,990	29	10	—	—
1949	Albert, Frank	260	129	49.6	1,862	27	16	—	—
1950	Albert, Frank	306	155	50.7	1,767	14	23	52.6	8
1951	Albert, Frank	166	90	50.7	1,116	5	10	60.2	8
1952	Tittle, Y.A.	208	106	51.0	1,407	11	12	66.4	5
1953	Tittle, Y.A.	259	149	57.5	2,121	20	16	84.0	3
1954	Tittle, Y.A.	295	170	57.6	2,205	9	9	78.4	7
1955	Tittle, Y.A.	287	147	51.2	2,185	17	28	56.5	4
1956	Tittle, Y.A.	218	124	56.9	1,641	7	12	68.5	7
1957	Tittle, Y.A.	279	176	63.1	2,157	13	15	79.6	6
1958	Tittle, Y.A.	208	120	57.7	1,467	9	15	59.1	3
1959	Tittle, Y.A.	199	102	51.3	1,331	10	15	58.2	4
1960	Brodie, John	207	103	49.8	1,111	6	9	57.8	5
1961	Brodie, John	283	155	54.8	2,588	14	12	84.5	4
1962	Brodie, John	304	175	57.6	2,272	18	16	78.1	6
1963	McHan, Lamar	195	83	42.3	1,243	8	11	54.3	15
1964	Brodie, John	392	193	49.2	2,498	14	16	64.3	12
1965	Brodie, John	391	242	61.9	3,112	30	16	95.2	3
1966	Brodie, John	427	232	54.3	2,810	16	22	65.5	8
1967	Brodie, John	349	168	48.1	2,013	11	16	57.5	11
1968	Brodie, John	404	234	57.9	3,020	22	21	77.9	3
1969	Brodie, John	347	194	55.9	2,405	16	15	74.9	7
1970	Brodie, John	378	223	59.0	2,941	24	10	93.9	1/1
1971	Brodie, John	387	208	53.7	2,642	18	24	64.7	12/6
1972	Spurrier, Steve	269	147	54.6	1,983	18	16	76.2	8/5
1973	Spurrier, Steve	157	83	52.9	882	4	7	59.2	21/13
1974	Owen, Tom	184	88	47.8	1,327	10	15	54.8	25/11
1975	Snead, Norm	189	108	57.1	1,337	9	10	77.2	11/5
1976	Plunkett, Jim	243	126	51.9	1,592	13	16	62.8	17/8
1977	Plunkett, Jim	248	128	51.6	1,693	9	14	62.1	17/8
1978	DeBerg, Steve	302	137	45.4	1,570	8	22	39.8	28/17
1979	DeBerg, Steve	578	347	60.0	3,652	17	21	70.3	13/5
1980	Montana, Joe	273	167	64.5	1,795	15	9	87.8	5/4
1981	Montana, Joe	488	311	63.7	3,565	19	12	88.2	4/1
1982	Montana, Joe	346	213	61.6	2,613	17	11	87.9	5/3
1983	Montana, Joe	515	332	64.5	3,910	26	12	94.6	5/3
1984	Montana, Joe	432	279	64.6	3,630	28	10	102.9	2/1
1985	Montana, Joe	494	303	61.3	3,653	27	13	91.3	3/1
1986	Montana, Joe	307	191	62.2	2,236	8	9	80.7	9/2
1987	Montana, Joe	398	266	66.8	3,054	31	13	102.1	1/1
1988	Montana, Joe	397	238	59.9	2,981	18	10	87.9	6/3
1989	Montana, Joe	386	271	70.2	3,521	26	8	112.4	1/1
1990	Montana, Joe	520	321	61.7	3,944	26	16	81.0	7/3
1991	Young, Steve	279	180	64.4	2,517	17	8	101.8	1/1
1992	Young, Steve	402	268	66.7	3,465	25	7	107.0	1/1
1993	Young, Steve	462	314	68.0	4,023	29	16	101.5	1/1
1994	Young, Steve	461	324	70.3	3,969	35	10	112.8	1/1
1995	Young, Steve	447	299	66.9	3,200	20	11	92.3	5/4
1996	Young, Steve	316	214	67.7	2,410	14	6	97.2	1/1

*NFL/NFC Rank

QUARTERBACK SACK LEADERS (Since 1971)

Year	Player	Sacks	Sack Yardage	Year	Player	Sacks	Sack Yardage
1971	Hardman, Cedrick	18	-NA-	1986	Haley, Charles	12	109
1972	Hart, Tommy	17	-NA-	1987	Haley, Charles	6	42
1973	Hardman, Cedrick	9	-NA-	1988	Haley, Charles	11.5	77
1974	Hardman, Cedrick	9	-NA-	1989	Haley, Charles	10.5	88.5
1975	Hardman, Cedrick	15	-NA-		Holt, Pierce	10.5	85.5
1976	Elam, Cleveland	14	-NA-	1990	Haley, Charles	16	107
1977	Elam, Cleveland	17.5	-NA-	1991	Roberts, Larry	7	50
1978	Hardman, Cedrick	10.5	-NA-		Haley, Charles	7	49
1979	Board, Dwaine	7	52	1992	Harris, Tim	17	116
1980	Stuckey, Jim	8.5	49.5	1993	Stubblefield, Dana	10.5	61.5
1981	Dean, Fred	12	106.5	1994	Stubblefield, Dana	8.5	53.5
1982	Dean, Fred	3.5	28.5	1995	Jackson, Rickey	9.5	49
1983	Dean, Fred	17.5	151.5	1996	Barker, Roy	12.5	74.5
1984	Board, Dwaine	10	82				
1985	Board, Dwaine	11.5	95.5				

About the 49ers Foundation
Director, Lisa DeBartolo

The 49ers Foundation was established in July 1991. It is a not-for-profit organization founded by the San Francisco 49ers to provide grants and aid to charitable activities and causes of civic concern.

The San Francisco 49ers are committed to extending their community involvement and good will throughout the Bay Area. The 49ers Foundation is one of many projects instituted to achieve this objective. The fund financially aids a wide variety of groups and organizations through grants.

It is the hope of the San Francisco 49ers to acknowledge and assist many of the worthy Bay Area charities. The fund serves as an additional vehicle of monetary support to the efforts of those groups helping the needy.

To apply for a grant:
The 49ers Foundation will accept written requests for grants from public charities and foundations. All applicants must be exempt from taxation under Section 501 (c) (3) of the Internal Revenue Code. Your request should be no more than two pages including:
- A brief description of your organization.
- What project will be funded through the grant.
- Who your other major funders are.

Additionally, enclose a copy of your IRS determination letter granting your organization tax-exempt status.

The letters of request must be submitted between January 1 and April 30. They will be reviewed by the administrators of the foundation, and grants will be awarded based upon the recommendations of the foundation administrators. The grants will be announced in May.

Unfortunately, not all funding requests can be filled. Also, there are areas that do not fit 49ers Foundation specifications, such as: land purchase, building and equipment, endowments, political campaigns, religious organizations, loans or scholarships, raffles and banquets. Also requests from groups or organizations outside of the Bay Area cannot be filled. Send requests to:

Lisa DeBartolo
Director, 49ers Foundation
c/o San Francisco 49ers
4949 Centennial Boulevard
Santa Clara, CA 95054